Windows 11

Simplified Beginners Guide with Step by Step Illustrations

Andy Kissinger

Copyright © 2024 Andy Kissinger

All rights reserved.

This book references various trademarks, including Microsoft Windows 11, which is a registered trademark of Microsoft Corporation. All other trademarks are the property of their respective owners. The author, Andy Kissinger, is independent of any products or vendors mentioned, and trademarks are used here for clarification only.

Table of Contents

CHAPTER 1 1
  INTRODUCTION 1
  What You Get From Windows 11 Version 22H2 2
  Windows 11 System Minimum Requirements 13
  Choosing the Right Edition of Windows 11 15

CHAPTER 2 18
  WINDOWS 11 UPGRADE, DOWNLOAD, AND INSTALLATION 18
    Backing Up Files and Syncing with OneDrive 20
    Windows 11 Installation Assistant Method 21
  Windows 11 Clean Installation Option 24
  How to Prepare your PC for a Clean Installation of Windows 11 25
    Creating a Bootable USB for a Clean Windows 11 Installation 28
    Windows 11 Clean Installation 33

CHAPTER 3 37
  GETTING STARTED WITH WINDOWS 11 37
  Windows 11 Desktop Lock Screen 37
  Taskbar Features 40
    The Windows 11 Start Button 41
    The Search Icon 42
    The Virtual Desktop or Task View 44
    Widgets 45
    Teams Chat 46
    File Explorer 47
    Edge Browser 47
    Microsoft Store 49

The Taskbar Notification Area 50
Task Bar Animation Features 50

CHAPTER 4 52

TASKBAR PERSONALIZATION 52

How to Change the Taskbar Position 53
How to Pin Installed Application 56
Removing Pinned Application 59
System Tray and Corner Overflow on the Taskbar 63
How to Hide the Taskbar Automatically 67
Displaying Badges on Taskbar Icons 68
Displaying Taskbar Across Multiple Screen 70

CHAPTER 5 74

THE START MENU AND ITS FEATURES 74

Searching for Applications and Files 76
The Start Menu Search Box 76
Pinned Apps on the Start Menu 80
Recommended Apps 82
All Apps 83

Start Menu Quick Setting 85
Editing Profile Photo 86
Start Menu Power Buttons 88
Accessing the File Explorer Through the Start Menu 90

CHAPTER 6 93

THE START BUTTON RIGHT-CLICK FEATURES 93

Installed Apps- How to Uninstall Apps 94
Mobility Center 95
Power Options Access to Power Consumption 97
Event Viewer, Explore Windows Messages 99

Device Manager, Know Your Hardware 100
Network Connections, on Your Computer 101
Disk Management 102
Computer Management 104
Windows Terminal/ Powershell 105
Task Manager at Your Fingertips... 106
Settings Option 108
Access to File Explorer.. 109
Search Option 110
Access the Run Command 111
Shut Down or Sign Out Options 112
Desktop 114

CHAPTER 7 115

NAVIGATING THE FILE EXPLORER FOR FILE MANAGEMENT 115

UNDERSTANDING FILES AND FOLDER.. 115

What is a File? 116
What is a Folder? 117
Benefits of Using the File Explorer 118

HOW TO ACCESS THE FILE EXPLORER 119

THE FILE EXPLORER INTERFACE 121

The Title Bar 121
The ToolBar 122
The Address Bar 124
The Search Box 125
Details Pane.. 126
The Navigation pane 129
Home Page 131

MASTERING SORTING AND GROUPING IN FILE EXPLORER 134

LAYOUT AND VIEW OPTIONS 137

COPYING, MOVING FILE(S) OR FOLDER(S) 142
   Drag and Drop Method of Moving or Copying 144
   Toolbar Method of Copying or Moving Item(s) 146
   The Mouse Method of Copying or Moving Item(s) 147

DELETING FILE(S) OR FOLDER(S) 149

CREATING A FOLDER 151

RENAMING A FILE OR FOLDER 153

THE RECYCLING BIN 155
   How to Open the Recycle Bin 156
   Sorting Deleted Files or Folders 156
   Restoring Deleted Items 157
   Permanently Deleting Files 158
   Emptying the Recycle Bin 159

CHAPTER 8 .... **160**

SYSTEM NOTIFICATIONS AND QUICK SETTINGS 160
   Types of Notifications in Windows 11 161
   Accessing the Notification Settings 163
   How to Turn Off/On All Your Notifications 165
   Do Not Disturb Settings 165
   Priority Notification Settings 170
   Focus Mode Settings 173

CHAPTER 9 .... **177**

QUICK SETTINGS PANEL 177
   How to Access the Quick Settings Panel 178
   Wi-Fi and Bluetooth Device Setting 179
   Airplane Mode Setting 181
   Battery Saver Setting 182
   Night light Setting 183

   Accessibility Setting 185
   Screen Casting (Wireless Display) Setting 188
   Mobile Hotspot Setting 190
   Nearby Sharing 193
   Audio Volume Control 195
   The Volume Mixer 196
 EDITING THE QUICK SETTINGS PANEL 199

CHAPTER 10 201

 FILE SHARING IN WINDOWS 11 201
   Benefits of File Sharing: 201
   Choosing the Right Sharing Method 202
   Security Considerations for File Sharing 203
 FILE AND PRINTER SHARING 203
   What is a Workgroup 204
   How to Check Your Computer Workgroup 204
   How to Check Your Computer Name 207
   How to Change the Name of Your Computer 211
   How to Activate Files and Printers Sharing 212
 HOW TO SHARE YOUR FILES 214
   Determining the Destination of the Files 216
 NEARBY FILE SHARING 217
   How to Use Nareby Share 220
 ONEDRIVE FILE SHARING 221
   Advantages of Using OneDrive 223
   Comparing OneDrive to the Competition 224
   OneDrive Files and Folders 225
   OneDrive Personal Vault 229

CHAPTER 11 232

BASIC INTERNET CONNECTION 232
Types of Internet Connections 232
How to Add a Hidden or Private Wi-Fi Network Manually 234

SECURING YOUR CONNECTION 239

CHAPTER 12 242

EXPLORING MICROSOFT EDGE IN WINDOWS 11 242
The Microsoft Edge Browser & Tab Controls 244
The Search Field and Address Bar 244
Accessing the Microsoft Edge Menu 246
Microsoft Edge Browser Tabs 247
Microsoft Edge Favourites Tabs 248

MICROSOFT EDGE EXTENSION BAR 251
How to Enable the Extension Icon 251
Frequently Installed Extensions 253
Installing and Removing Extensions 255
Extensions Settings Page 256

CHAPTER 13 259

SECURING YOUR WINDOWS 11 259

IMPORTANCE OF WINDOWS UPDATES 259

THIRD-PARTY ANTIVIRUS PROGRAM 264
Popular Third-Party Antivirus Options 266

BEST PRACTICES FOR ONLINE SAFETY 272

USER ACCOUNTS 273
How to Create a User Account 274

PARENTAL CONTROLS 275
How to Create a Family Account 275

CHAPTER 1

INTRODUCTION

Welcome to your one-stop guide to the exciting world of Windows 11! Whether you are an experienced computer user or a novice making your first journey into the digital realm, this comprehensive guidebook will help you unlock the full potential of the Windows 11 operating system.

In this book, you will discover clear, step-by-step instructions and insightful tips to pave the way for a smooth and enriching learning experience. From mastering the fundamentals to unlocking hidden functionalities, this guidebook will equip you with the tools to harness the full potential of Windows 11.

Windows 11 is built on the same foundation as Windows 10 and delivers astounding value to commercial users. Within Windows 11, you will discover new features, performance enhancements, and a completely redesigned interface. Microsoft is committed to enhancing your experience and will continuously roll out updates to provide an even better Windows 11 experience.

What You Get from Windows 11 Version 22H2

Windows 11 includes at least 30 new features. The following are the main new features:

- **An Overhauled User Interface**

   Microsoft continues to make significant changes to Windows 11 to make it more pleasant and easier to use. The interface looks much cleaner and more modern, with smoother movements and sharper visuals for your apps.

   You can also customize the Start Menu according to your preferences. You can pin your favorite apps, files, and even websites to find them all in one place, just like arranging your favorite things on your desk for easy access.

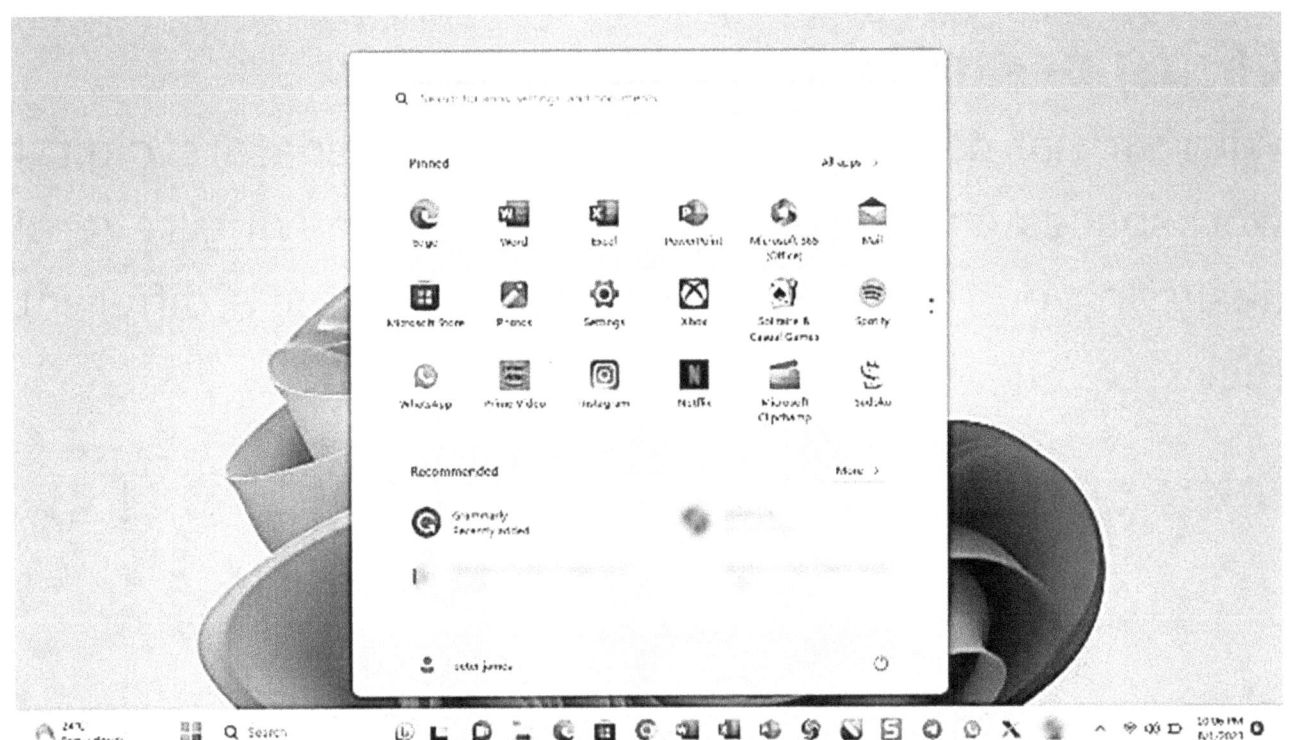

Windows 11 has a centralized notification center that displays all your alerts and lets you quickly change settings, just like having your central command center for your computer. It also comes with a Dark Mode option that changes the background to a darker color, making it easier on your eyes and helping you relax when using your computer in the evening. This can even help save your laptop battery life if it comes with an OLED screen.

- **Virtual Desktops**

  With virtual desktops, you can set up separate digital workspaces on your computer. It's like having several desks in your office, each one set aside for a different task.

  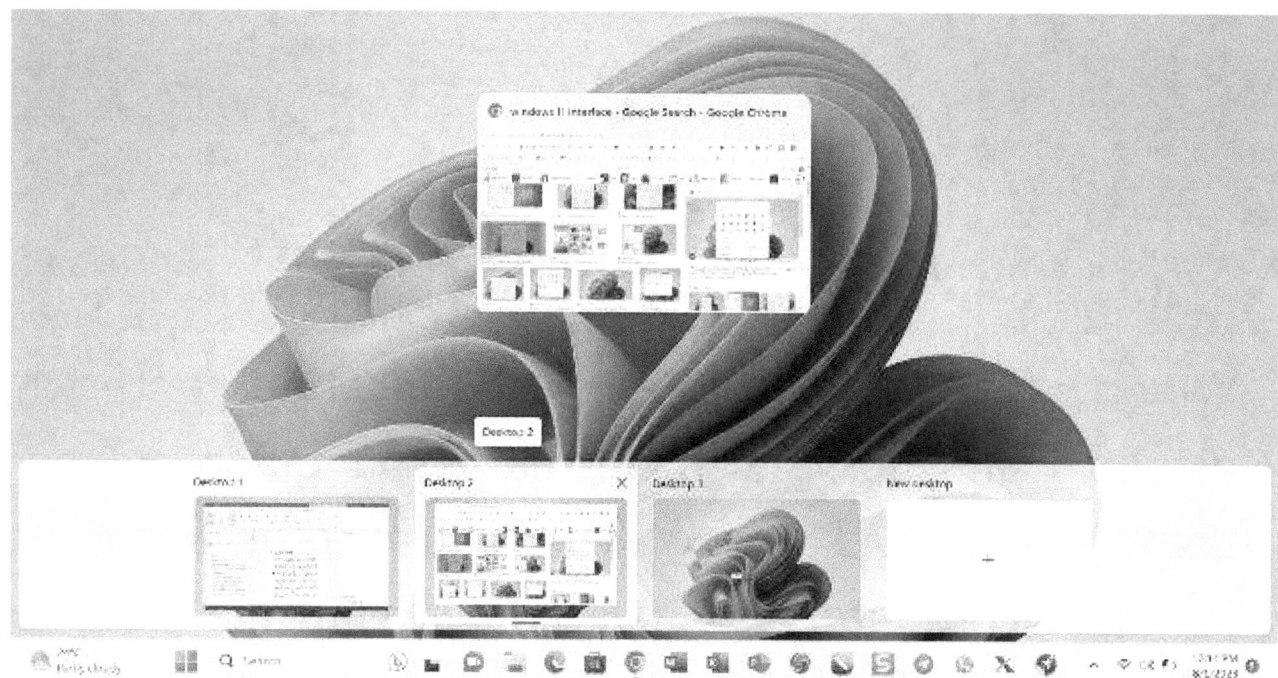

  You can use one desktop for work, another for personal projects, and even one for entertainment. This keeps things in order and reduces distractions so you can work on one thing at a time.

  You can easily move between these desktops, just like you would between real desks. You can even move apps between them without closing and reopening them.

This feature is excellent for people who have a lot of things to do or complex projects to work on at once because it keeps everything organized and easy to find, which makes you more productive all day.

- **New Multitasking Options**

With Windows 11, it's easier to do more than one task at once, like comparing documents or doing research online. You can now quickly snap windows to specific spots on your screen, either next to each other or in four squares, which is similar to how you would arrange windows on a desk.

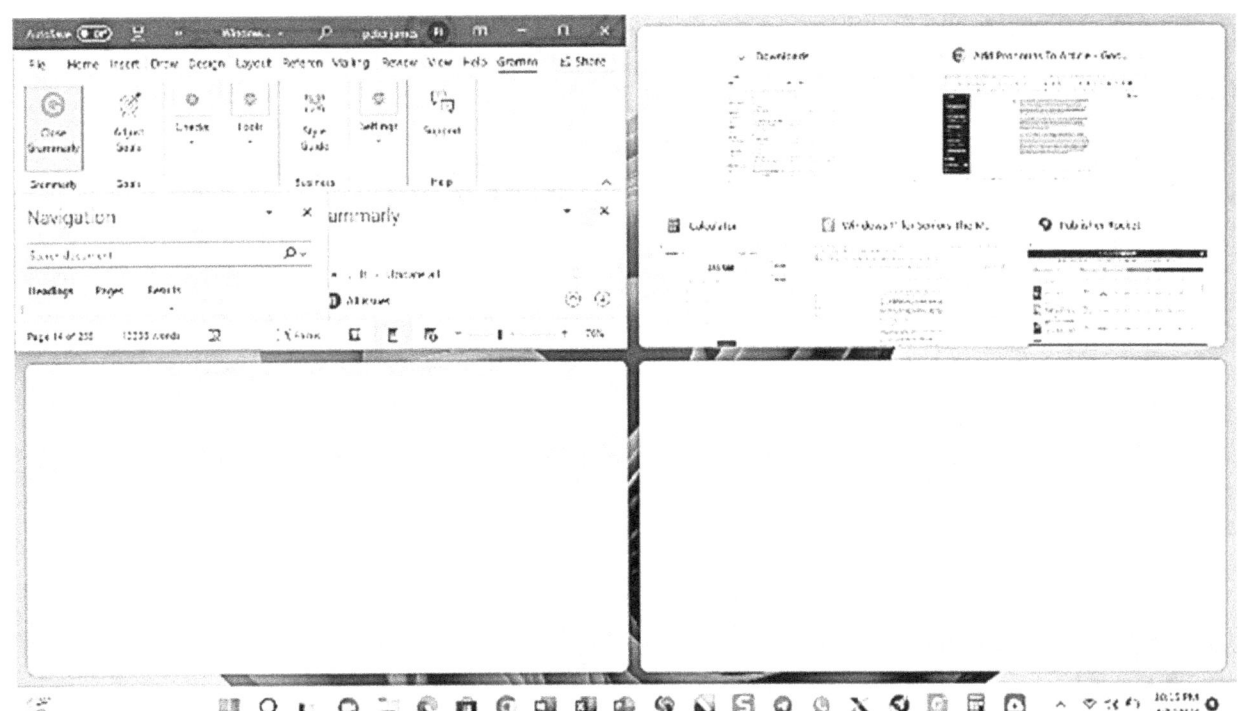

This keeps you from switching between windows and lets you see everything at once.

- **Widgets and Android Apps**

  Windows 11 brings incredible new features to your desktop, making it more personal and valuable. You have little boxes on your screen that show you the weather, the news, and your list of things to do all at once. These are called widgets, and you can pick which ones to show. If you use a touchscreen device, swipe left to view the widgets.

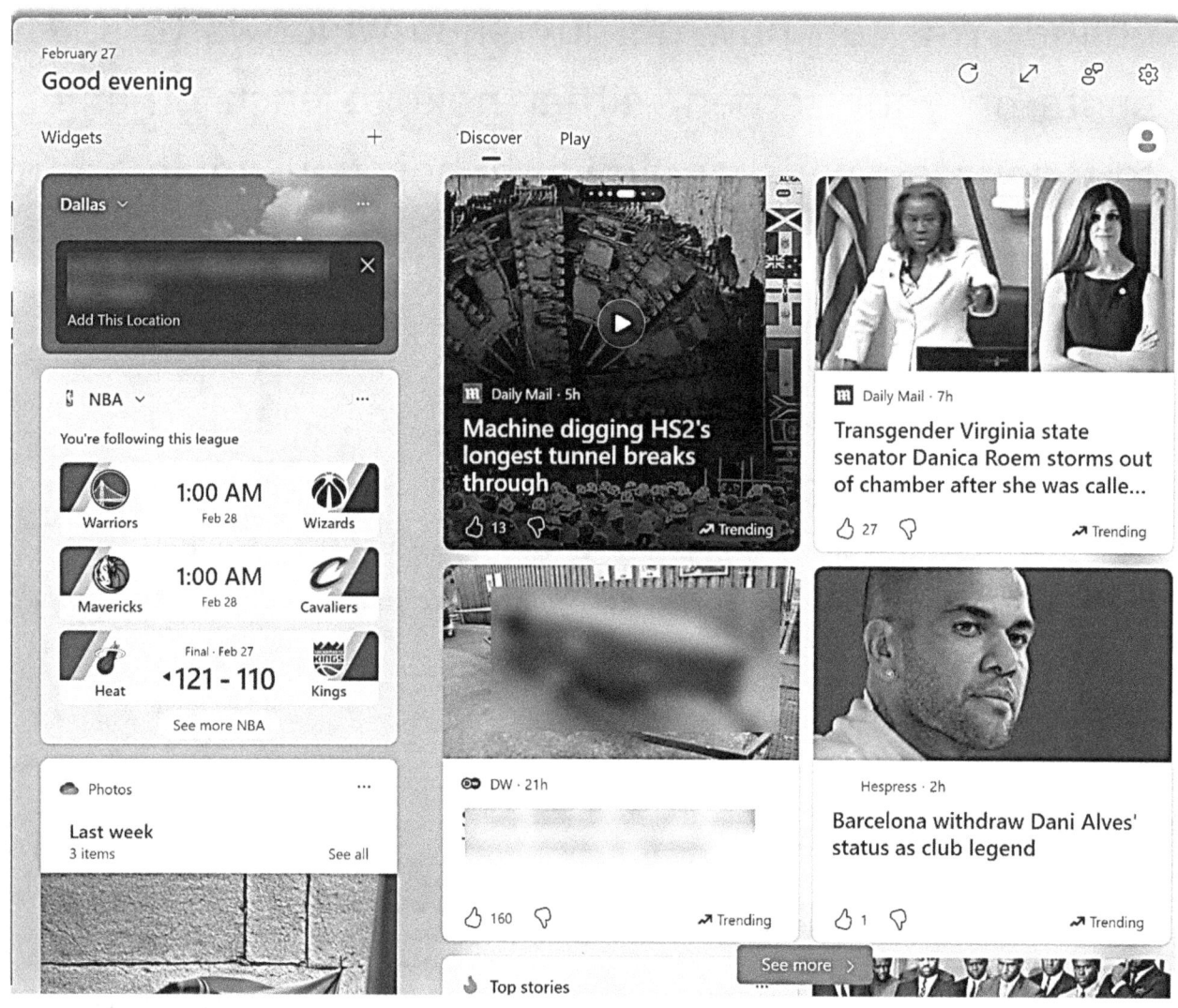

The integration of Android apps adds even more possibilities, as you can now run your favorite mobile apps directly on your desktop. With widgets and Android app integration, your desktop becomes a central hub of information and functionality, which helps to boost your productivity and accessibility to essential content and apps. This transformative feature enhances your computing experience by providing a unified and efficient workspace that adapts to your needs.

- **Integrated Teams Chat**
"**Teams**" is an integrated app in Windows 11 that facilitates easy communication and connection with others, whether for personal or professional purposes.

Imagine being able to use just one app for all of your messaging. Teams lets you talk about work projects, share files, and even make video calls with other team members in one app.

So you don't have to switch between apps like email and videoconferencing platforms, and you can keep everything in one place.

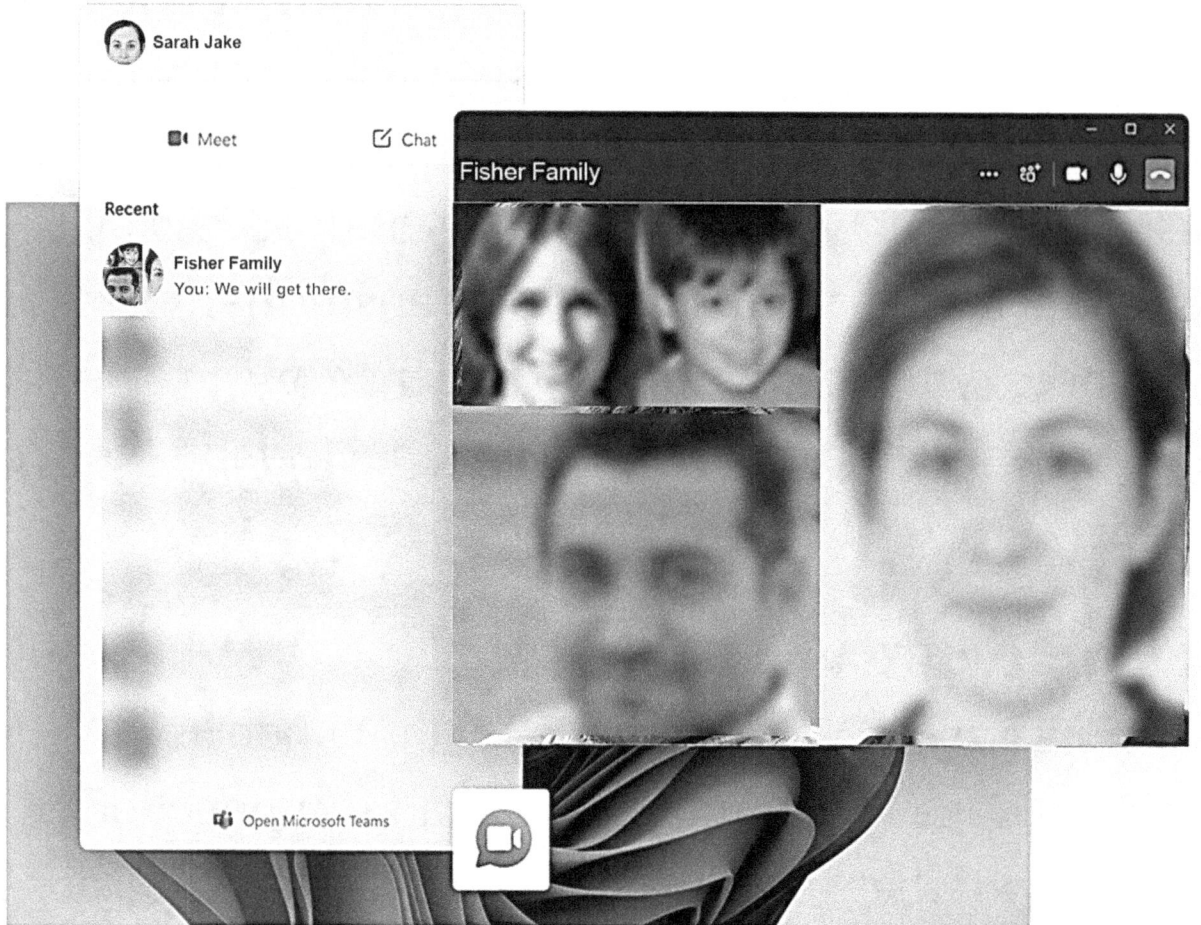

Teams is not just for work, though! It also lets you talk to family and friends who live far away. Teams make it easy to switch between personal and work conversations, whether you are talking about projects with coworkers or spending time with family after a long day. With this feature, your computer becomes a hub for all your communication needs.

- **Improved Gaming Experience**

    With Windows 11, you can play games better than ever. If your computer hardware meets the minimum requirements, Windows 11 will get more power out of it. This will make all your favorite games run more smoothly and at higher frame rates. It is like putting a solid engine under your car's hood, which makes it go faster and smoother.

    In addition, Windows 11 adds new features like DirectX 12 Ultimate, which makes games that work. Windows 11 also has a mode called "Game Mode" that puts all your computer's power into the game you are playing and shuts down any other programs running in the background to avoid interruptions.

- **Reorganized Settings Menu**

    Windows 11 makes things a great deal simpler. Rather than having infinite options, settings are grouped like those of clear shelves at a store.

    Consider each shelf to be a specific category, such as "Display" or "Personalization." You have a variety of toys in the "Toys" department, which are stored on these shelves and organized into smaller groups.

In this manner, locating what you require is like browsing through areas familiar to you in a store.

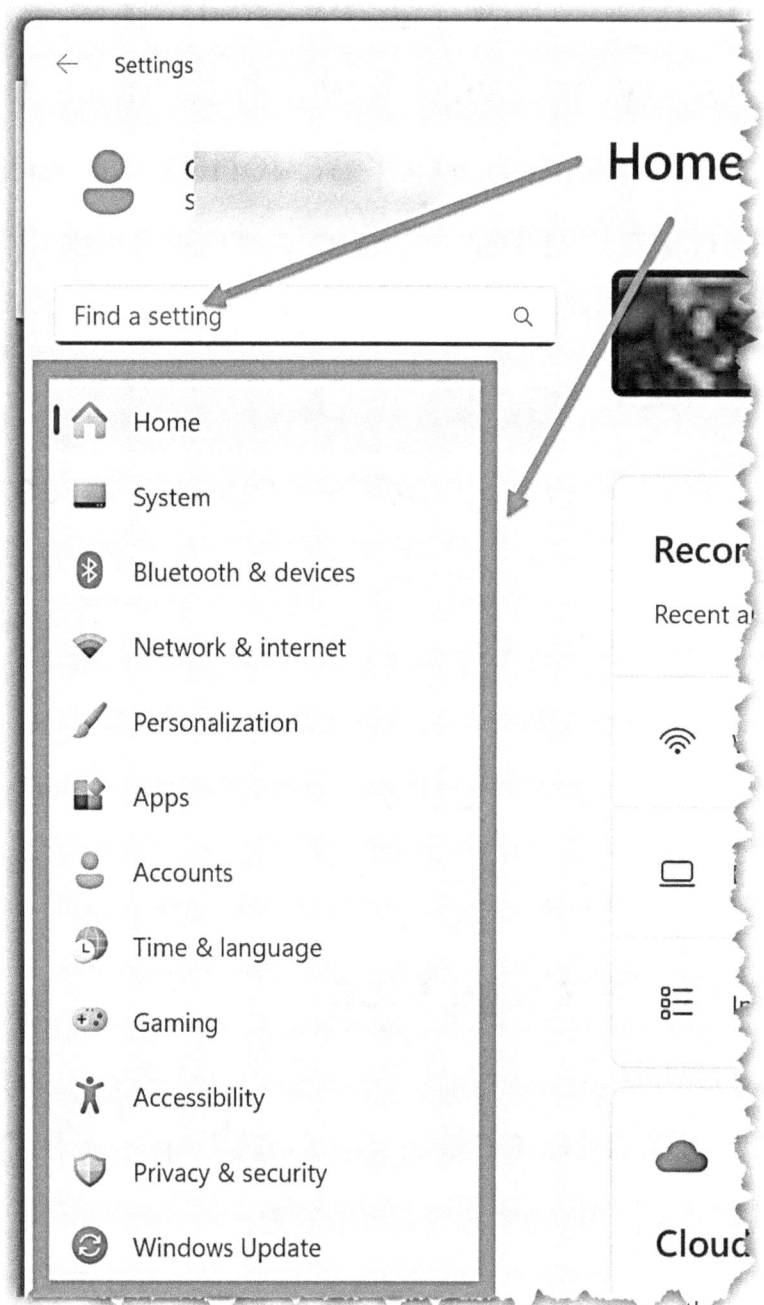

If you are unsure about what you are looking for, use the search bar at the top right corner, and the settings app will guide you.

- **A Better Memory Management System**

    Ensuring that your computer's memory is managed effectively is necessary to guarantee the system will run smoothly. Memory leaks and RAM allocation are challenges that are addressed by Windows 11's memory management system, which has been optimized to address these concerns.

    Memory leaks are instances in which programs installed on your computer fail to release memory that they no longer use, resulting in a slow decline in performance. These leaks are something that Windows 11 addresses, which will free up important RAM for use by other apps.

- **AI- Powered Assistant**

    You get access to the revolutionary feature known as Copilot with Windows 11 version 22H2. Your work experience will be completely transformed by this cutting-edge assistant powered by artificial intelligence.

    Copilot is your assistant, supplying you with relevant information, producing new ideas, and giving helpful tools while operating within the applications you already have.

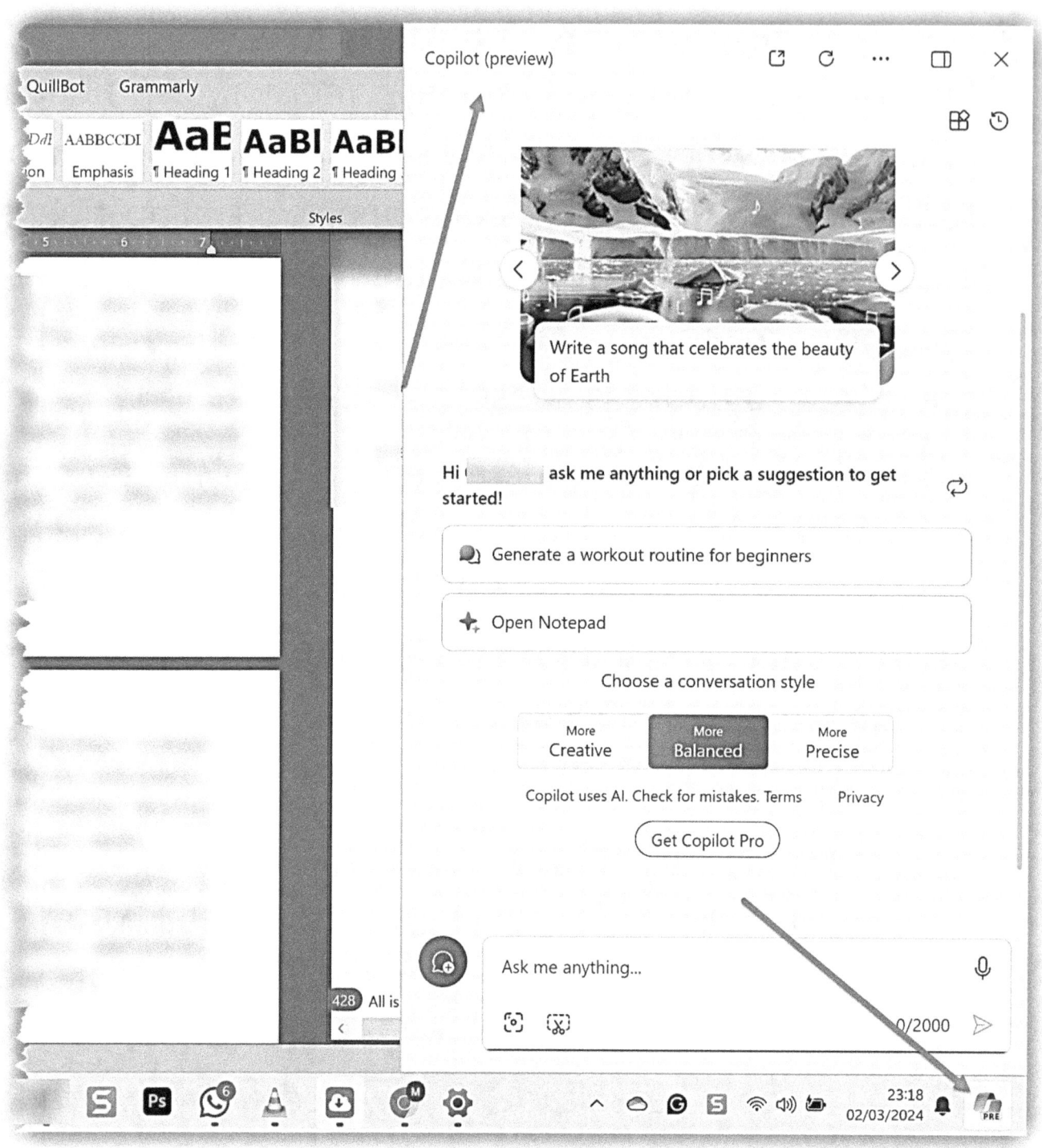

Imagine the frustration of juggling between multiple open apps and endless web searches for information. Copilot eliminates this struggle by instantly fetching data points and research tailored to your needs.

Windows 11 System Minimum Requirements

Microsoft has established minimum system requirements for running Windows 11 on your computer.

Beyond these essentials, certain features in Windows 11 have been enhanced beyond these minimum requirements as outlined below:

- **Processor:**

    The system processor should have a clock speed of 1 Gigahertz (GHz) or more, featuring multiple cores on a well-suited 64-bit processor or System on a Chip (SoC).

- **RAM:**

    A minimum of 4 gigabytes (GB) of RAM is needed to keep operations smooth and responsive.

- **Storage:**

    A 64 GB or larger storage device ensures ample space to install the operating system and applications.

- **System firmware:**

    UEFI (Unified Extensible Firmware Interface) and Secure Boot capability are crucial components for a secure and efficient system.

- **TPM:**
  Version 2.0 of TPM is a necessity, contributing to enhanced security features.
- **Graphics card:**
  A graphics card well-suited with DirectX 12 or later, featuring a WDDM (Windows Display Driver Model) 2.0 driver.
- **Display:**
  A high-definition (720p) display exceeding 9 inches diagonally, with 8-bits per color channel for vibrant visuals.
- **Internet connection and Microsoft accounts:**
  A Microsoft account and active internet connection are required to install Windows 11 on a PC. By establishing this link, your computer will be fully integrated into Microsoft's larger ecosystem.

Windows 11 will work as long as your computer meets the minimum requirements, but some features have been fine-tuned to provide an even better experience. These additions aren't strictly necessary, but they help the OS run smoother and faster overall.

Choosing the Right Edition of Windows 11

Windows 11 is available in various editions, each tailored to meet a particular set of requirements. To help you decide which one is best for your computer, we will compare and contrast the seven primary editions:

- **Windows 11 Home:** This is the basic edition, which is ideal if you are a home user who will use your computer regularly and require an operating system that is easy to use for activities such as browsing the web, working on documents, and enjoying entertainment.

- **Windows 11 Pro:** This edition has additional capabilities for enterprises and power users. These features include joining your company networks, encrypting data to ensure it is safe, and remotely administering other machines.

- **Windows 11 Pro Education:** The purpose of this edition is to cater to educational institutions, just like the Pro edition does. It frequently offers special discounts and other features that are pertinent to schools, such as the ability to manage student accounts.

- **Windows 11 Pro for Workstations:** This specialist edition was developed for high-performance computers that are utilized for labor-intensive applications such as scientific research or video editing.

- **Windows 11 SE:** Explicitly designed for educational institutions, this simplified edition provides a more streamlined user interface and more stringent security features to handle student devices.

- **Windows 11 Enterprise:** The Enterprise version focuses on security, management, and lots of deployment features. It is designed specifically for large businesses and organizations. This edition was developed to fulfill the rigorous requirements that are present in corporate settings.

- **Windows 11 Mixed Reality:** The Windows 11 Mixed Reality operating system was designed to target users engaged in immersive experiences, thereby revealing the potential of virtual reality. This edition places an emphasis on compatibility with mixed-reality devices, which expands the scope of computing to include a new dimension.

Choosing the Right Version:

- **Windows 11 Home** is the best option for you if you are a **home** user.

- Consider using **Windows 11 Pro** if you require functionality for sophisticated work or use in a commercial setting.

- **Windows 11 Pro Education** or **Windows 11 SE** is suitable for educational institutions.

- **Windows 11 Pro for Workstations** is the way to go when it comes to producing powerful workstations.

CHAPTER 2

WINDOWS 11 UPGRADE, DOWNLOAD, AND INSTALLATION

Microsoft provides you with three different installation choices to choose from when it comes to installing Windows 11 on your PC:

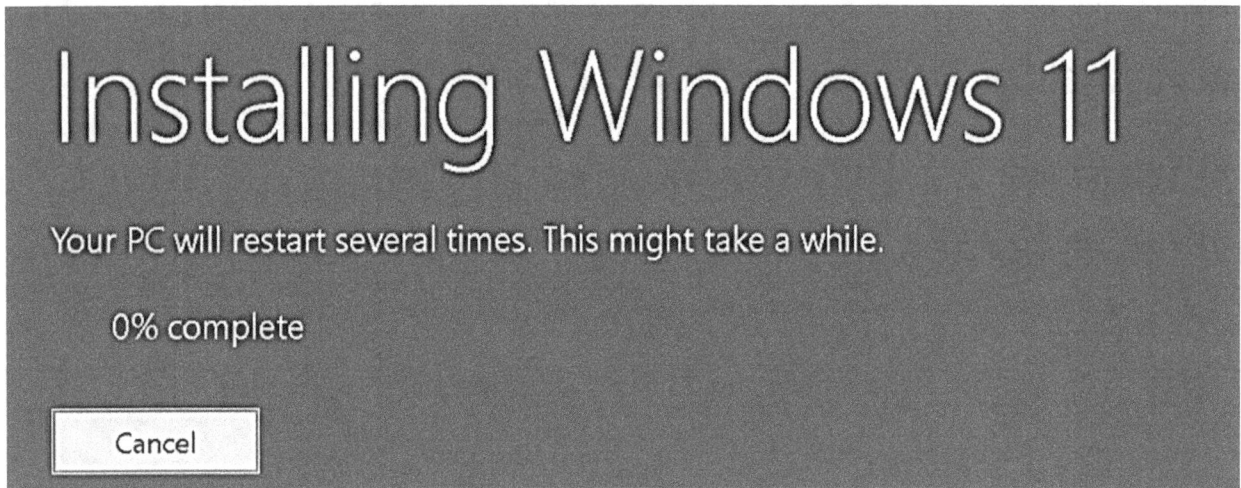

- **Windows Upgrade:** This is the least complicated option if you are already running Windows 10. It ensures that all of your files, programs, and settings are preserved, which makes the process of upgrading to Windows 11 extremely easy and uncomplicated. Because it saves time and guarantees the security of your data, this is the option that is suggested for the majority of users.

- **Windows 11 Clean Install:** With this option, your computer's hard drive will be entirely wiped clean, and Windows 11 will be installed over it. You will find this helpful if you are beginning with a new computer or if you are looking for a blank slate. In spite of this, it is of the utmost importance to remember to create backups of all of your essential files before proceeding with this process, as these files will be deleted altogether.
- **Custom Install:** With this option, there is more control over the installation process, but it is also more complicated. When installing Windows 11, you can select which parts of your old system files or programs will be moved to the new installation. This option is recommended for users with more experience who wish to have more specific control over their system configuration.

Backing Up Files and Syncing with OneDrive

Before upgrading to Windows 11, it is wise to take preventative measures like creating multiple backups of all your essential data. This preliminary step is crucial because it protects against unforeseen complications during the upgrade.

There are several methods available for securing your files. The tried-and-true method requires you to copy all your data to an external hard drive, a physical and offline storage space separate from your computer.

However, OneDrive is a modern alternative that provides safe cloud storage for your files and makes them available from any computer with an internet connection.

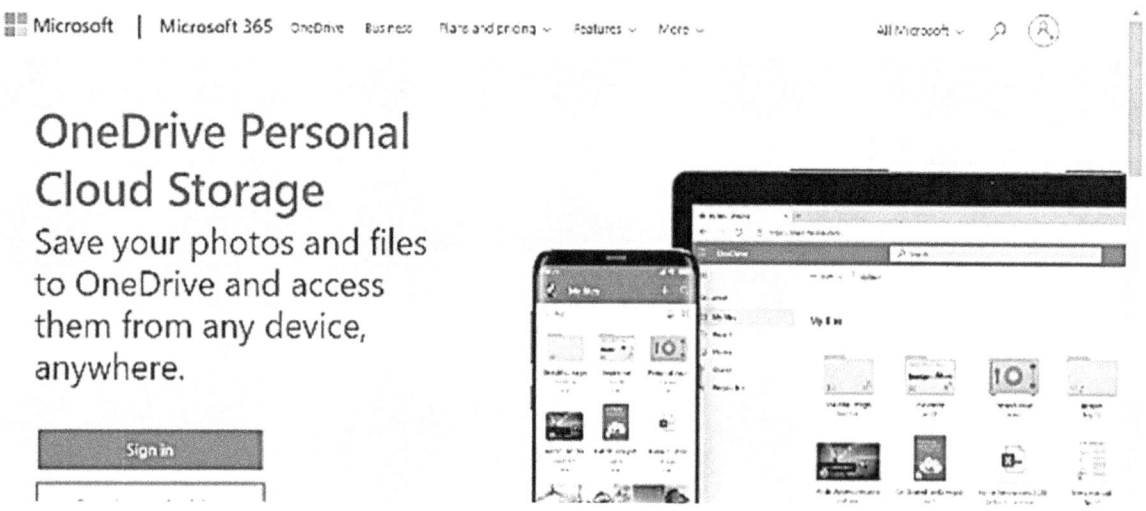

Both methods come with their own set of benefits and drawbacks.

An external hard drive is better if you prioritize offline access and complete control over your data. On the other hand, cloud storage services may be the best option if you place a high importance on ease, accessibility from any device, and automatic backups.

Windows 11 Installation Assistant Method

As a beginner, the **Installation Assistant** option is a simple way to update to Windows 11.

- Go to Microsoft's Download Windows 11 web page.

    https://www.microsoft.com/en-us/software-download/windows11

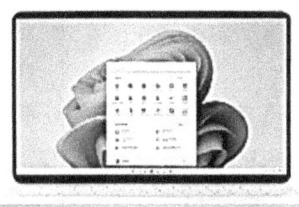

- Under the Windows 11 Installation Assistant column, click the **Download Now** button. Ensure your internet connection is stable before doing this.
- After the download, open the **.exe** file and follow the on-screen instructions.

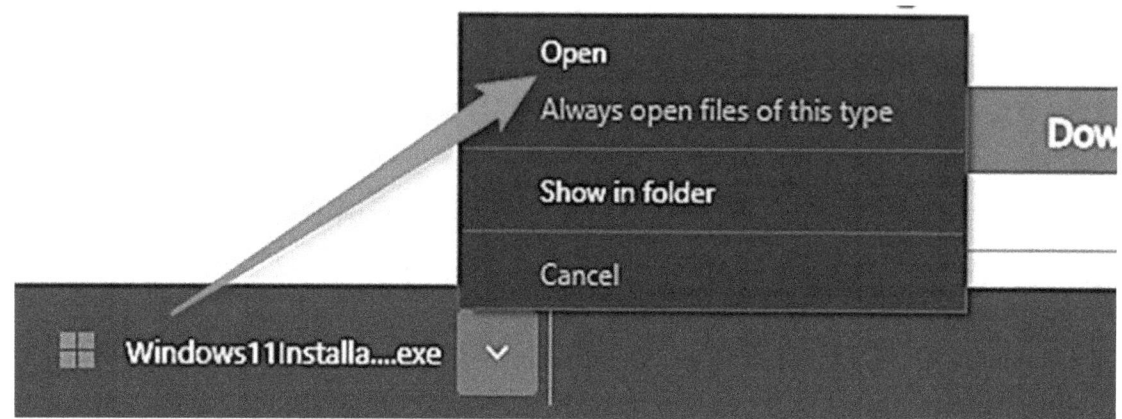

- Click the **Accept and Install** button to start the installation process.

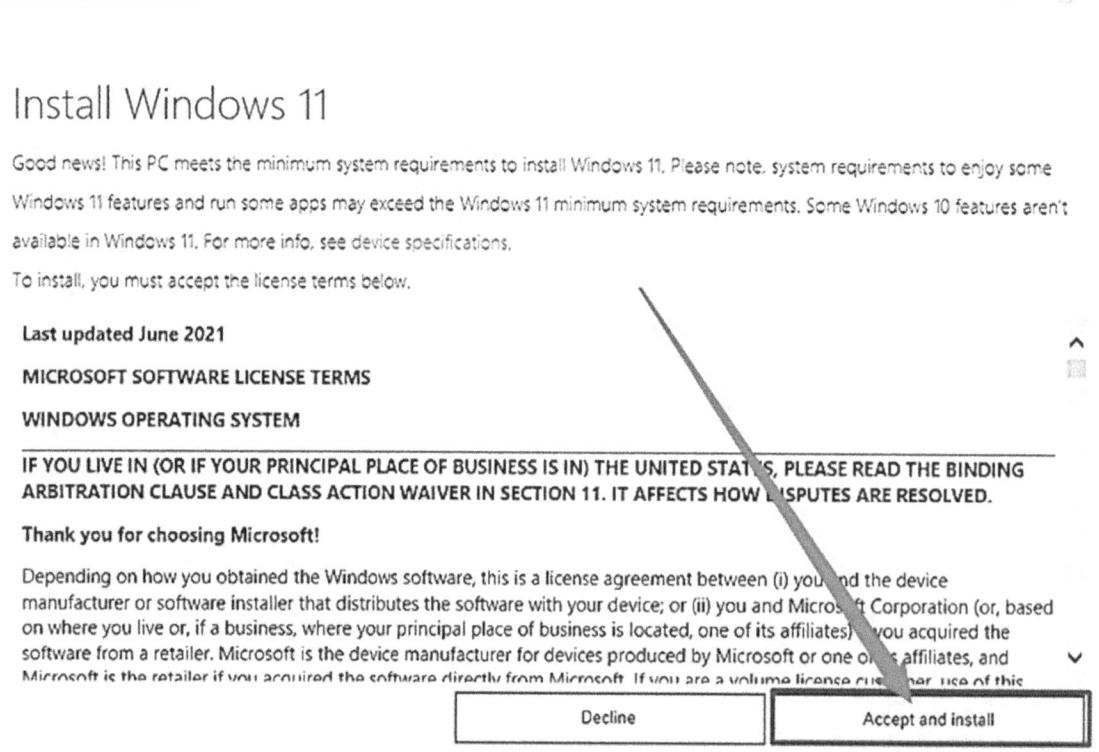

- Depending on your computer's memory and speed, wait a while for Windows 11 to be installed.

Step 3 of 3: Installing

It's OK to keep using your PC, but we'll restart your PC 30 minutes after we reach 100% on this screen, so be sure to save your work frequently.

Percent complete:

79%

After completing the update to Windows 11, all your files and applications should remain in their original locations. Though some programs and folders may have a new visual appearance, such as rounded corners on apps and folders, everything should function as expected.

Windows 11 Clean Installation Option

To configure a new laptop or desktop computer, a clean installation of Windows 11 involves completely wiping the computer's hard drive and installing a fresh copy of the operating system. This method is also helpful in fixing problems with an existing setup.

Additionally, a clean installation of Windows 11 can significantly improve battery life and is the most effective way to remove viruses and spyware from the system.

For new PCs, starting over with a clean installation is an effective way to deal with bloatware that comes pre-installed with the original factory image.

A clean installation ensures a fresh, stable, and optimized operating system, which will help enhance the overall system performance and extend your device's battery life in the case of a laptop. It is also useful when dealing with malware or unwanted software that may have been present in the previous setup.

Moreover, it gives you a cleaner and more efficient system without unnecessary pre-installed programs often found in factory configurations.

However, it is crucial to remember that a clean installation will erase all data from the hard drive, so be sure to back up your important files before proceeding.

So, if you are not confident performing the process yourself, seeking assistance from a knowledgeable individual or a professional is advisable to ensure a successful and smooth setup.

How to Prepare your PC for a Clean Installation of Windows 11

Performing a clean installation of Windows 11 provides your computer with a fresh start, but it also comes with a huge drawback: all of the data that is stored on the hard drive will be deleted. During this process, it is essential to take appropriate safeguards to avoid data loss by accident.

Before you proceed, create a backup of your crucial files. This is a highly recommended step. This includes all files you would not want to lose.

However, earlier discussed, when it comes to copying your data, you have two primary choices:

- **External storage device:** Your data will be copied onto a physical storage unit, such as an external hard drive or a USB flash drive. This setting assures that you will have access to your data even when you are not connected to the internet.

- **OneDrive:** Microsoft provides its customers with a cloud storage service. You are able to upload your files to OneDrive, and they will be stored online, making them accessible from any device that has an internet connection. Even though it is convenient, this option requires a connection to the internet to view your data.

On an old operating system like Windows 10, you can confirm the activation status of your Windows by following these steps:

1. Right-click on the Start menu and select "**Settings**."
2. In the Settings menu, click on "**Update & Security**."

3. Choose "**Activation**" from the menu on the left.

4. The activation status of your current version of Windows can be viewed here.

When it comes to Windows activation and your Microsoft account, there is a significant distinction that you need to be aware of: even if your Windows 10 is active, it may not be linked to your Microsoft account. This circumstance can arise when the activation is based on a digital license, activating the operating system but not instantly connecting it to your personal account.

Although your Windows operating system is fully functional and usable, the license will not immediately transfer to a new device if you log in with your Microsoft account on that device. This is because Windows does not have an association with other operating systems. Awareness of this difference is essential, particularly if you intend to swap devices or wish to alter your Windows license's settings through your Microsoft account.

To ensure that the Windows 11 installation goes on smoothly, I recommend you disconnect all peripherals that are not necessary, such as USB drives, printers, cameras, scanners, and Bluetooth devices.

Please ensure that your monitor, mouse, keyboard, and internet connection are all plugged in while the process is being carried out. During the installation process, this helps make sure that there are no potential conflicts or problems.

Creating a Bootable USB for a Clean Windows 11 Installation

For a fresh installation of Windows 11, you will need to create a USB bootable media. The Microsoft Media Creation Tool helps make bootable USB drives.

Create Your **Windows 11 bootable USB** drive

To use **Microsoft Media Creation Tool** to create a Windows 11 USB bootable media requires a USB flash drive with a minimum of 8GB storage space. Next, you follow the steps below:

1. Go to the Microsoft Windows Download web page.

https://www.microsoft.com/en-us/software-download/windows11

2. Scroll to the "**Create Windows 11 Installation Media**" section and click the ***Download Now*** button to download the **.exe** file on your device.

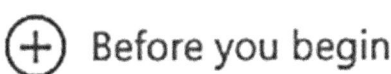

3. Once the download is complete, locate the MediaCreationToolW11.exe file to run the tool on your computer.
4. Go through the License Terms and click on the Accept button to proceed.

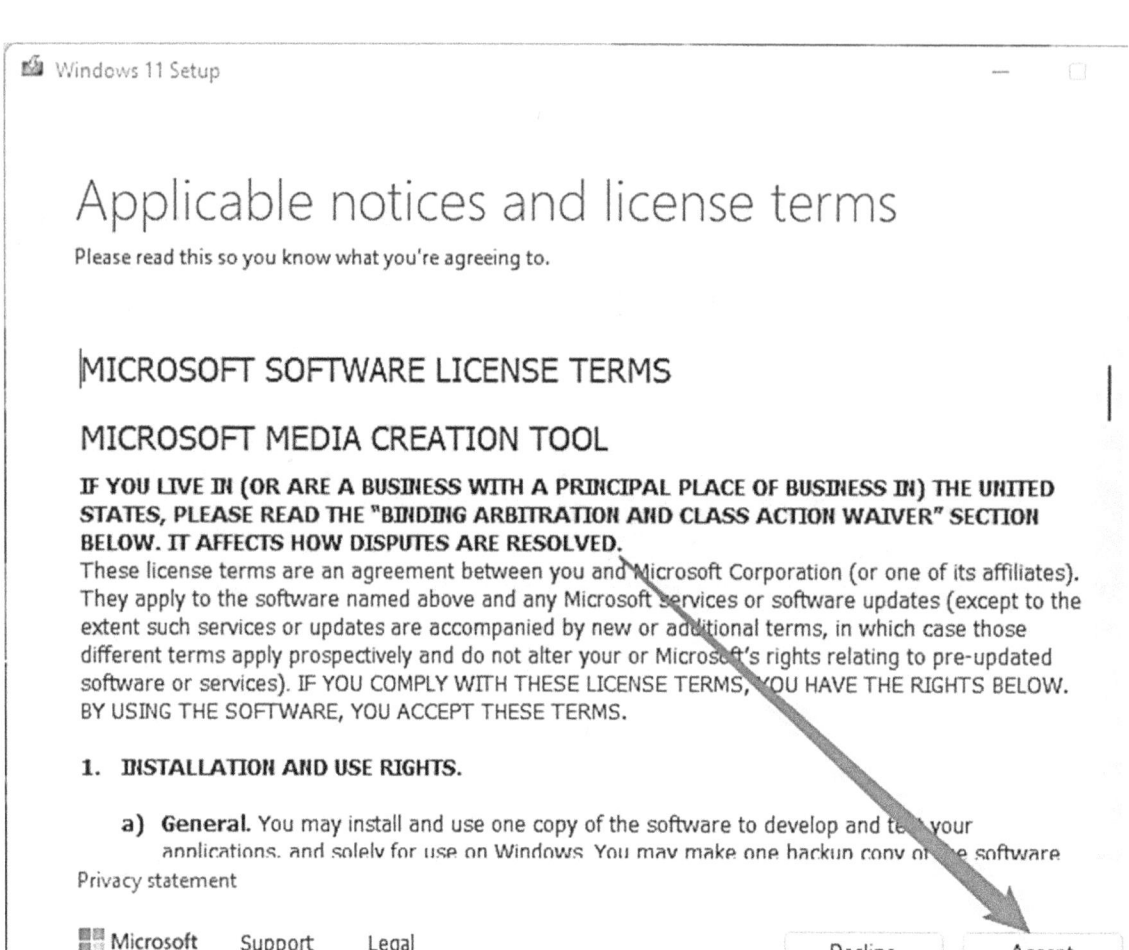

5. Select your preferred language and Windows 11 edition. ***Uncheck*** the "**Use the recommended options for this PC**" box.

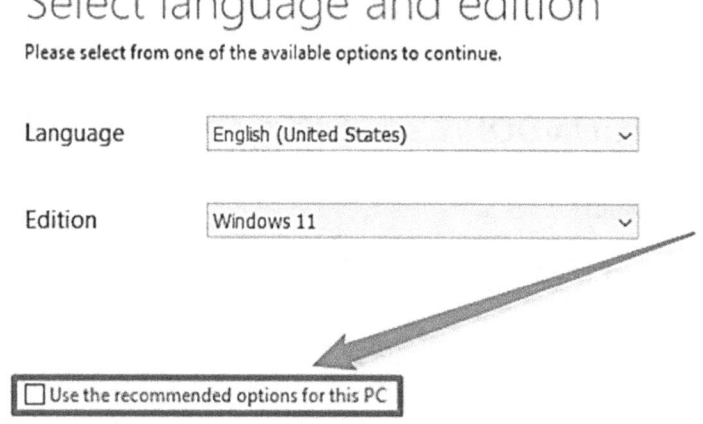

6. Click on **Next** button to continue.

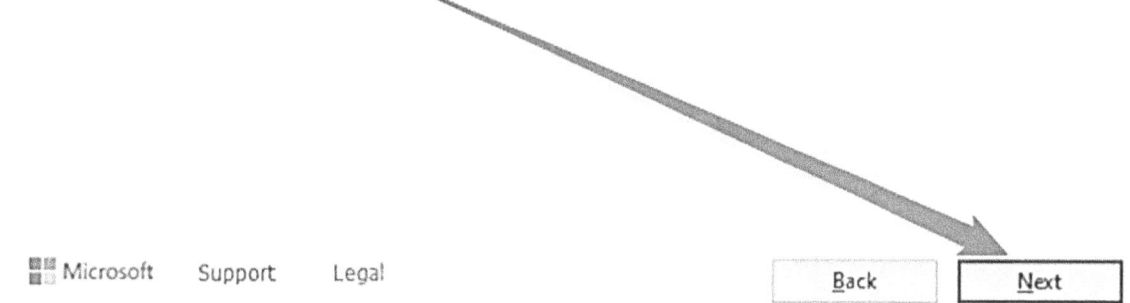

7. Select the USB flash drive option.

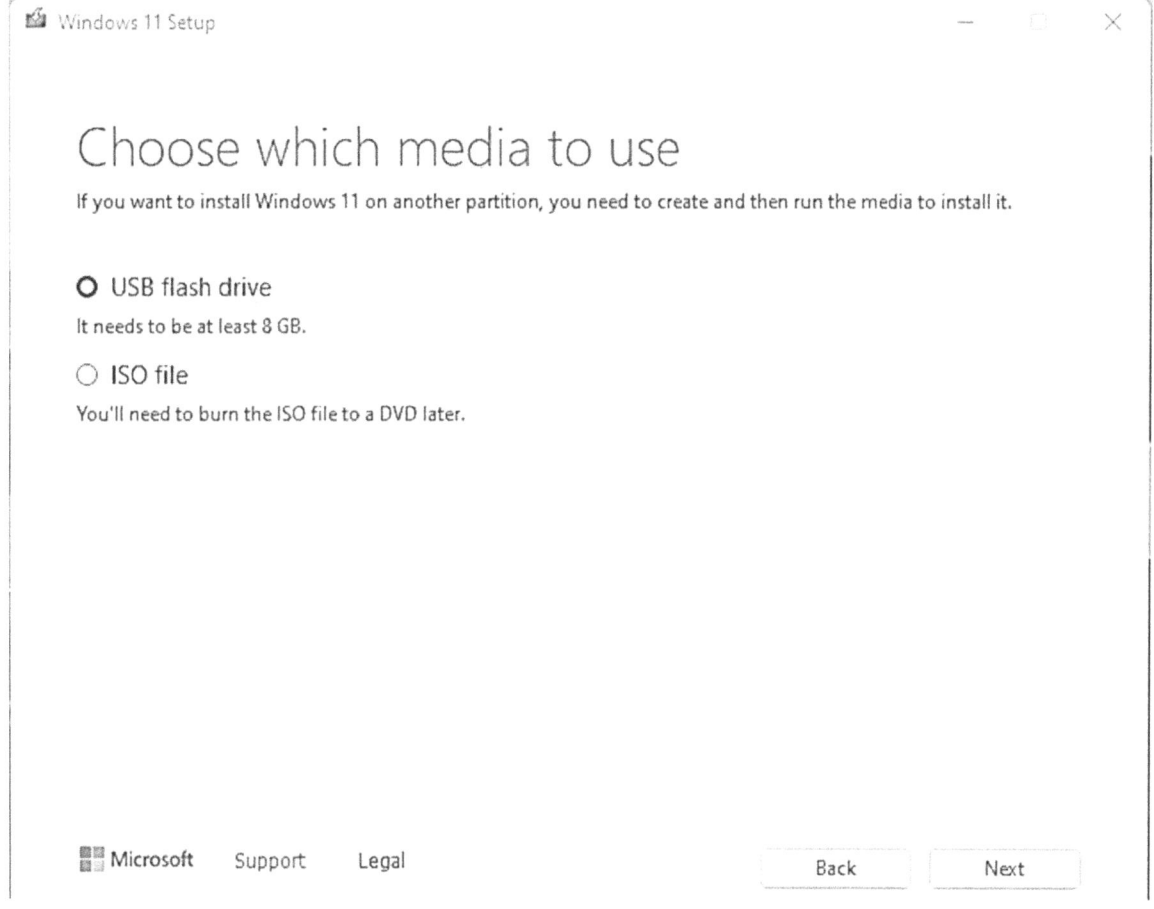

Note that using a USB flash drive requires a minimum of 8GB of storage. The ISO file option will require an additional task to create a bootable media

8. Click on Next button, and then select the USB Flash Drive.

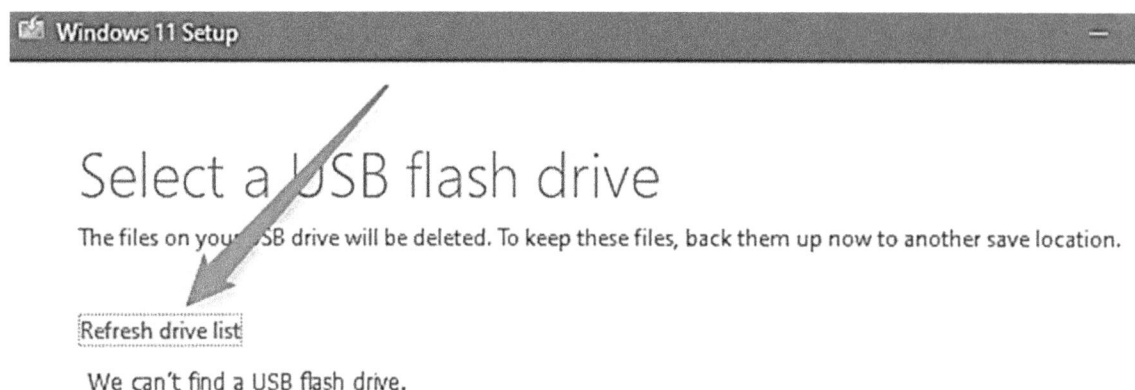

If the USB Flash Drive you want to use is not found, click on the **Refresh drive list** link.

9. Click on the **Next** button, and then click on the **Finish** button.

After completing these steps, the application will download and create an installation media. The bootable USB flash drive contains files to boot your computer and install a fresh copy of Windows 11.

Windows 11 Clean Installation

You can now install Windows 11 after preparing a bootable USB flash drive.

This process will erase all the data on your hard drive, so you may have to back up all your files before you proceed.

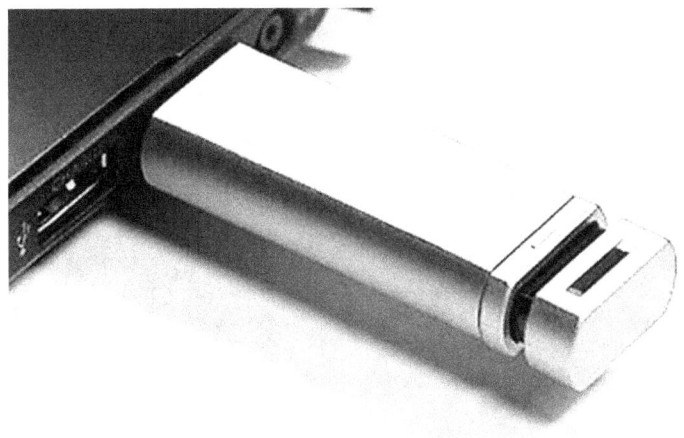

Follow the steps below for a clean installation process.
1. Connect the Windows 11 bootable USB flash drive to your computer and start the PC.
2. Next, your computer will prompt you to press any key to boot from the USB drive. Press any key to continue.

3.Select your language, time format, and keyboard.

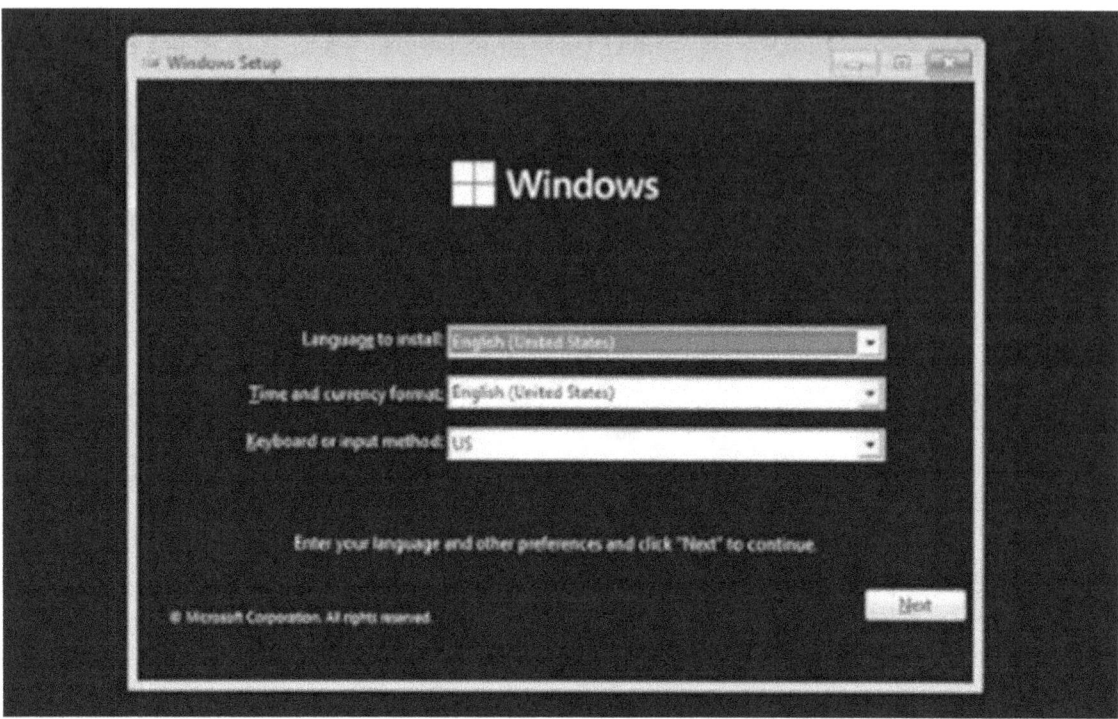

4.Click on the **Next** button to continue.

5.Click on the **Install now** button on the next screen.

6.On the next screen, click on the "**I don't have a product key"** link to continue if you are reinstalling.

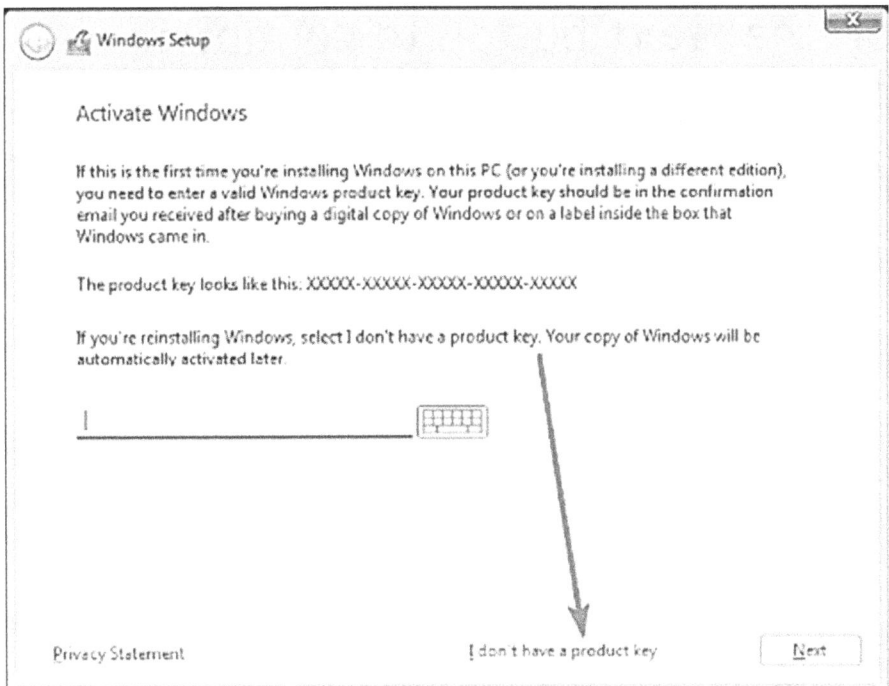

If the Windows 11 installation is the first, you will need to enter the product key. You can skip and select the ***I don't have a product key*** link to enable you to continue and later on add the key.

7. Click the **Next** button and select the Windows 11 edition you want to install.

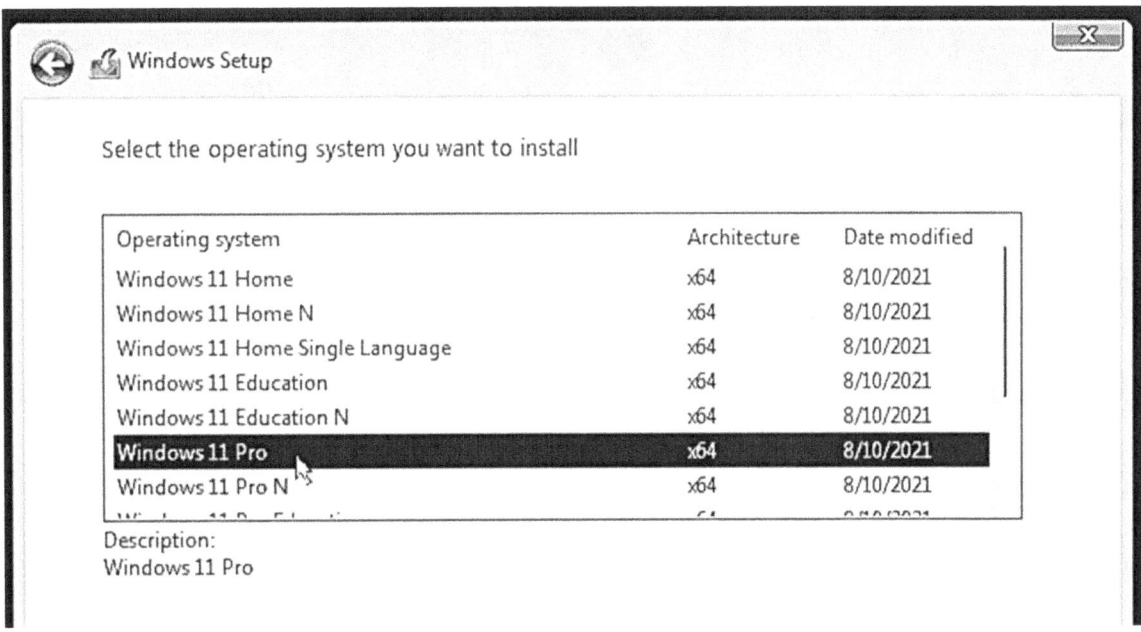

Click on the **Next** button to continue.

8. Accept the license terms to continue. On the next screen, select **Custom** for a fresh installation.

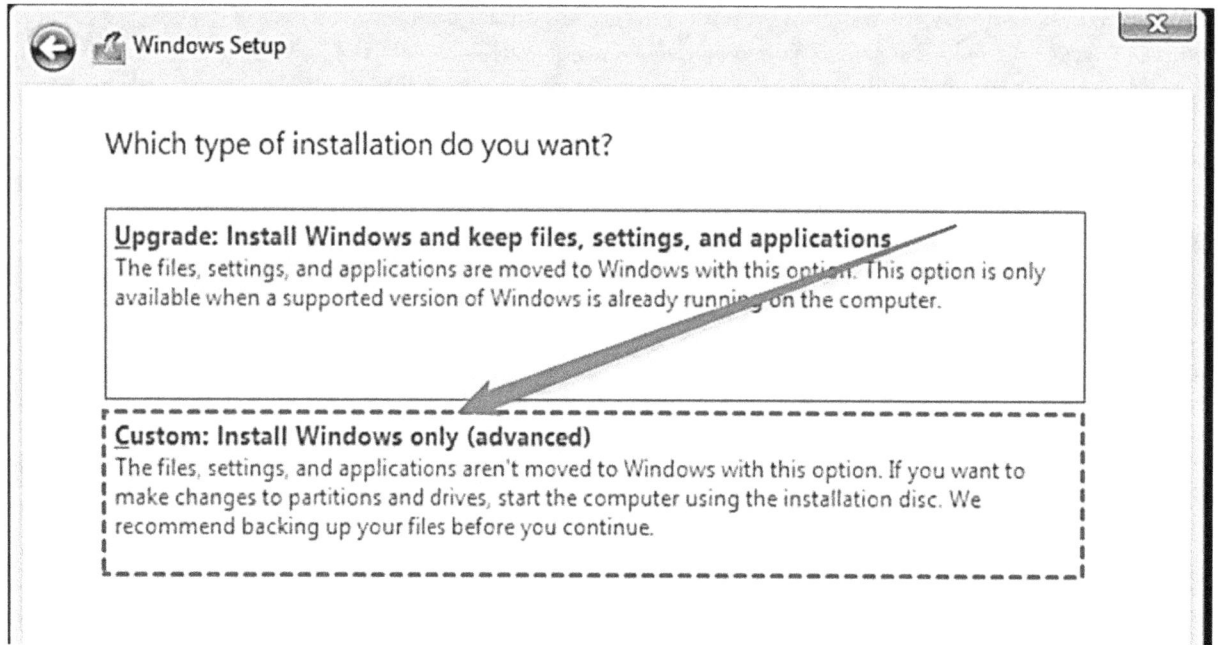

9. Choose the disk partition, click Next to start the installation, and wait for it to complete.

CHAPTER 3

GETTING STARTED WITH WINDOWS 11

Windows 11 Desktop Lock Screen

When you first turn on or wake up your computer, the Windows 11 operating system will boot and display the Desktop Lock Screen.

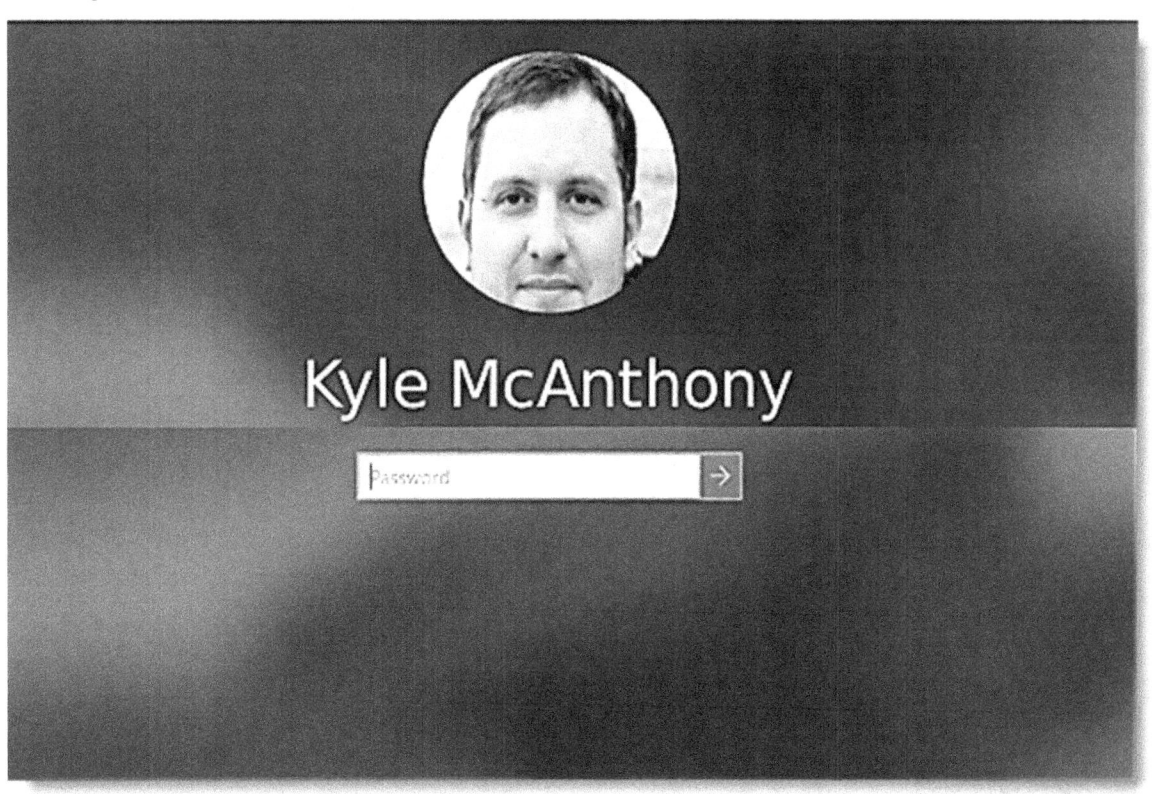

To unlock the Windows 11 Lock Screen, you must perform the appropriate authentication method, such as typing your password, entering your PIN, or using your biometric credentials. These are security features Microsoft has put in place.

After successfully unlocking the Lock Screen, you will be taken to the Windows 11 desktop.

The Windows 11 Desktop

The desktop on your screen is the central hub of your computer. It is the first thing that appears when you log in, and it offers a space that can be customized to suit your digital life.

The main area of the desktop displays your background image or wallpaper, which sets the visual tone for your workspace.

The great thing about the desktop is that it can change to fit your needs. You can put your favorite program's icons, folders, and shortcuts anywhere you want. This lets you make your workspace your own, making it quick and easy to find what you need.

The wallpaper may first draw your attention to the desktop, but it is more than just pretty. One essential desktop component is the Taskbar located at the bottom of the screen. The Taskbar provides quick access to features like the Start menu, system notifications, open apps, and the system tray.

Taskbar Features

Windows 11 offers a significantly better user experience with a modern Start menu and a redesigned Taskbar that preserves the comforts of Windows 11. The Taskbar provides access to the Start Menu, Windows Search, Virtual Desktops, Windows Explorer, and applications, among other essential operating system functions.

The Start menu, located in the Taskbar's lower-left corner, is the preferred interface for opening apps, navigating settings, and performing searches.

Start Menu

The Taskbar also displays icons representing running applications, allowing you to switch between them efficiently.

This user-friendly feature streamlines the process of managing and navigating through active applications.

Hovering over an icon displays a thumbnail of the application's window.

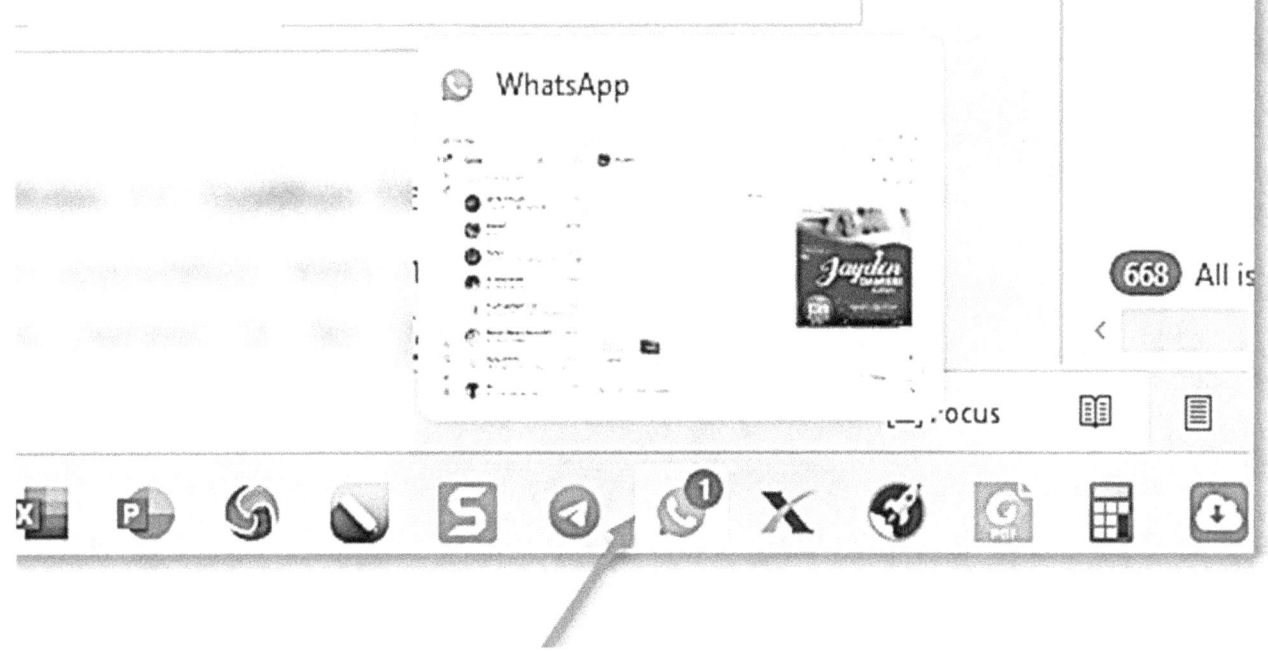

The Windows 11 Start Button

The **Start Button** is the first icon on the Taskbar's far-left (with four white rectangles).

The Start Menu gives you access to all the programs on your computer.

The Search Icon

Next to the start button is the s*earch icon* that looks like a magnifying glass.

The **Search** icon allows you to look for files, programs, and settings on your computer.

To search for an item, click the search icon and type in the word on the search bar.

A result of your search will appear below the search bar.

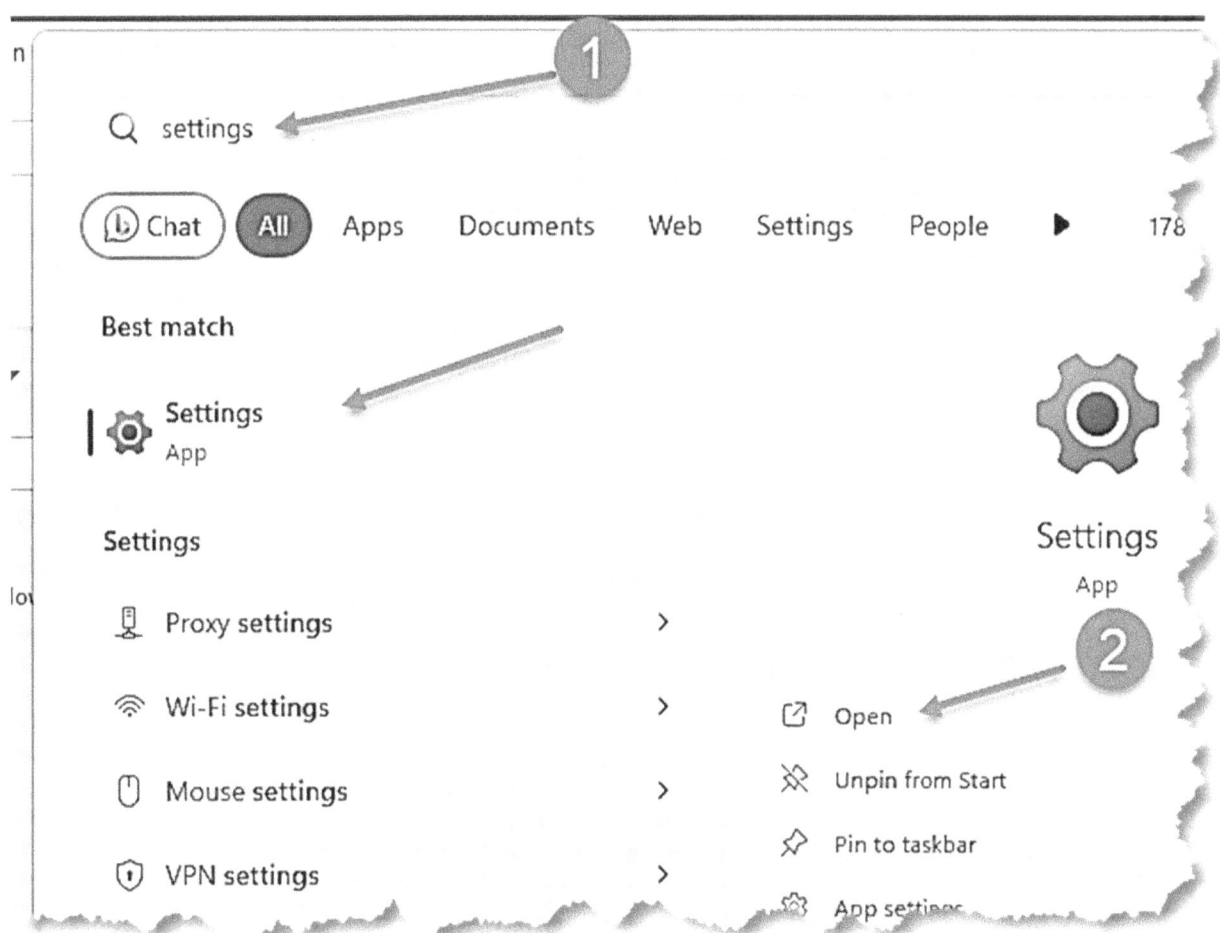

As seen in the example above, when you type "**Settings**" in the search bar, the **Best match** panel will appear along with the contents of your computer that contain the searched term.

Let's say you are looking for a particular file on your computer. Under such circumstances, you can click the search icon, type the file name into the search bar, and hit Enter to display the best match result for your search.

The Virtual Desktop or Task View

Next beside the Search bar is the **Virtual desktop** or **Task View**.

Task View lets you quickly see what programs are active, and you can switch from one desktop to another within your computer using the Task view.

Since its inception, this function has undergone numerous refinements. In addition to quickly switching between programs, you can pick up where you left off in any activity. Use Task View with virtual desktops for a streamlined method of handling related tasks.

Widgets

Widgets are a collection of apps with graphic displays that you can access right from the Windows 11 taskbar. Widgets provide quick access to information such as news, sports results, stocks, weather, and so on.

You can access the Widgets menu in Windows 11 by clicking on the widget's icon on the taskbar.

Next, click on the item you want to view, either sport, news, weather, etc.

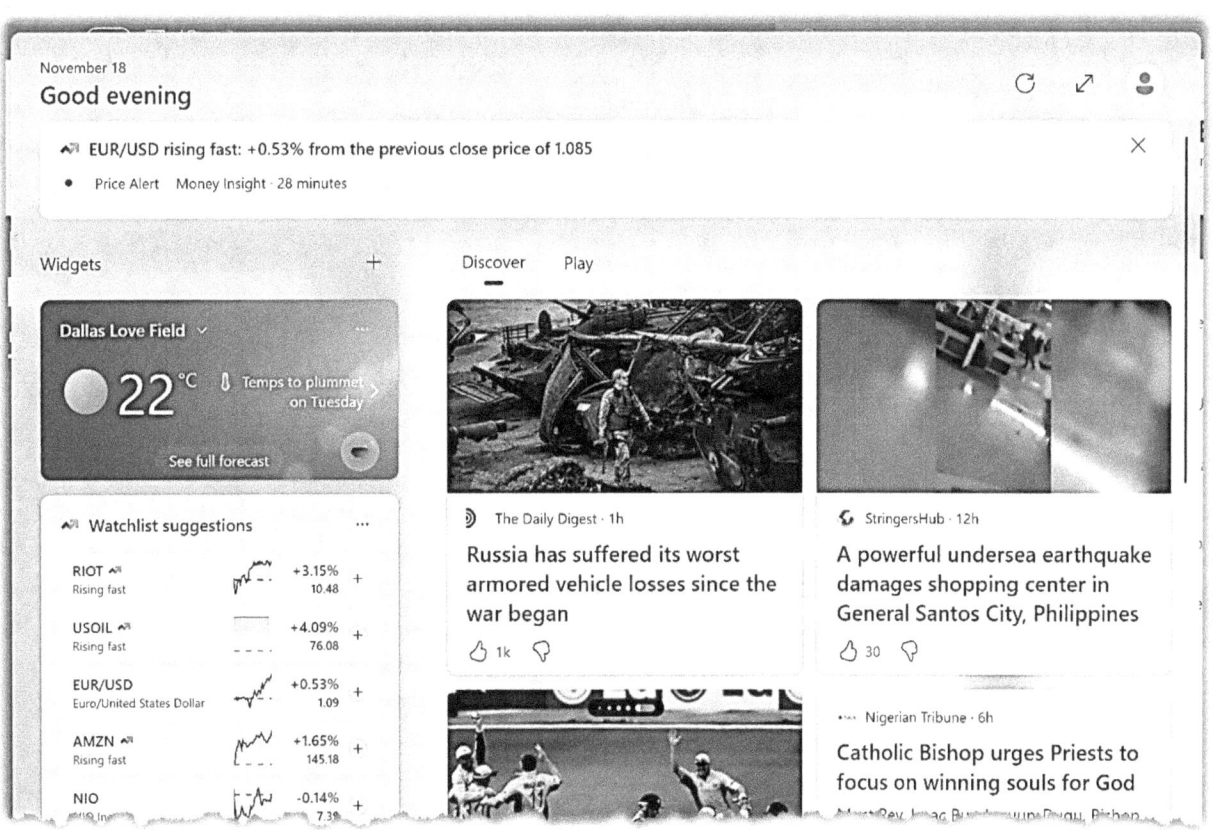

However, an active internet connection is required to use this feature. The customizable widget menu allows you to configure settings and display only widgets aligned with your interests.

Teams Chat

With Windows 11, you have access to Microsoft Teams, a central hub for all your online communication, and it lets you easily reach out to the people who matter most via text, voice, or video call on any device running Windows 11.

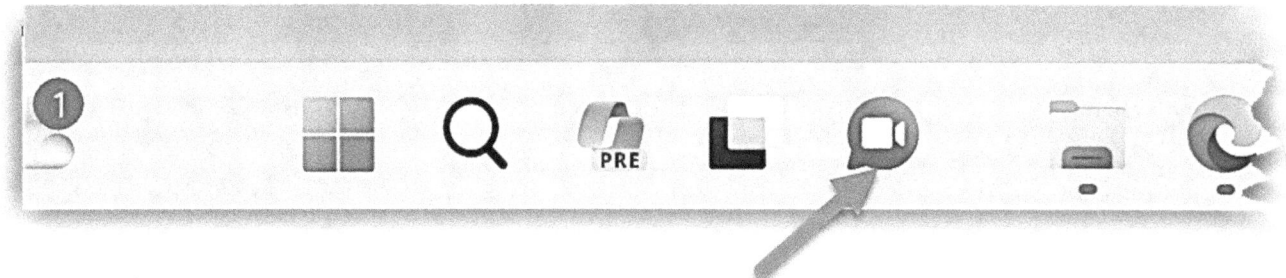

Your contacts can join you from any computer, smartphone, or tablet with access to the web.

The Teams Chat icon on the taskbar gives you access to Microsoft's Teams chatting and video conference.

File Explorer

One of the most essential features of Windows 11 is the addition of the File Explorer shortcut to the Taskbar.

Clicking the icon gives you access to your device's file system, which allows you to navigate through folders and files easily. You can easily organize and retrieve your digital content in this way, saving time and effort over conducting exhaustive manual searches.

In another chapter, we will dive deeper into the file explorer, promising you an enriched understanding of this essential tool in Windows 11.

Edge Browser

Microsoft's Edge icon lets you launch the operating system's default browser.

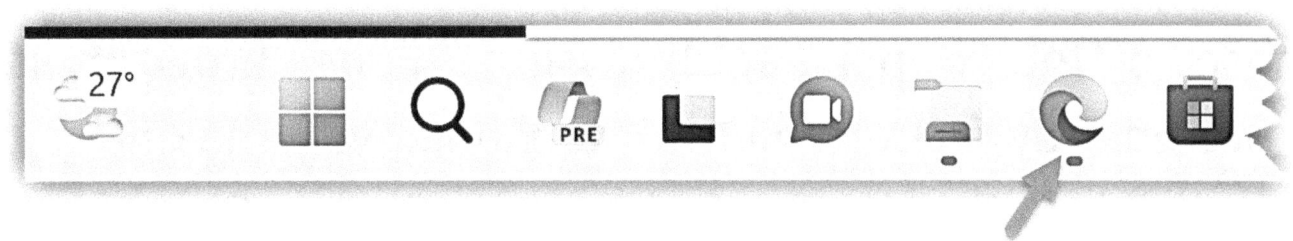

Microsoft has heavily invested in upgrading the Edge browser, which reflects their desire to encourage Windows 11 users to adopt Edge as their preferred browser.

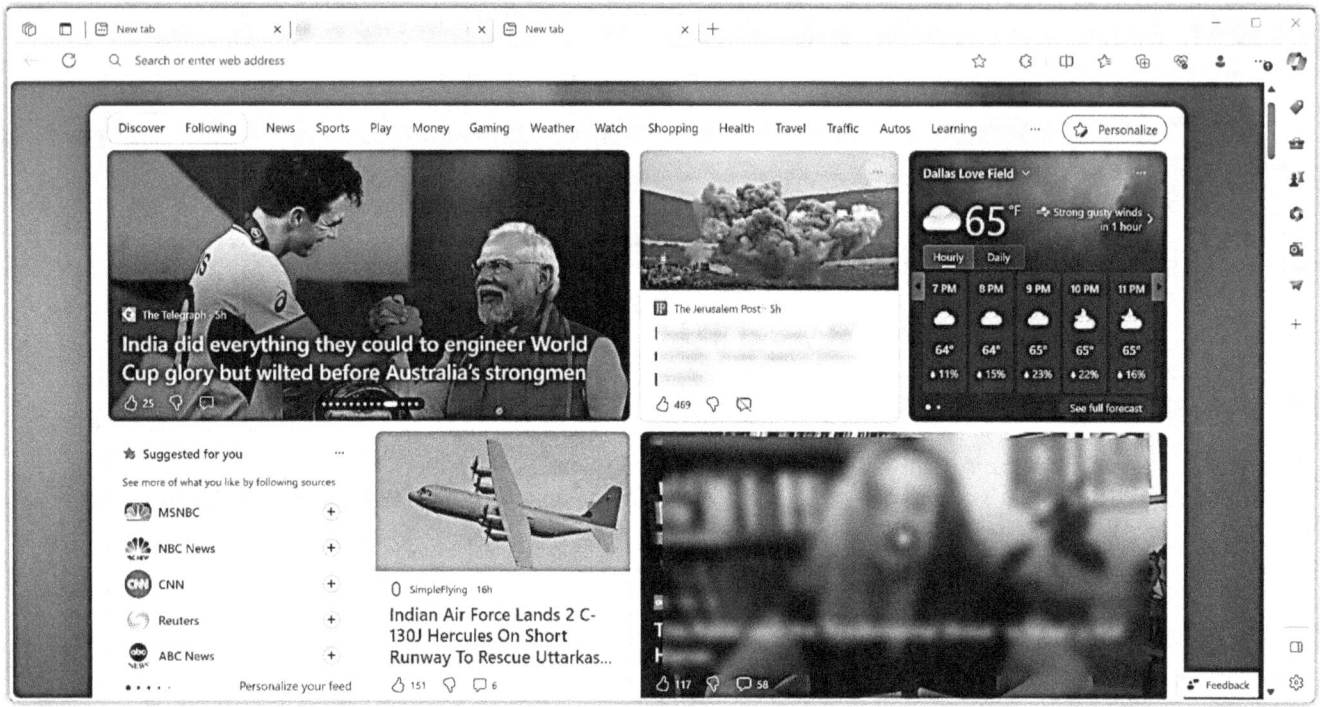

While the choice ultimately rests with the user, Microsoft's efforts highlight its commitment to providing a strong and competitive browsing experience within the Windows ecosystem.

There are several benefits to making Microsoft Edge your primary browser, as its features are competitive with those of other popular browsers. Edge browser is powered by "Chromium" technology, making it compatible with add-ons designed for Google Chrome.

Microsoft Store

The Microsoft Store icon in Windows 11 is your portal into a lively online marketplace.

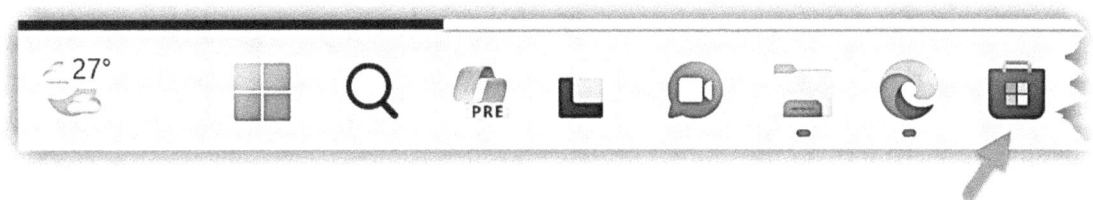

Once you click on this button, a world of possibilities opens up, including an easy and streamlined method of downloading apps.

The ability to sign in with a Microsoft account online adds a granular level of customization, letting you effortlessly access preferred apps and settings across all of your devices. With this integrated experience, installing apps is a personalized journey where you can look into available apps and pick the ones that best fit your needs and interests.

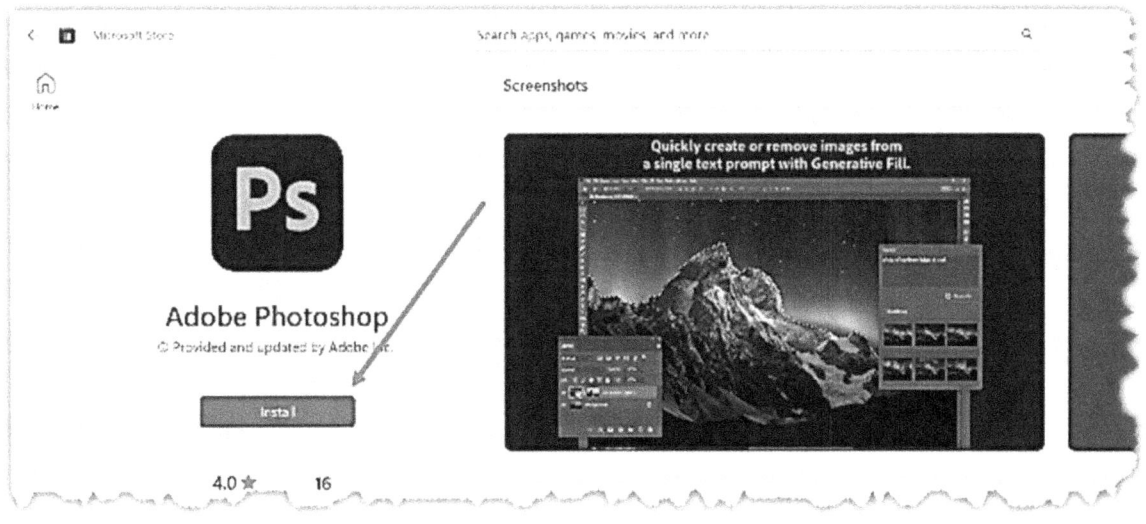

The Taskbar Notification Area

The notification area is at the right end of the taskbar in Windows 11.

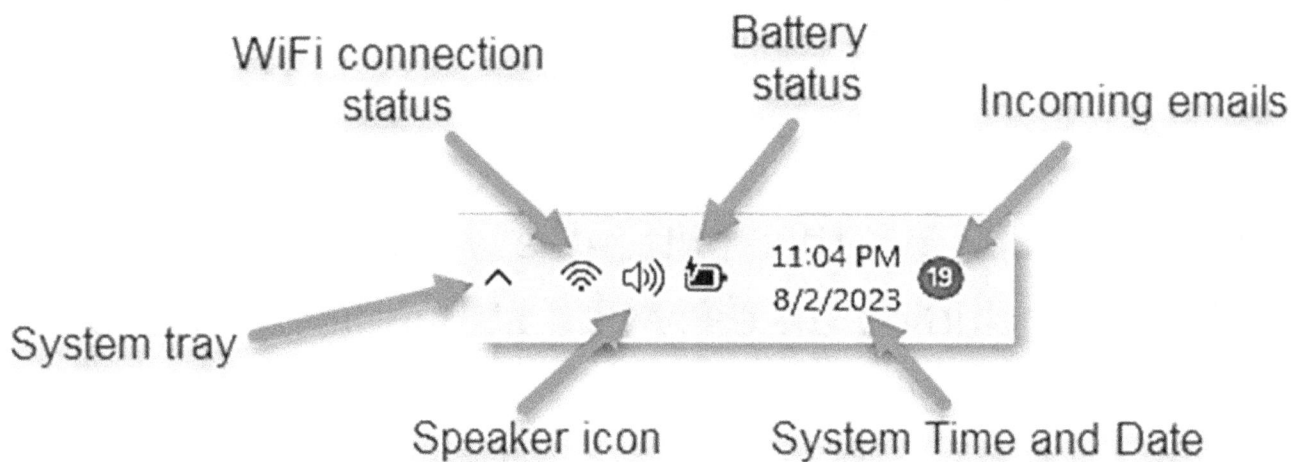

The taskbar notification area shows things like the status of your WiFi connection, new emails, Windows software update alerts, the battery life of your laptop, the speaker icon, taskbar corner icons, and the system time and date.

There are only a few icons in the Notification area, but you can hide, show, or change the icons of apps you use often. To see hidden icons, click the system tray arrow.

Task Bar Animation Features

Windows 11's Taskbar goes beyond just providing access to your apps. It also incorporates subtle animations to enhance your user experience.

When you launch any app, its icon on the Taskbar changes, adding some animation. This visual clue gives the app personality and lets you know it is being used.

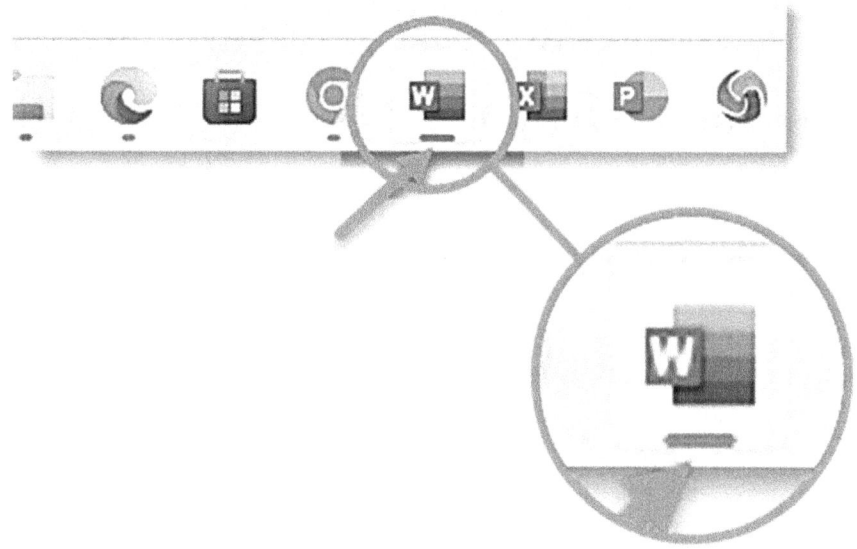

A small pill-shaped icon is at the bottom of each active app icon on the Taskbar. This indicator isn't still; it comes to life with small animations. Compared to older versions of Windows, this makes the interface feel more lively and exciting.

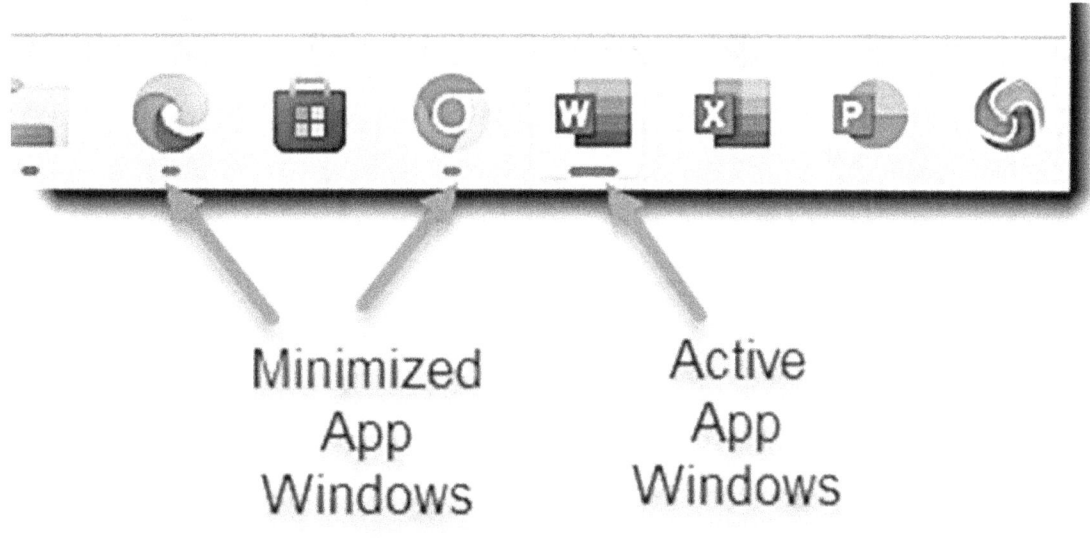

CHAPTER 4

TASKBAR PERSONALIZATION

Windows 11 knows that not all users are the same, especially regarding how you work. The bar at the bottom of your screen, the Taskbar, is no different. It can be changed to fit your workflow and screen layout needs.

One of the most useful customization options is the ability to move the Taskbar to the left or right side of your screen from its usual spot at the bottom. This can help users who like a more vertical layout or have a widescreen monitor. The size of the Taskbar can also be changed to fit your screen and needs better. There is more room for icons in a bigger size, but a smaller size looks better.

Auto-hide is an important feature if you want to maximize your screen space. Once this setting is made active, the Taskbar will disappear when not in use, making more screen space available. To make it appear again, you hover over it with the mouse.

How to Change the Taskbar Position

To change the position of the taskbar in Windows 11, follow these steps:

1. Right-click on an empty area of the taskbar. (An empty area is anywhere on the taskbar that does not contain an icon or an open application.)

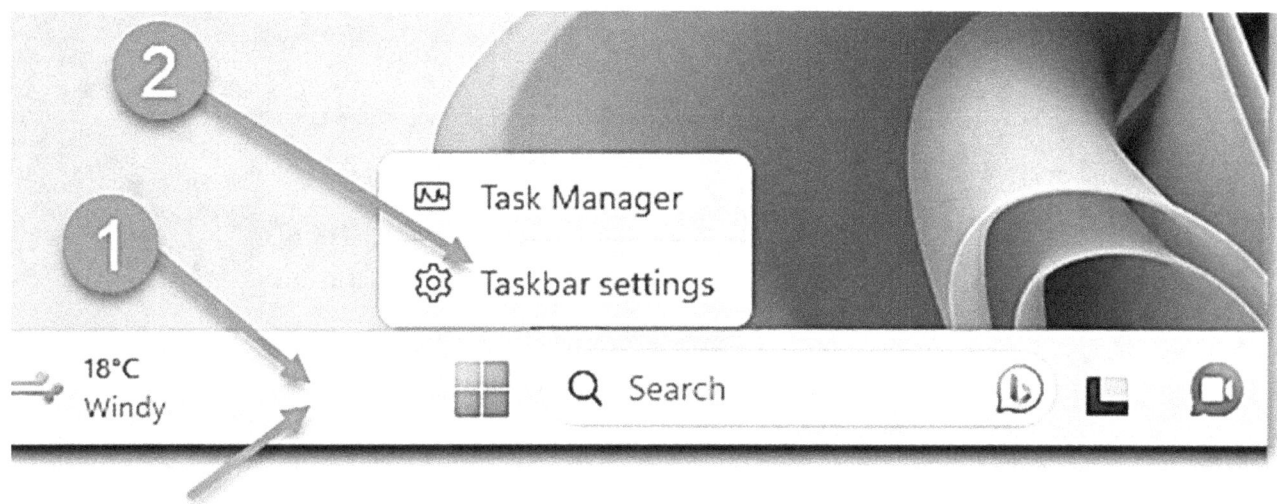

Empty area

2. From the context menu that appears, click on "**Taskbar settings**."

3. Scroll down and click "**Taskbar settings**".

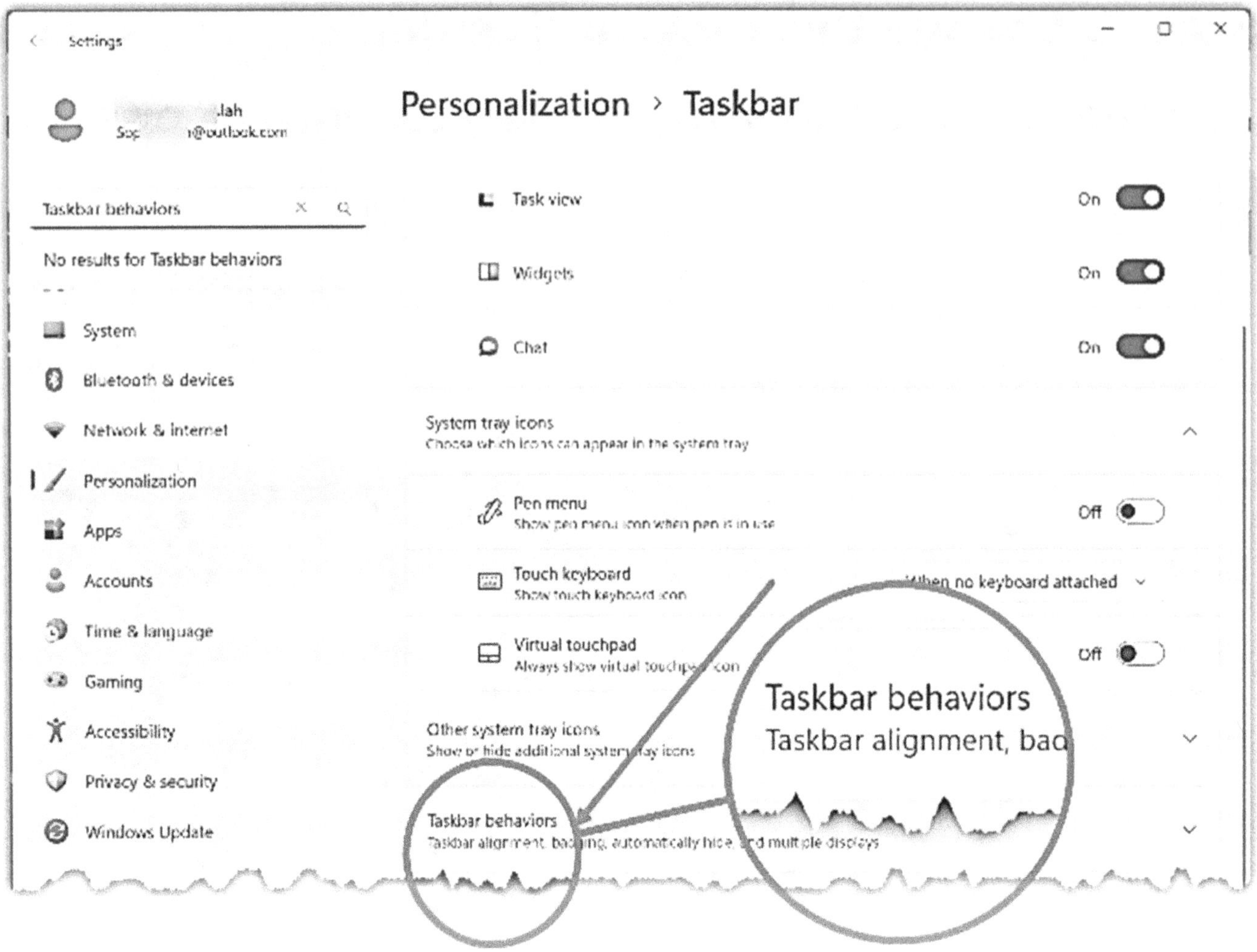

4. Under "**Taskbar behaviors**," you will find the "**Taskbar alignment**" option, which allows you to choose the taskbar's position on the screen.

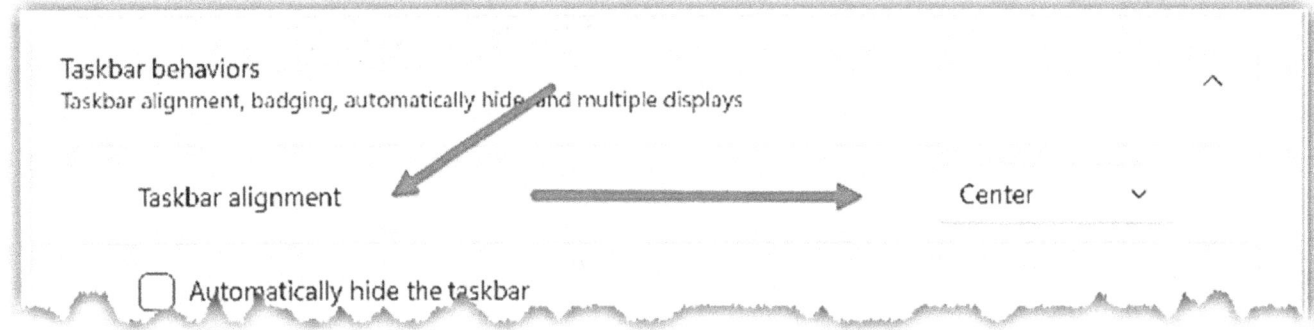

5.Click on the drop-down menu under "**Taskbar alignment**" and select your preferred position for the taskbar.

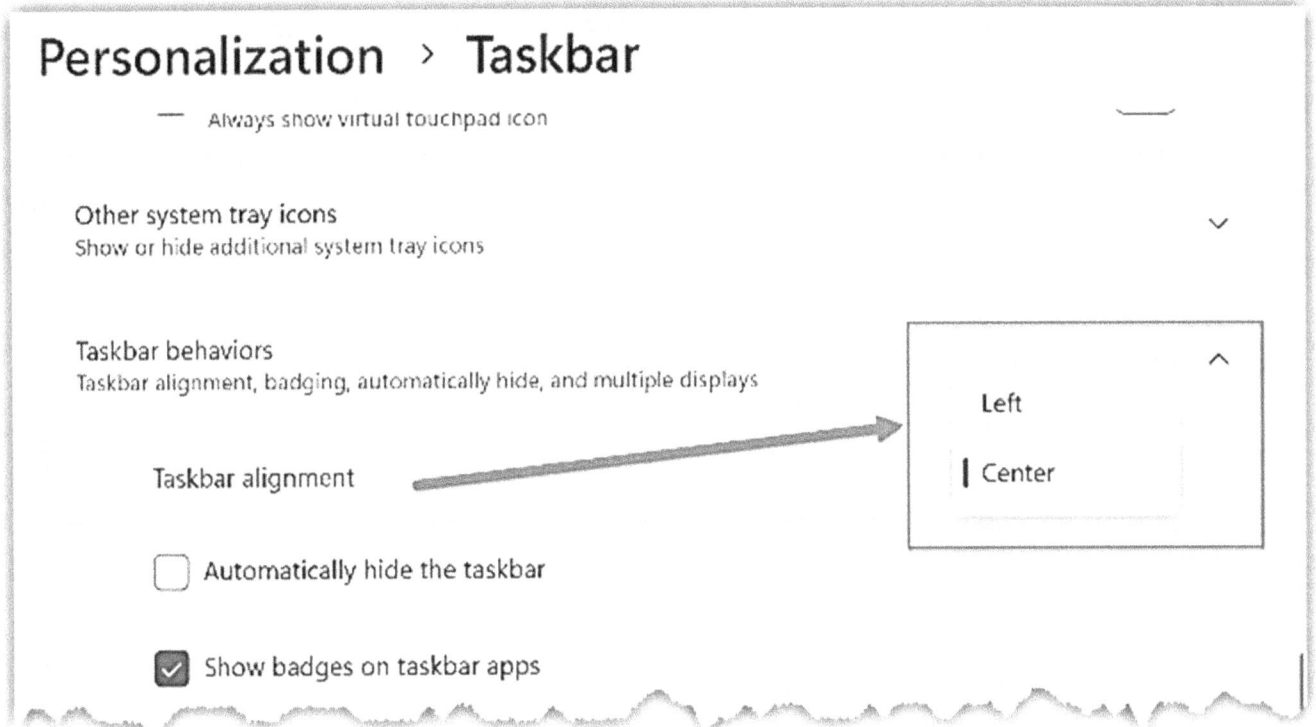

How to Pin Installed Application

The Taskbar is where you can access and manage all your running apps.

When you start up an app, its icon shows up on the Taskbar to let you know that it is currently running. This makes it simple and quick to see which apps are running on your computer.

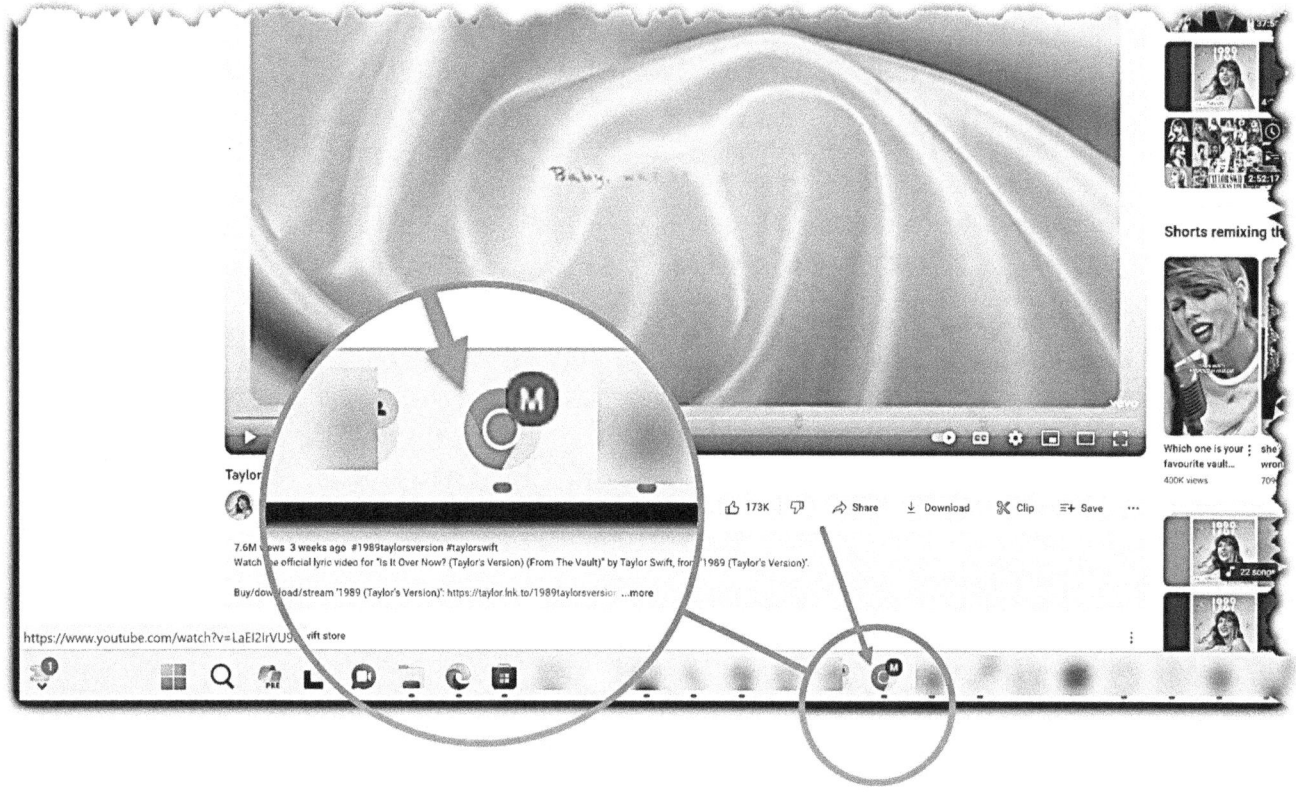

When you close an app, its icon goes away from the Taskbar on its own. This keeps the Taskbar clean and organized by only showing the icons of programs that are running or that have been pinned for quick access.

However, you can pin application icons to the Taskbar so they are easy to find when you need them. This makes sure that the icon stays even after you close the program, so you can quickly open it again with just one click.

To pin an application in the taskbar, ensure the application is running, then **right-click** on the app's icon as it appears in the taskbar and select **Pin to taskbar**.

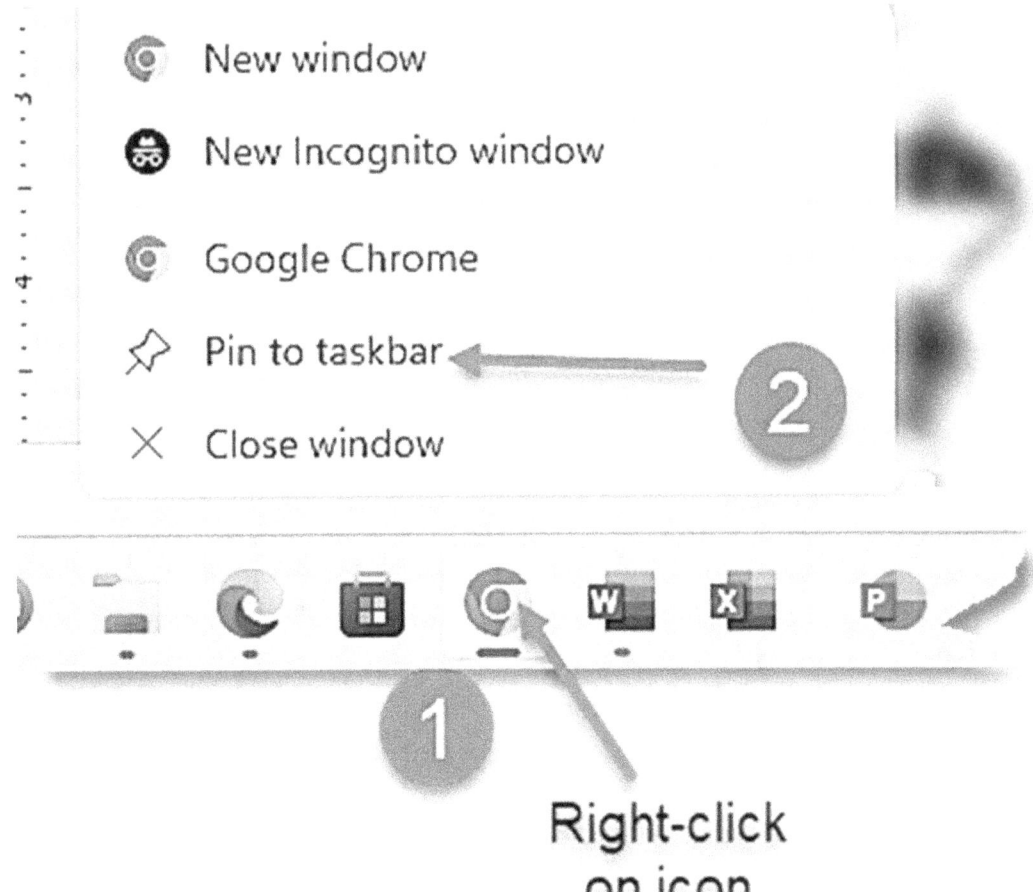
Right-click on icon

Only applications whose icons you pinned remain displayed even when the application is not opened or running in the background.

Another method you can use to pin an application icon in the taskbar is using the desktop.

If the application has its icon on your Desktop, **Right-click** on the icon, and then select **Show more options** at the bottom.

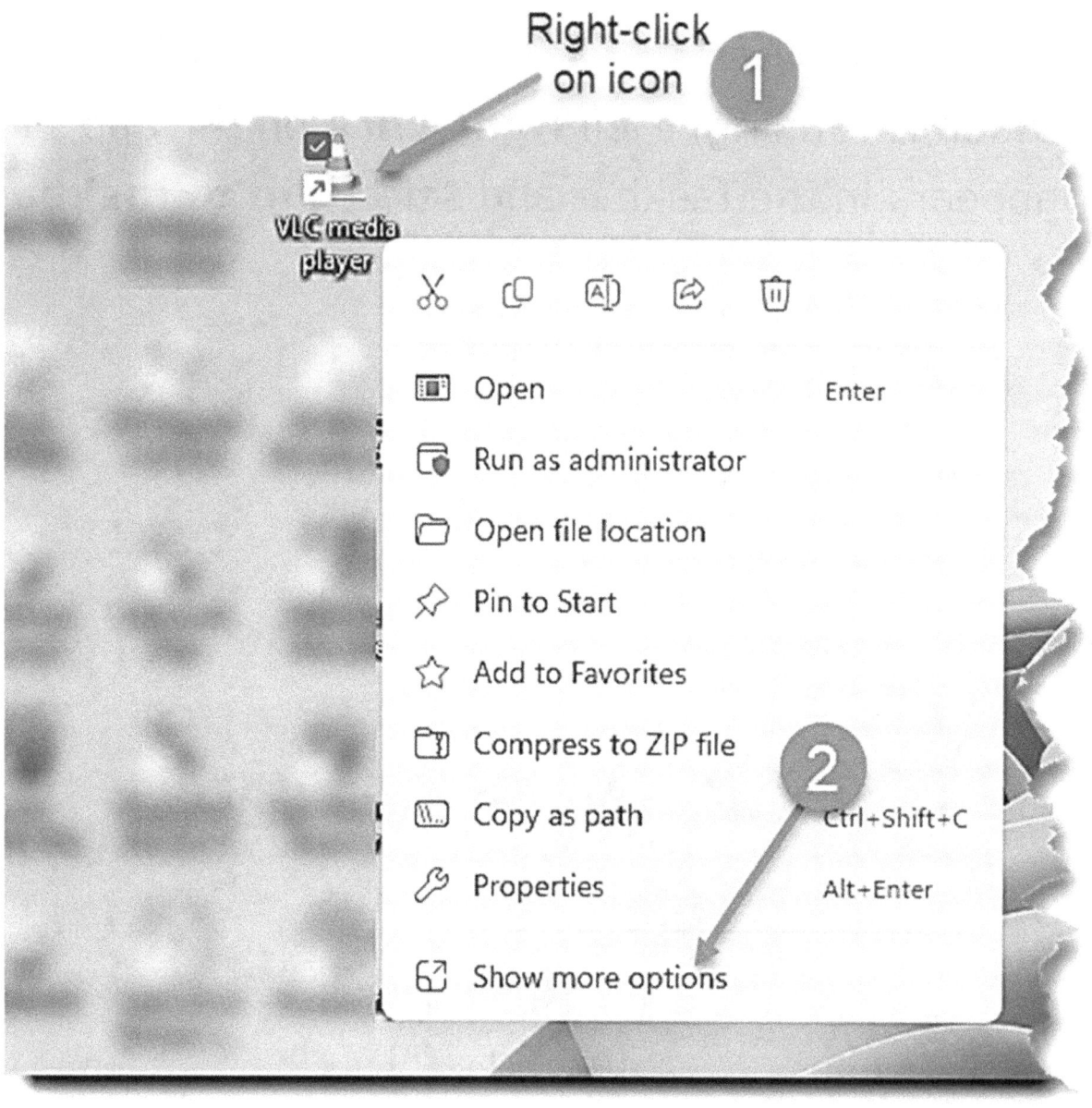

Next, click on **Pin to taskbar** from the list of options displayed to complete the process.

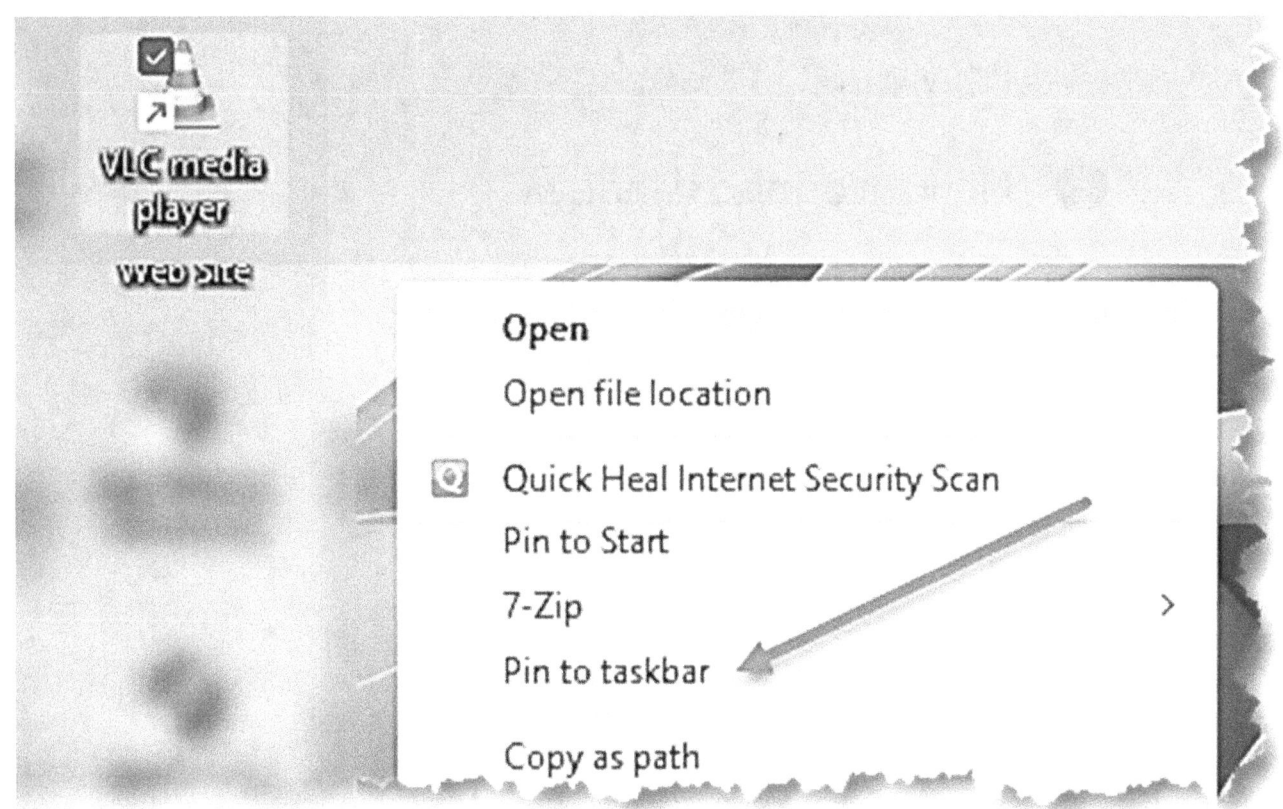

Removing Pinned Application

By default, in Windows 11, the Start menu, Search, Copilot, Desktop, Widget, Chat, and Microsoft Store icons are pinned to the taskbar.

If you wish to disable or unpin an application's icon from the taskbar, you can follow these steps:

Right-click on the app's icon and select **Unpin from the taskbar**.

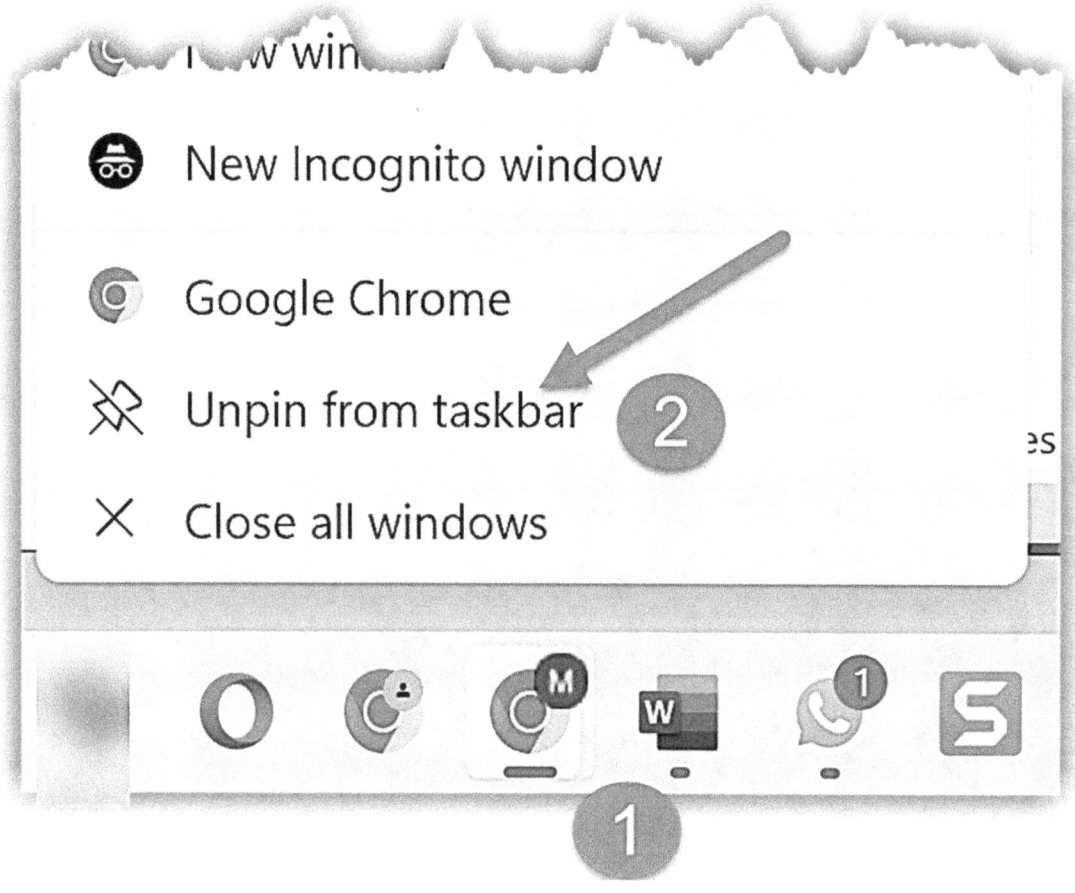

To remove any of the other default icons,

1. Move your mouse cursor to the taskbar.
2. Right-click on any empty space on the taskbar. Make sure you don't right-click on an app icon or an active application. Choose an area without any existing icons.

Empty area

3. After right-clicking, a context menu will appear. In the context menu, click Taskbar settings.

4. On the personalization panel, the **Taskbar items** hold the default icon settings. Amongst these icons, you can toggle off the icons you don't want.

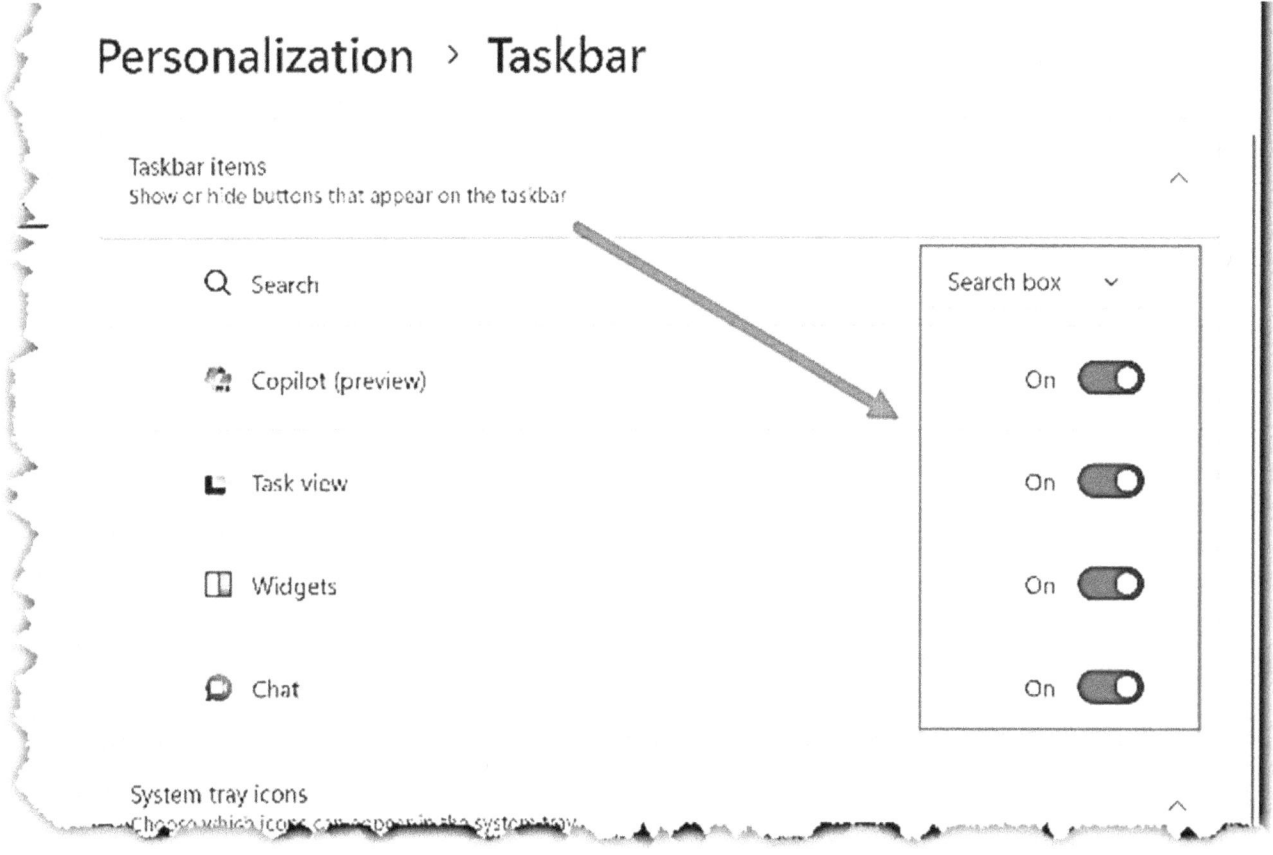

Any of the items you toggle off will not appear on the taskbar.

Meanwhile, the search box will require you to change the option to Hide by clicking the drop-down arrow.

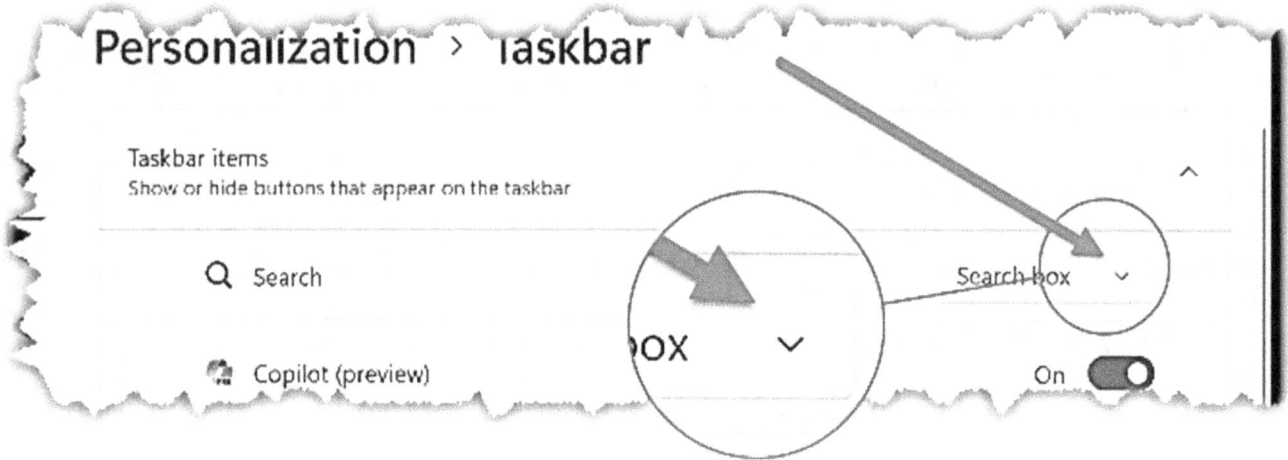

From the list, you select Hide.

System Tray and Corner Overflow on the Taskbar

The system tray is a handy tool for navigating your computer's functionality. It is located on the right side of the taskbar, starting with the **Show hidden icons**.

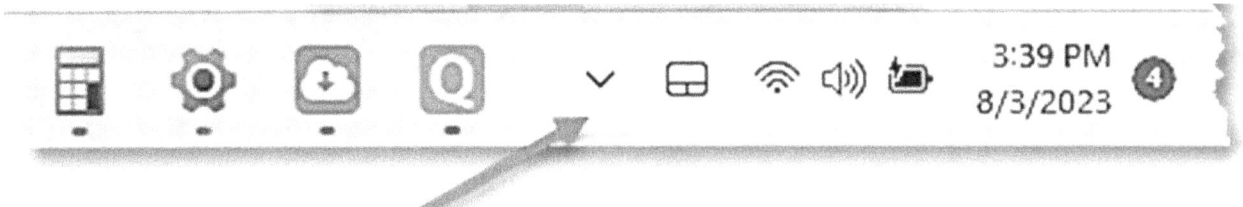

The system tray is where you can access system utilities, get live notifications, and monitor tasks running in the background. It is like a small control center that lets you quickly get to important features without searching for them or going through menus.

However, not all the icons are immediately visible. You can reveal a hidden list of additional icons by clicking the small arrow (^) on the right-hand side of the taskbar.

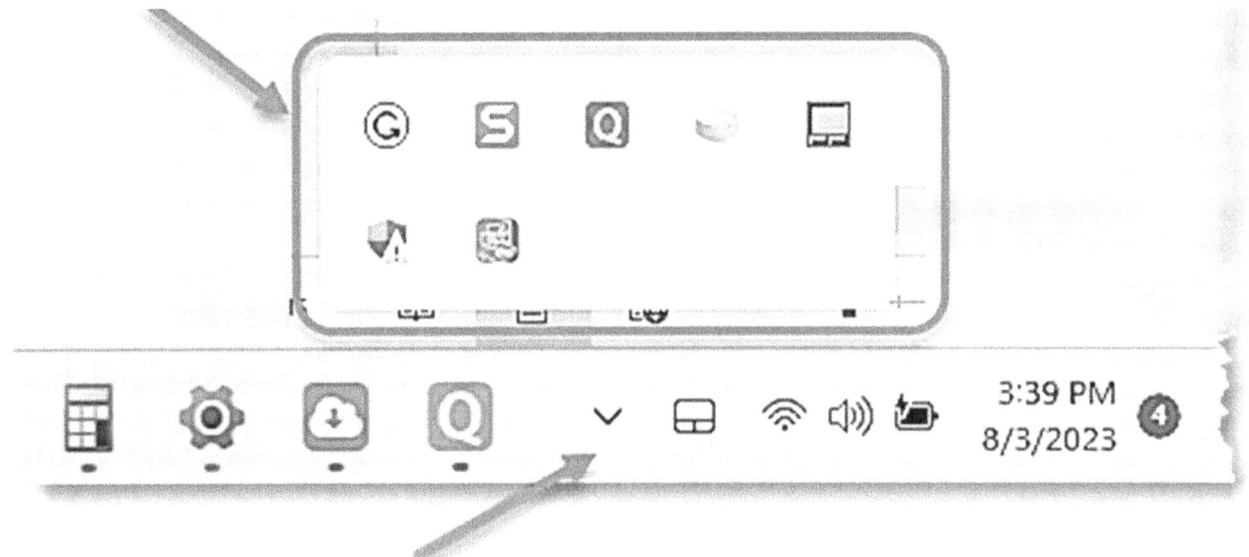

The taskbar also has the **Taskbar Corner Overflow** feature in the bottom right corner just after the "Show hidden icons" arrow.

It is a multipurpose tool that helps you manage the clutter on your taskbar while providing easy access to essential applications and system functions. By default, Windows 11 shows only a few icons in the system tray, keeping the rest hidden in the taskbar corner overflow.

Clicking on the small arrow next to the "Show hidden icons" section allows you to view the hidden icons within the Taskbar Corner Overflow.

To customize your layout, you can then drag and drop icons between the system tray and the overflow area.

With this feature, you can make your taskbar more organized by hiding icons you don't use very often and leaving the ones you use easy to find. So, your workspace will stay clean and organized, and you will always have what you need close at hand.

How to Customize the Taskbar Corner Overflow

1. Go to any space on the taskbar and right-click, then select **Taskbar.**

2. In the Taskbar personalization panel, scroll down to **Other system tray icons**. Here, you will see a list of icons currently hidden or shown in the system tray.

3. To show an icon in the overflow, toggle on the switch next to it.

4. To hide an icon in the taskbar corner overflow, toggle off the switch next to it.

5. You can also rearrange icons between the system tray and the taskbar corner overflow by clicking on the **show hidden icons** (^) and dragging your desired icon to the corner overflow area.

To move a Icon, Click and drag the icon to the **Taskbar overflow corner**

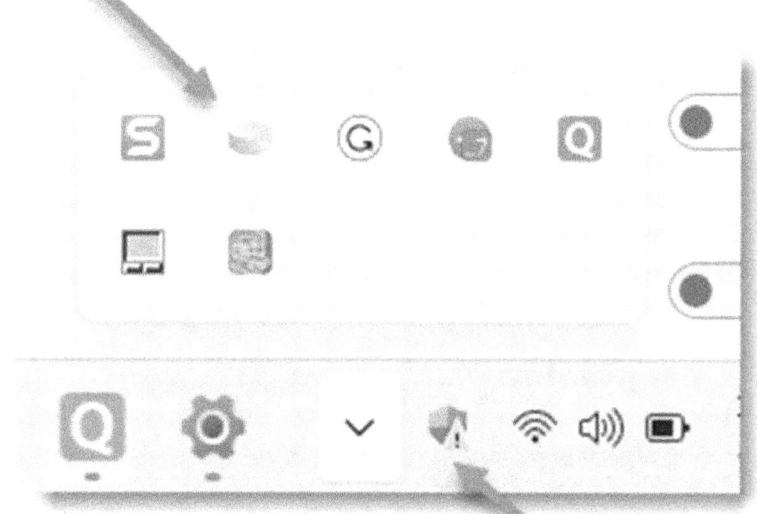

To move a Icon, Click and drag the icon on the **Taskbar overflow corner**

How to Hide the Taskbar Automatically

If you run out of screen space on your computer, you can utilize the "**auto-hide**" feature. Enabling auto-hide automatically hides the taskbar whenever you are not actively using it. This means it disappears from the bottom of your screen and is suitable for times when you need as much space as possible, like when you are editing photos, watching videos, or writing documents.

Here's how to set up the auto-hide feature for the taskbar in Windows:

1. Right-click on an empty area of the taskbar.

2. From the context menu that appears, select "**Taskbar settings**."

3. In the "**Taskbar settings**" window, scroll down to the "**Taskbar behaviors**" section.

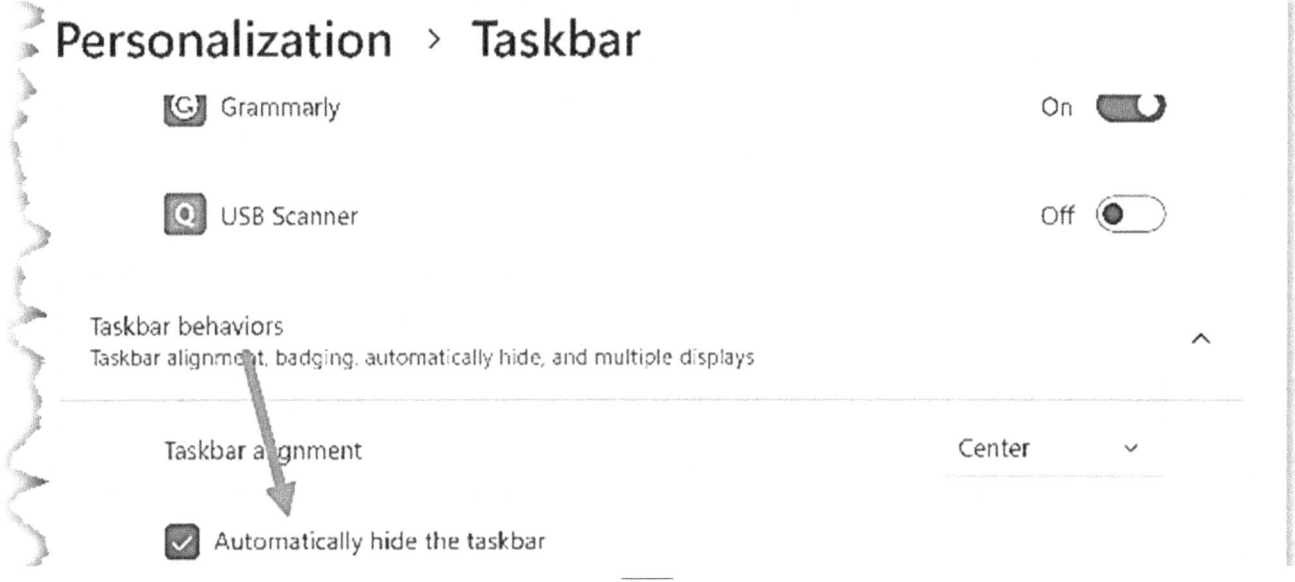

4. Click the check "**Automatically hide the taskbar**" chek box.

5. Once enabled, the taskbar will automatically hide when you are not using it.

6. To access the taskbar, move your cursor to the bottom of the screen, and the taskbar will reappear.

Displaying Badges on Taskbar Icons

The taskbar also serves as a vital information hub through badges displayed on app icons.

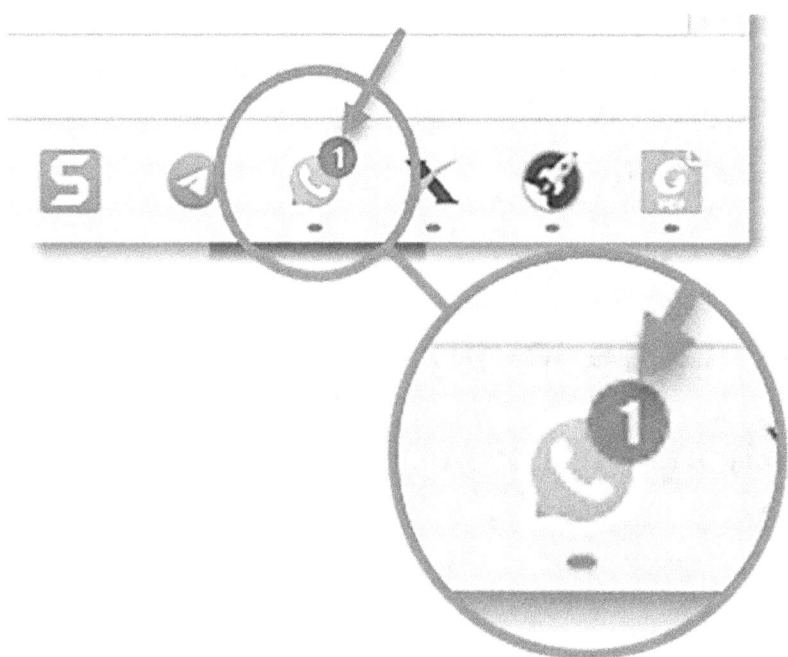

Badges appear as small numbers or symbols on top of app icons in the taskbar. They act as visual cues, indicating that something within the app requires attention.

These badges will stay on the app icon until you respond to the notification within the app. This way, you won't miss any vital information and can keep up with your work.

For instance, if you have the Whatsapp app for desktop running in the background, a number badge may appear on its taskbar icon, indicating the number of unread messages.

To disable the badges for taskbar applications, follow these steps:

1. Right-click on any space on the taskbar.

2. From the context menu that appears, select "**Taskbar settings**."

3. In the "**Taskbar settings**" window, click on "**Taskbar behaviors**."

4. Uncheck the "**Show badges**" box to turn off application badge notifications.

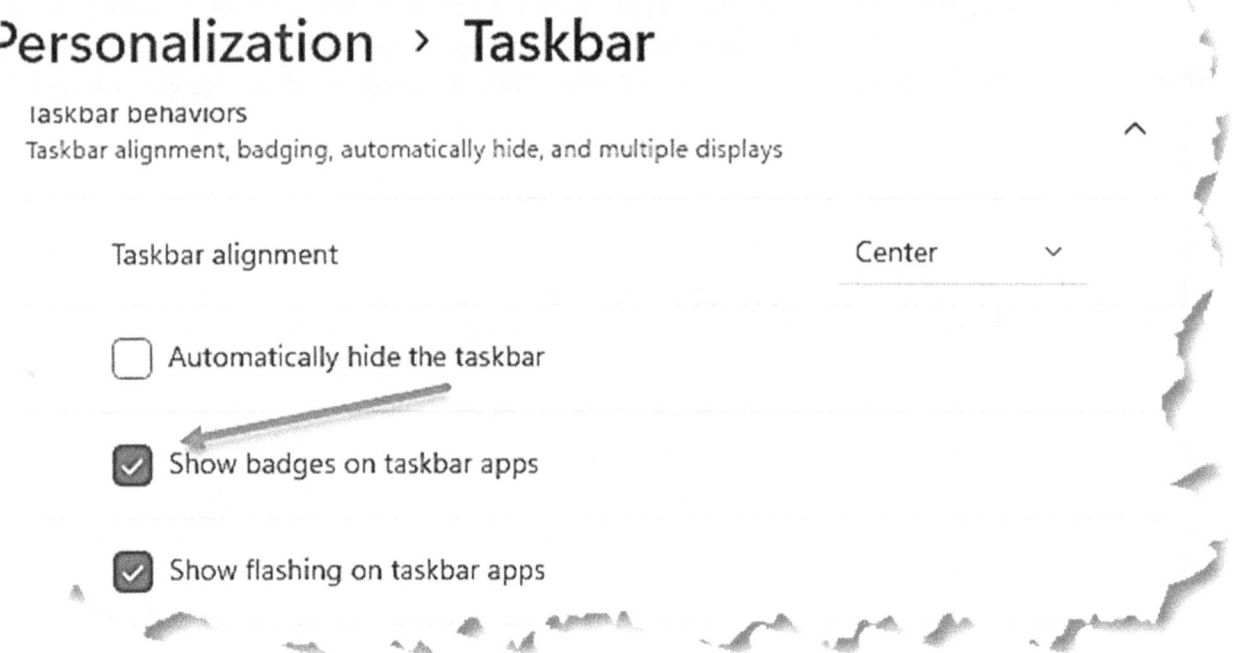

Remember that you can always enable the badge notifications by following the same steps and checking the "**Show badges**" box again.

Displaying Taskbar Across Multiple Screen

Keeping your workflow organized and efficient is crucial when working with multiple monitors. The taskbar offers a valuable customization option to enhance your multi-monitor experience.

By default, the taskbar appears only on your primary monitor.

This means you must switch the focus to the primary screen to open apps or check system notifications. If this setting doesn't work, Windows 11 lets you make the taskbar span across all your connected monitors.

This means that the taskbar will be copied on all monitors, giving you easy access to your programs and system features no matter which screen you use.

Follow these steps to configure the Taskbar to appear on all connected monitors:

1. Right-click on any empty area of the Taskbar.

2. From the context menu, select "**Taskbar Settings**."

3. In the "**Taskbar settings**" window, navigate to the "**Taskbar behaviors**" tab.

4. Locate the "**Show my taskbar on all displays**" checkbox and ensure it is checked.

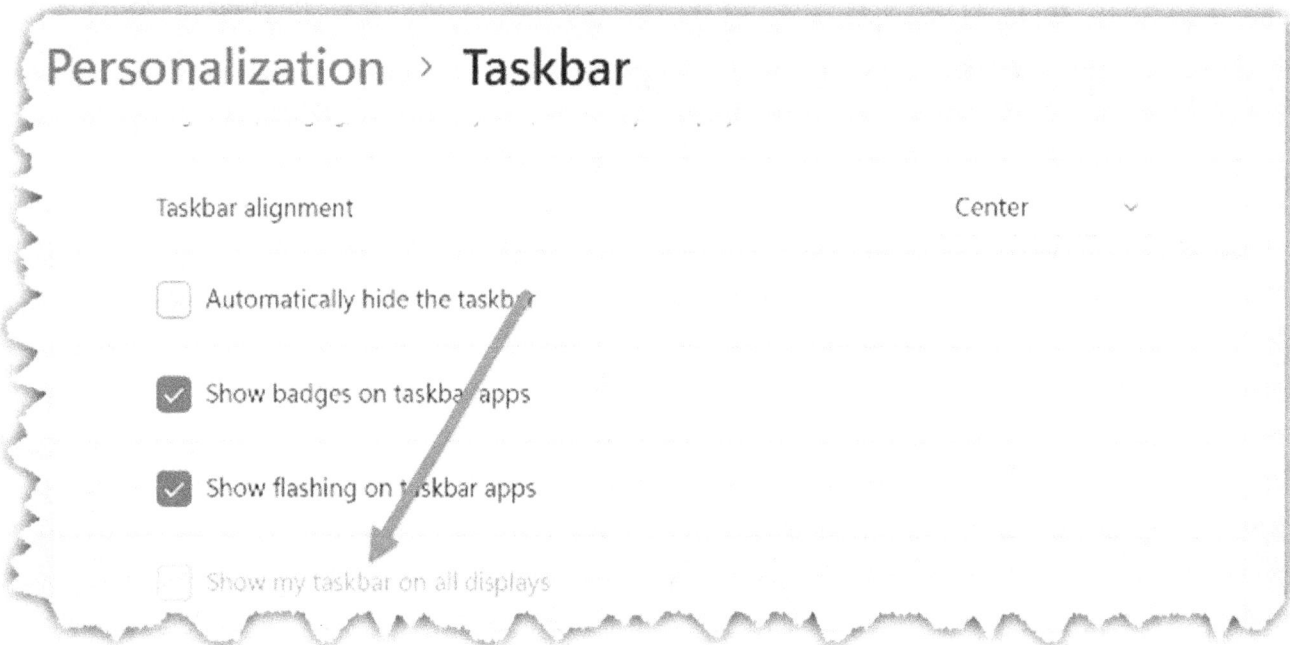

5. Beneath the checkbox, find the "**When using multiple displays, show my taskbar apps on**" drop-down menu.

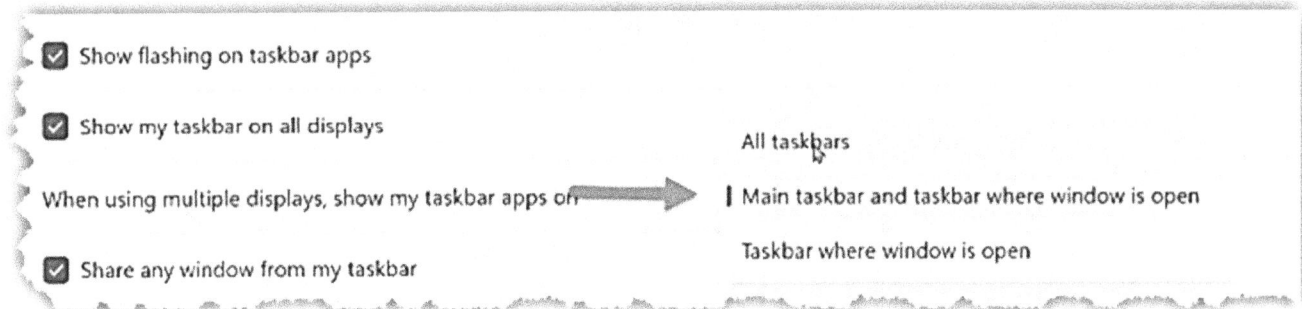

6. From the drop-down, select "**All Taskbars**."

CHAPTER 5

THE START MENU AND ITS FEATURES

The Start Menu has been an essential part of Windows since its introduction in Windows 95 and until its controversial removal in Windows 8.

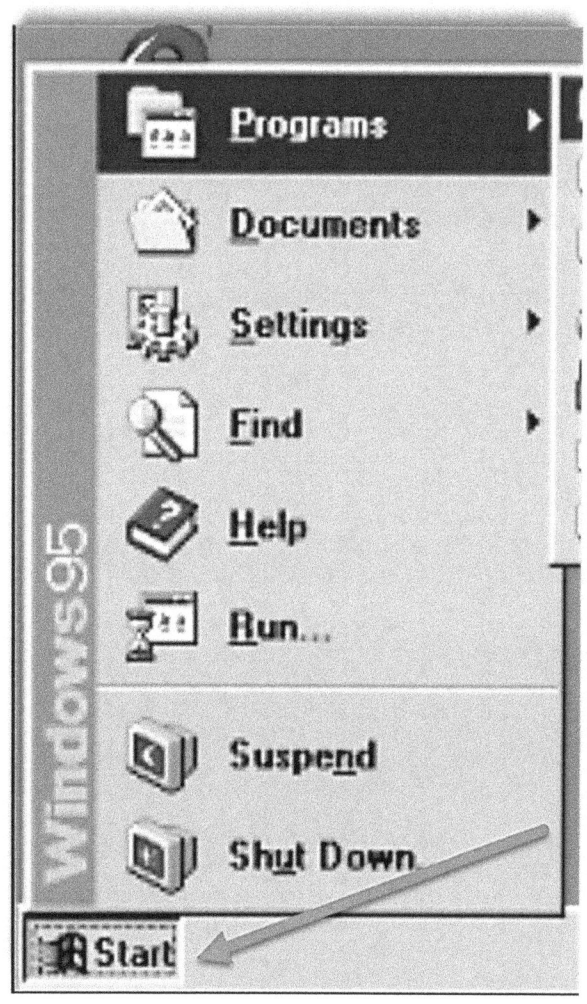

When Windows 8 added the Start Screen, the standard Start button, which was loved for being easy to use, went through a big change.

As a result of the general dislike of this major change, Microsoft gradually re-introduced the familiar Start Menu in later updates.

In Windows 11, the evolution continues with a Start Menu placed in the middle of the screen to make things more straightforward. This new version tries to find the right balance between simplicity and usefulness. It offers a streamlined experience while keeping the most important features, all wrapped in a modern design that goes with Windows 11's overall look.

Clicking the Start button, as illustrated below, or pressing the Windows key on your keyboard will launch the Start Menu.

Start Button

The Start button provides a convenient way to browse and launch your installed applications, access important files, and explore other functionalities offered by Windows 11.

Searching for Applications and Files

The Windows 11 Start Menu is a built-in tool that includes search functionality. This makes it a one-stop shop for quickly finding files and starting programs.

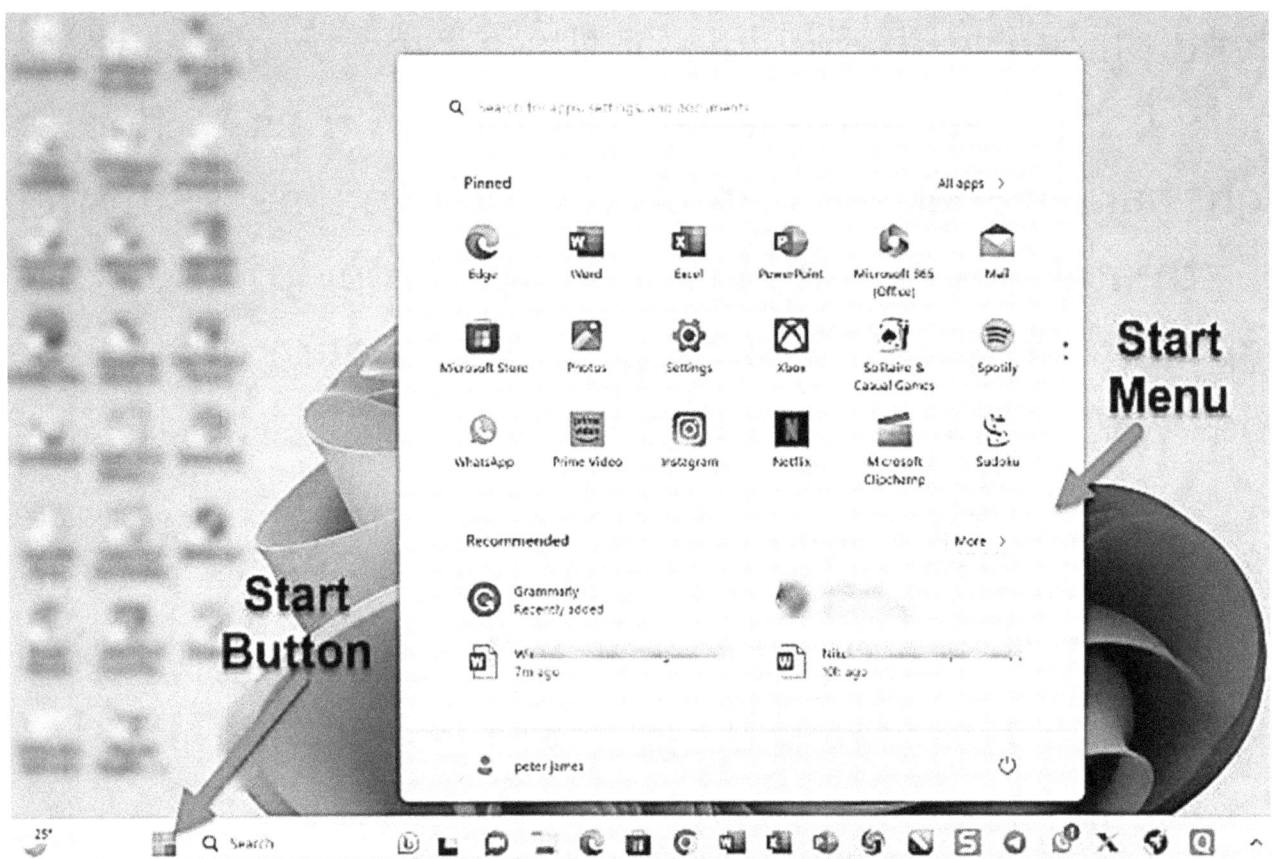

Let us look at how you can use the start menu in Windows 11 to get a lot more done when using the operating system.

The Start Menu Search Box

The Start menu's Search Box Section lets you quickly find files, applications, and settings on your computer.

Click on the **Start button** to open the **Start Menu**; you will find the search bar at the top.

Once you click inside the search bar, the Start Menu switches to the default Windows search interface, similar to that of Windows 10, as illustrated below.

Enter a description of the file or application you are looking for in the search bar, and Windows will display a list of suggested results that match your search.

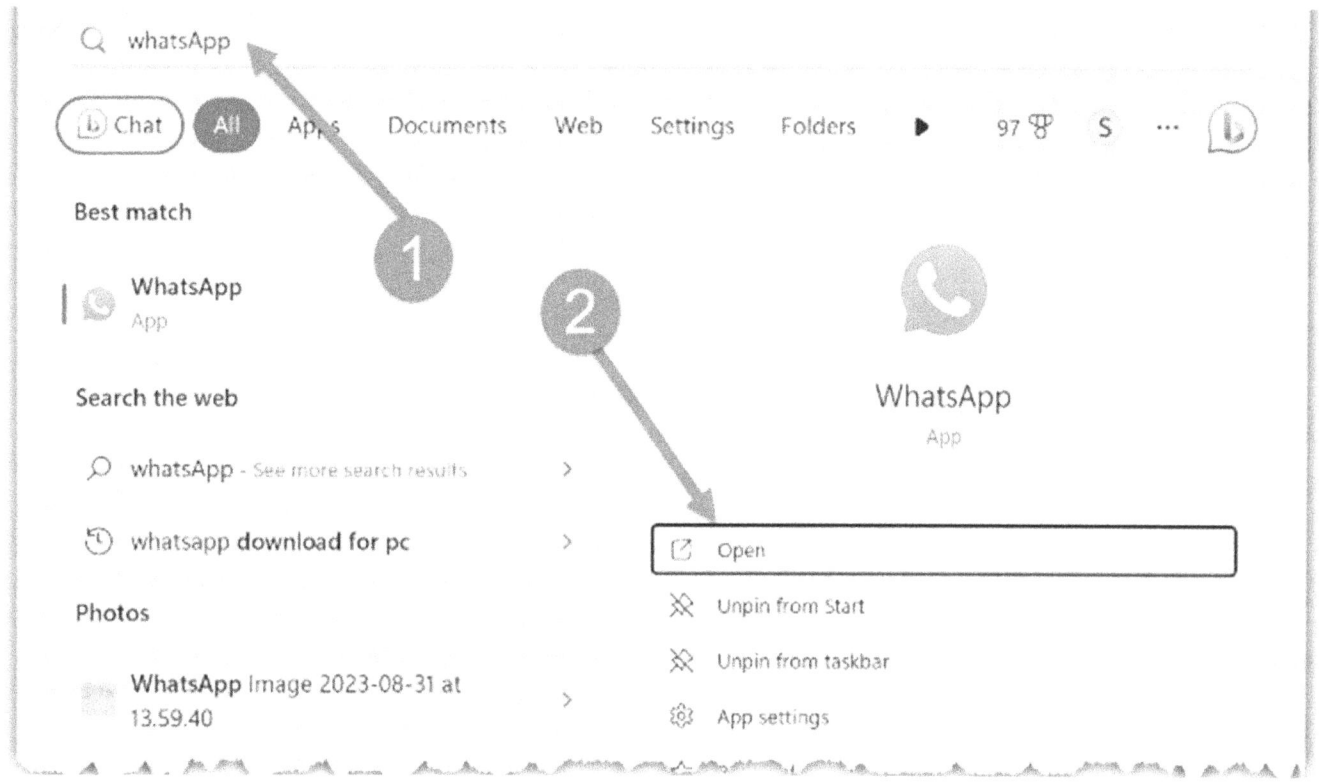

Click on the relevant result to run the related application or open a file.

Alternatively, to narrow your search to a specific category, click on the format of what you are searching for.

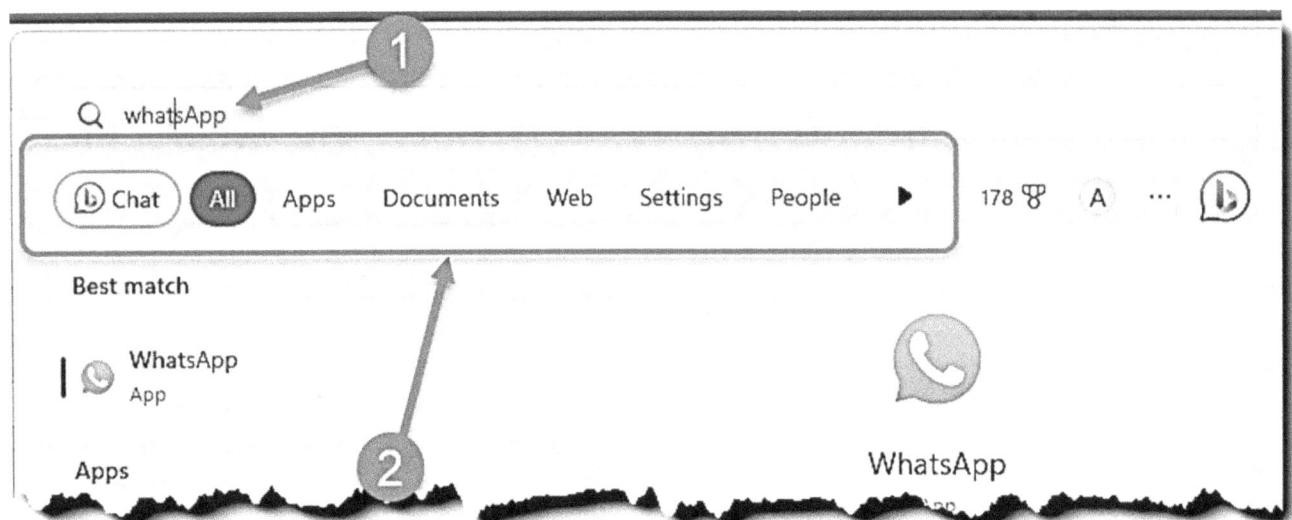

For example, if you are looking for a document saved on your computer, click on the Document tab after entering your search content, and Windows will display all the files that match your entry.

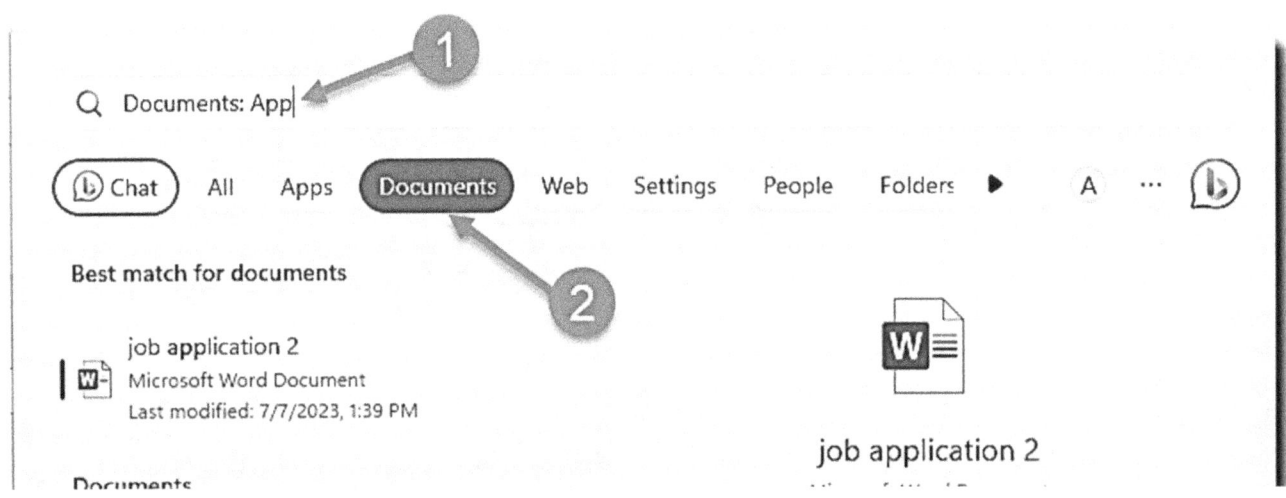

- For documents, click on the "**Document**" tab to display all matching files.
- To find installed applications, click on the "**Apps**" tab.
- For web pages, click on the "**Web**" tab.
- The **Settings** button is used to access specific settings or perform tasks for which you are unsure of the exact location.

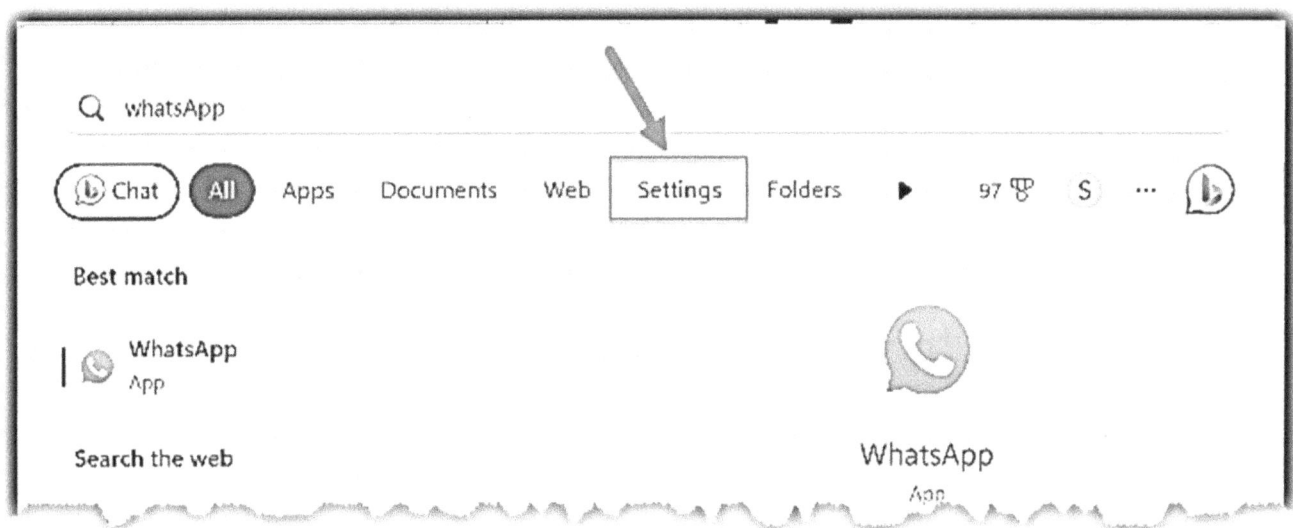

Suppose you want to configure your computer's wireless connection but don't know how to access the relevant Windows settings. Click the **Settings** button and enter the keyword "**wireless**" in the search bar.

This method is like having your computer's GPS when finding technical stuff.

- To see more search options, click on the "**Scroll Arrow**."

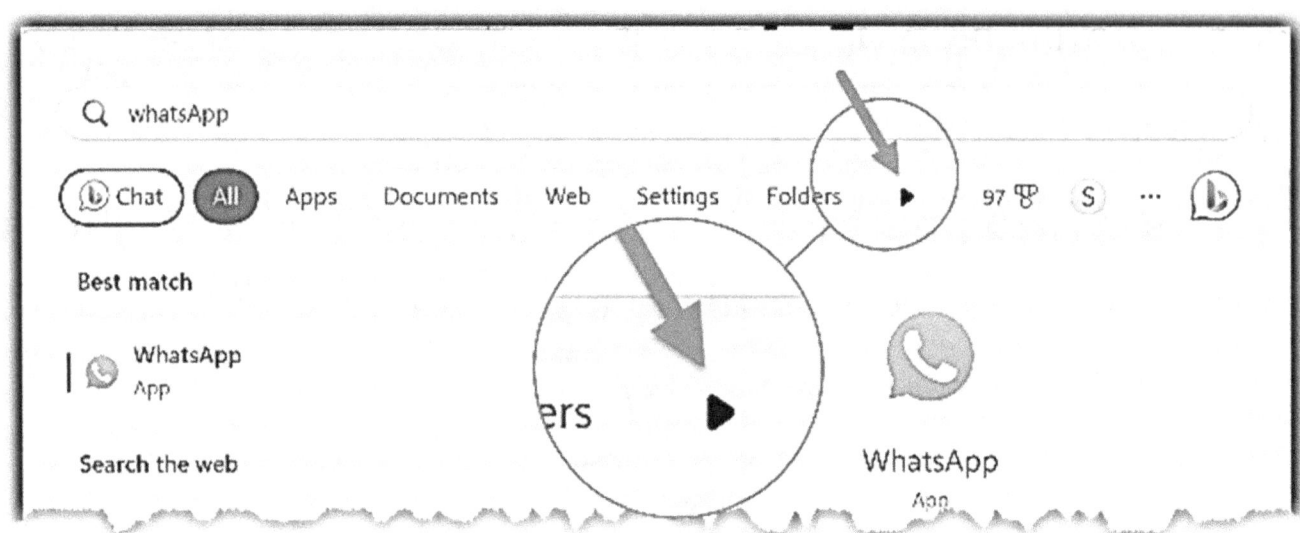

Pinned Apps on the Start Menu

Below the search bar on the start menu is another section used to display your pinned apps.

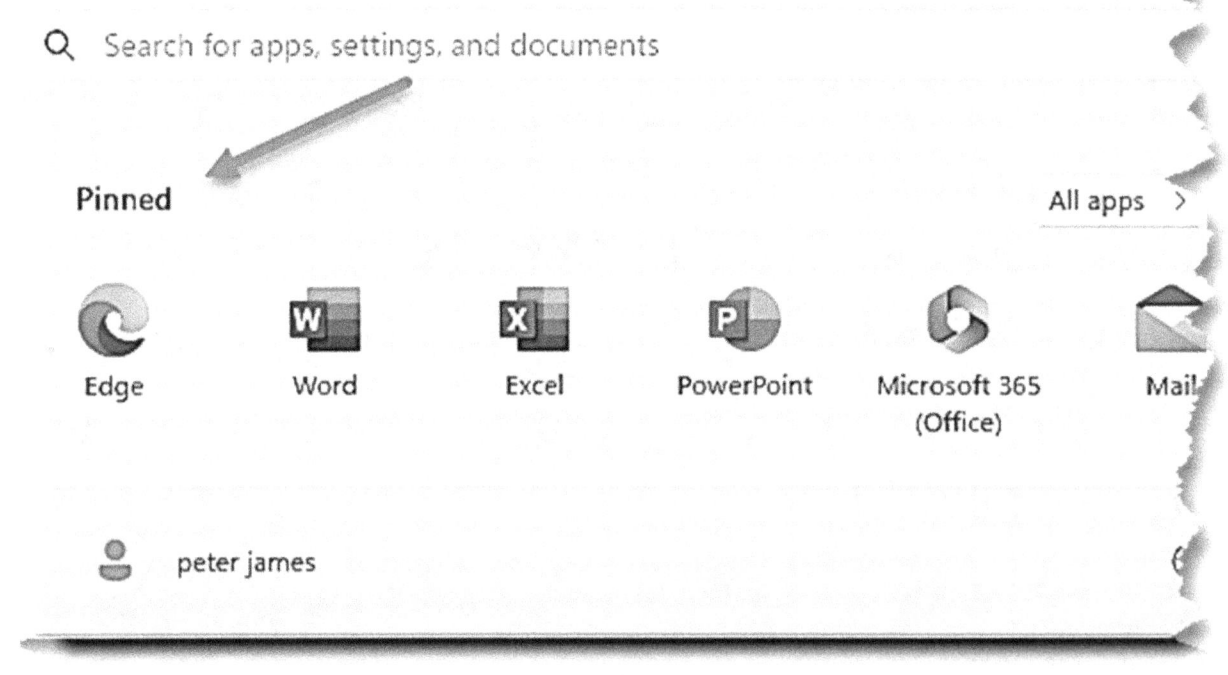

The term "**Pinned**" refers to applications that you frequently use and are kept in this section on the start menu for easy access. You can personalize the experience by pinning or unpinning apps according to your preferences.

To unpin an app from the start menu, right-click the particular app icon and select **Unpin from Start,** as illustrated below.

Recommended Apps

The **Recommended** section shows apps that the system thinks you will like based on how you have used them and Microsoft's intelligent suggestions.

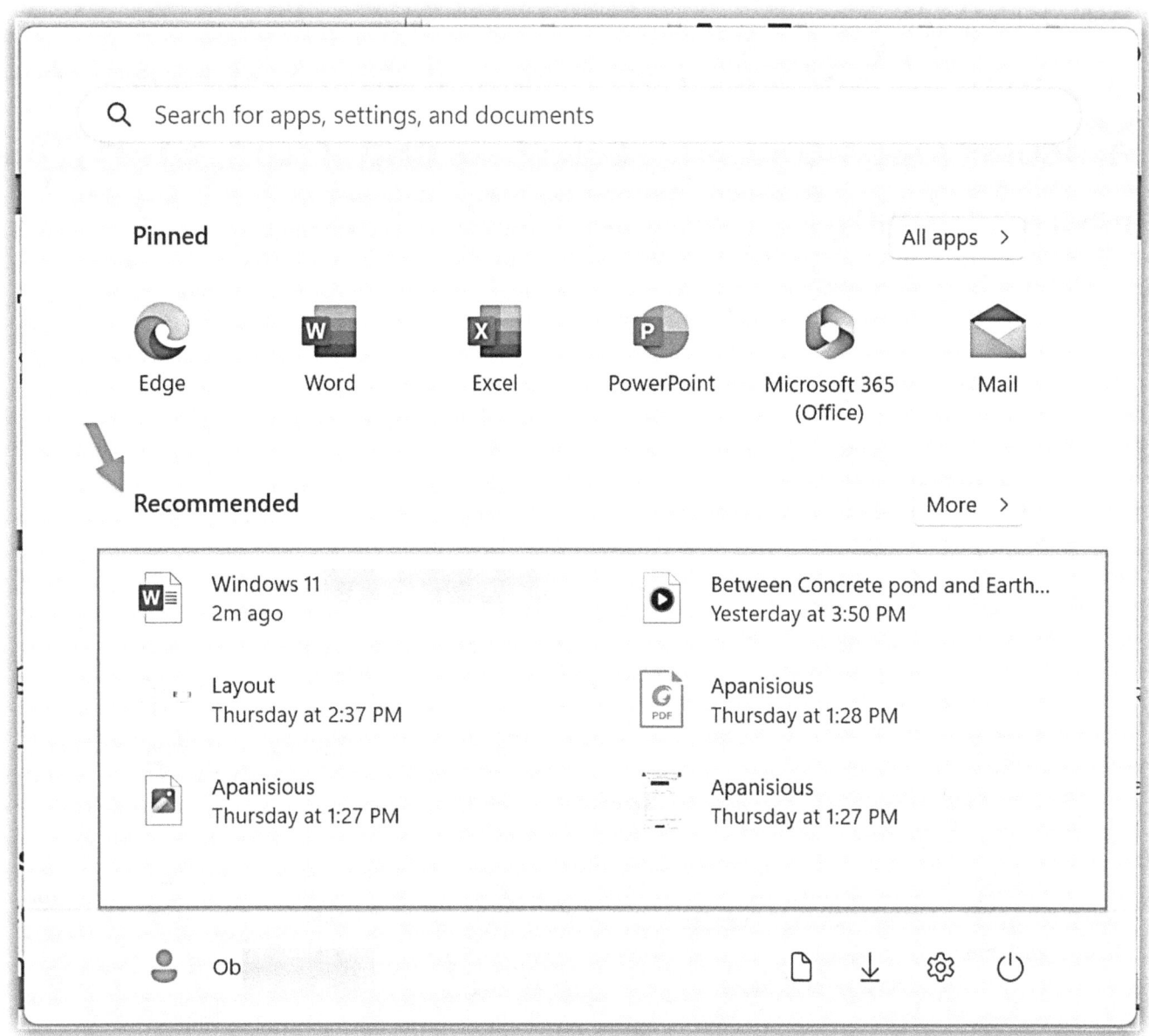

You might find one of these apps useful. All it takes is a click to open the suggested app.

All Apps

The "**All Apps**" section in the Windows 11 Start Menu gives you access to a comprehensive list of all the applications installed on your computer.

This list includes Windows 11's default apps and any additional applications installed on your computer. It provides a convenient way to find and launch any specific application without pining it to the Start Menu or the taskbar.

When you click the "**All Apps**" section, the apps are arranged automatically in numeric-alpha order, which makes it easier to find the one you want to use.

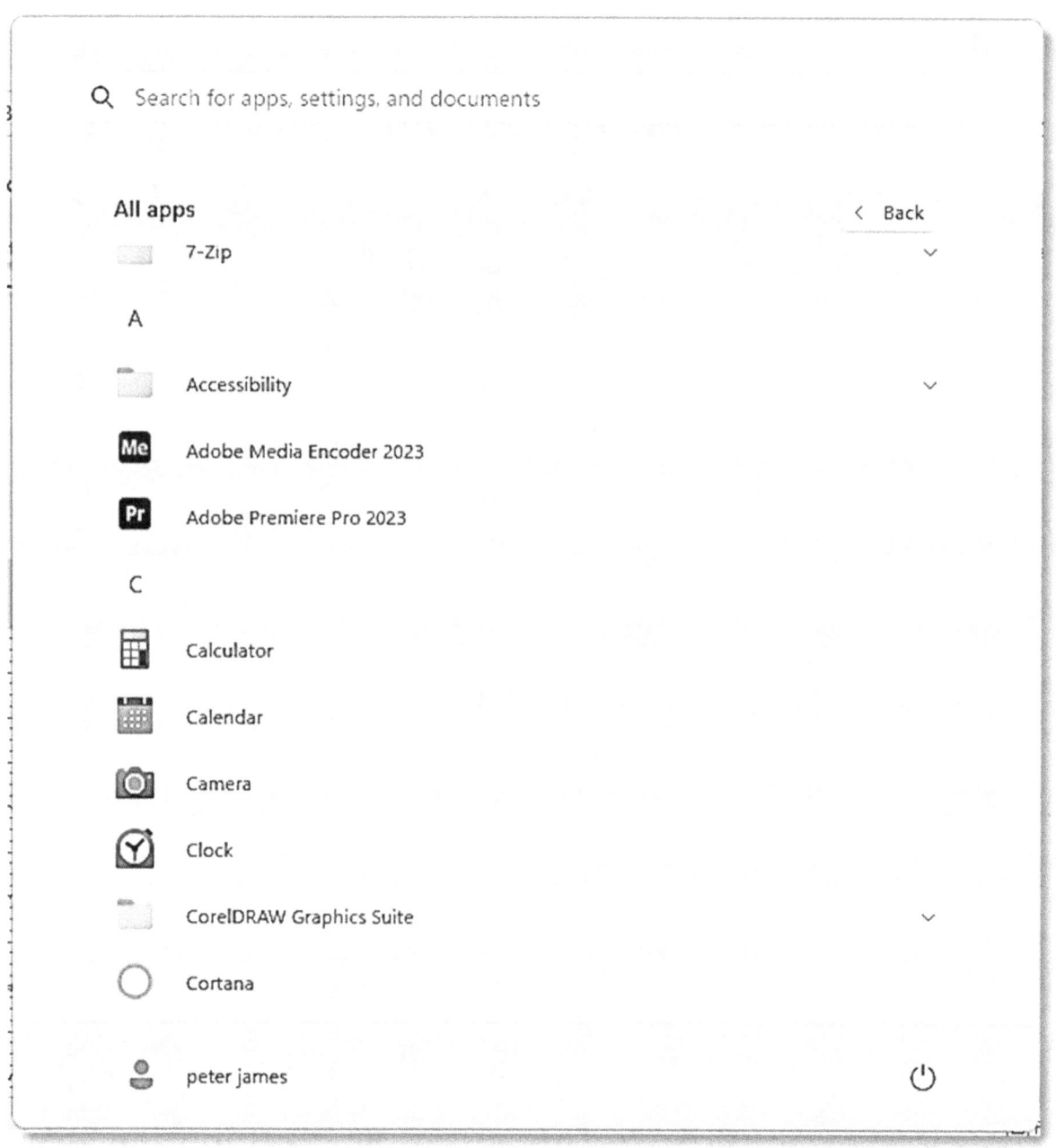

You can scroll through the list or use the search bar at the top to quickly find the app you need by entering its name in the search bar.

Start Menu Quick Setting

Your profile picture and name are in the bottom left corner of the Windows 11 Start Menu.

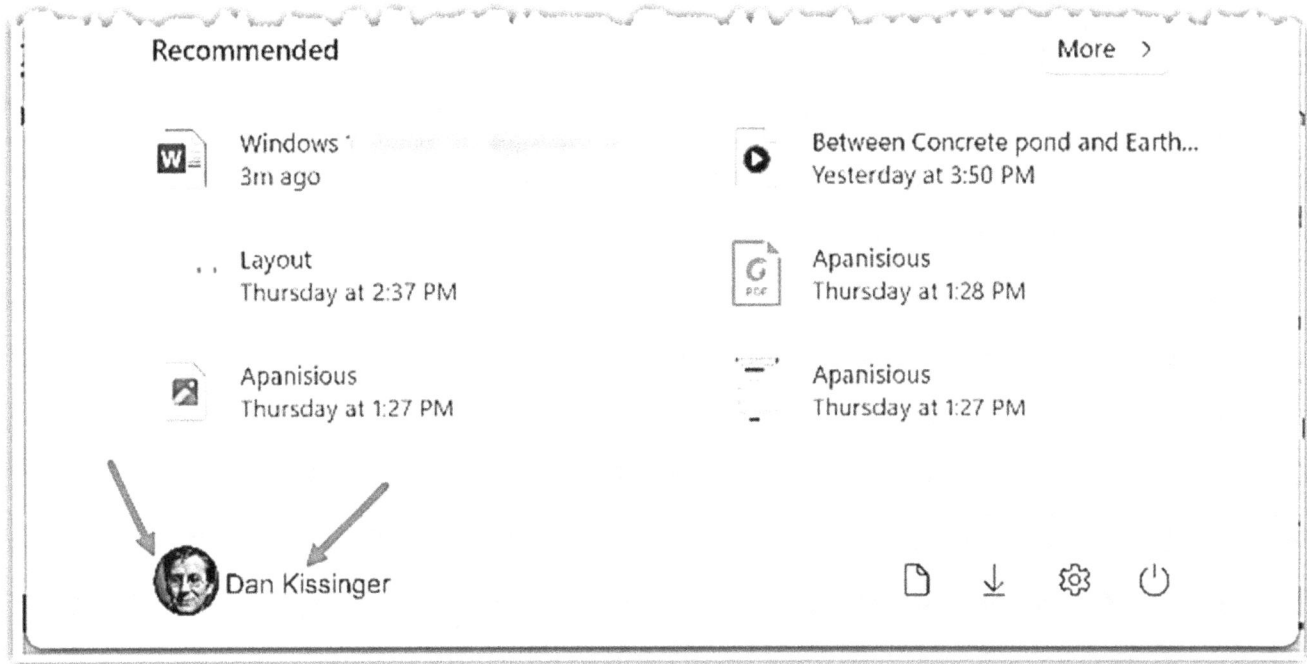

When multiple Microsoft accounts are registered on your computer, each account holder must log in using their passwords.

The Start Menu's user profile photo and name indicate which account is active. Think of it as your digital welcome sign.

Editing Profile Photo

In Windows 11, you can edit your profile photo directly from the Start menu.

To make changes to your profile photo, follow these steps:

- Click the Start button to access the Start Menu.
- Click on your profile picture at the bottom of the Start Menu.
- Next, click on **Change account settings**.

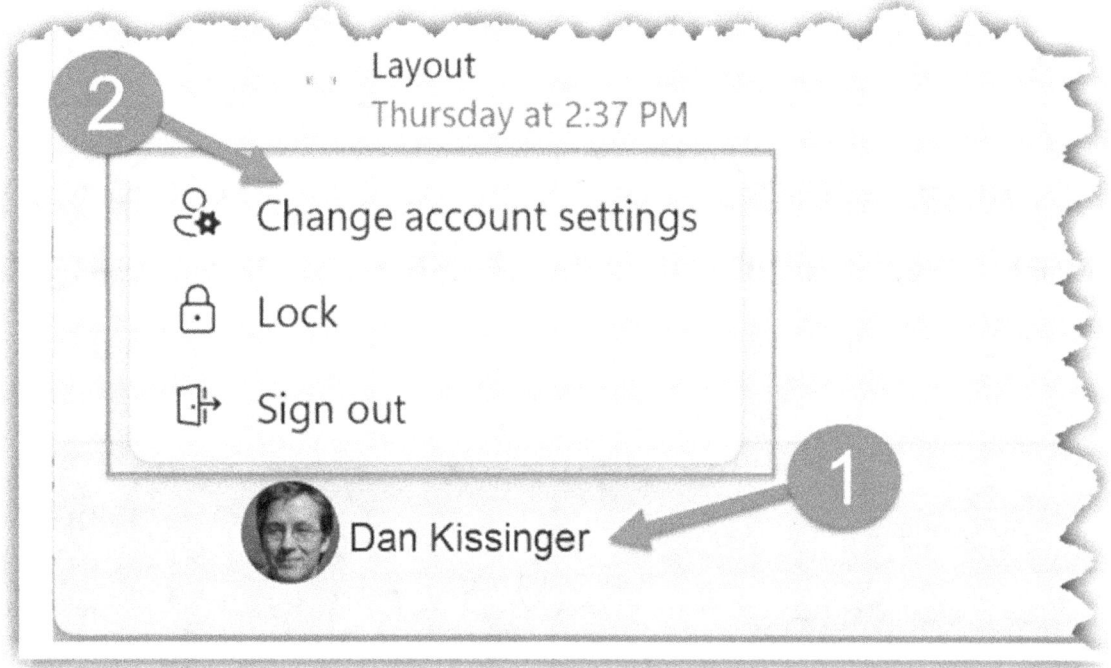

- Next, click on **Change account settings**.
- To change your photo, you capture the image from your device camera or upload the image file.

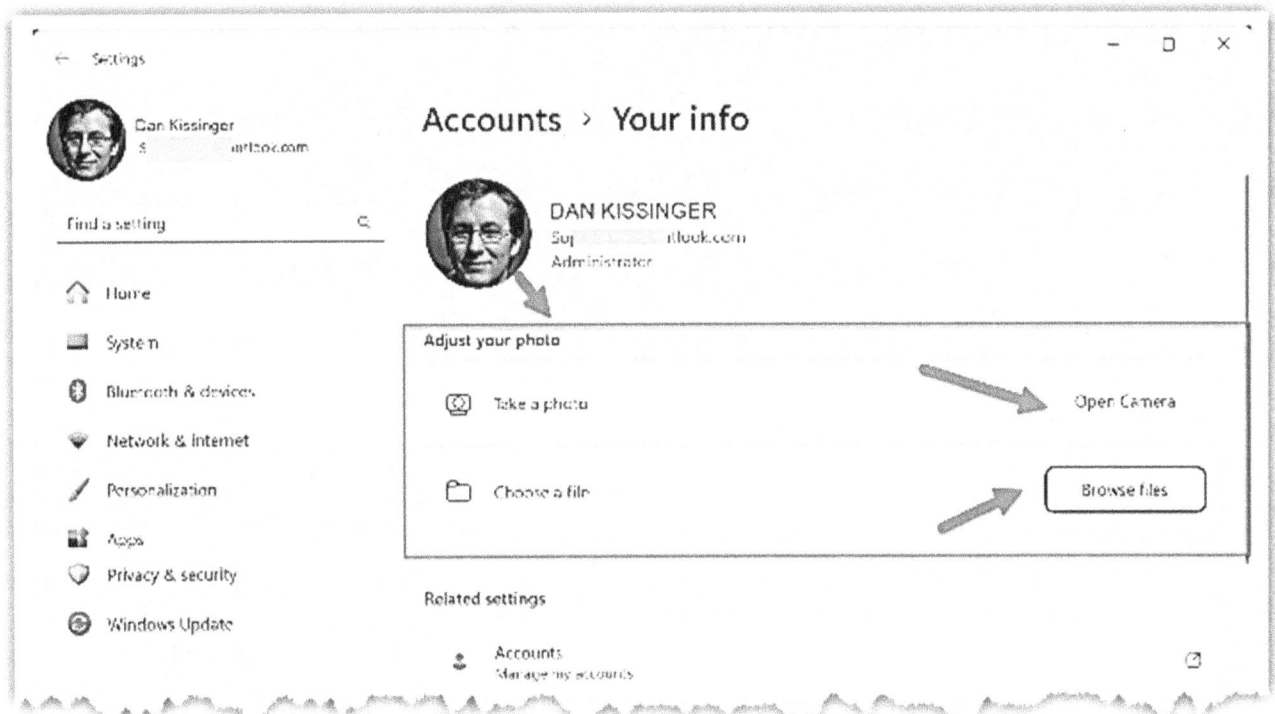

The browse files button allows you to search within your computer for the picture file you want to use for your Profile photo.

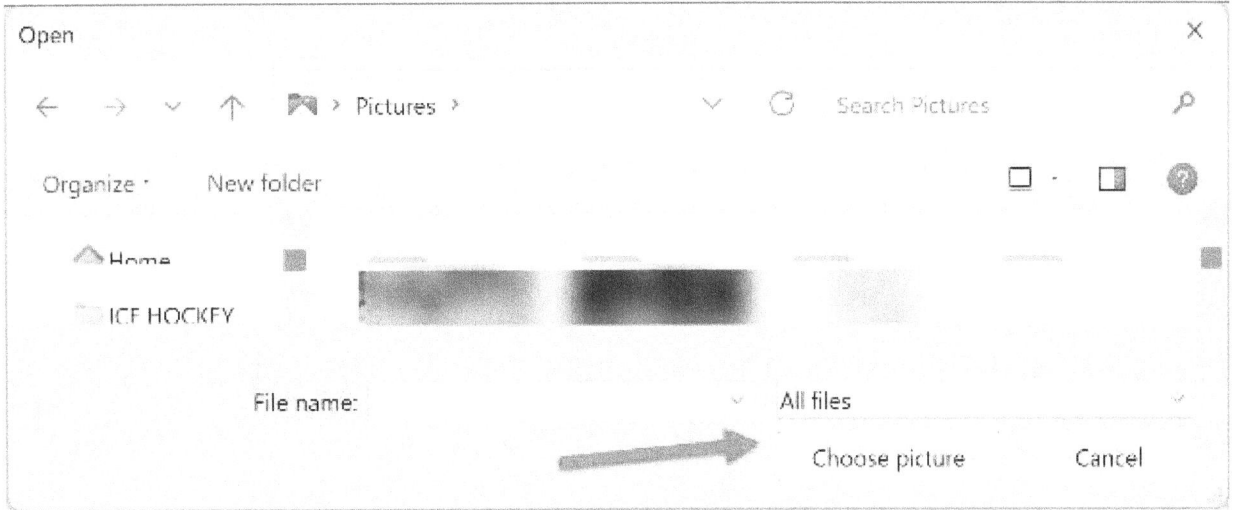

Click on the **Choose picture** button when done to upload the photo.

Start Menu Power Buttons

The Power button in the bottom right corner of the Windows 11 Start menu is the only button by default. The Sleep, Shut down, and Restart buttons are all embedded in the Power button.

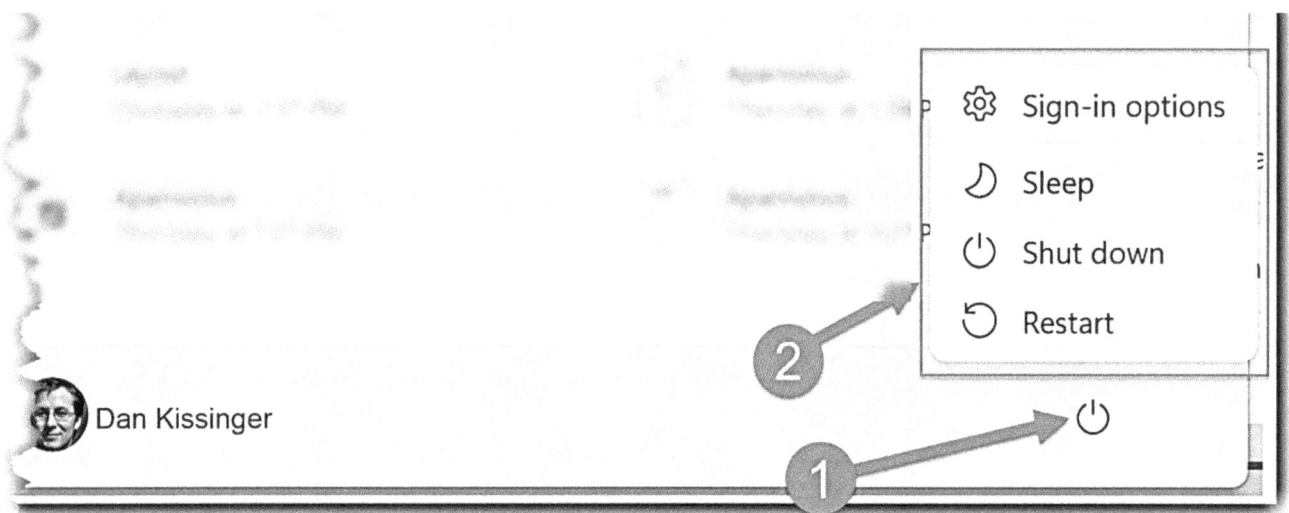

To access them, click the Power button and move the cursor to any of the options you want to use.

- **Sleep:** This option puts your computer to sleep so you can take a break from work without having to close or restart any programs. You can pick up where you left off when you come back.

- **Shut down:** If you want to turn off your computer, use this button. Ensure you have saved all of your work and closed all your programs.

- **Restart:** This option turns off your computer and restarts it automatically. It comes in handy when your computer is not working right or when a newly installed app needs a restart to make changes take effect.

Alternatively, you can access the power button by right-clicking the Start button. From the drop-down menu, click "**Shut down or sign out**."

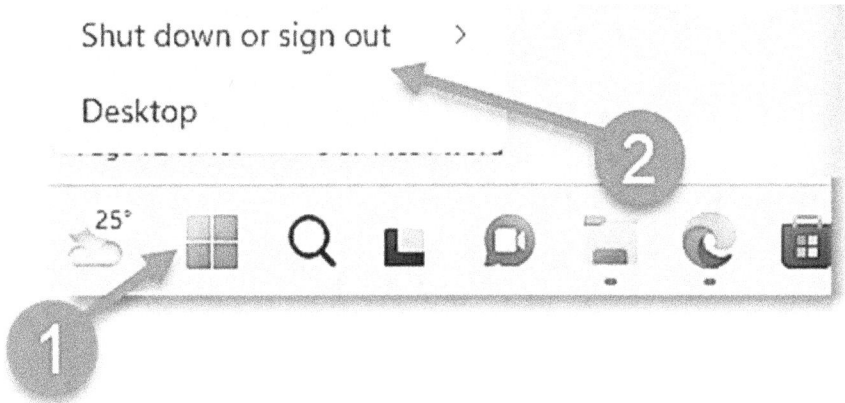

This will present you with four options to choose from:

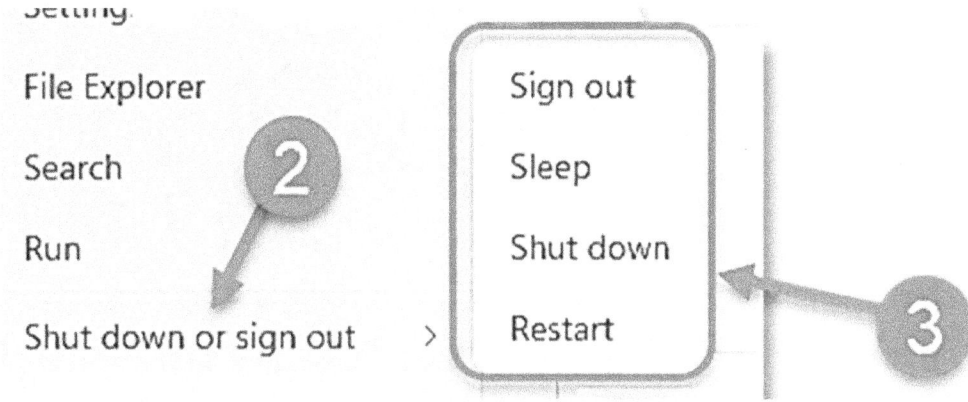

Accessing the File Explorer Through the Start Menu

The File Explorer in Windows 11 is a file management app that allows you to navigate through existing files and folders on your computer.

To make the File Explorer easily accessible through the Start menu, you can pin it to the Start menu using the following steps:

- Click on the Start button to open the Start menu.
- Click on the "**All Apps**" button to display a list of all installed applications.

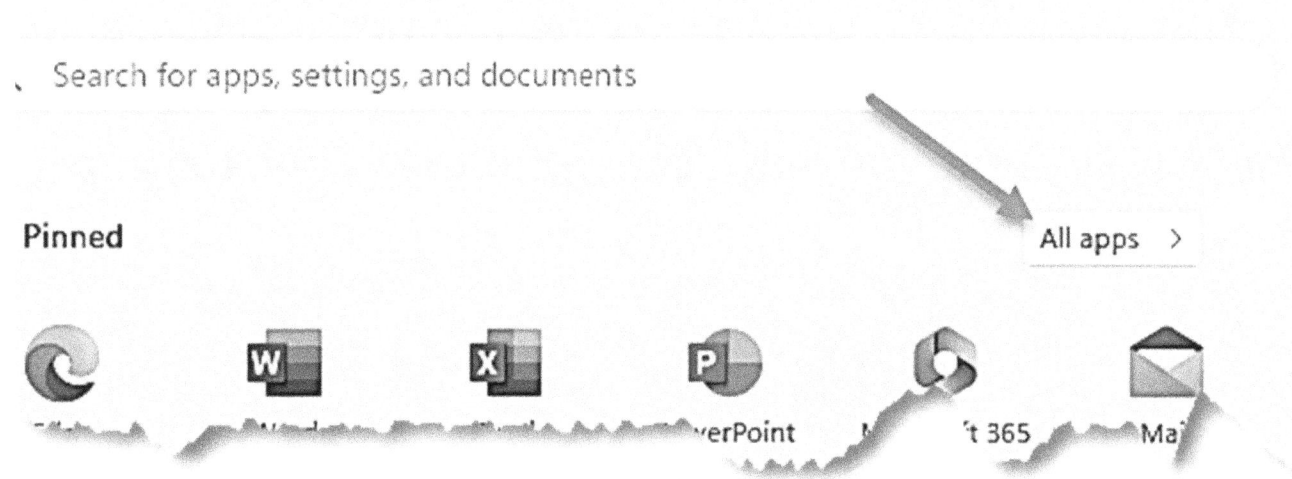

Scroll through the list and locate the File Explorer icon.

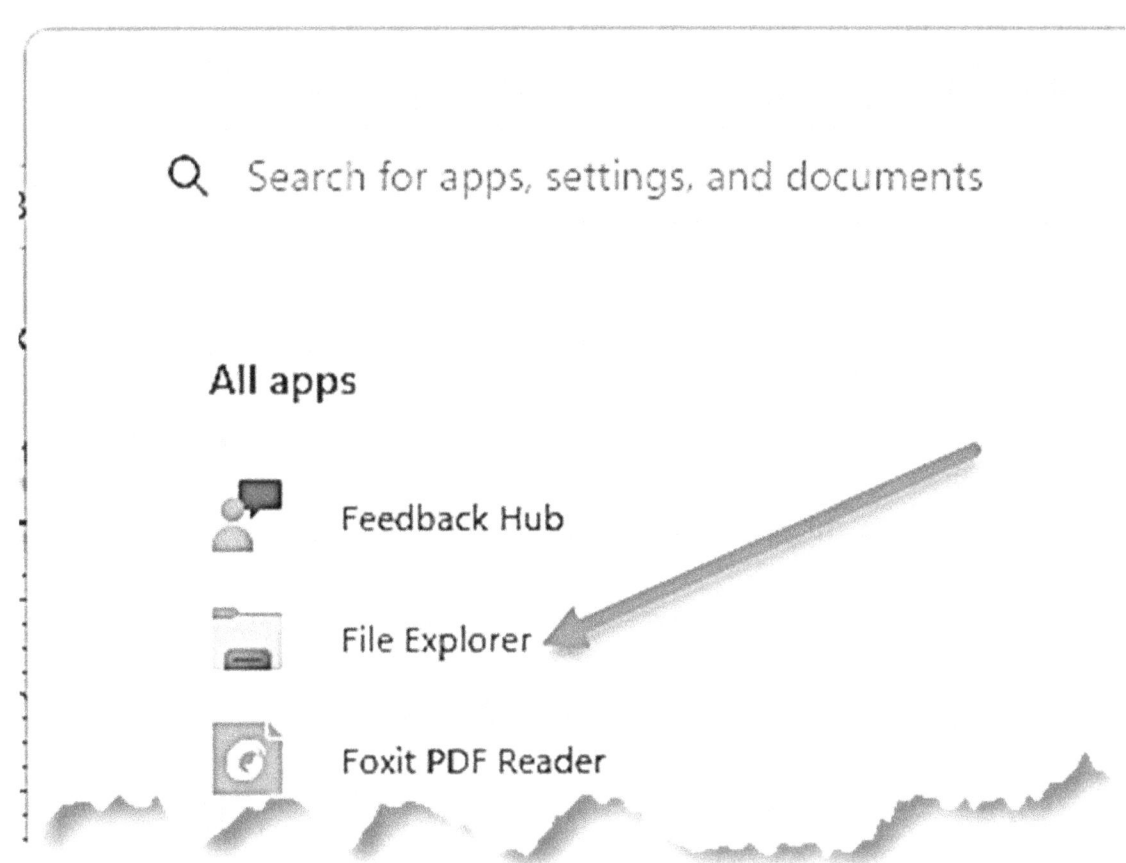

- Right-click on the **File Explorer** to open a context menu. From the options that appear, click on "**Pin to Start**."

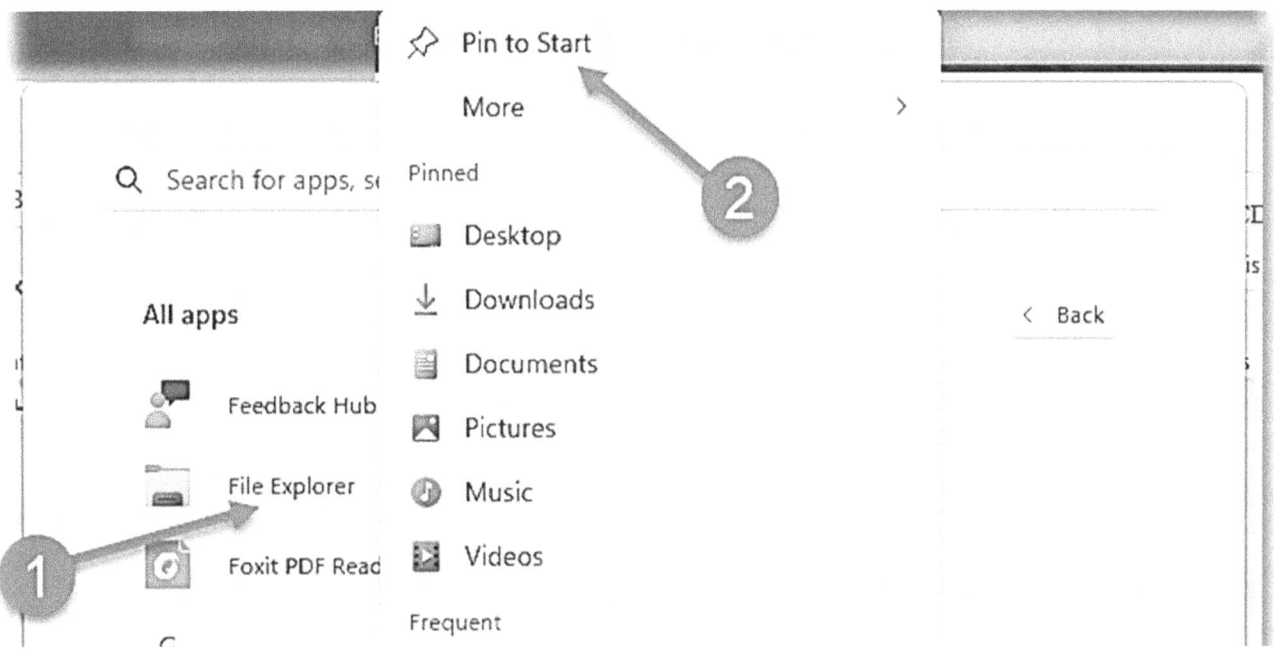

Returning to the Start menu, you will see the File Explorer icon among the pinned applications.

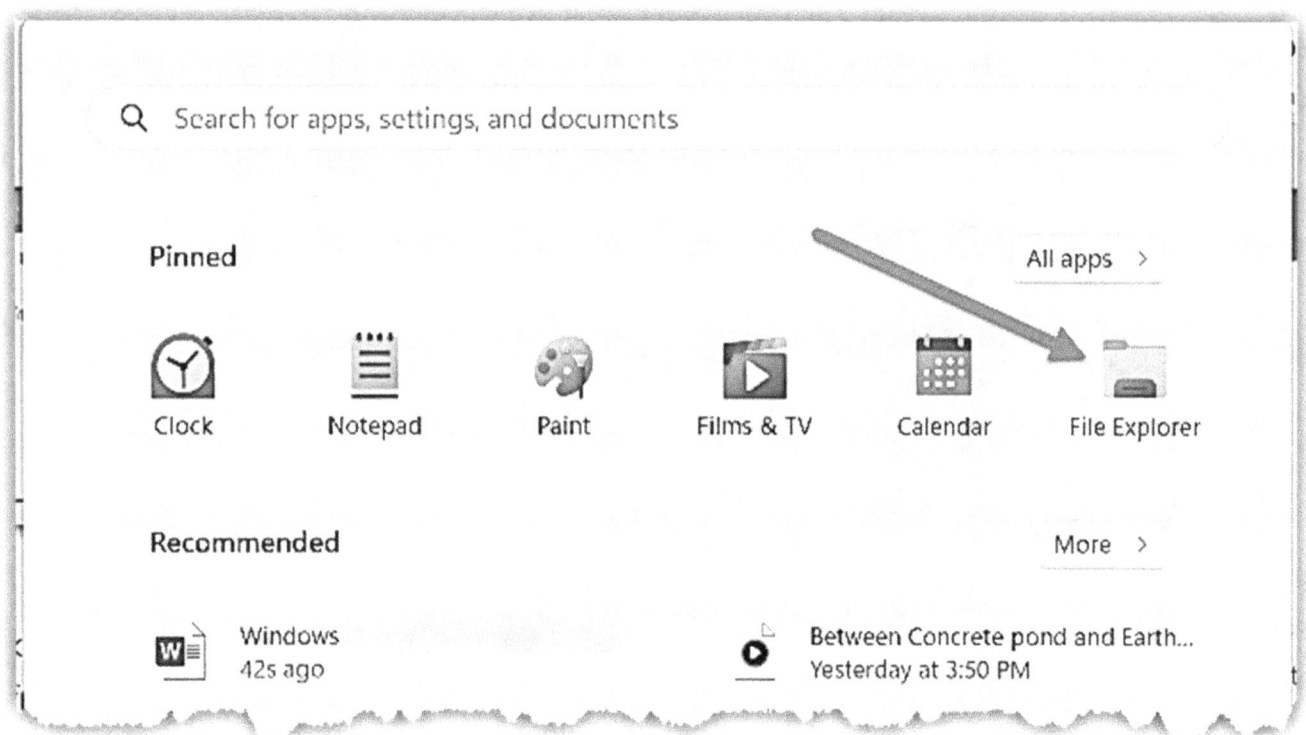

This makes accessing the File Explorer directly from the Start menu quick and easy without navigating other menus.

CHAPTER 6

THE START BUTTON RIGHT-CLICK FEATURES

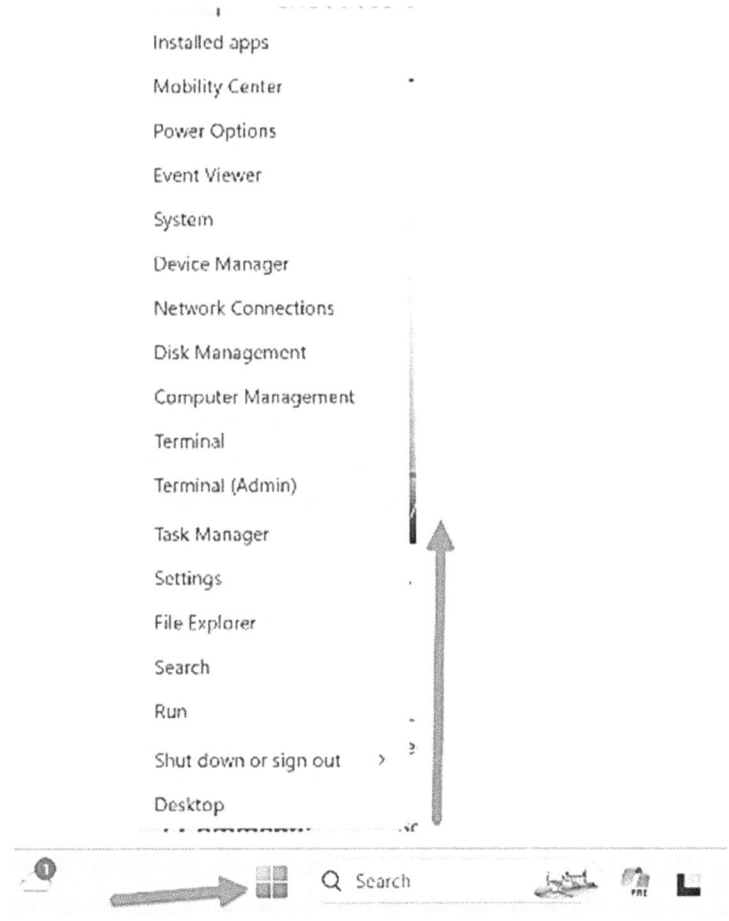

When you right-click the Start button, a treasure chest of choices that are meant to make your experience easier pops open, this menu serves as a central hub, providing quick access to important tools, system settings, and customization choices.

This intuitive design empowers you to navigate and manage your Windows 11 environment efficiently, saving you time and effort to find the needed options.

Installed Apps- How to Uninstall Apps

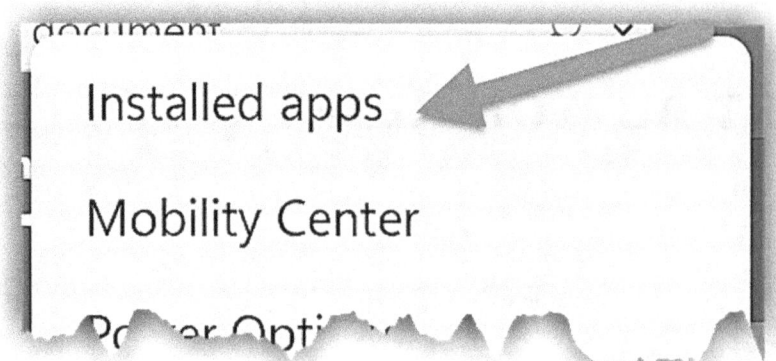

The "Installed apps" feature offers two key functionalities:

- It lets you quickly view a complete list of all the apps you have installed on the device. You won't have to look through files or menus, saving you time and effort.

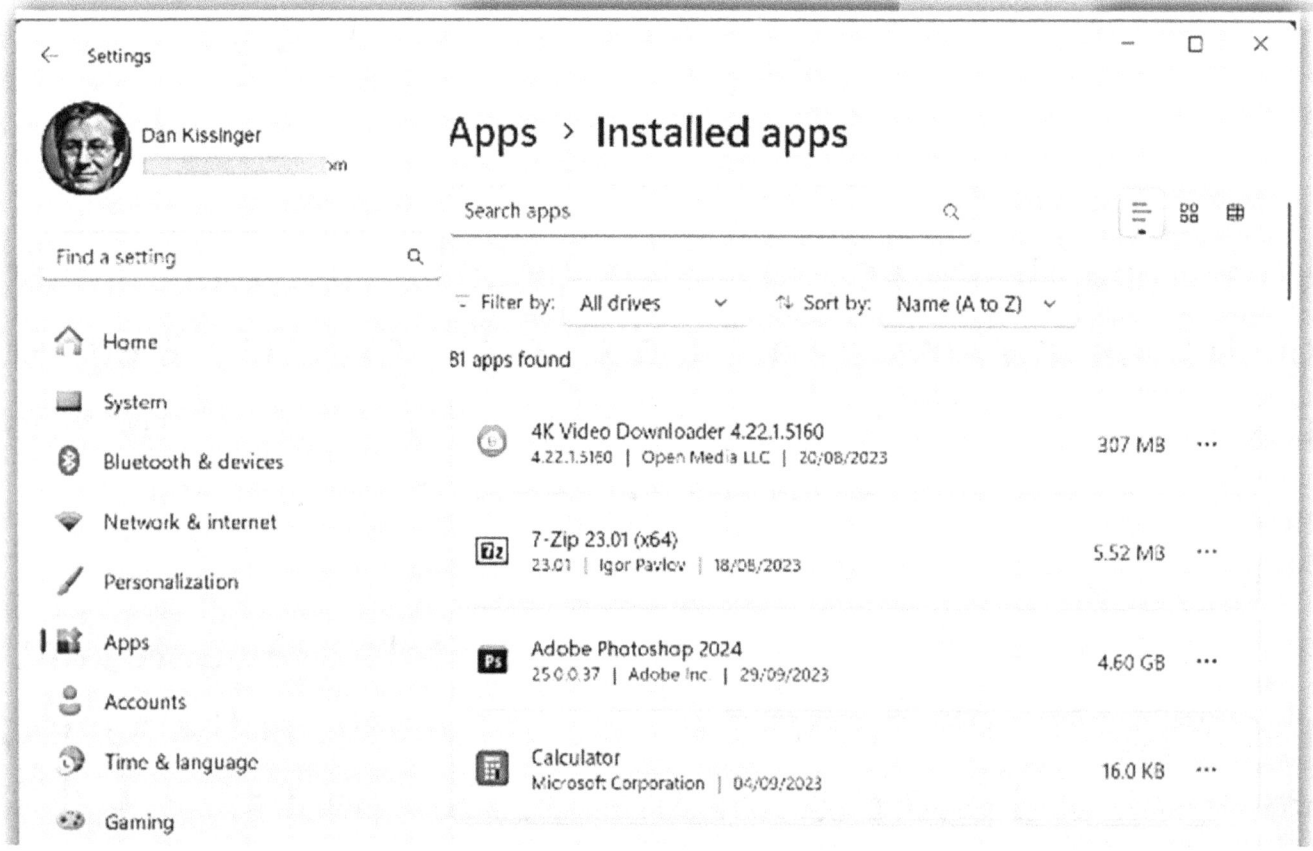

- You can easily uninstall apps using the "Installed apps" tool.

  To uninstall any apps on your computer, click on the **three-dots** along the particular app's tab and then select **Uninstall,** as illustrated below.

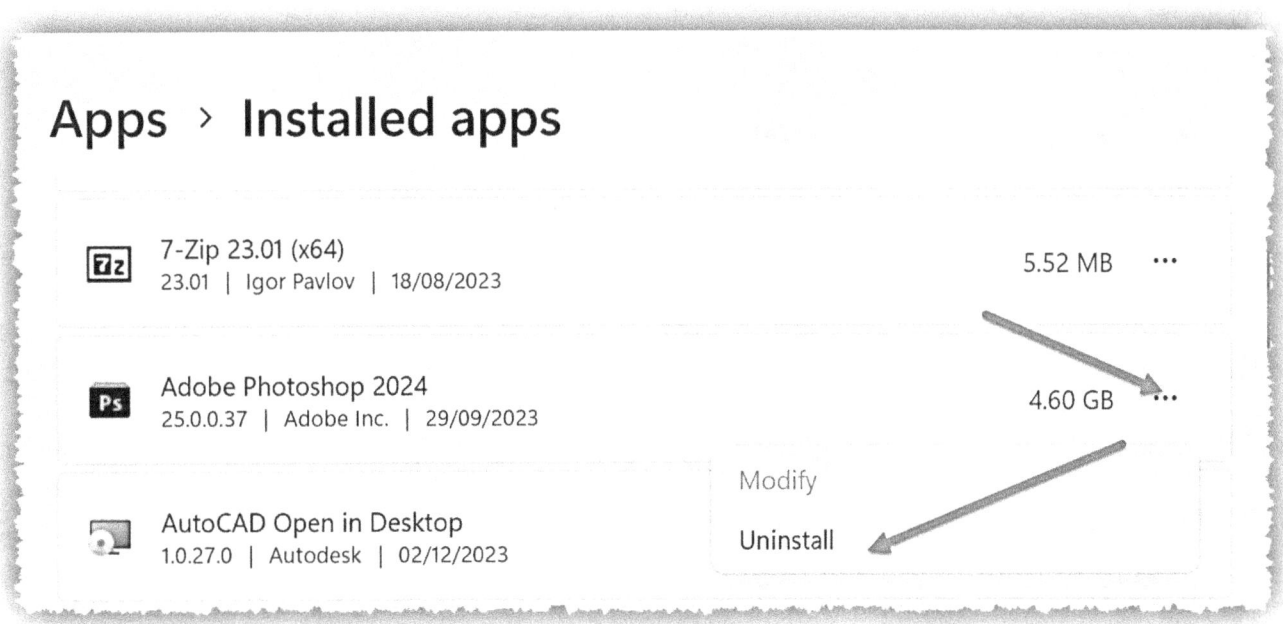

Mobility Center

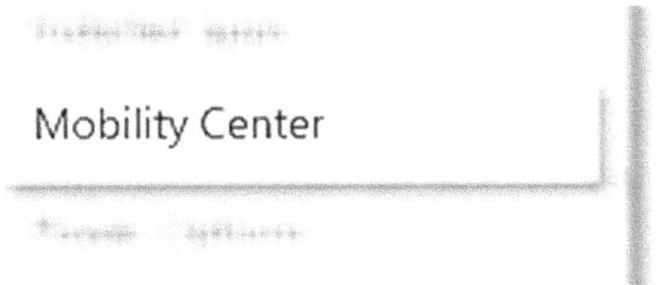

Like your phone's control center, the Mobility Center is like a central hub for managing your laptop's portability and usefulness.

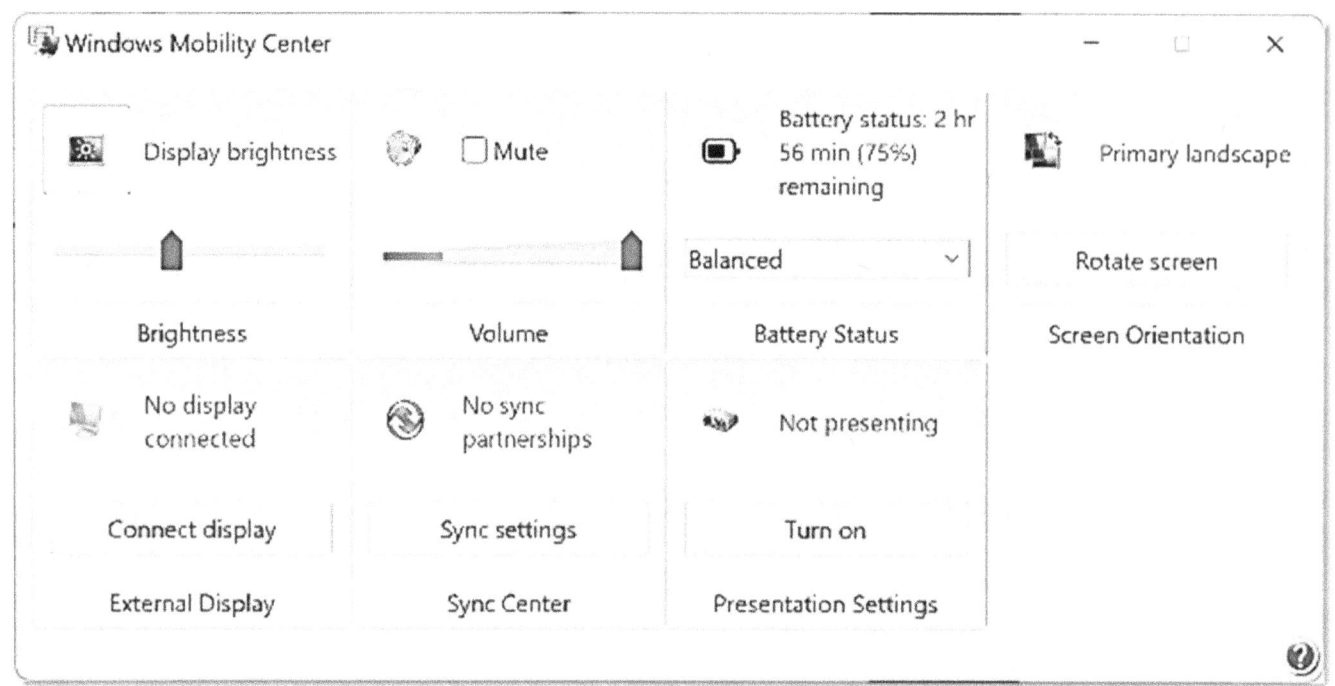

You can easily access essential settings like battery life, wireless connectivity, display options, and even a presentation mode in one convenient location. This feature allows you to optimize your laptop's performance and settings on the go. A range of options available on the mobility center include:

- **Brightness:** It allows you to use the slider to adjust the brightness of your screen to suit your taste, giving you the ability to create the ideal amount of illumination.

  - **Volume:** It allows you to adjust your computer speaker volume and make any other necessary adjustments to your audio settings.

- **External Display:** If you are making use of an additional screen, you can configure and set it up in a seamless manner through the use of this option.

- **Presentation Mode:** When you have a presentation, you can prepare it by adjusting the settings on your computer to correspond with the connected device's requirements.

- **Battery Status:** This setting allows you to closely monitor your device's battery to gain insight into its current state and decide how power is managed.

Power Options Access to Power Consumption

This setting is crucial in managing your computer's power consumption when using its battery as the power source.

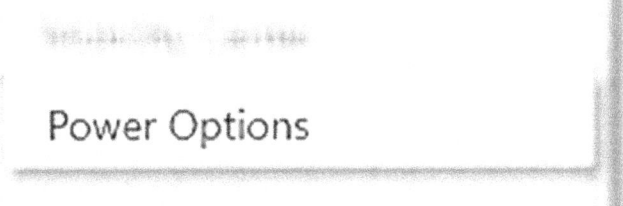

It guides your computer on its power usage and can make a real difference in its performance and battery duration.

Upon selecting the power option, a window dedicated to your device's Power and Battery settings will appear.

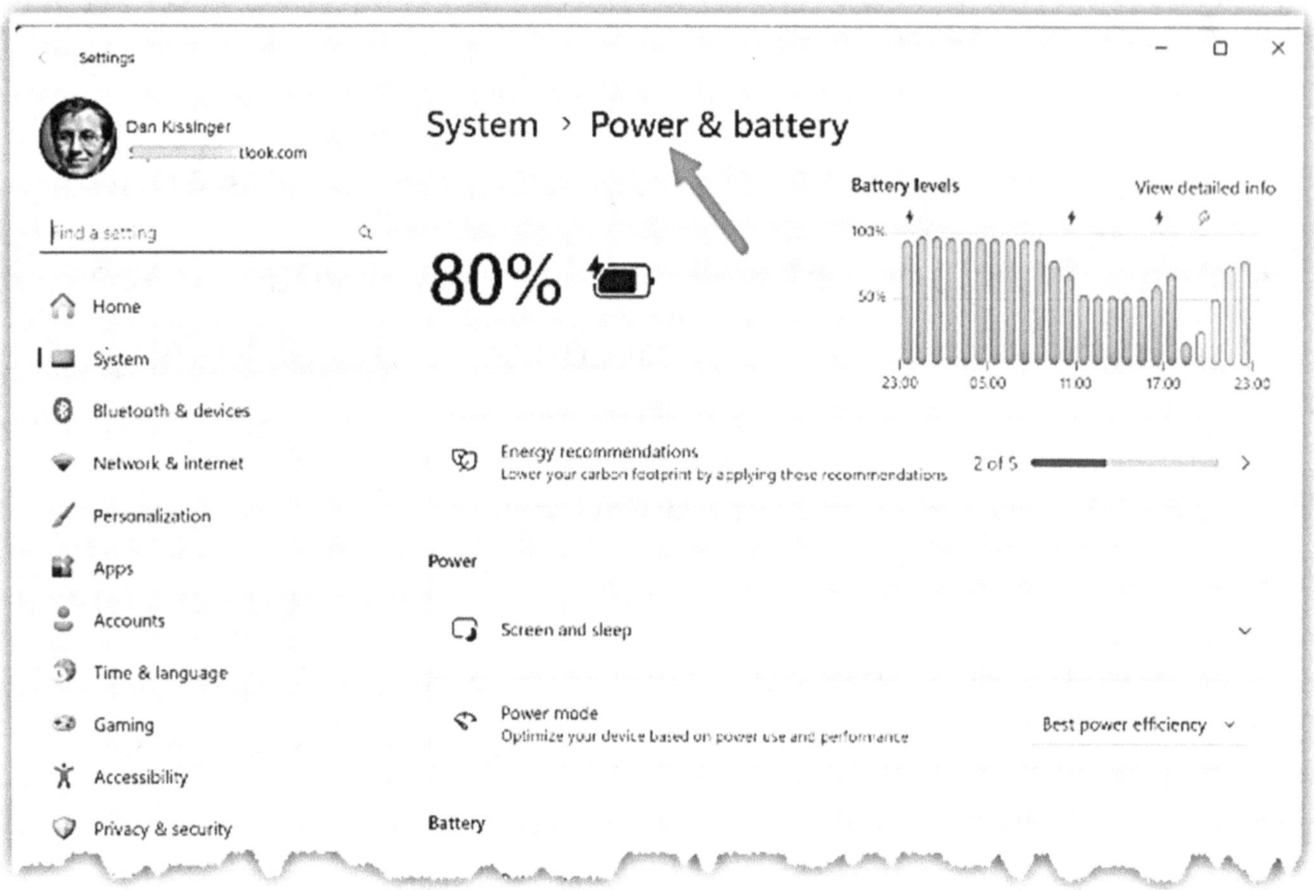

If you are using a laptop, you can quickly check the current mode of usage and the battery level by simply looking at the power option.

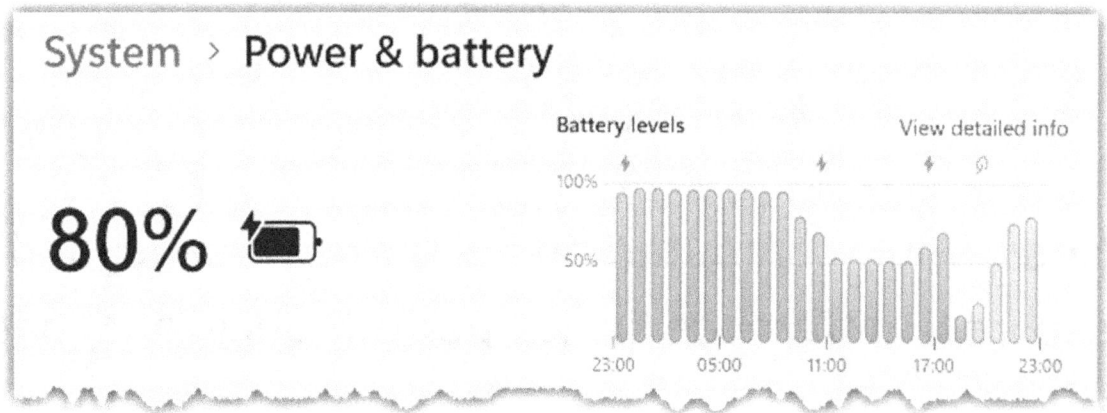

The battery level in percentage. It is similar to getting a real-time status update on how your device manages its power resources.

Event Viewer, Explore Windows Messages

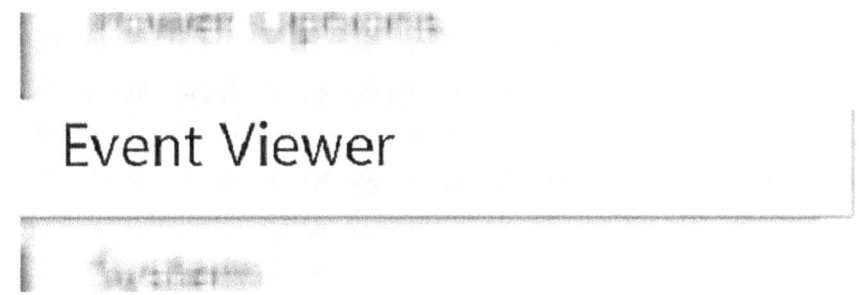

Event Viewer acts like your tech detective, meticulously recording every operation and program action on your computer. Whether you are a seasoned techie or a curious beginner, the Event Viewer offers something for everyone.

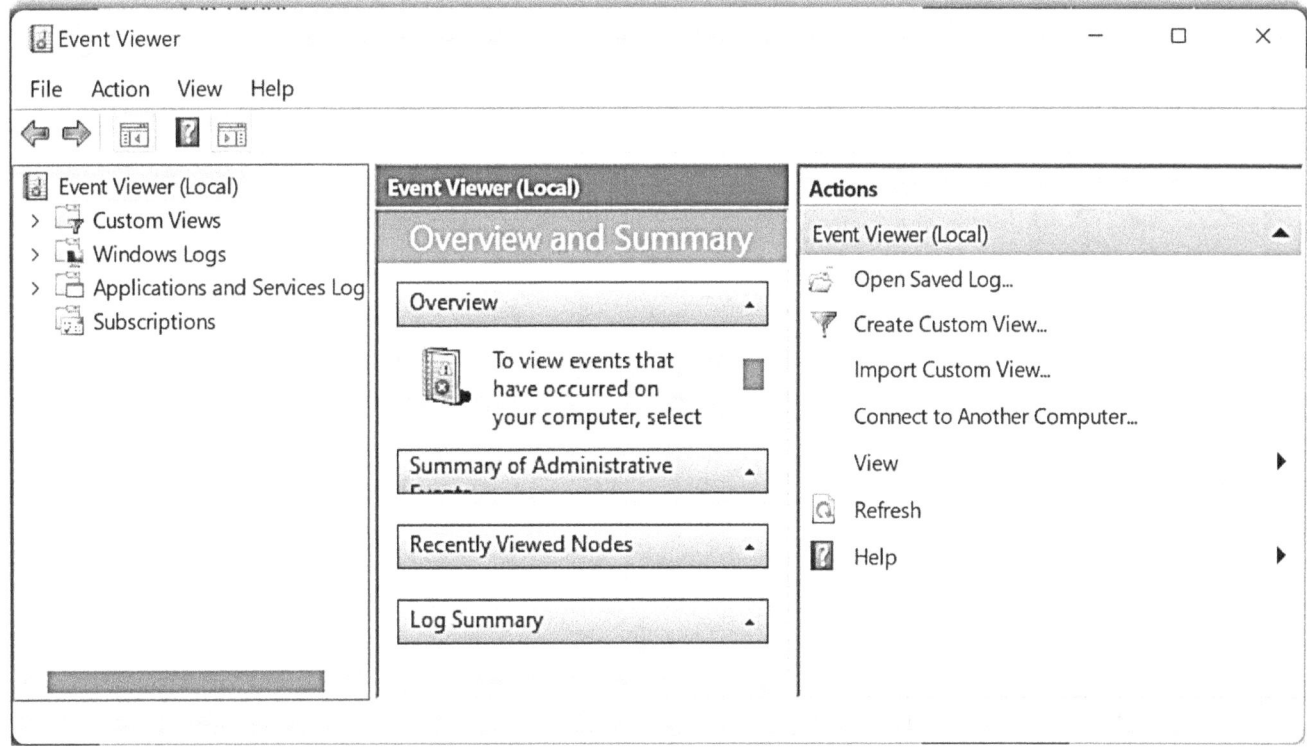

For a tech enthusiast, the Event Viewer unveils the intricate workings of your system, allowing you to delve deep into troubleshooting task.

On the other hand, as a beginner, you can gradually explore its features as you learn more about your computer to satisfy your curiosity and aid your digital learning journey at your own pace.

Device Manager, Know Your Hardware

Device Manager gives you a complete picture of all the hardware connected to your computer, making it like a virtual control panel.

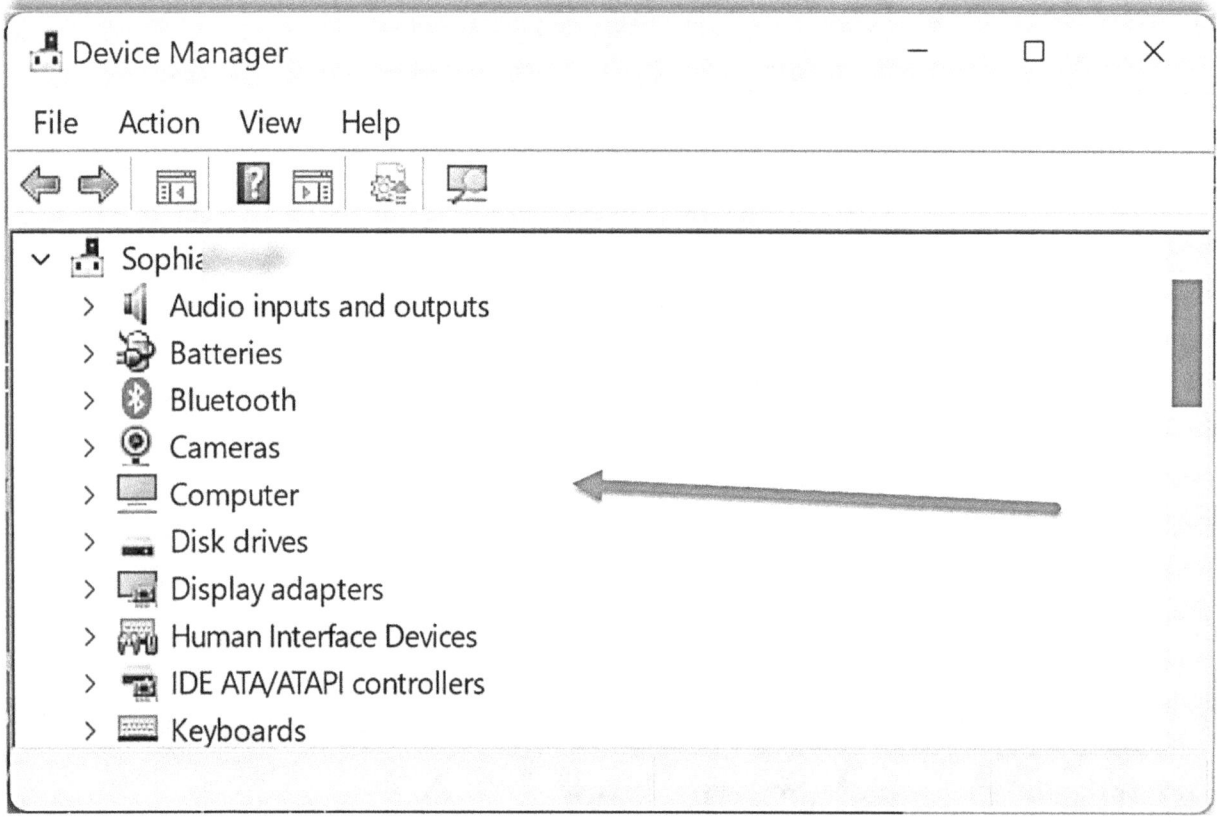

From basic hardware like the keyboard and screen to more complex hardware like network adapters and printers, the Device Manager is where you can view information, fix problems, and handle device drivers. With this tool, you can learn how your system works and keep it running at its best.

Network Connections on Your Computer

Network Connections is like a hub for all of your connections.

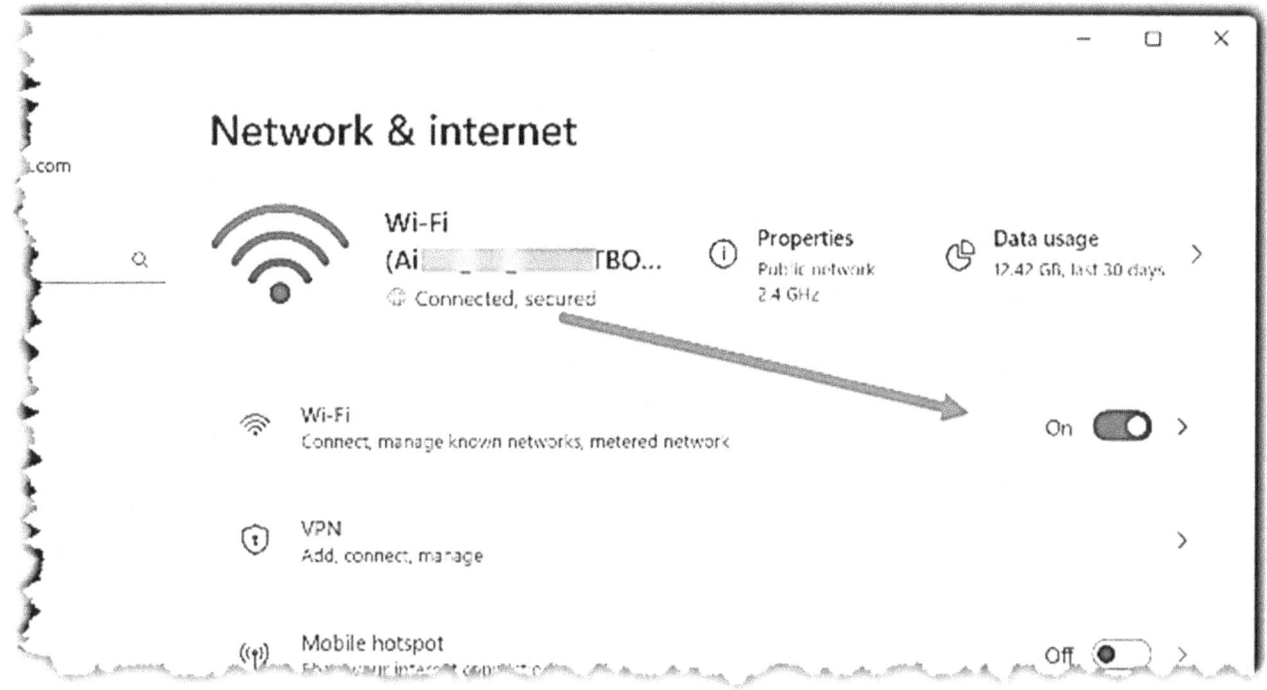

It gives you a view and control over how your computer connects to the internet. This tool manages all incoming and outgoing links, much like an air traffic control tower. Whether connected via Wi-Fi or a wired Ethernet cable, the Network Connections window lets you change settings, fix problems, and oversee different parts of your internet connection, ensuring you stay online.

Disk Management

Disk management is designed to function like a specialized space planner: it helps you keep your computer's storage space organized.

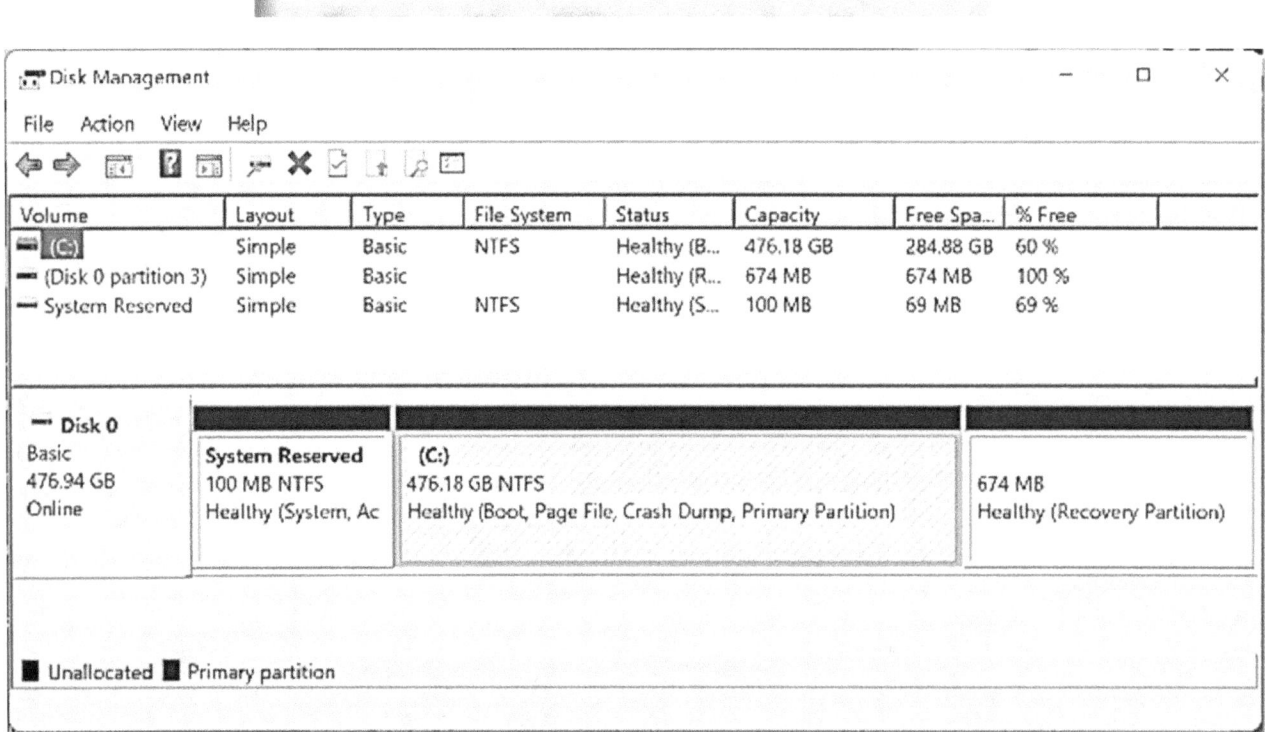

Disk Management makes it easy to see all of your hard drives. This includes your main hard drive, where your operating system and important files are kept, and any USB flash drives, memory cards, or external hard drives connected to your computer.

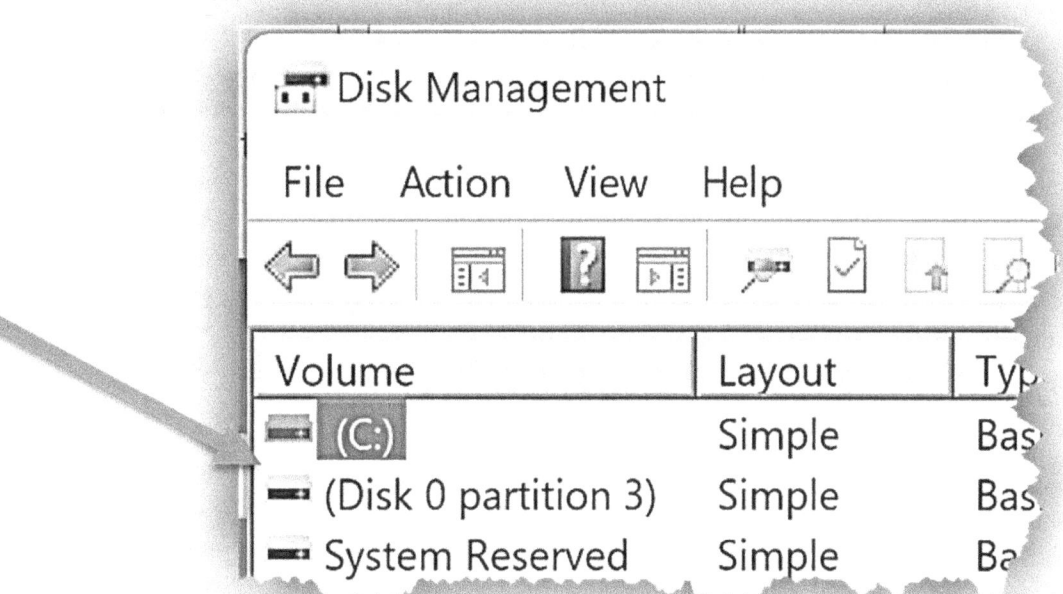

This tool also allows you to create or format partitions on your drives, so you can change how your storage is set up to make the best use of it.

Computer Management

Computer Management is the hub where you can find intelligent tools that will help you get better at using your computer.

This multifaceted tool serves as a central hub, a gateway leading you to a suite of sophisticated utilities that can transform you into a computer expert.

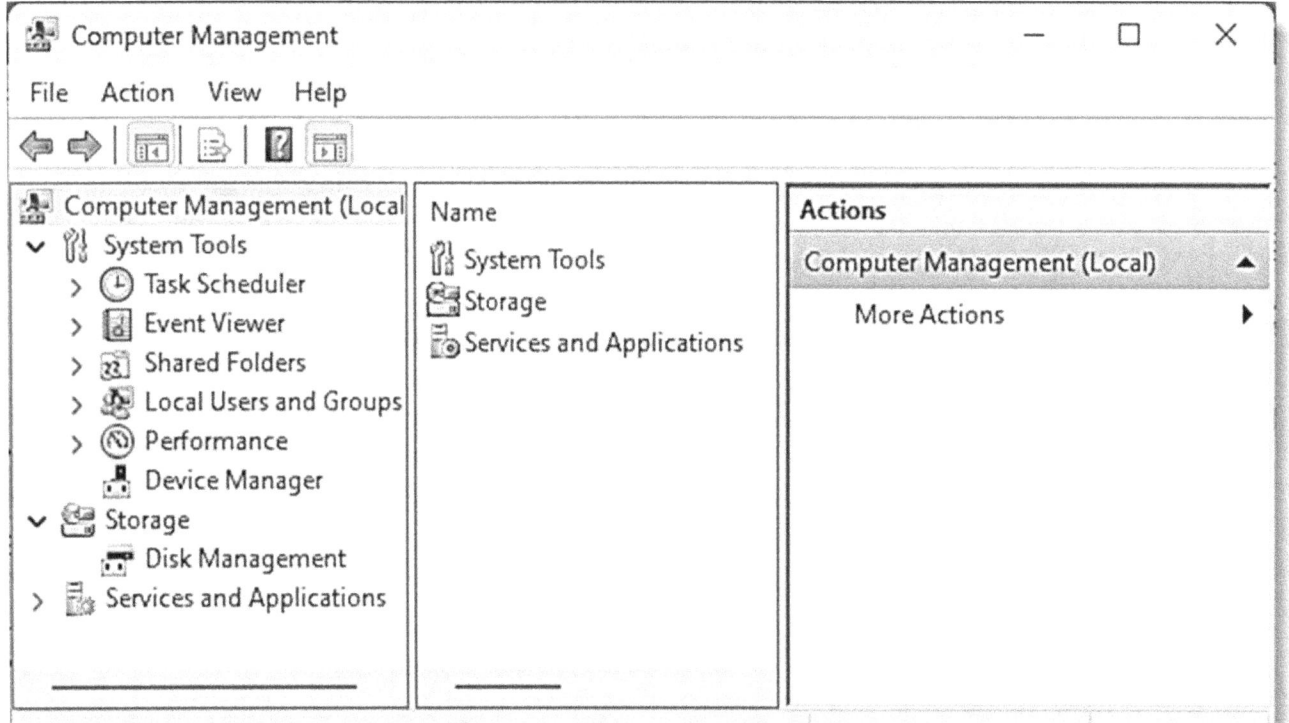

As a beginner, you might not have to go deeper into these settings.

Windows Terminal/ Powershell

Windows Terminal is your computer's secret language decoder. It's like having a direct line of communication with your computer's brain.

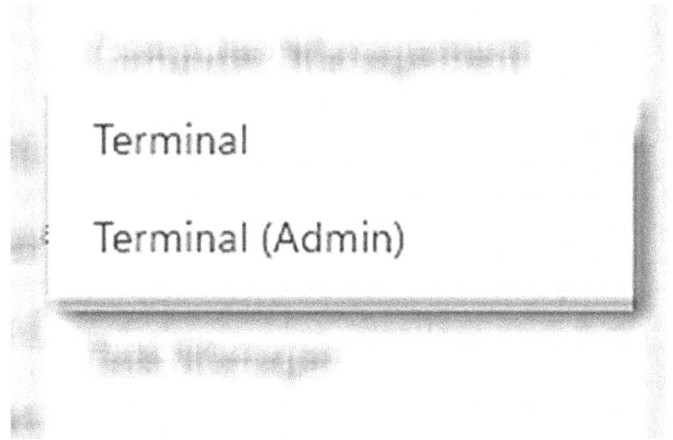

This tool takes different command-line tools and bundles them up in a single, powerful package.

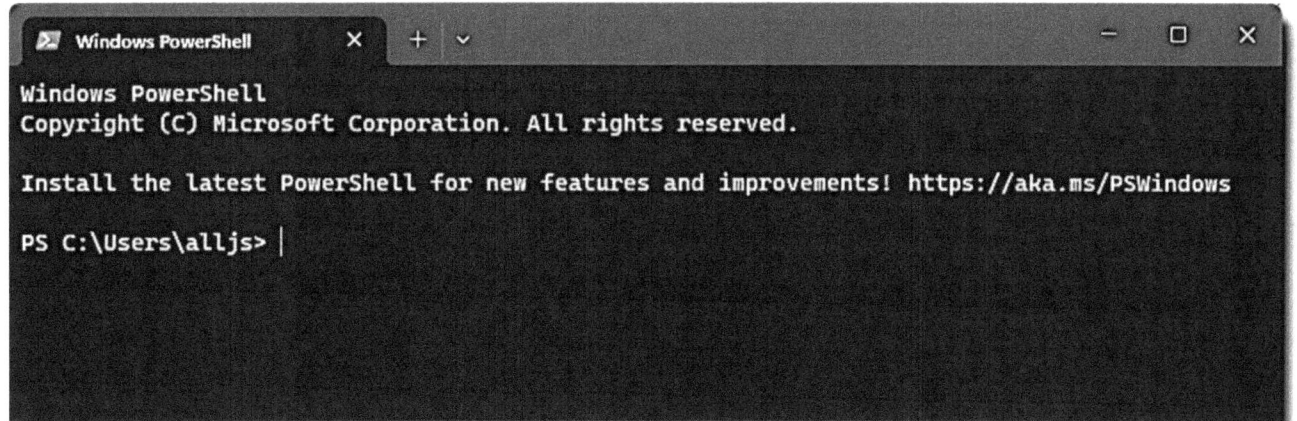

The Windows Terminal Admin lets you go beyond the usual limits. This mode elevates you to an admin wizard, giving you the authority to use the available tools in the Windows Terminal app with no restrictions.

Task Manager at Your Fingertips

The task manager allows you to view what goes on behind the scenes of your computer and manage all the tasks and processes seamlessly.

The Task Manager monitors the performance of your computer; It keeps track of CPU usage, memory usage, disk activity, and network activity.

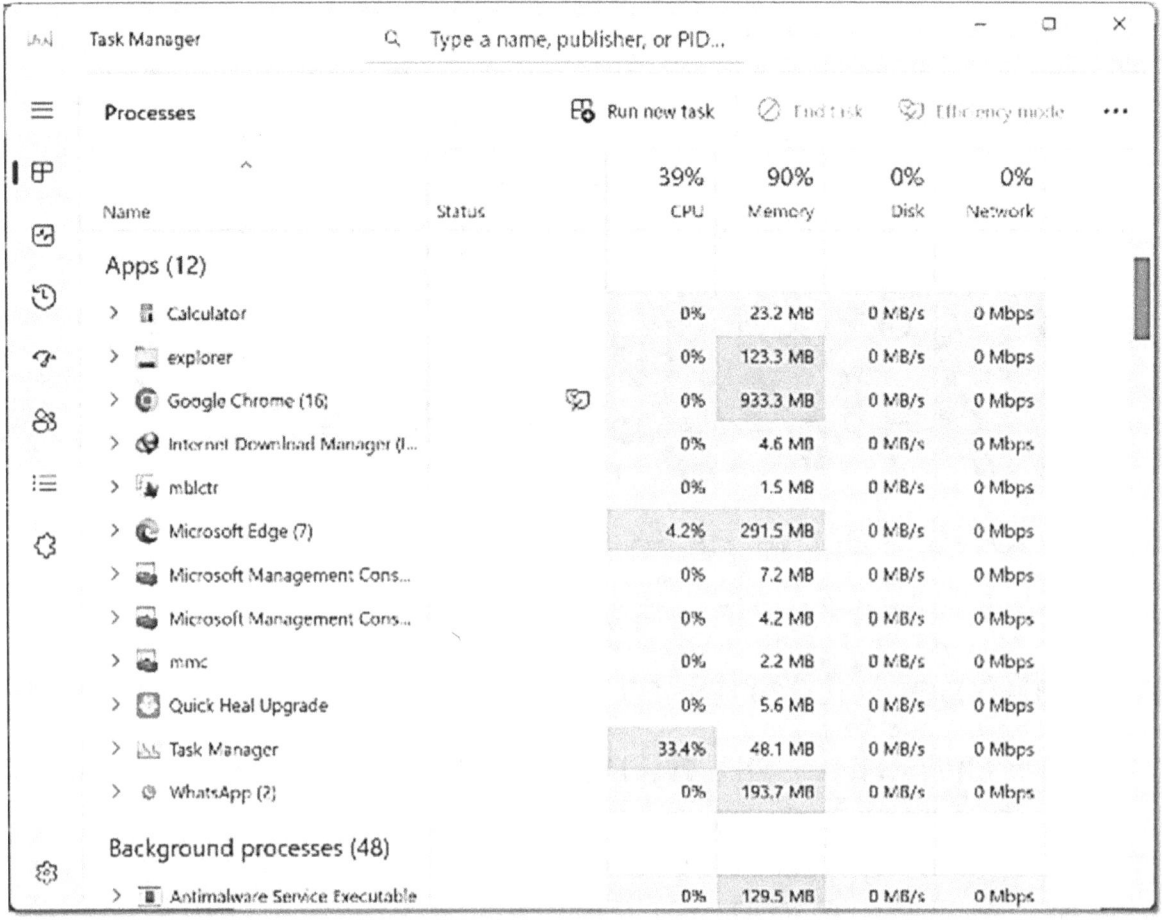

You can quickly identify bottlenecks or resource-hungry applications that might slow down your computer.

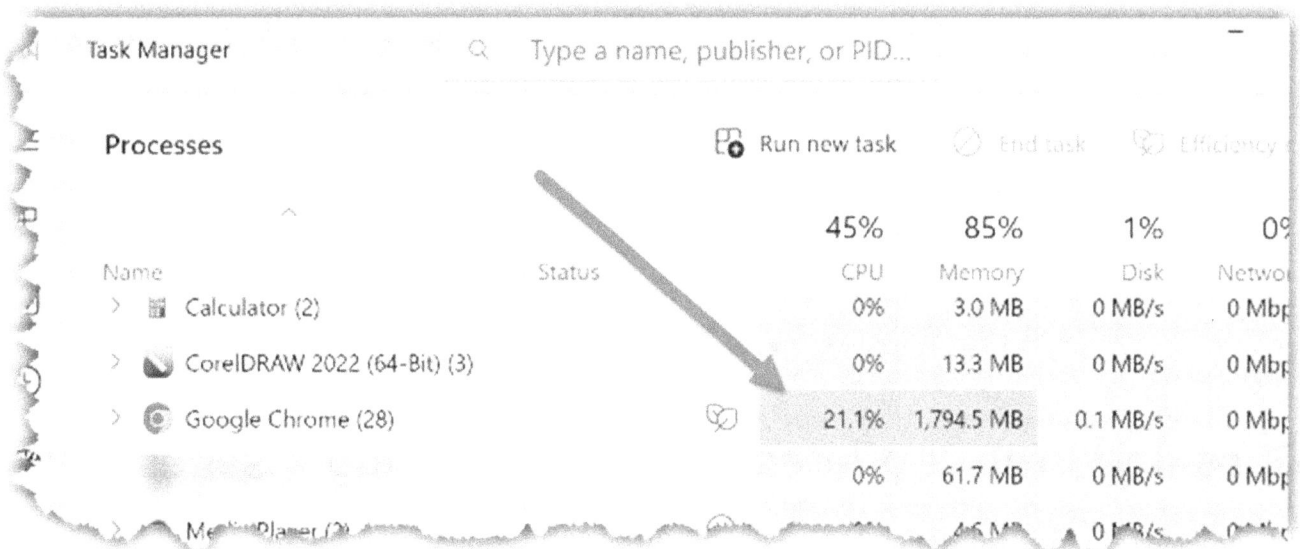

The Task Manager is the tool that will come to your aid if you are experiencing a frozen application that will not close, regardless of what you undertake. With just a few clicks, you can end the app that is not responding to your commands and get back to work.

Settings Option

The Settings option allows you to adjust various aspects of your computer, including all connected devices, your internet connection, accounts, privacy, etc.

Checking for updates, troubleshooting issues, and accessing options are possible when you click Settings.

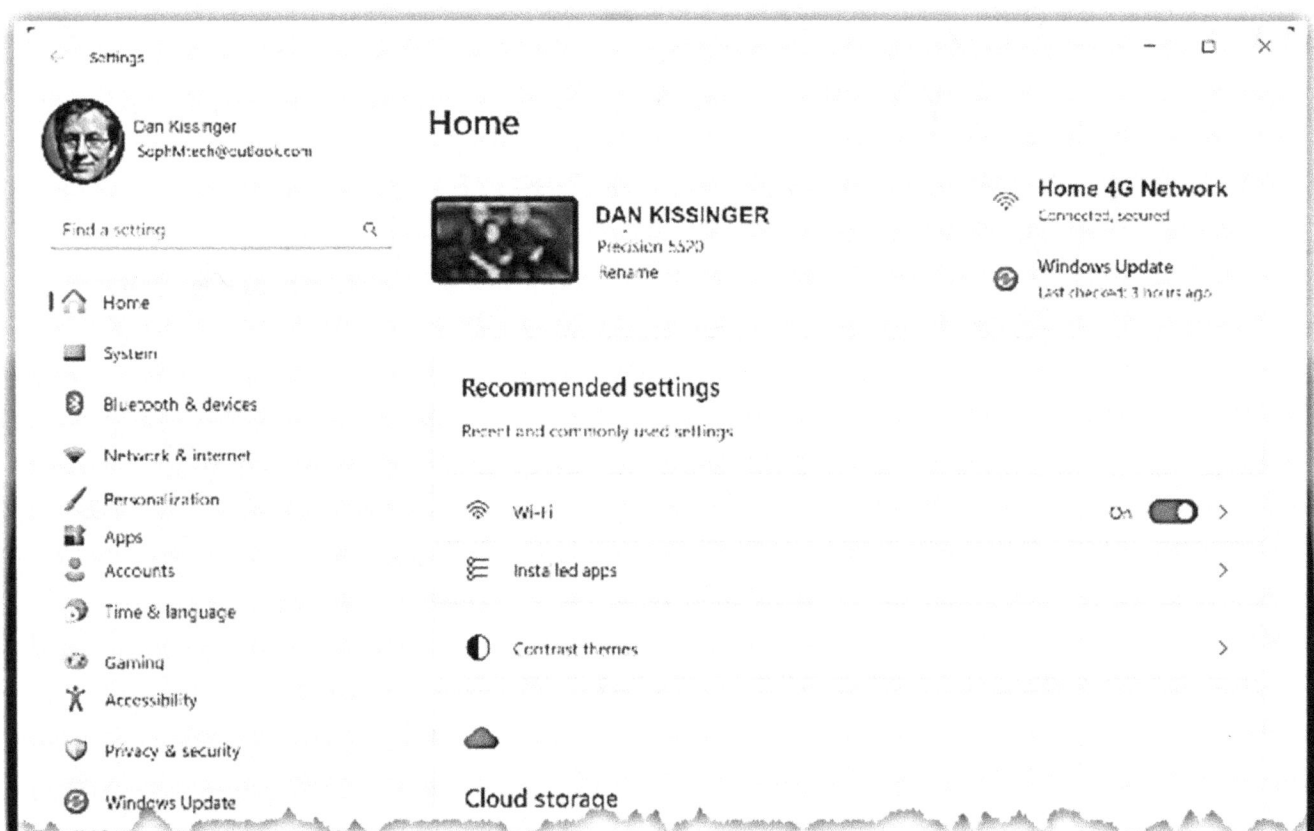

The Settings window is also user-friendly and intuitive.

Access to File Explorer

This tool gives you direct access to the File Explorer window, an essential component for efficiently managing files and folders.

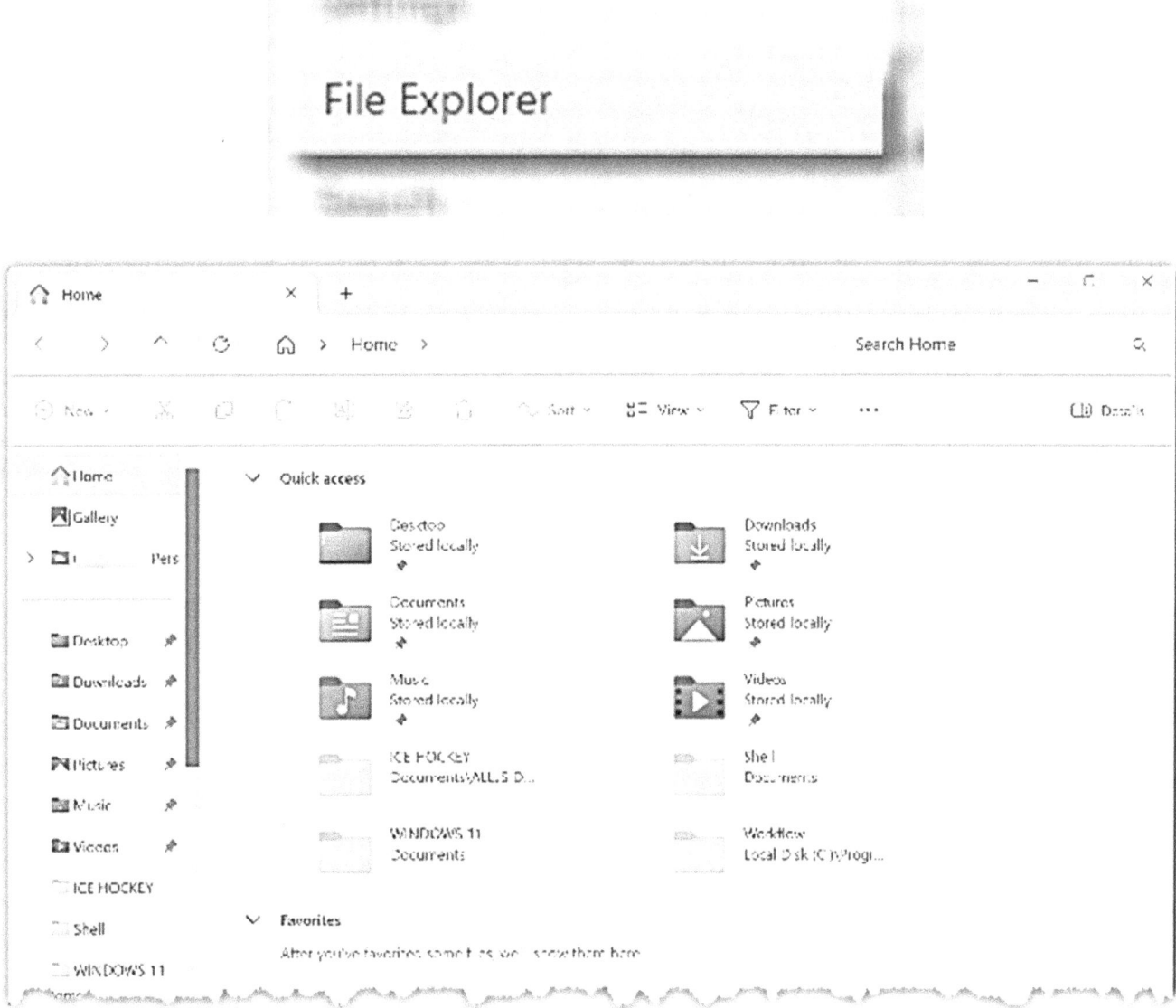

Chapter 7 will focus on more information regarding the file explorer.

Search Option

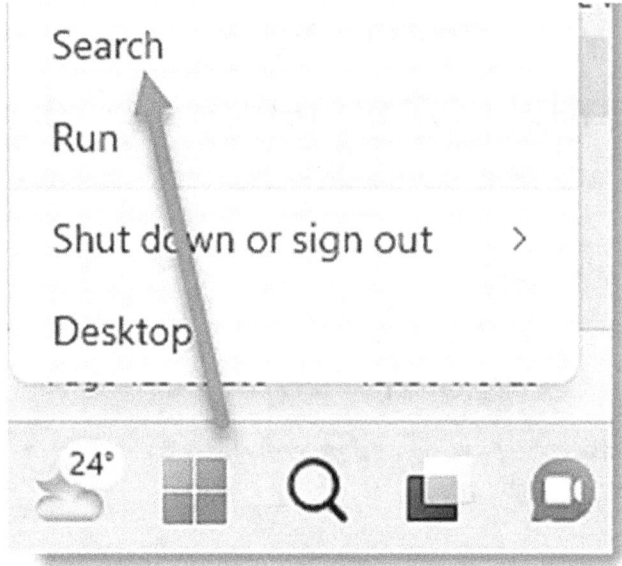

This enhanced search feature empowers you to find anything you need on your computer.

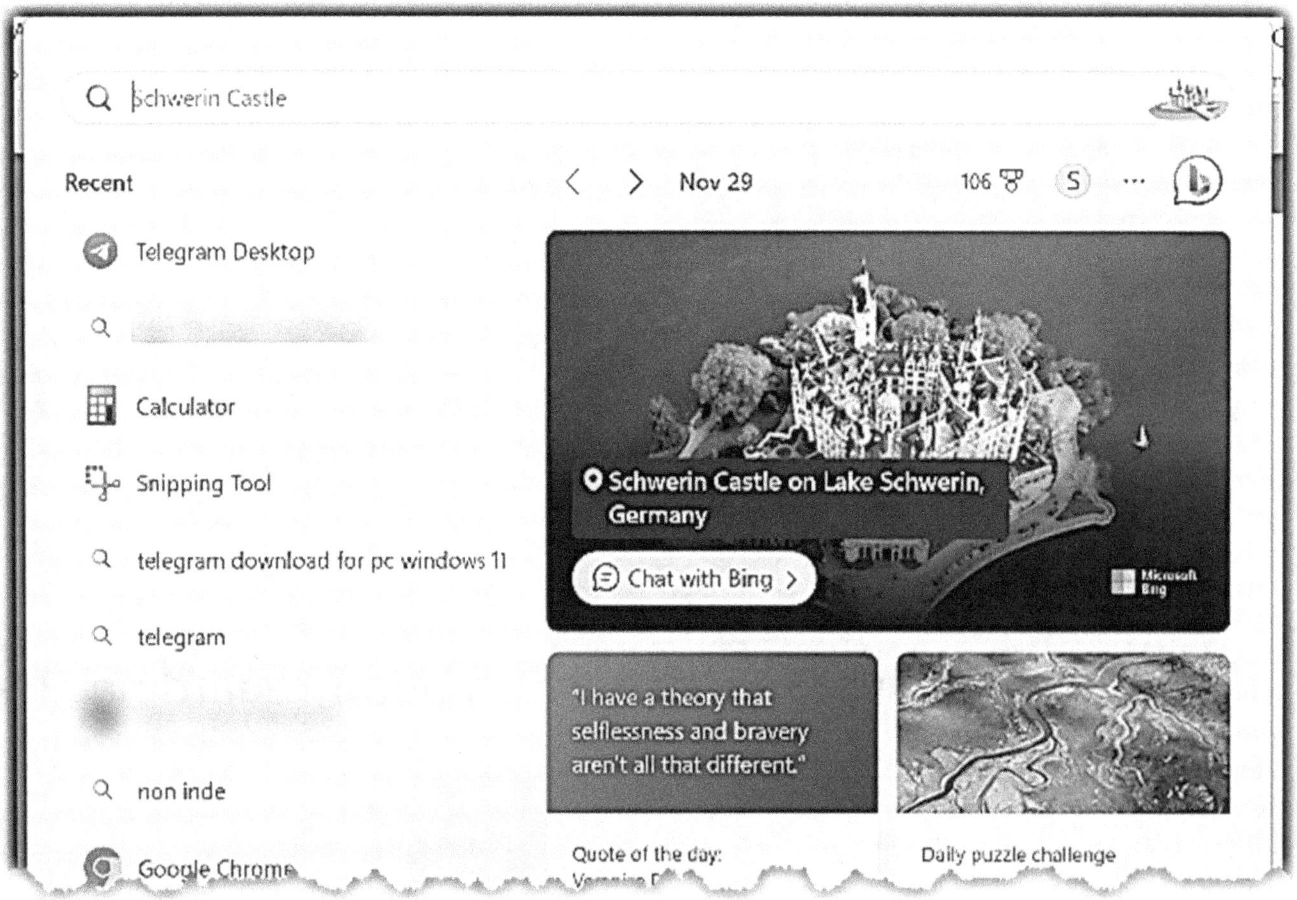

This feature is there to assist you in getting the most out of your workflow and increasing your productivity. It doesn't matter if you are looking for a document, an email, or an application; the power of search is at your disposal. You won't have to waste time conducting manual searches or struggling to find your way through the complex file system of your computer.

Access the Run Command

The RUN option is an excellent tool for getting around your computer quickly.

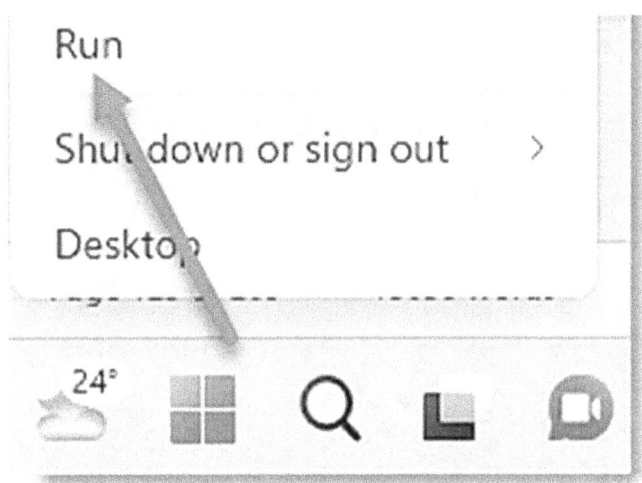

You can quickly access your files, folders, programs, and commands by typing their names or paths.

For example, entering "**control**" and then clicking the OK button, as illustrated below, opens the Control Panel.

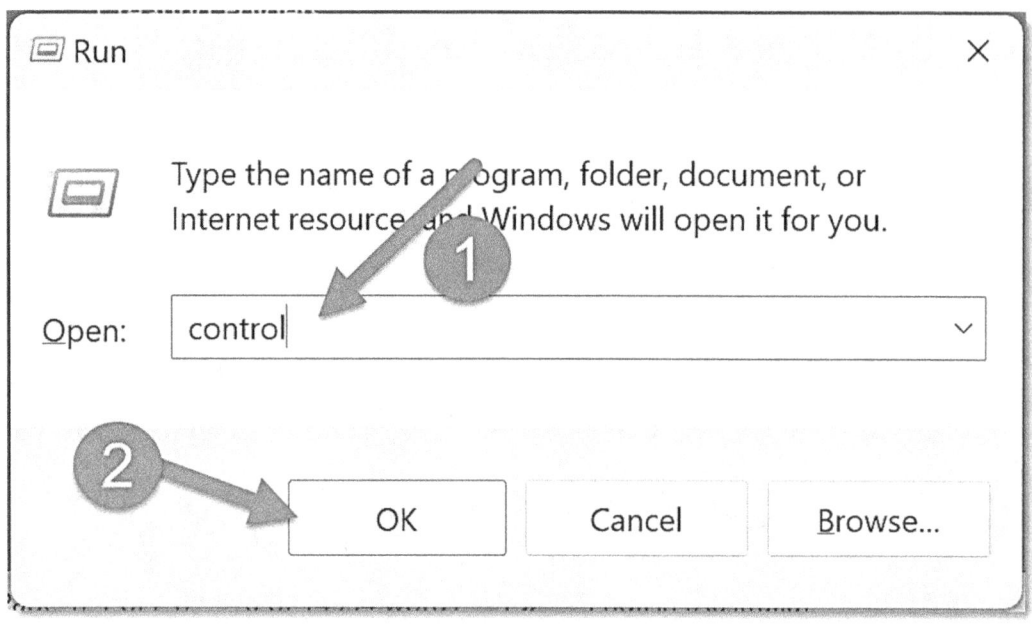

The RUN dialog allows power users to easily access commonly used apps and system tools.

Shut Down or Sign Out Options

On Windows 11, you can access the Shut Down or Sign Out menu by right-clicking the Start button.

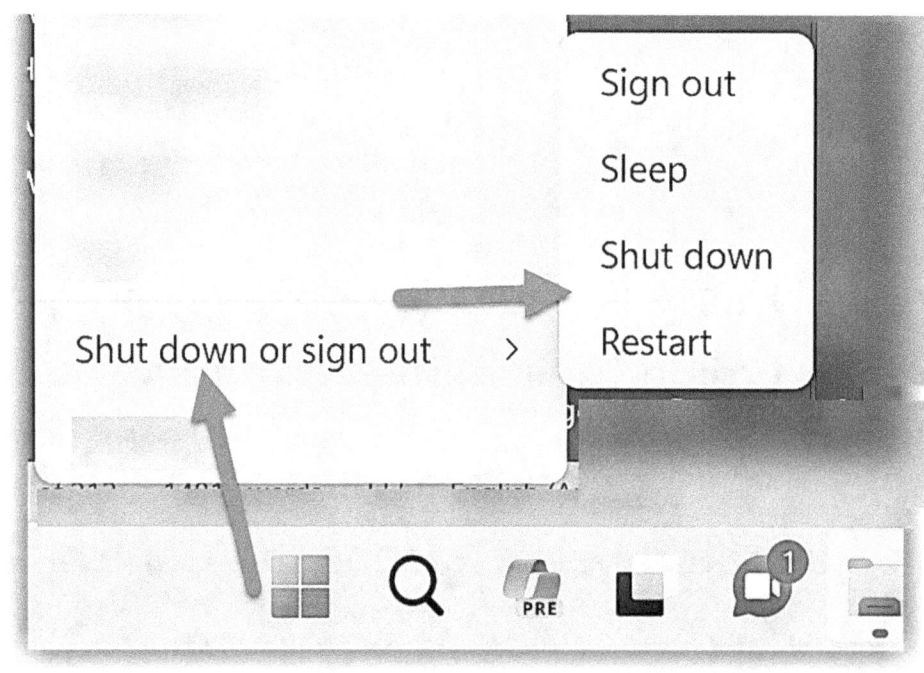

This menu allows you to control your computer's power state. There are many choices on this menu, so you can make use the right tool at a time.

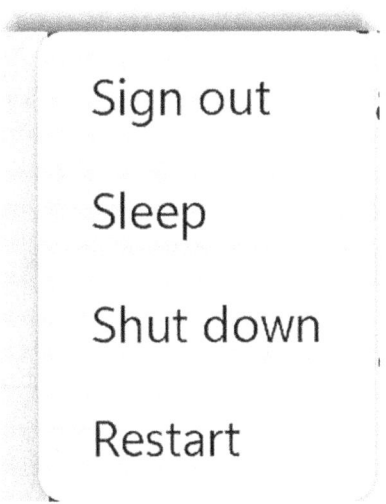

- **Shut Down**: If you want to turn your computer off, click on "**Shut down**." This is useful when you are done using your computer for the day.

- **Sleep**: If you plan to return to using your computer soon but want to save power, click on "**Sleep**." This saves energy on your computer without ending your work session. Your computer can be turned back on by clicking the power button.

- **Restart:** Sometimes, a restart is all you need to fix minor glitches or software updates. Selecting "**Restart**" reboots your computer and closes any open programs while reloading the operating system.

- ***Sign out***: This option allows you to switch user accounts without shutting down your computer if more than one person uses it. This allows other users to log in and access their files and settings while preserving your current session.

Desktop

Right-clicking the Windows 11 Start button and selecting "**Desktop**" minimizes all open apps windows, effectively hiding them to display the underlying desktop background.

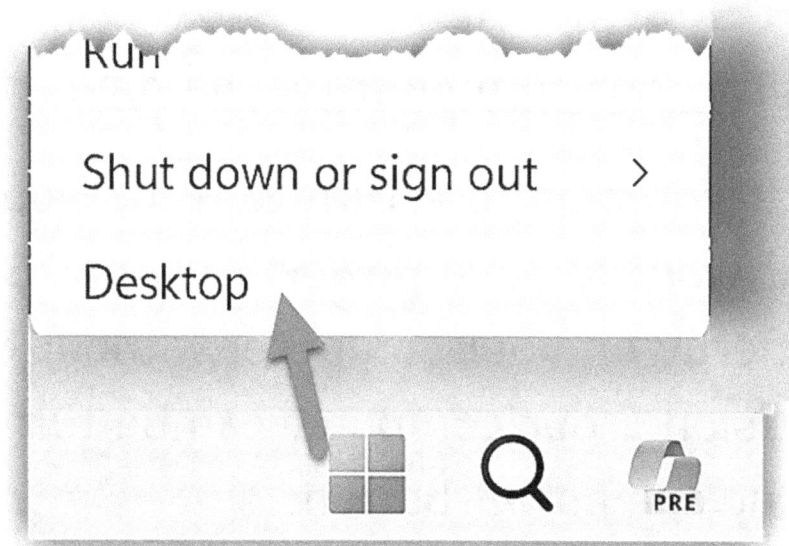

This provides a quick way to access files or gadgets on your desktop without manually minimizing each open app's window.

CHAPTER 7

NAVIGATING THE FILE EXPLORER FOR FILE MANAGEMENT

Windows File Explorer is a crucial tool for managing files and folders on your computer and OneDrive account. The File Explorer graphics interface lets you organize and interact with your device's file system. There have been several updates and simplifications to the File Explorer interface since earlier versions of the Microsoft operating system.

UNDERSTANDING FILES AND FOLDER

To successfully navigate your computer, it is essential to understand how to handle files and folders. As soon as you fully understand how these components operate, they will become indispensable to your computer activities. This chapter will walk you through the fundamentals of file manipulation; this covers tasks such as opening files, moving them into folders, and removing files from your computer.

What is a File?

One way to organize and save data in a digital format is in a file. Files can be in different formats like documents, photos, videos, or even executable programs.

A file's data type and the name that identifies it dictate what information it can store and how it can be processed.

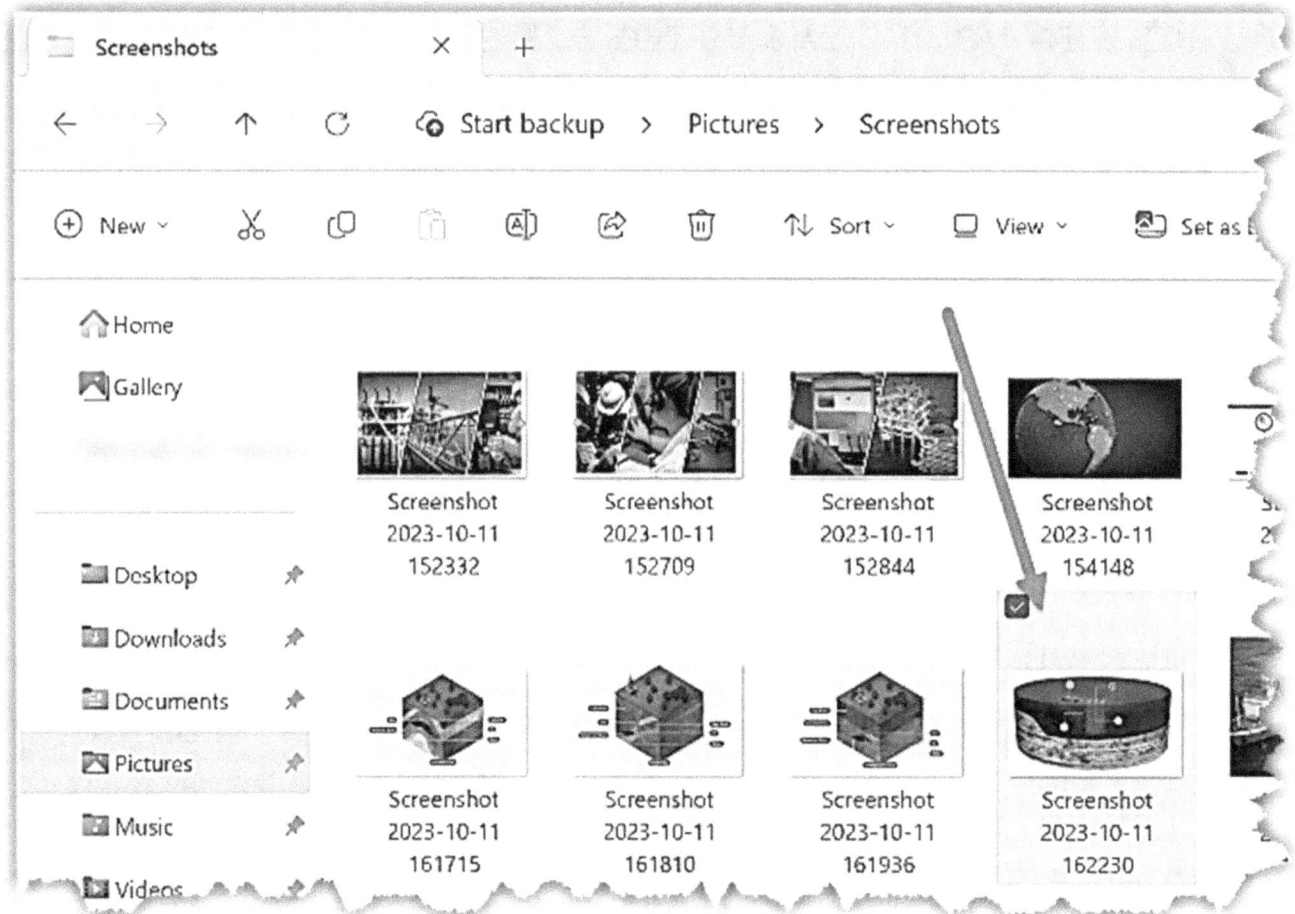

For example, you will need a photo viewer or editing program to open and view an image file. You can access and modify the contents of each file per its intended use.

What is a Folder?

The term "folder" refers to a virtual container that facilitates the organization of files, enabling you to organize documents, images, or any other digital content that is related to one another.

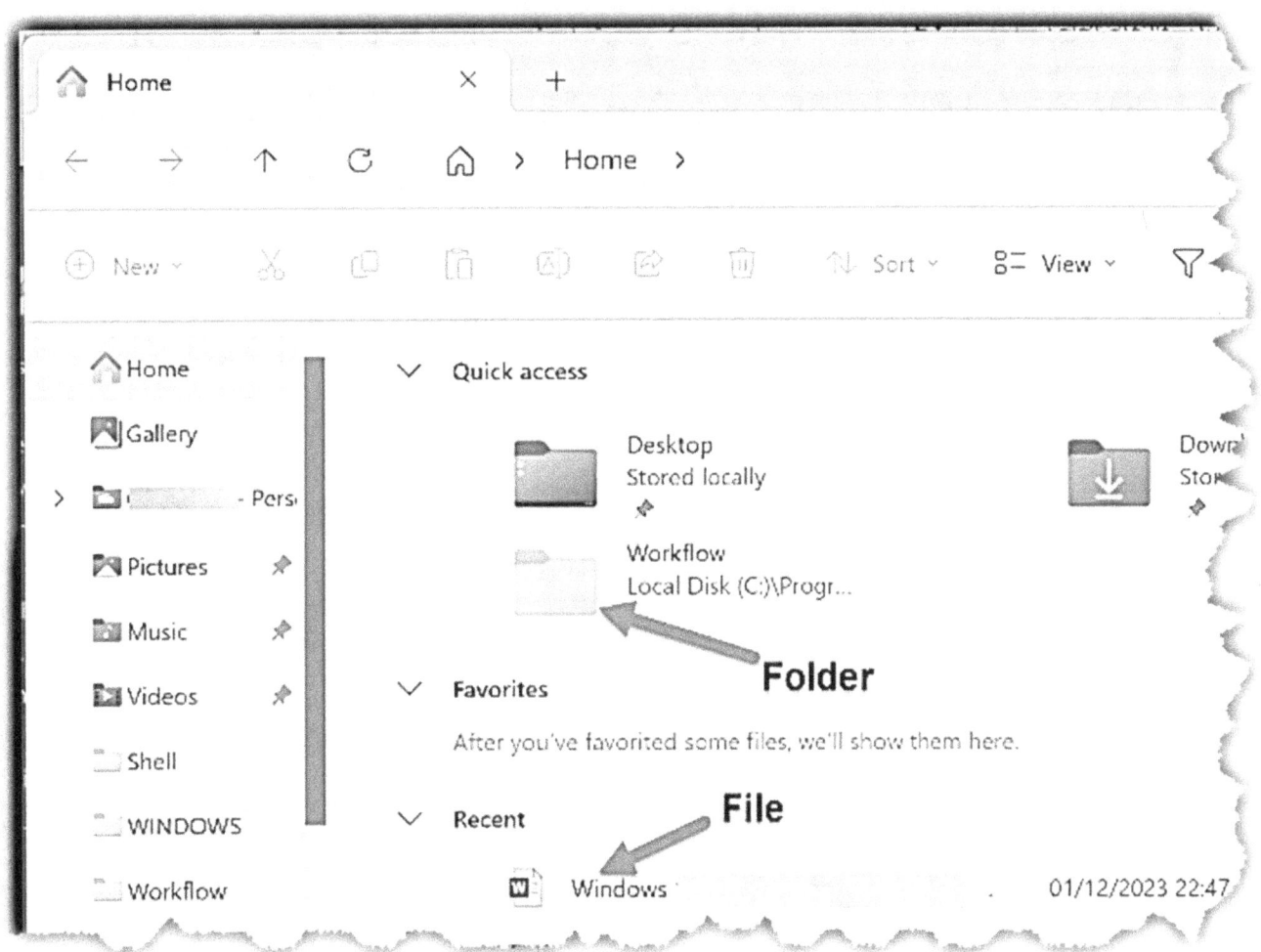

Consider it a digital filing cabinet, with each folder functioning as a drawer labeled and containing a particular category of information.

However, Files are structured hierarchically within folders to facilitate managing and retrieving your digital content.

Benefits of Using the File Explorer

Explorer gives you the ability to control your digital assets in the following ways:

- **Effortless Organization:** You can easily create new folders, move things around, and organize everything in a manner that makes sense. File Explorer offers a graphical representation of your data, making organizing it more straightforward and effective.

- **Seamless OneDrive Integration:** Within the File Explorer application, you can access and manage files that are saved in your OneDrive account. This guarantees that your essential data is always backed up and accessible from any internet-connected device you choose.

- **Swift File Searching:** The file explorer helps you avoid wasting time searching through infinite folders to search for your files by utilizing the File Explorer built-in search bar.

- **Simplified Interface:** Microsoft has made File Explorer more user-friendly over the years by streamlining its navigation and functionality. Even novices will find the user interface straightforward, uncluttered, and easy to understand.

HOW TO ACCESS THE FILE EXPLORER

The File Explorer can be accessed using a variety of methods. The Windows taskbar is one method; click the icon representing the "**File Explorer**" application.

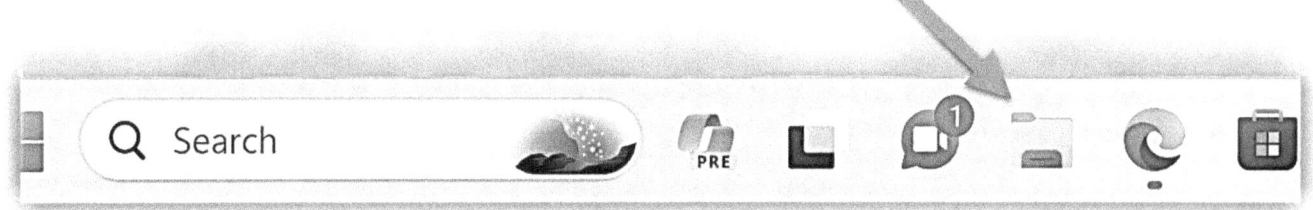

You can also use the Start button or Start menu to access the File Explorer. Right-click the "**Start**" button on the Windows taskbar to select File Explorer from the options available.

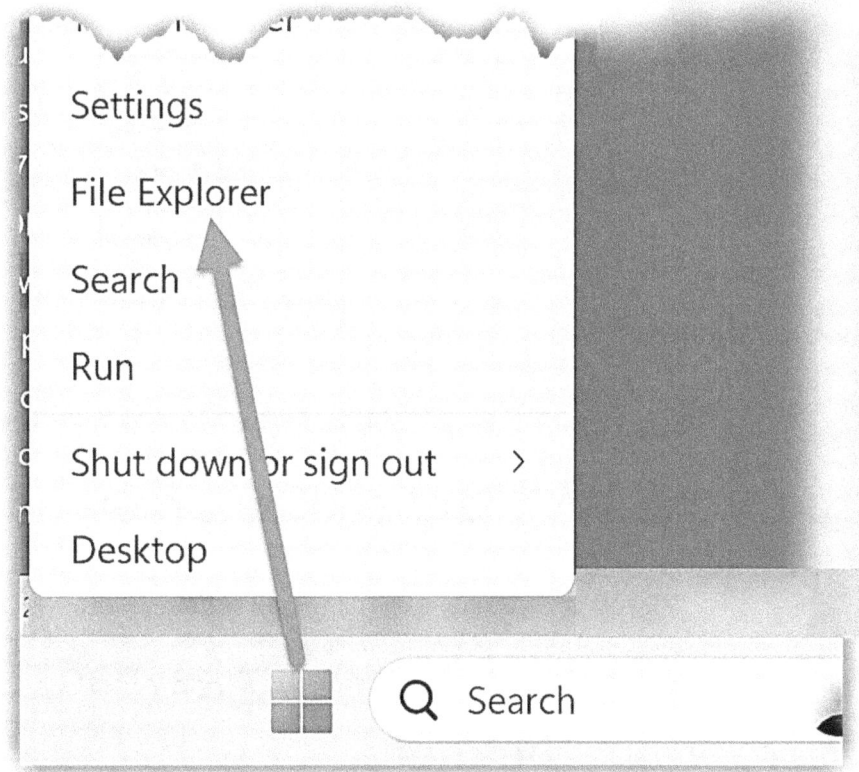

However, the Start menu approach requires you to locate and click the File Explorer icon amongst the Pinned items.

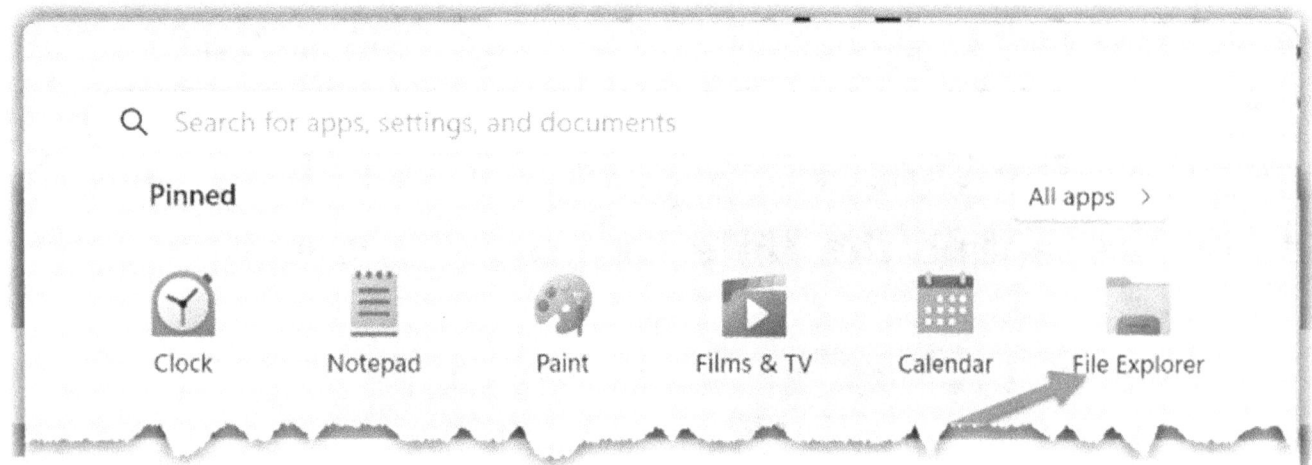

Another option is to use the **Search** bar. After seeing the application, use your mouse to click on it.

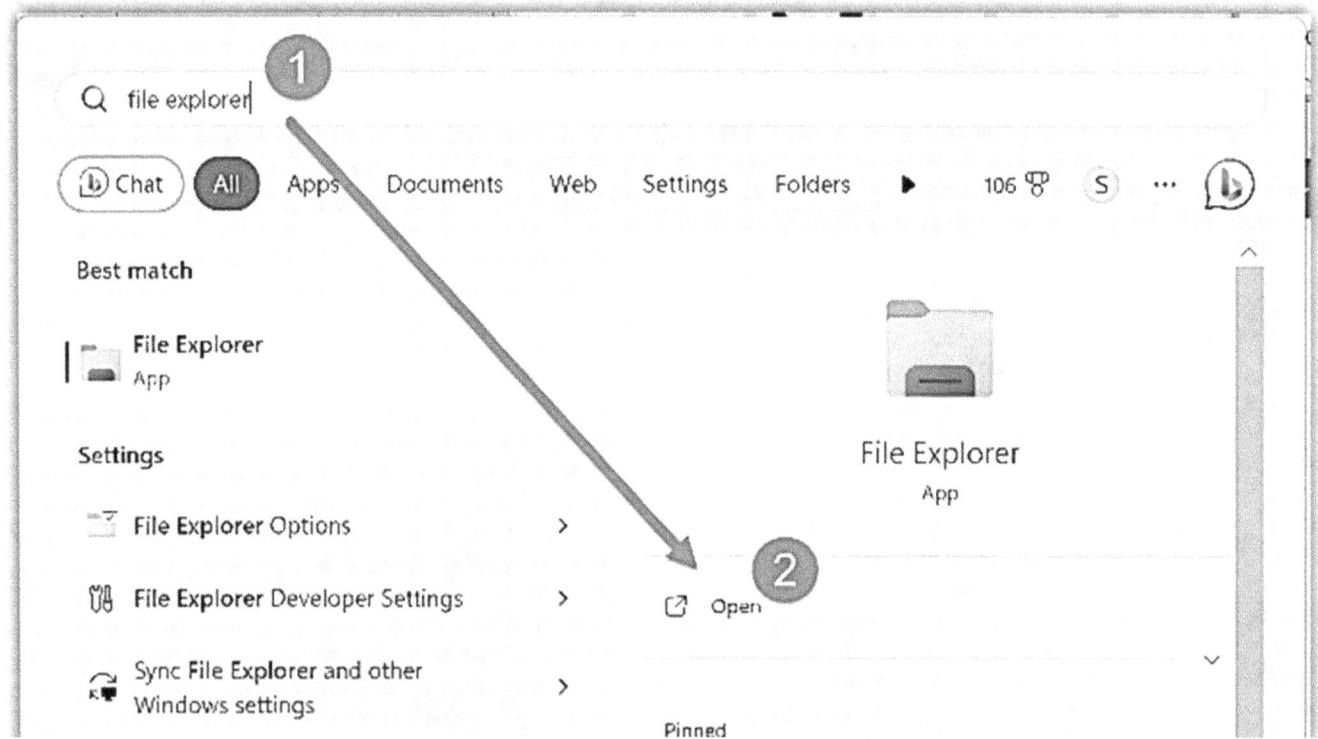

You can also try the keyboard shortcut method to launch File Explorer:

> Press **Windows Key** + **X** on your keypad, then select File Explorer from the menu.

THE FILE EXPLORER INTERFACE

In Windows 11, the File Explorer interface consists of several parts, as discussed below:

The Title Bar

The Title bar on the File Explorer in Windows 11 is a folder identification tool. This bar is the horizontal strip at the top of the File Explorer window that displays the active folder name.

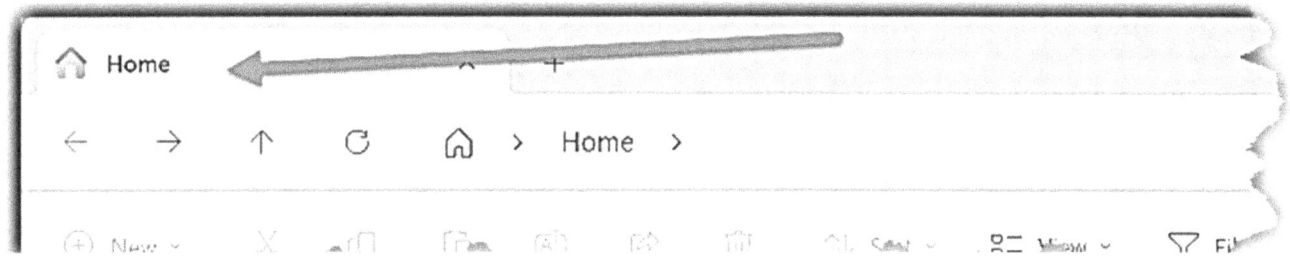

The **Quick Acess** page was the File Explorer default page until it was changed to **Home** in the Windows 11 2022 update.

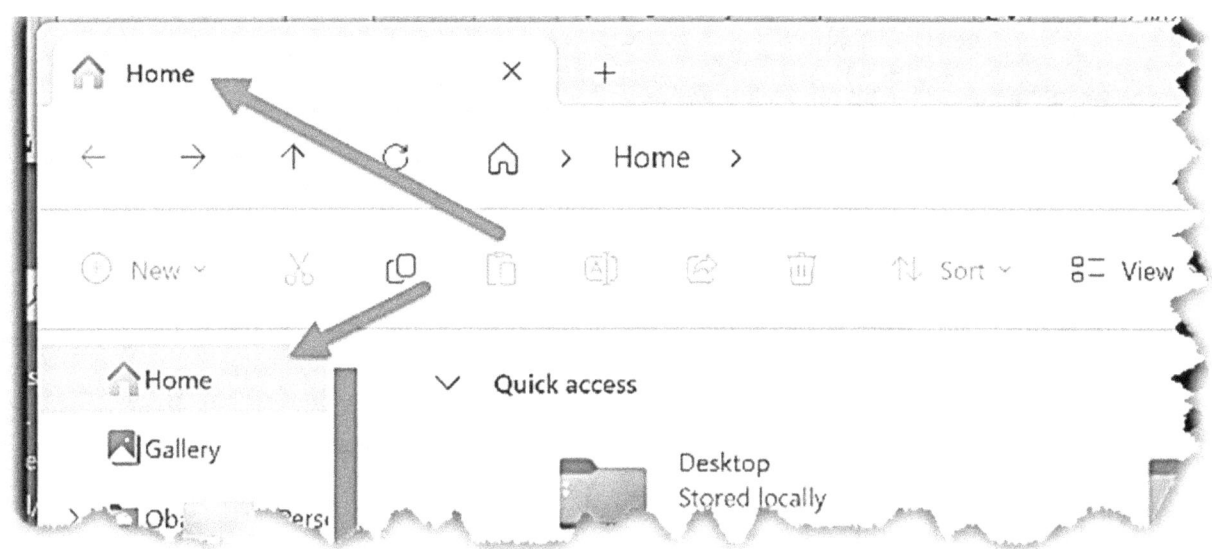

The ToolBar

The File Explorer Toolbar is located directly below the title bar and is one of the features you might want to investigate further.

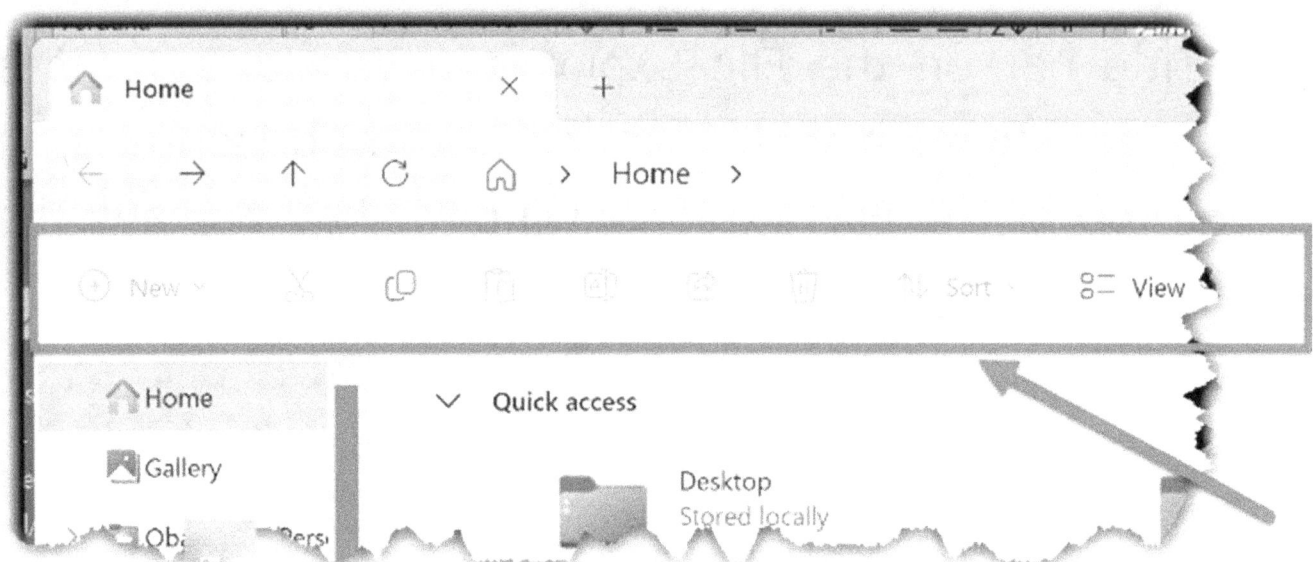

When it comes to managing your files and folders, the toolbar gives you access to a variety of commands and customizable options.

The icons on the toolbar include:

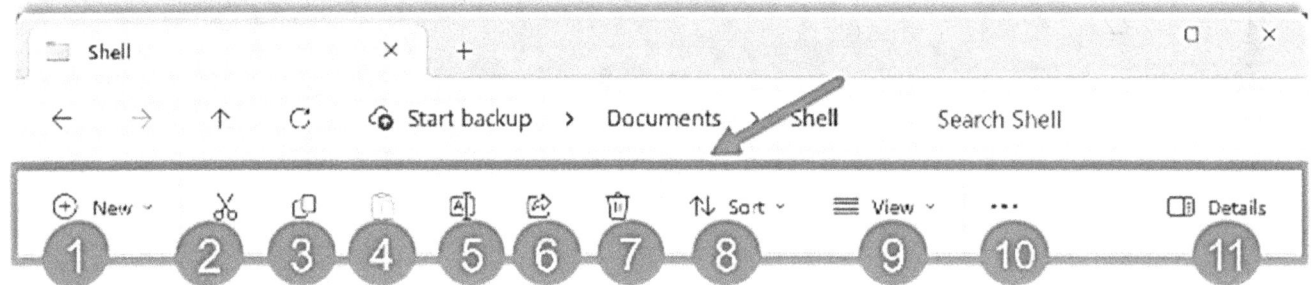

1. **New item** – use it to create a new item, e.g., a folder.

2. **Cut** - moves an item(s) in the file explorer content pane.

3. **Copy** - duplicates an item(s) in the file explorer content pane.

4. **Paste** – drops the item(s) that have been cut or copied to the new location on the file explorer content pane.

5. **Rename** – used to change the identity of a file or folder.

6. **Share** – used to share an item(s) from the file explorer to other platforms.

7. **Delete** – used to delete an unwanted item(s) in the content pane.

8. **Sort** – used this icon to arrange your items alphabetically or numerically with the help of their name

9. **Layout and View** – use this icon to set how you want your content pane to display items.

10. **See more** – allows you to see other hidden tools.

11. **Details** – allows you to view information on the file you selected on the content pane.

The Address Bar

The Address Bar shows the location of the selected folder.

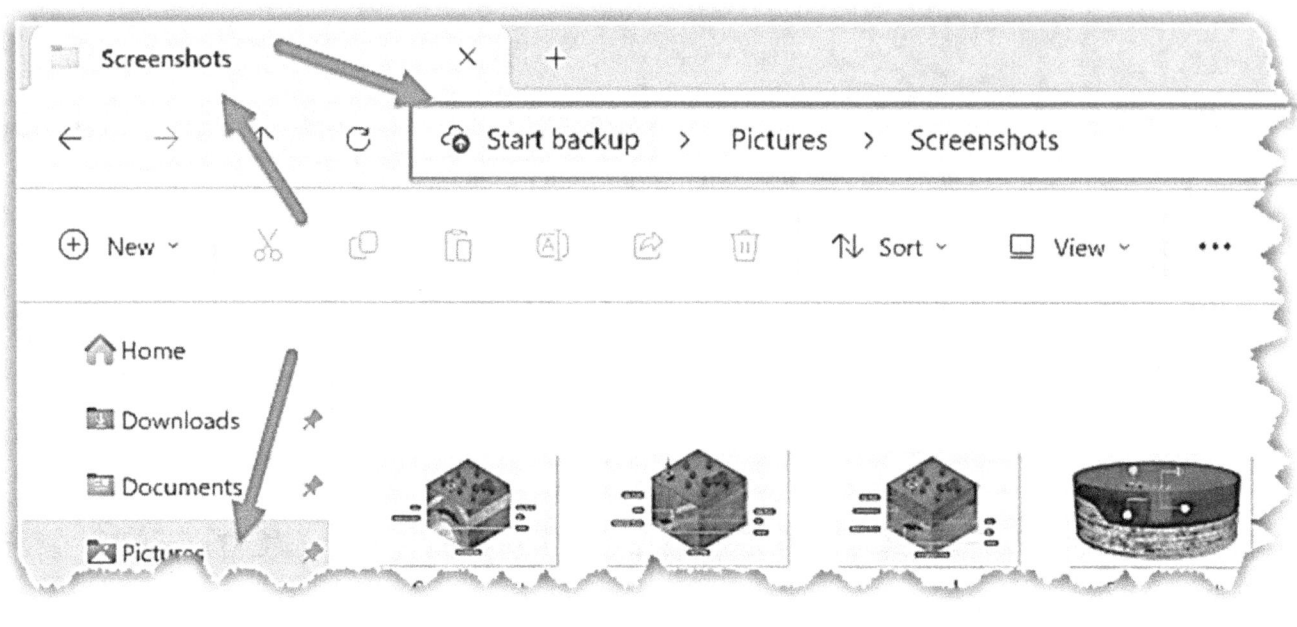

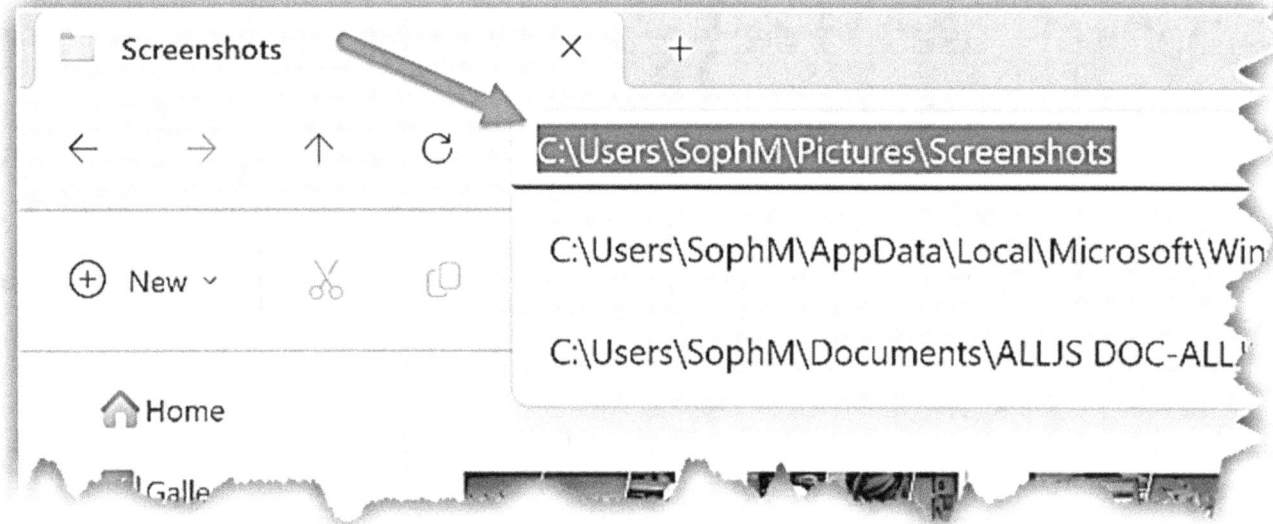

The Search Box

The search box is used to search for a particular file or folder in a folder location that you have selected in File Explorer.

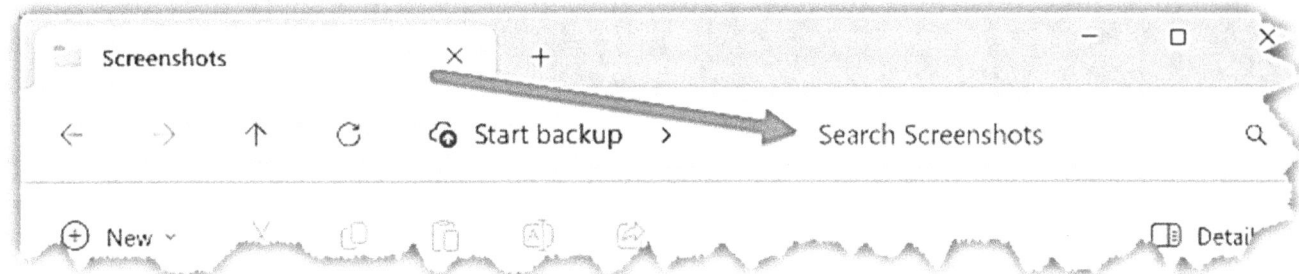

Click inside the Search bar and type the name of the file or folder or the first few letters of the file or folder name to start the search.

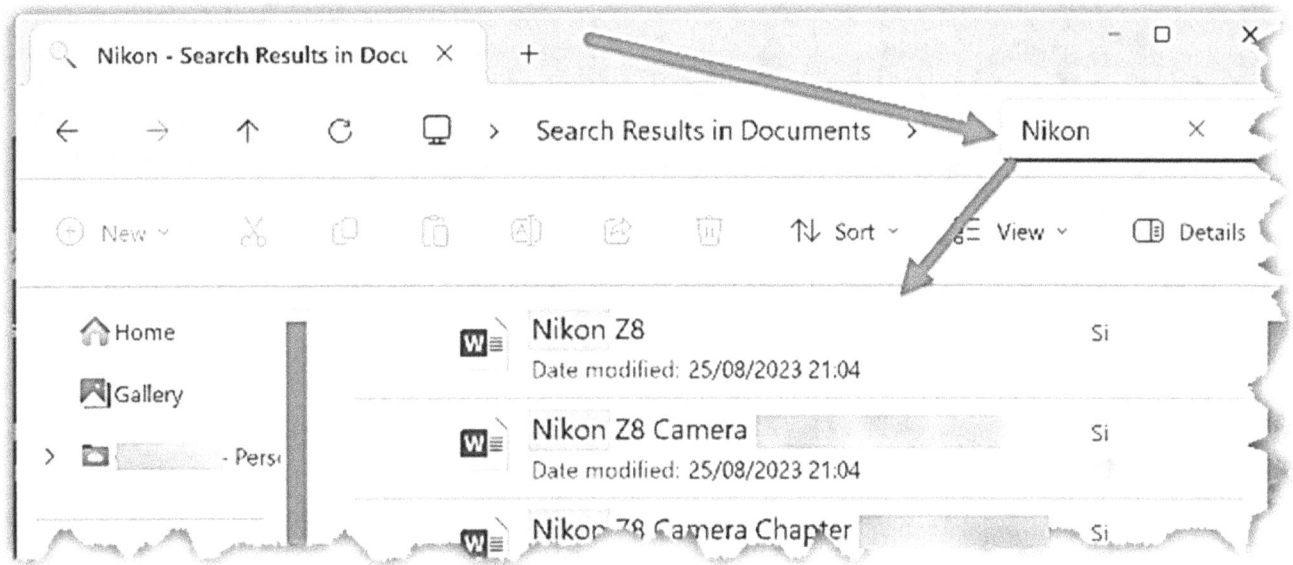

File Explorer will then search within the folder location you have selected for the item you are looking for.

Details Pane

The details pane allows you to view the properties that are most frequently associated with the file that you have selected.

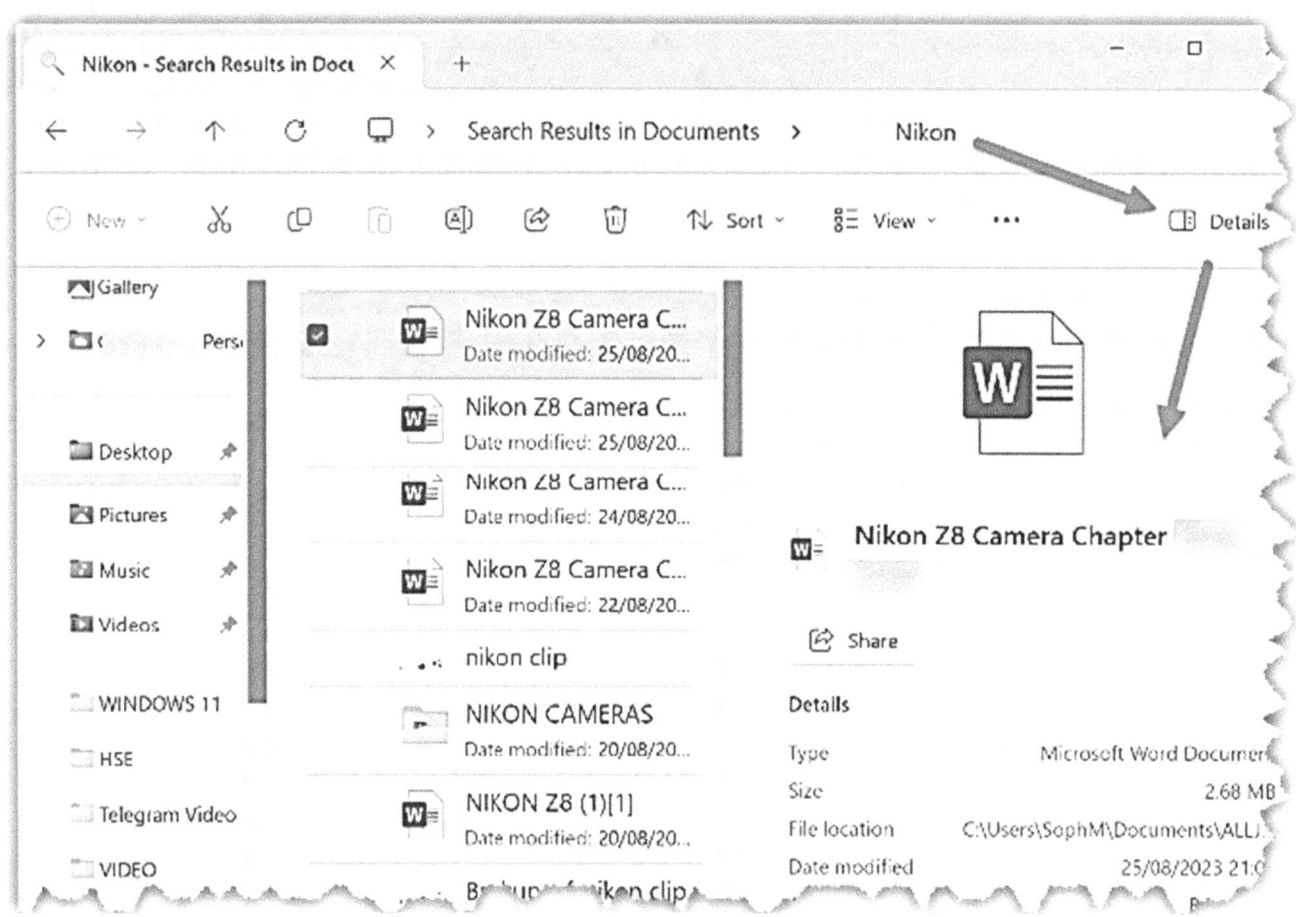

In addition to providing additional information about a file, file properties include the file's author, the date on which the file was modified, and any descriptive tags you may have created and added to the file.

If the details pane is not visible, you can access it by clicking the View tab and then selecting **Details Pane** from the menu.

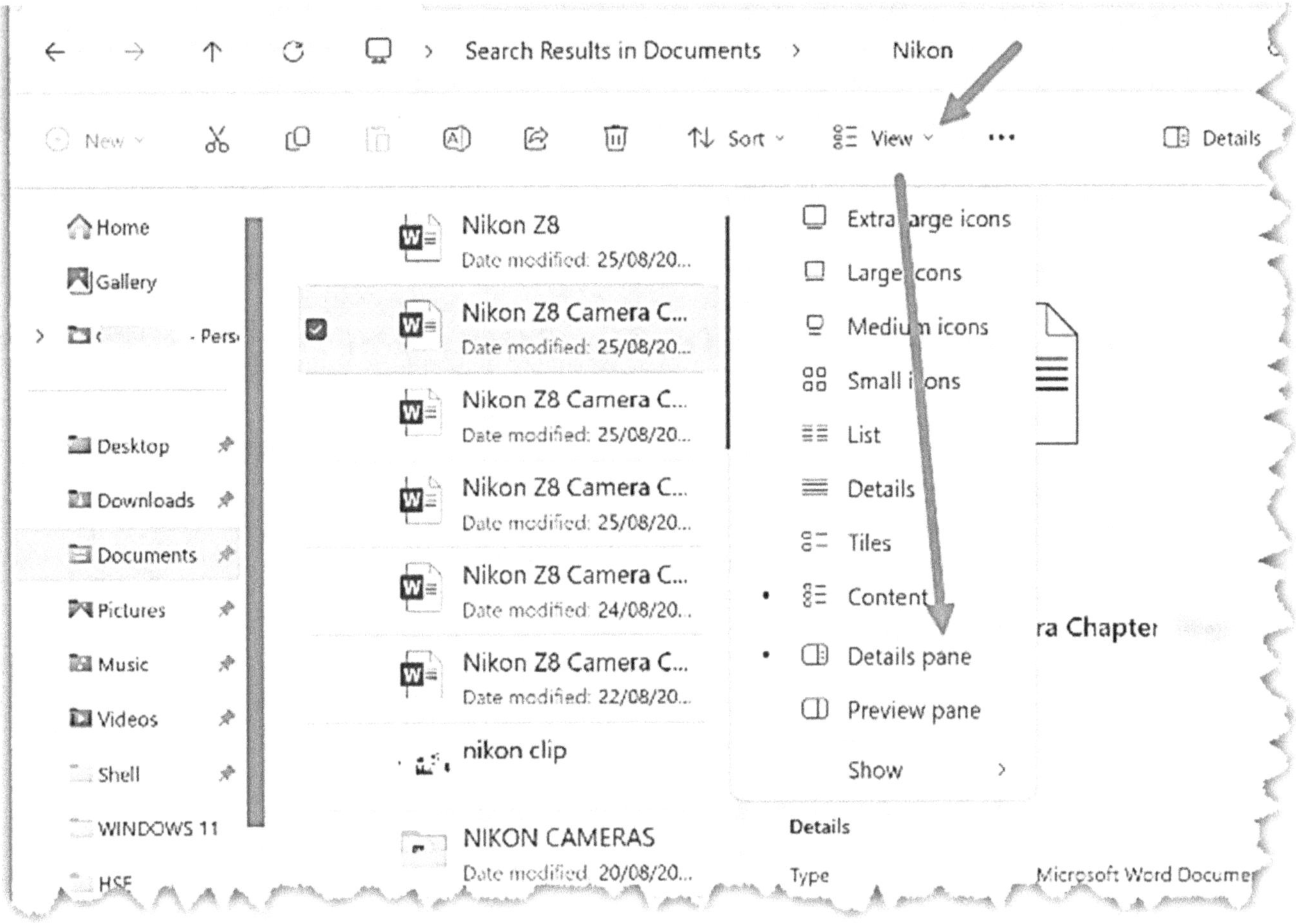

You can also **share** a selected file using the share button in the details pane.

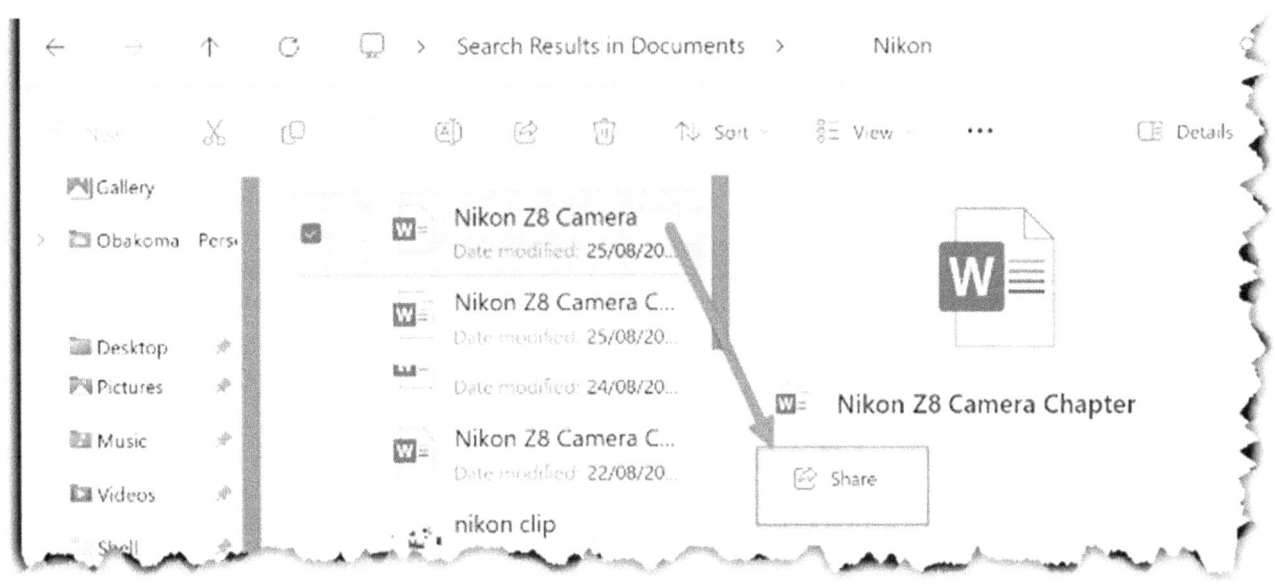

The options available to use in sharing your file include;
- The Share button, integrated with online sharing capabilities, enables you to share content with collaborators through email or link sharing. This applies to files stored on cloud services such as OneDrive.

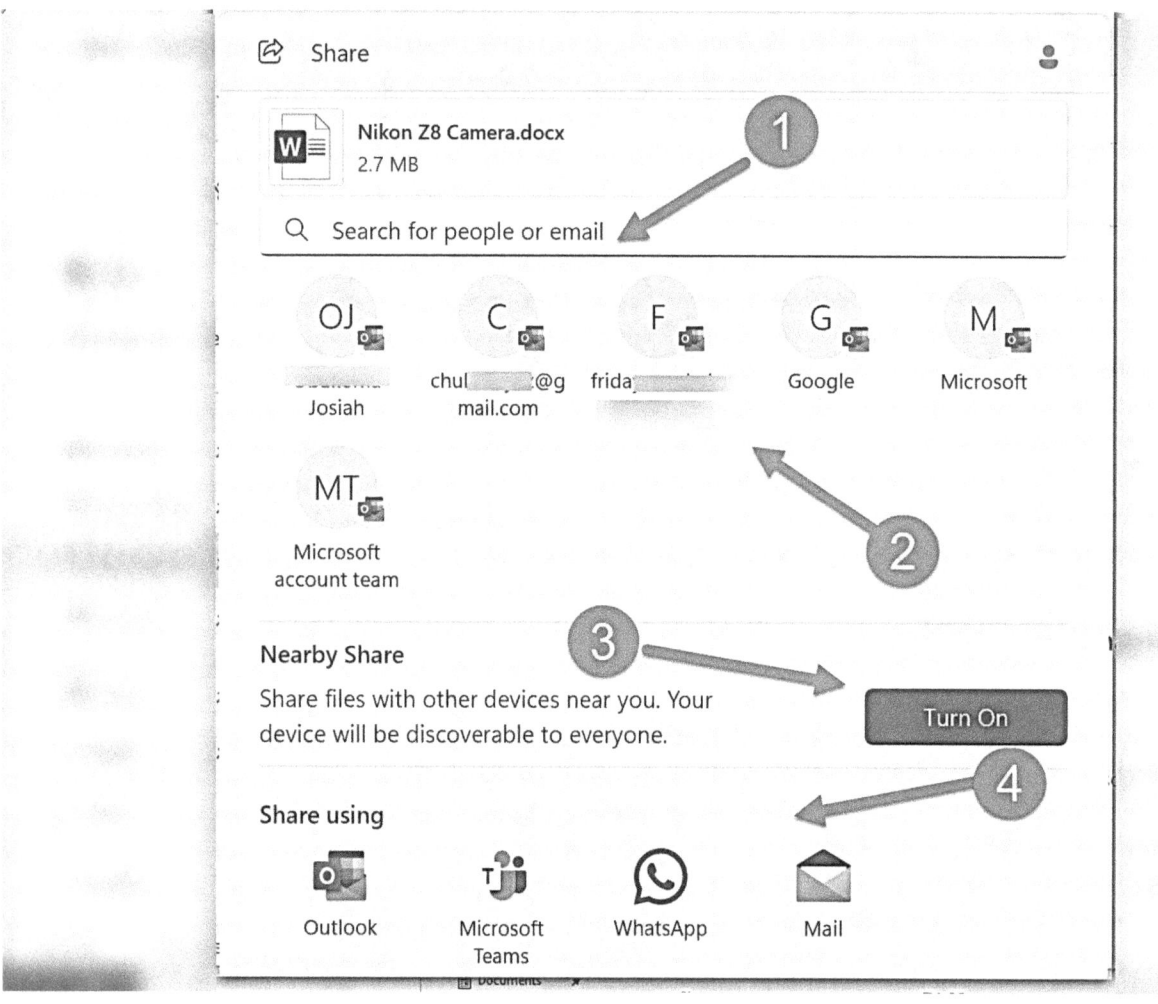

- You also have instant access to local sharing options, allowing you to share files with other users connected to the same network or device as you.

The Navigation pane

The Navigation pane is on the left side of your screen, allowing you to select folders and navigate your computer network folders and files.

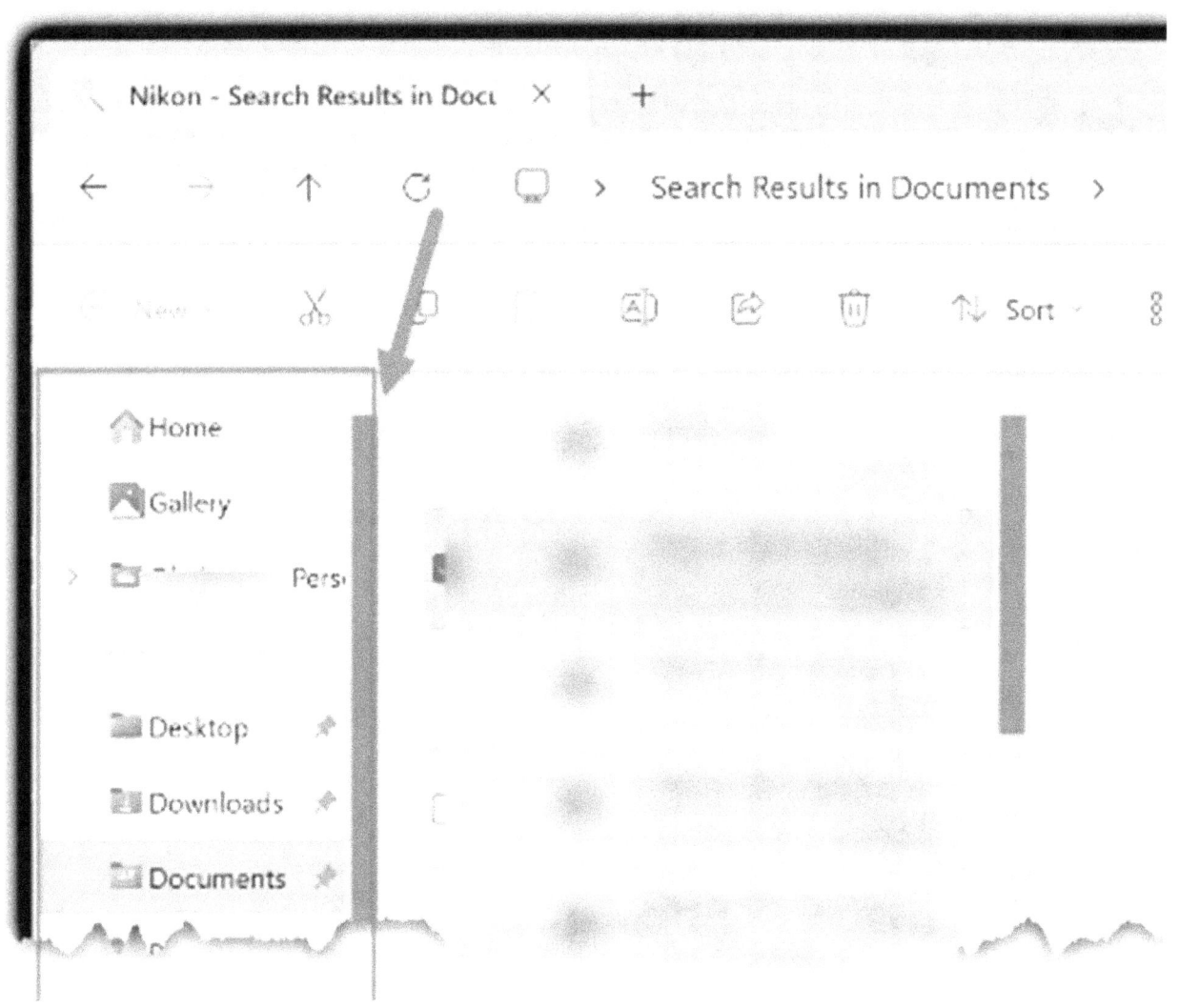

Areas frequently displayed in the Navigation pane include the Home page, OneDrive, This PC, and Network.

Other features include the Desktop, Documents, Pictures, Music, Videos etc.

You can use the arrows beside the names folders in the Navigation pane to expand and collapse their menu.

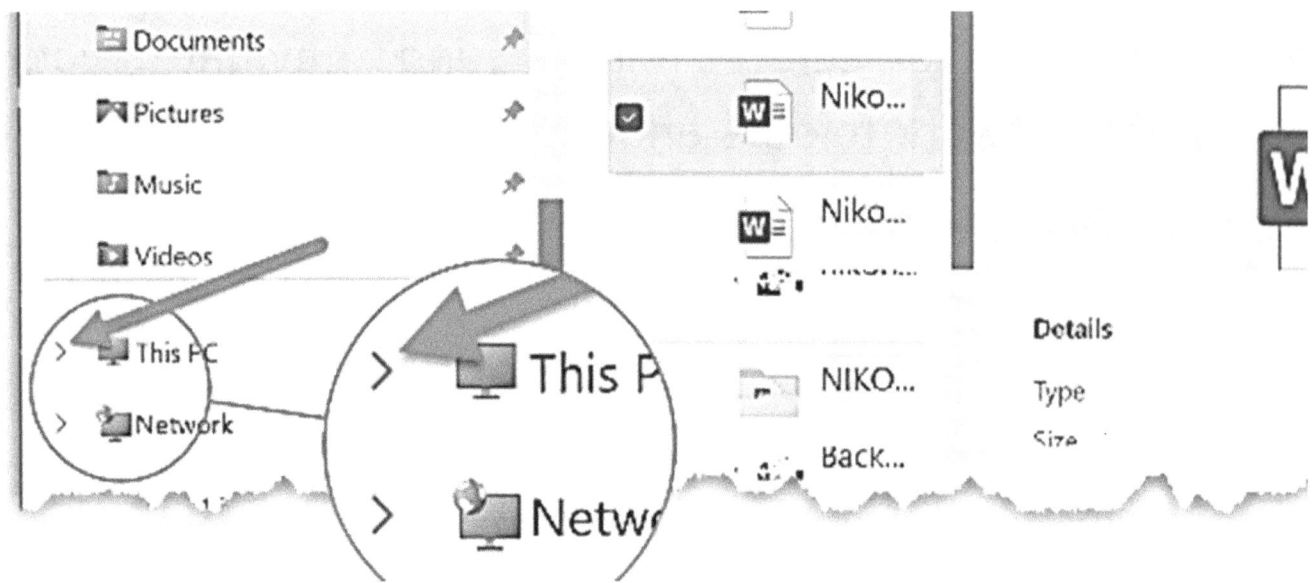

However, you can click the Back, Forward, or Up buttons to access the various sections you have visited in File Explorer.

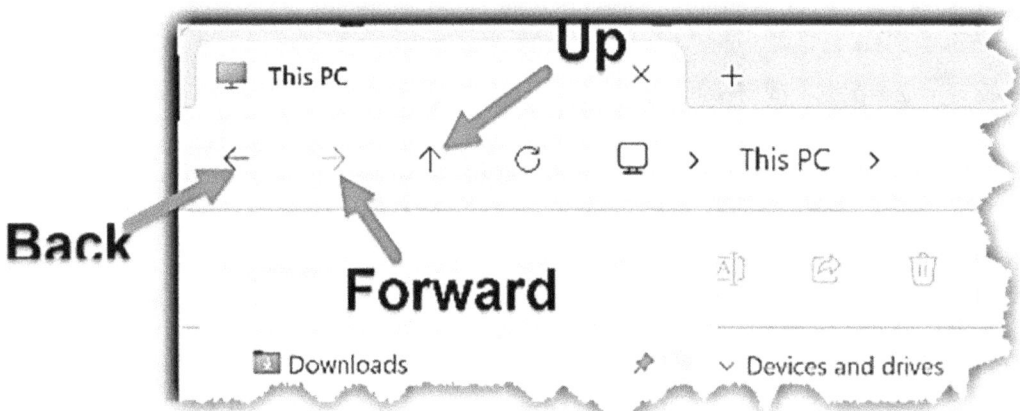

The Forward button will allow you to proceed forward once you have used the Back button. The Up button will allow you to advance one level within the folder hierarchy in the File Explorer window.

Home Page

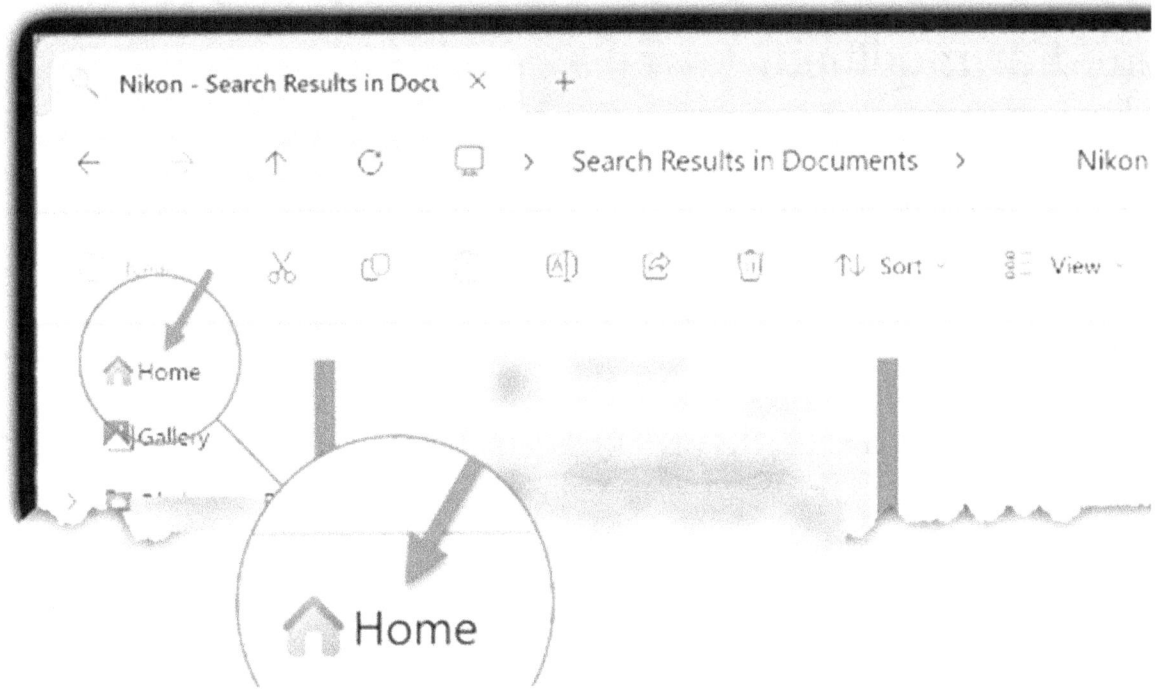

If you are using the updated version of Windows 11, you will see the Home page icon instead of what used to be Quick Access.

Upon launching the file explorer window, the Home page folder is automatically designated as the default page.

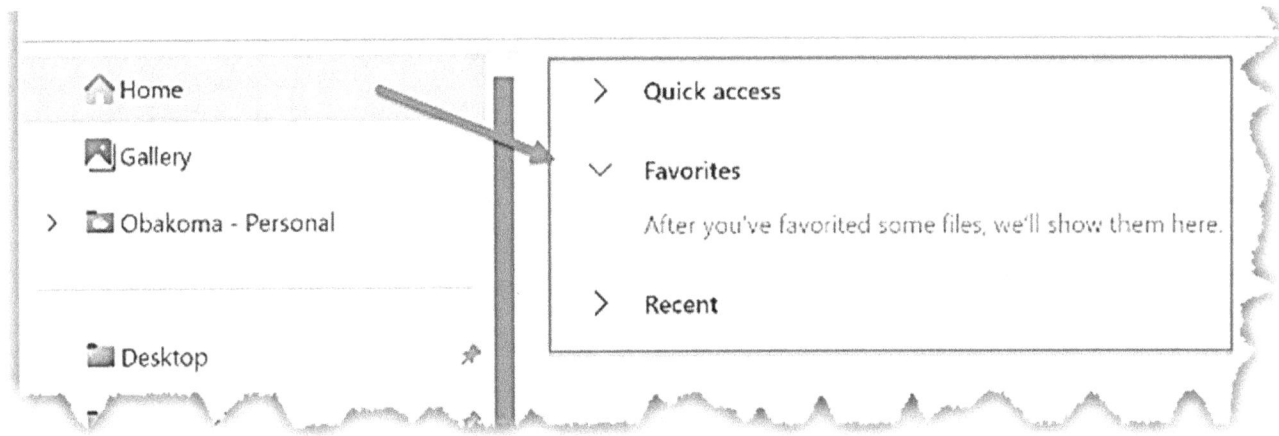

When you click on the Home Page icon, you can gain speedy access to documents that have been recently opened or modified.

- **Quick Access** tab displays items that you can quickly click on.
- **Favorites** tab displays files or folders you frequently open.
- **Recent** tab displays files or folders you just opened.

The arrows beside each tab enable you to hide or show their contents.

You can pin your favorite folders to the Home page, to enable you access frequently visited locations without needing additional navigation.

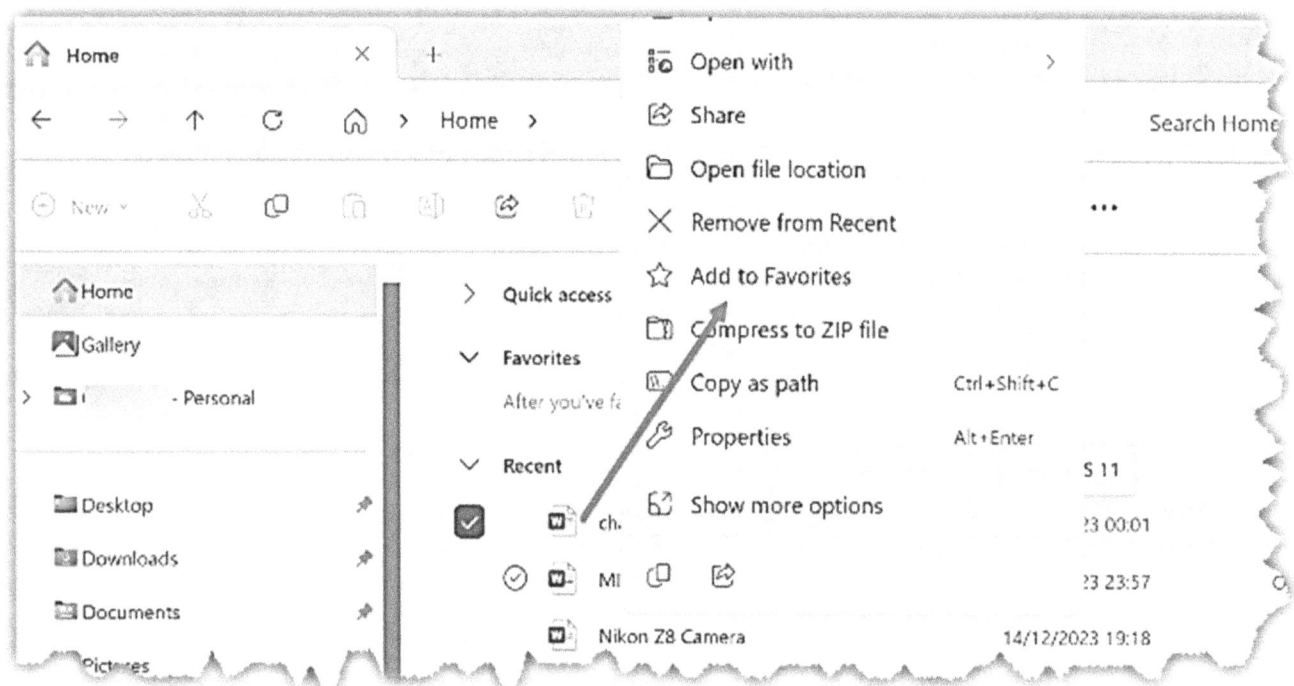

To do this, right-click on any folder or file and select **Add to Favorites.** This will make that particular folder or file appear under the **Favourites** tab.

When the time comes to view the content under any tab, you only need to click the tab once to view the contents under its column.

MASTERING SORTING AND GROUPING IN FILE EXPLORER

As you continue to use your computer, the system will produce a large number of files. At this point, you need an efficient file management system to keep things organized and make the most of your productivity. The Windows 11 File Explorer provides complete features for sorting and organizing your files.

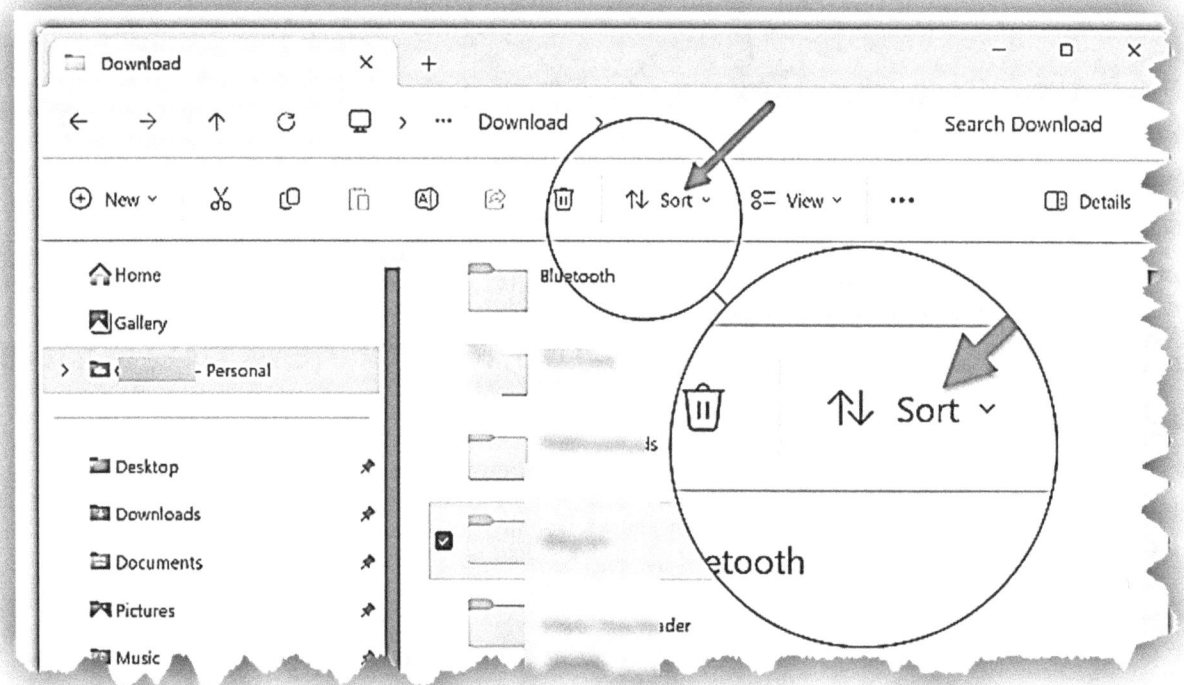

The sorting feature lets you put your files and folders in order based on predefined criteria and eliminates the need to sort files manually, thereby saving time and effort.

The File Explorer interface makes it easy to get to the sorting options on the toolbar, and you don't have to highlight your files or folders before sorting.

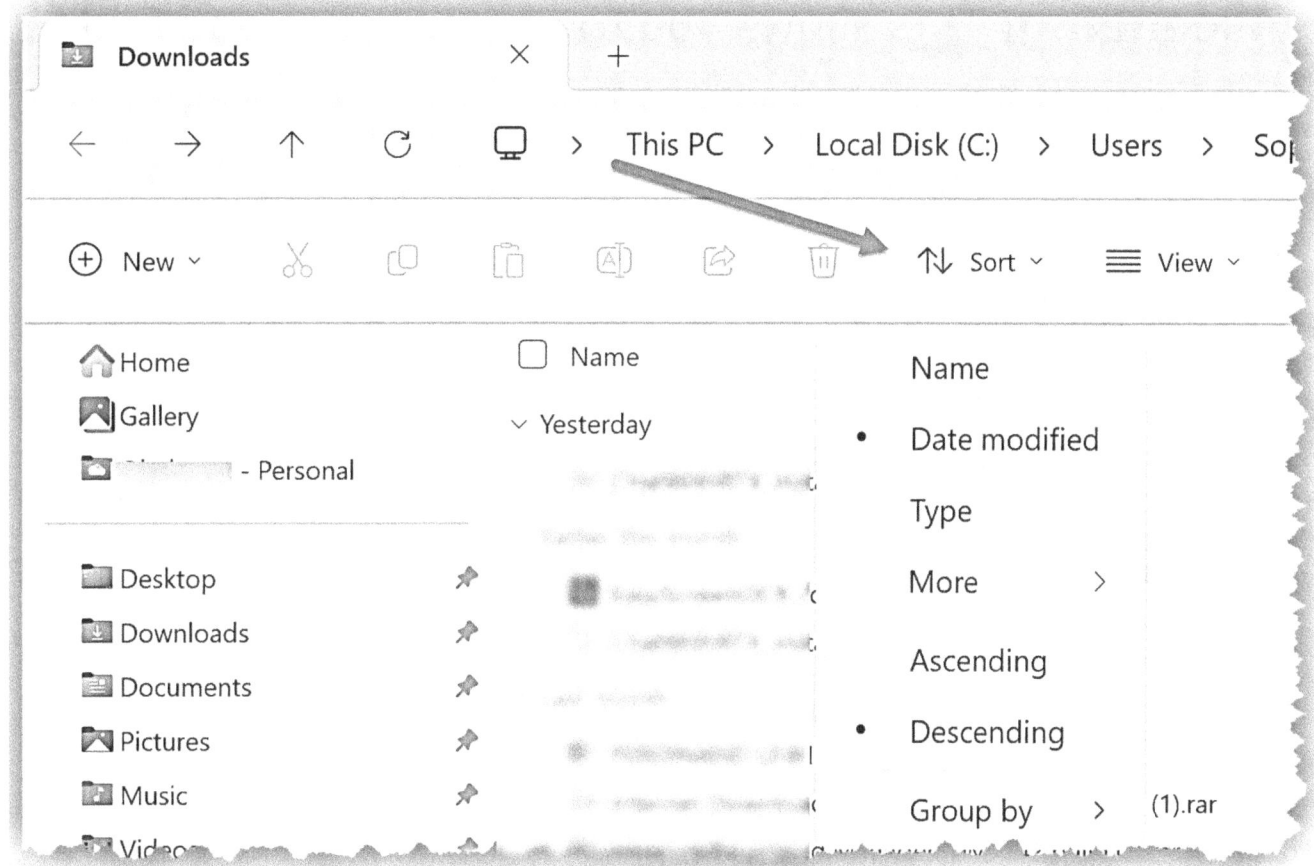

- **Name**: It organizes files and folders alphabetically, from A to Z, based on the names of the files and folders.

- **Type:** Helps with the identification and classification of files and folders more expediently by sorting them according to the type or format of the files.

- **Size:** Provides you with the ability to identify and manage large files more efficiently by organizing them according to their cumulative size.

- **Ascending:** This allows you to arrange files and folders in ascending order, providing a systematic arrangement from the smallest to the largest, A to Z, or in alphabetical order.
- **Descending:** This option allows viewing content from the largest to the smallest or Z to A. It arranges your files and folders in descending order.
- **Group By:** This feature allows you to organize files and folders according to a specific criterion, thereby fostering a hierarchical view that assists in improving organization.

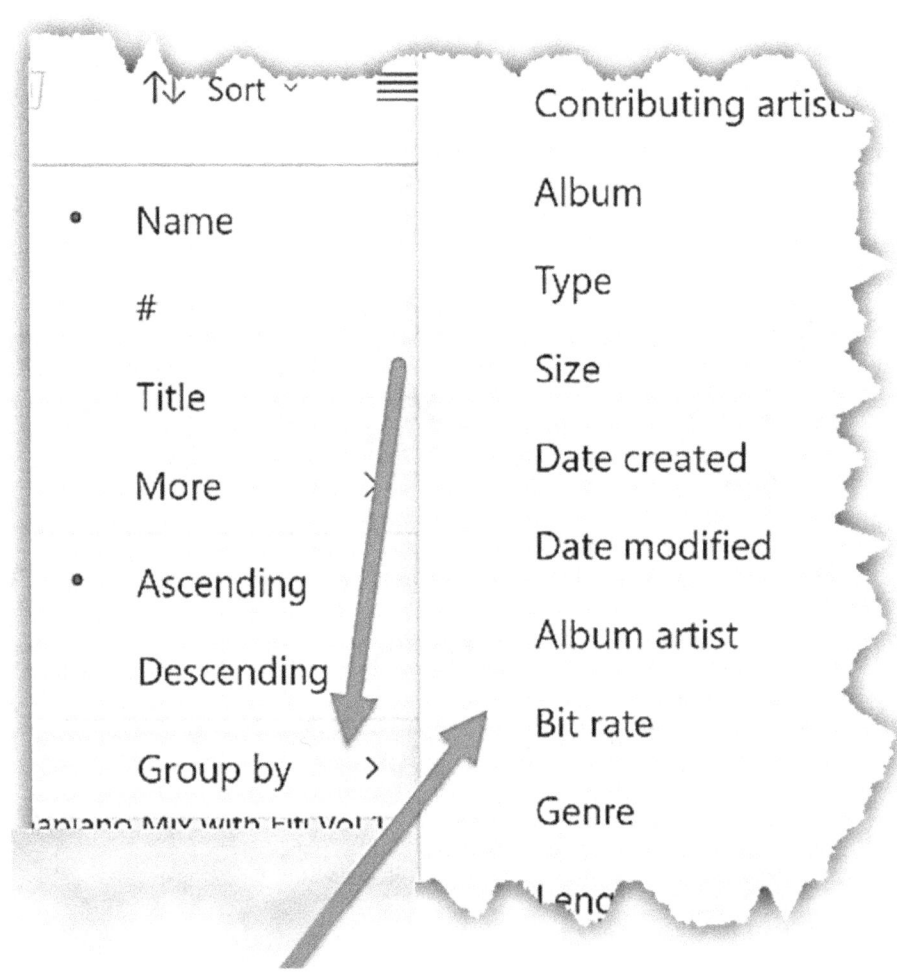

As a beginner, take your time and experiment with different combinations of sorting and grouping to customize the File Explorer view to meet your specific requirements.

LAYOUT AND VIEW OPTIONS

The updated Windows 11 File Explorer version has a new layout and view options that provide a flexible and adaptable environment. Whether you favor a detailed list view or a representation rich in icons, this feature allows you to customize your workspace to achieve the highest possible productivity. The icon to access this feature is right after the sort and grouping icon on the toolbar.

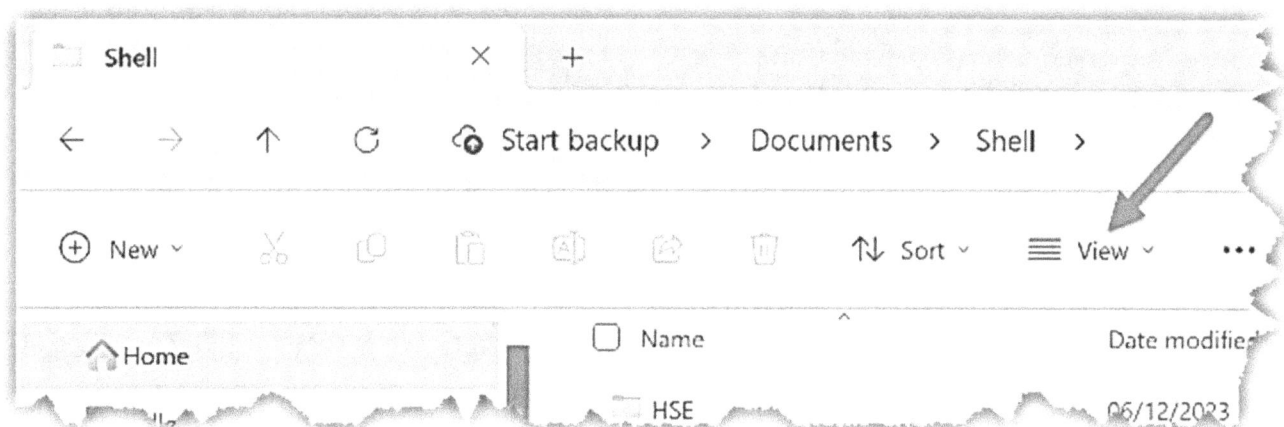

The options available include:
- **Extra Large Icons:** The icons are displayed very large, making them suitable for high-resolution screens or inspection of icons in greater detail.

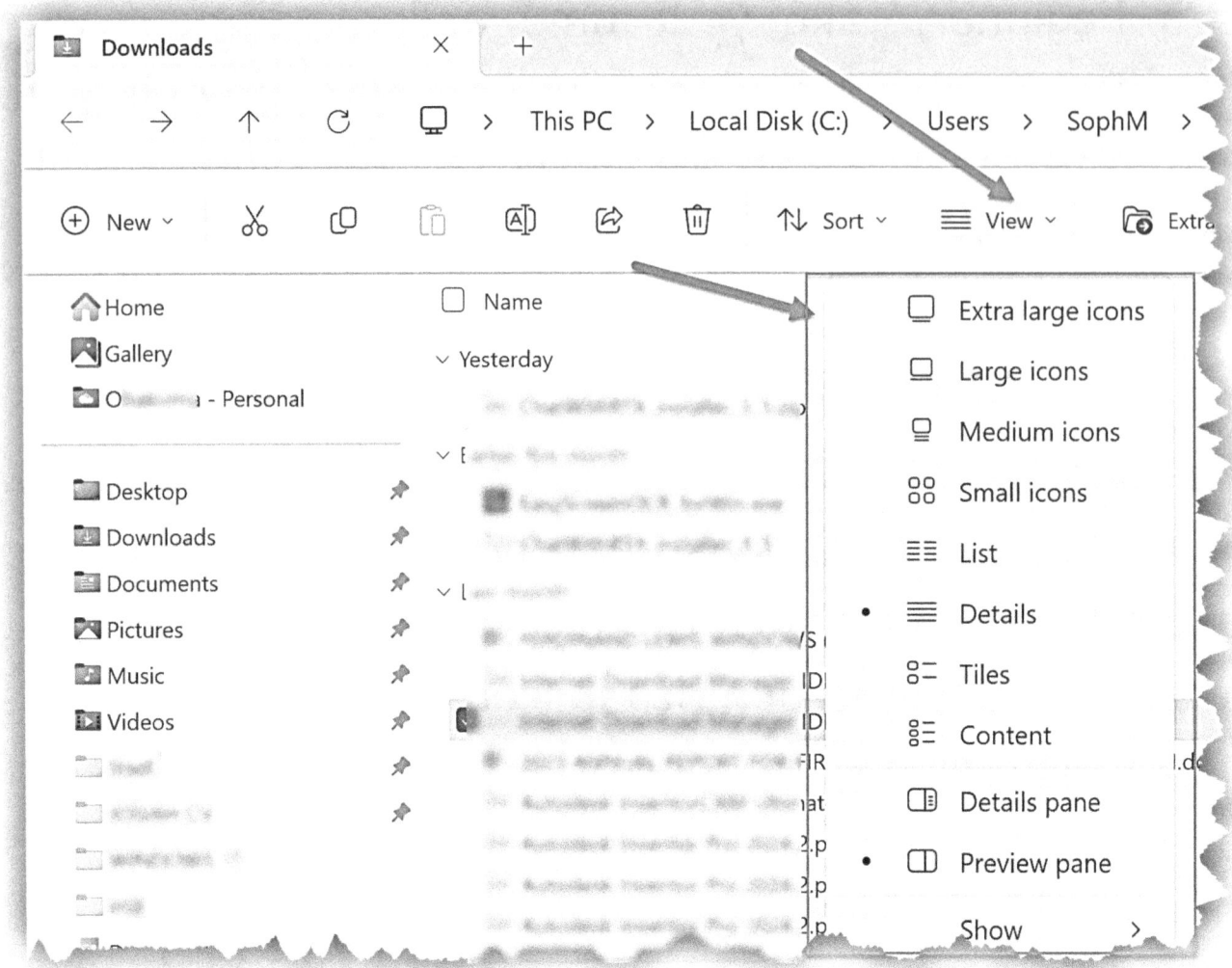

- **Large Icons:** This feature displays icons in a large size, which helps with clarity and visibility. This feature is useful when working with a large number of items.

- **Medium Icons:** Features an icon view that is of medium size, making it suitable for a variety of scenarios and the preferences of individual users.

- **Small Icons:** Provides a condensed overview while providing a compact view with small icons to maximize screen space.

- **List View:** The names of files and folders are displayed in a single column, making it possible to browse through a list of items quickly.

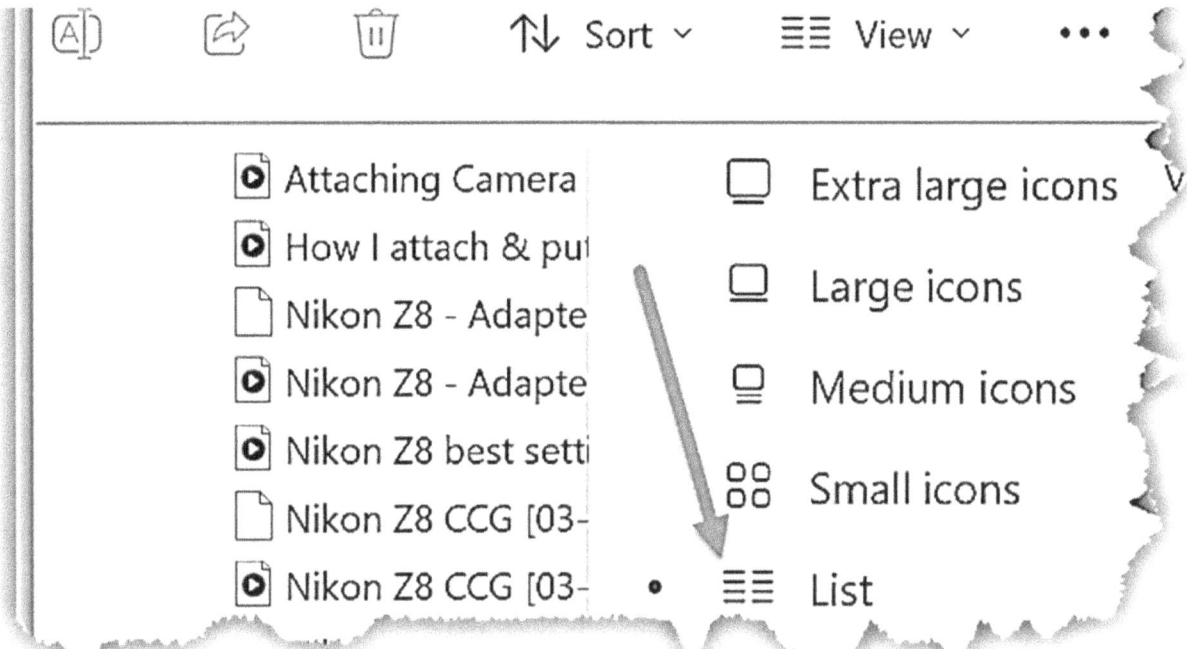

- **Details View:** This feature allows for easier sorting and filtering by displaying the details of your files and folders, as well as information such as your file size, type, and the date they were modified.

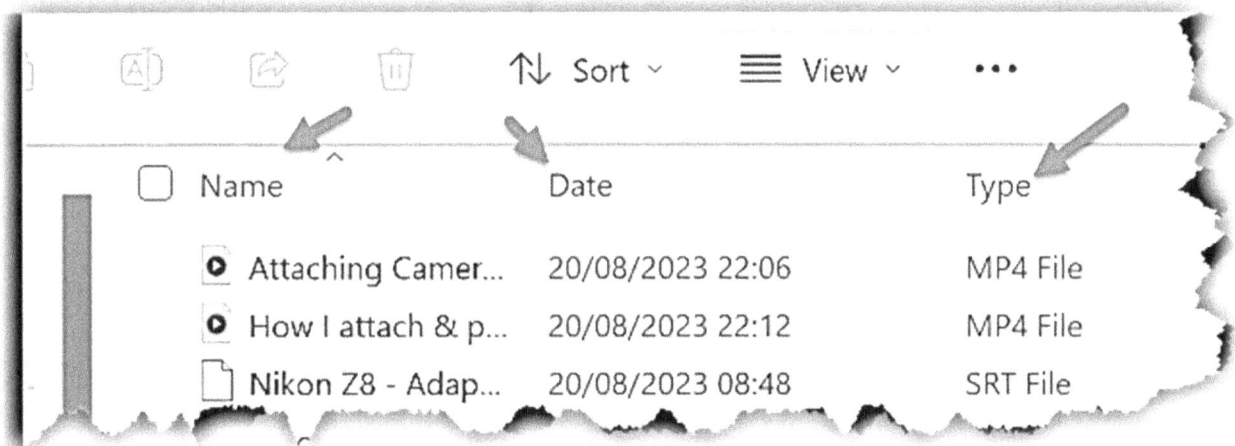

- **Titles View:** It provides a spacious view for both visual and text elements by displaying their names and large icons arranged in a grid view.

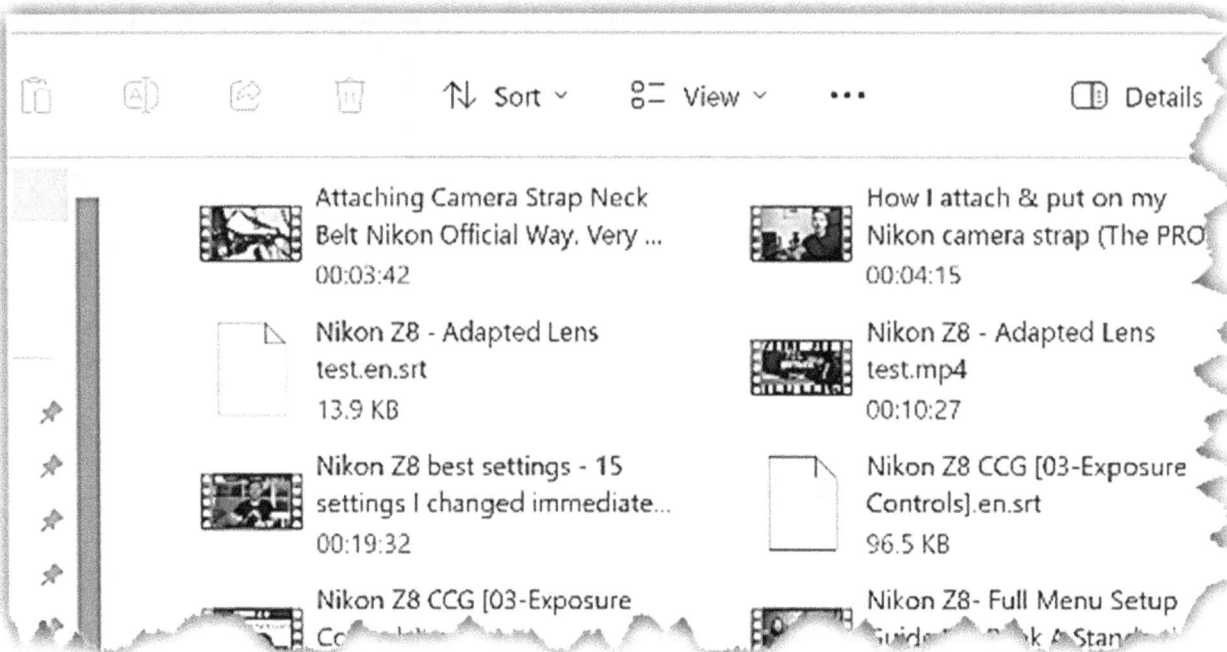

- **Content View:** This feature integrates small icons with additional metadata, such as tags, ratings, and authors, to display a comprehensive overview.

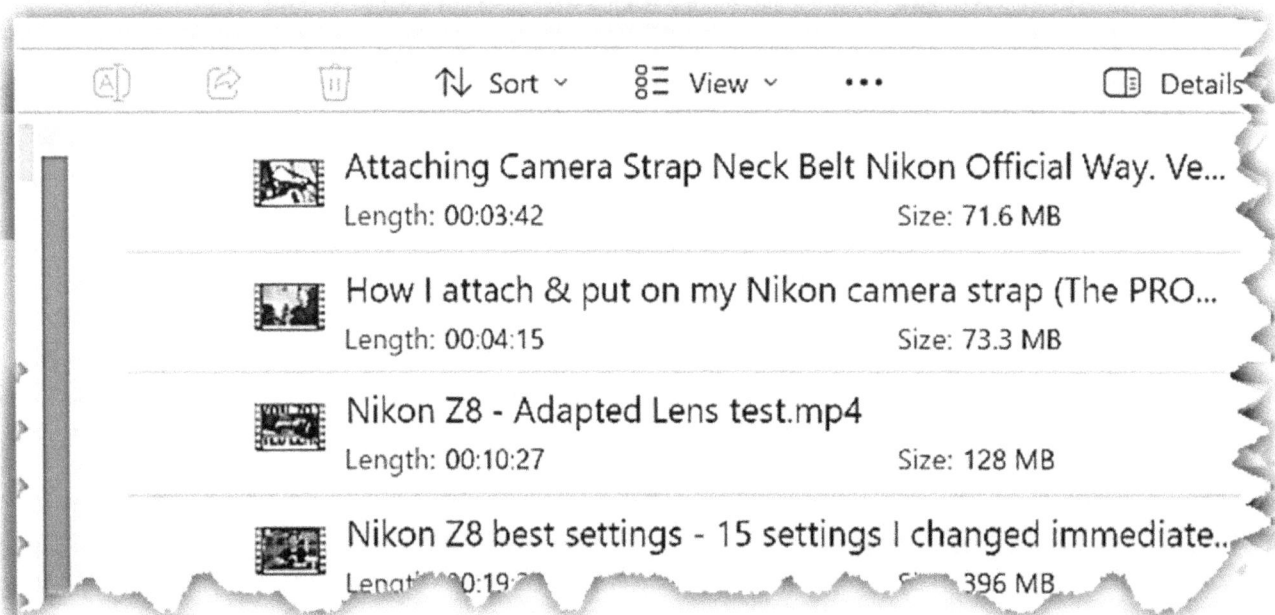

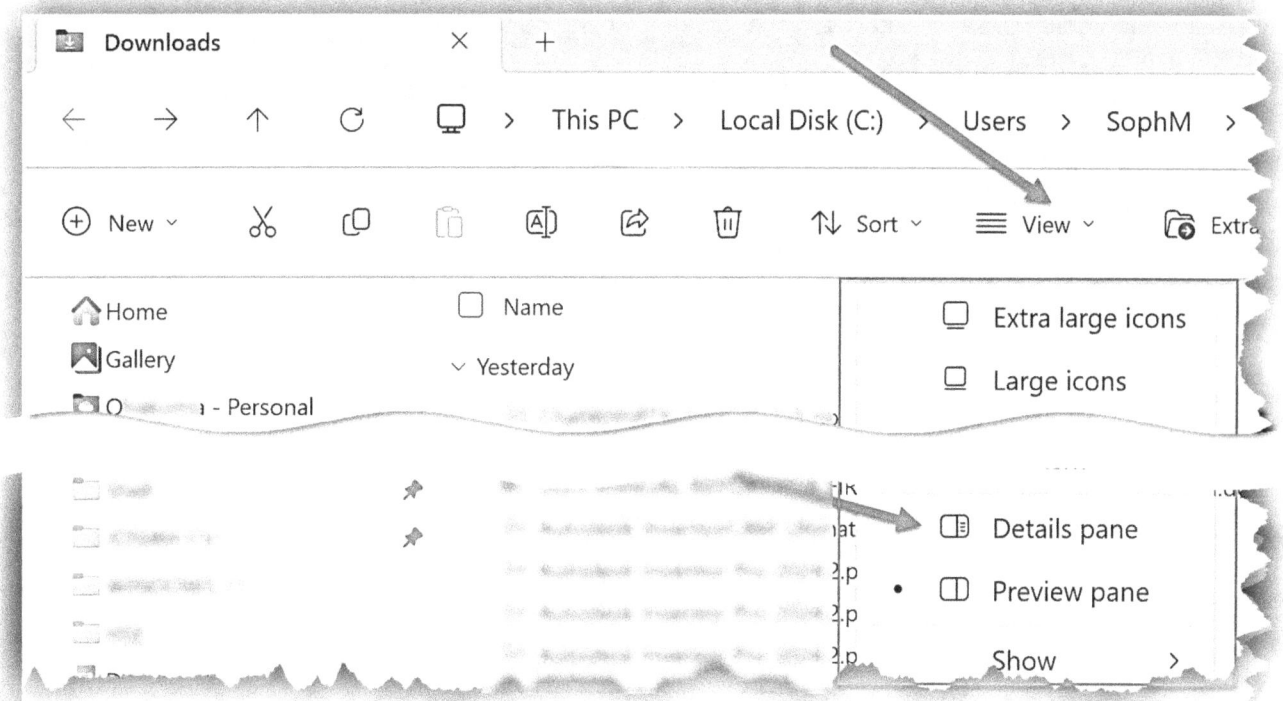

- **Details Pane:** This feature creates a pane on the right side of the File Explorer window and displays detailed information about your selected items. It enables you to carry out quick checks and edits on your file or folder property.

- **Preview Pane:** This feature displays a pane that previews the file you selected on the right side of the screen.

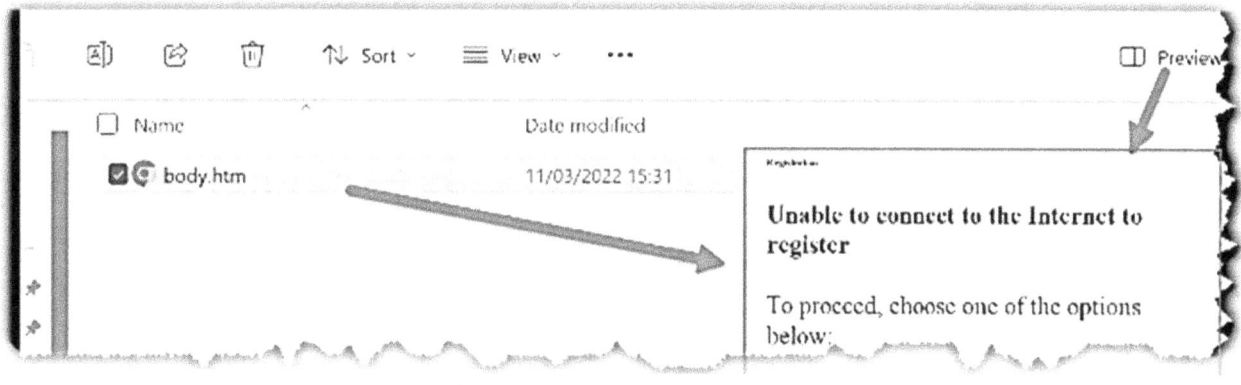

The preview pane lets you quickly glance at your selected content without opening the file.

- **Show**: This feature provides you with the ability to toggle the visibility of various elements within File Explorer, such as the ribbon, navigation pane, and status bar.

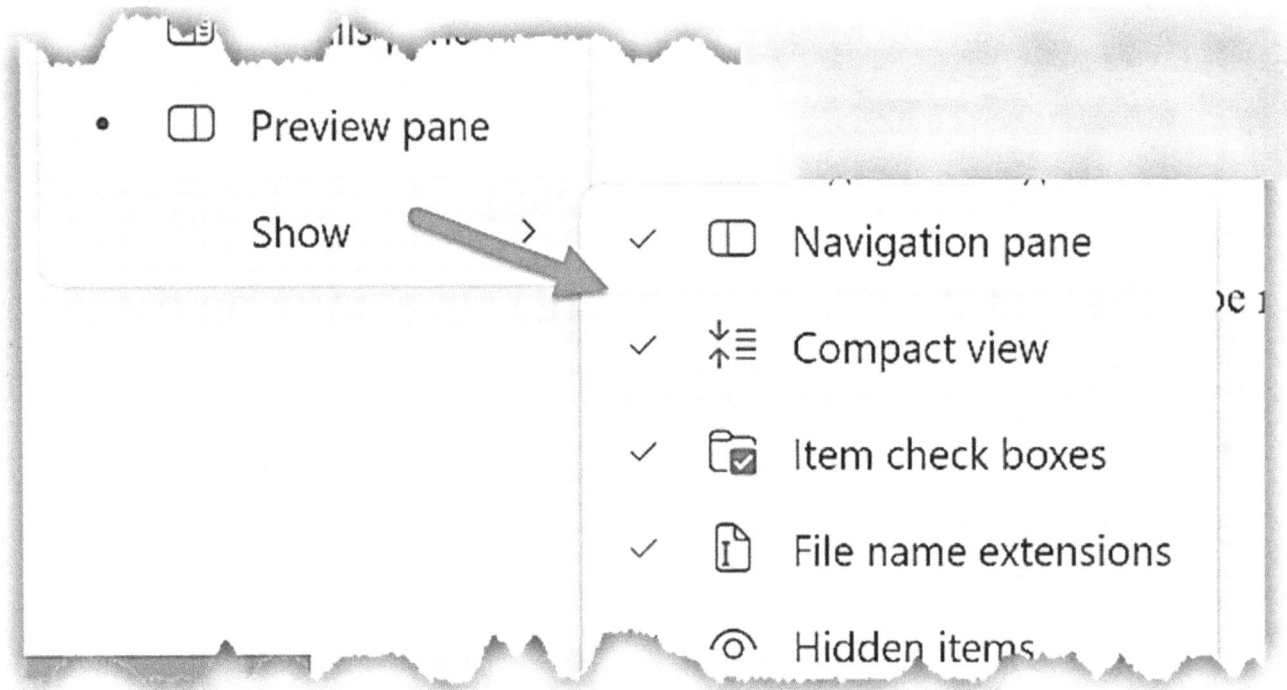

COPYING, MOVING FILE(S) OR FOLDER(S)

As the number of files on your computer grows, it becomes more important to keep things organized. The good news is that File Explorer makes managing files easier by giving you robust tools to keep your digital life in order.

However, knowing the difference between moving and copying files in File Explorer is vital in getting the most out of it.

Here's a breakdown of these two key actions:

- **Moving:** If you move a file or folder, you basically take it from where it is now to somewhere else. It's like taking a book off one shelf and putting it on another. The original copy is no longer in the place where it was before; it is now only in the new place. This is the best thing to do when you want to clean up a folder or put your files in a more reasonable order.

- **Copying:** By contrast, copying makes a copy of the chosen file or folder. Imagine photocopying a paper; you get two copies that are exactly the same. The original file stays where it is and is unchanged, while a copy of it shows up exactly where you chose. Doing this lets you keep a copy of a file in a different place or send a file to someone else without changing the original.

Drag and Drop Method of Moving or Copying

The most straightforward and efficient method of transferring a file or folder in File Explorer is clicking, dragging, and dropping.

You can quickly move or copy item(s) on the same drive or to a different location on a network.

Steps to Move or Copy a File or Folder:

- **Navigate to the Source Folder:** Locate the folder that contains the item(s) you want to transfer in File Explorer.

- **Open to the Destination Folder:** Open the destination folder where you want to transfer the item(s) in File Explorer.

- **Select the Item:** Select the item(s) by clicking on it once, or use the shortcut key **Ctrl+A** if you intend to move all the items in the source folder.

- **Initiate Drag and Drop:** Click and Hold the left mouse button while dragging the selected item(s) to the destination folder.

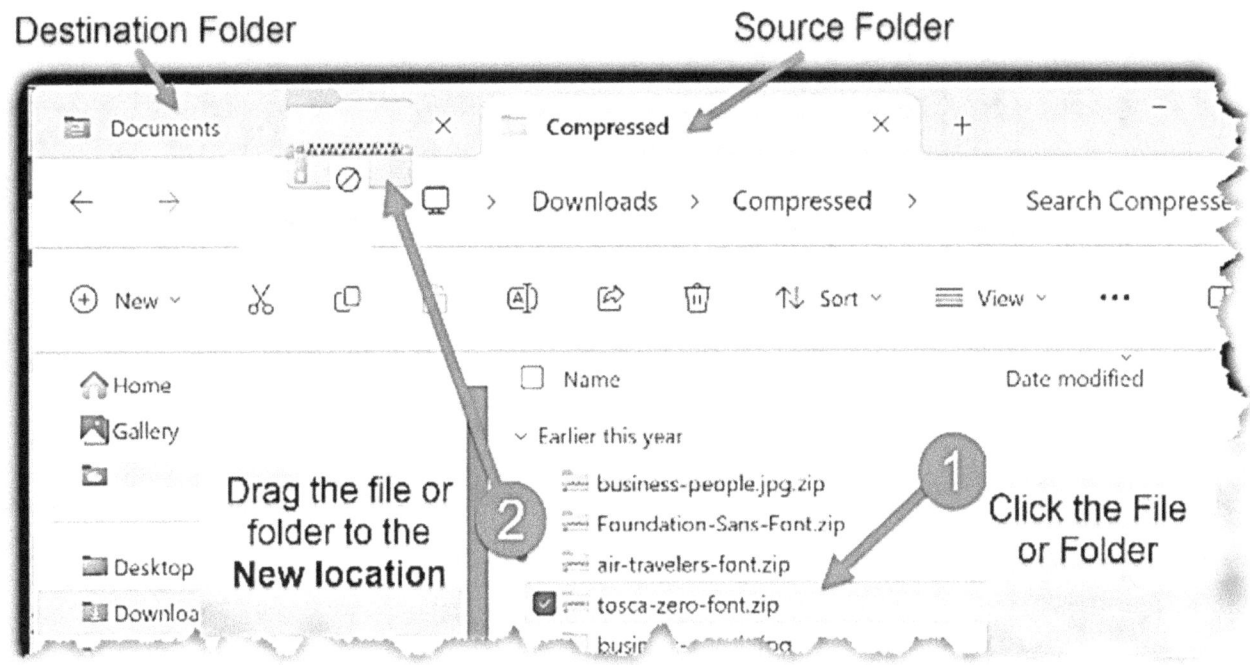

As you drag the item(s) into the destination folder, you will see the cursor tip showing **Move to**. Next, release the mouse button to complete moving the item(s).

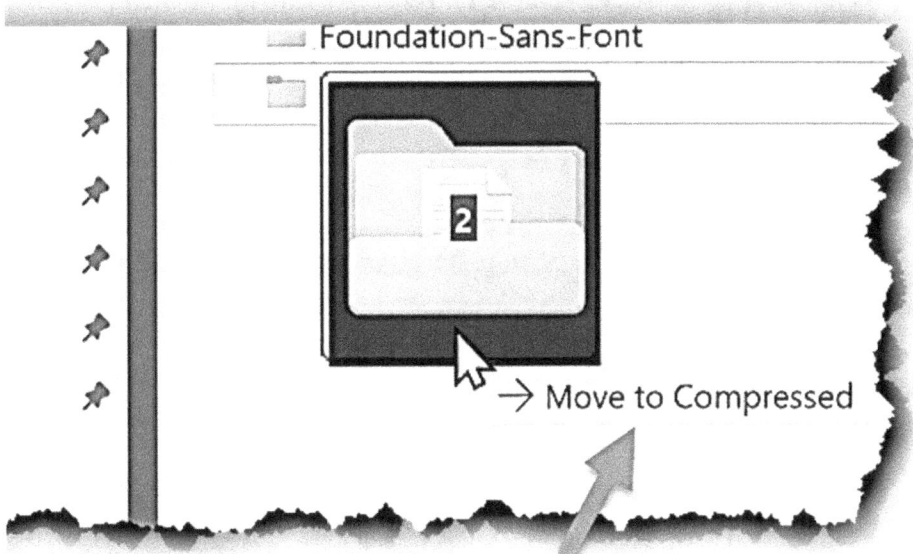

- But if you want to **Copy** the item(s), press the **Ctrl** key on your keyboard before you release the mouse button.

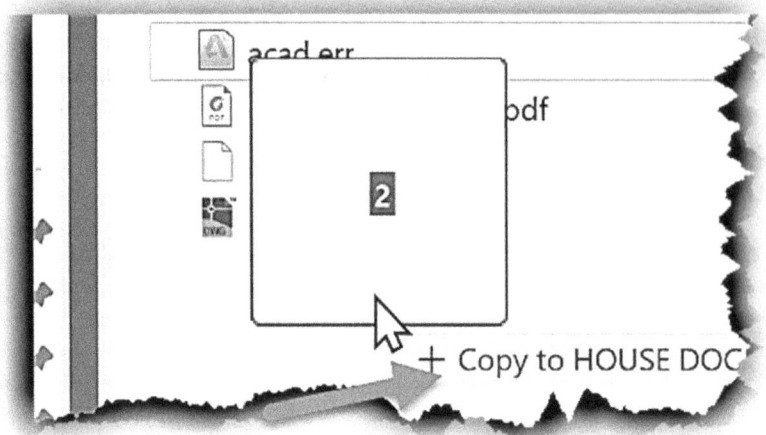

You will notice a plus sign (**+**) with the **Copy to** appear on the cursor tip.

Press the **Esc** button to exit the drag-and-drop operation if necessary.

Toolbar Method of Copying or Moving Item(s)

This method is much easier as well. You need to click the item(s) in the source folder and go to the toolbar to click the **Copy** or **Cut** icon.

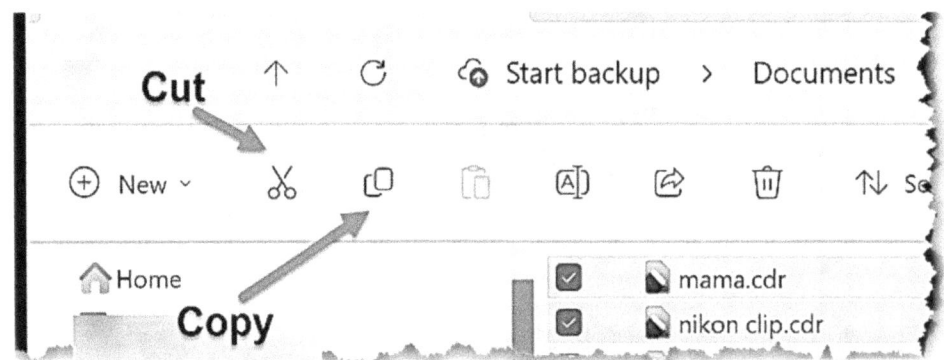

Remember, when you **Copy** the item(s), it remains in the source location (folder), but not when you **Cut** the item(s).

Next, you go to the Destination folder, and on the toolbar, you click the **Paste** icon.

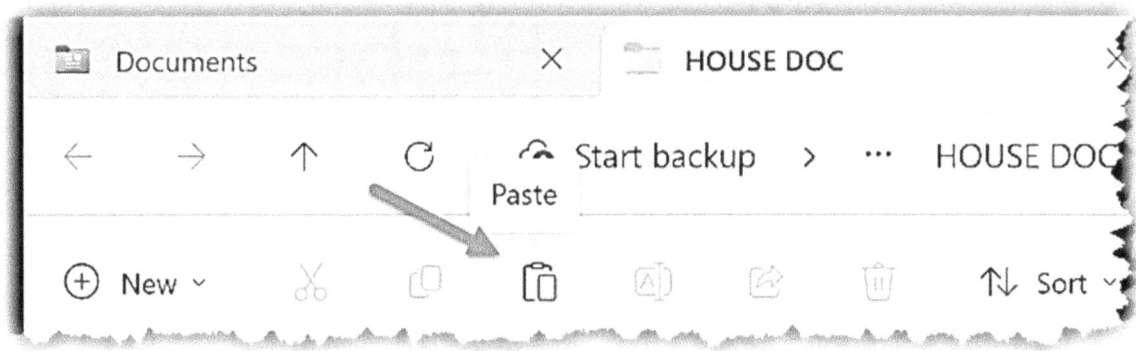

The Mouse Method of Copying or Moving Item(s)

This method requires you to select the item in the destination folder using your mouse.

You can also use the shortcut key **Ctrl** + **A** on your keyboard to select all the items. Next, right-click your mouse button and select **Copy** or **Cut** from the options.

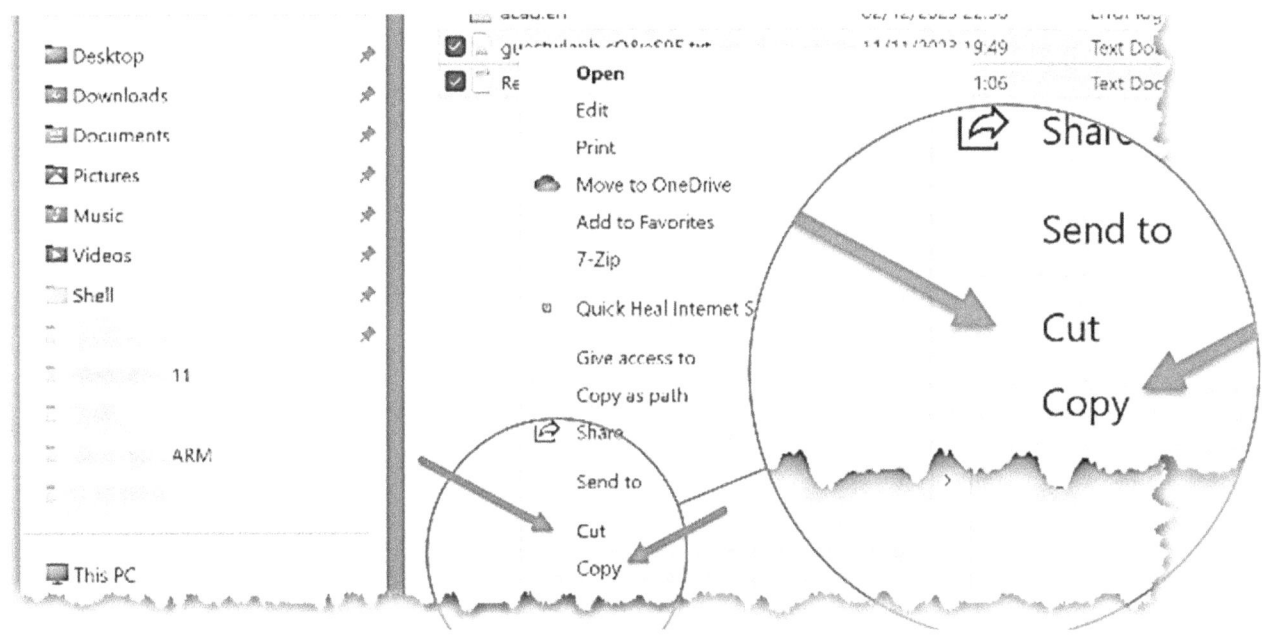

Next, go to the destination folder, right-click your mouse button, and select **Paste** from the options.

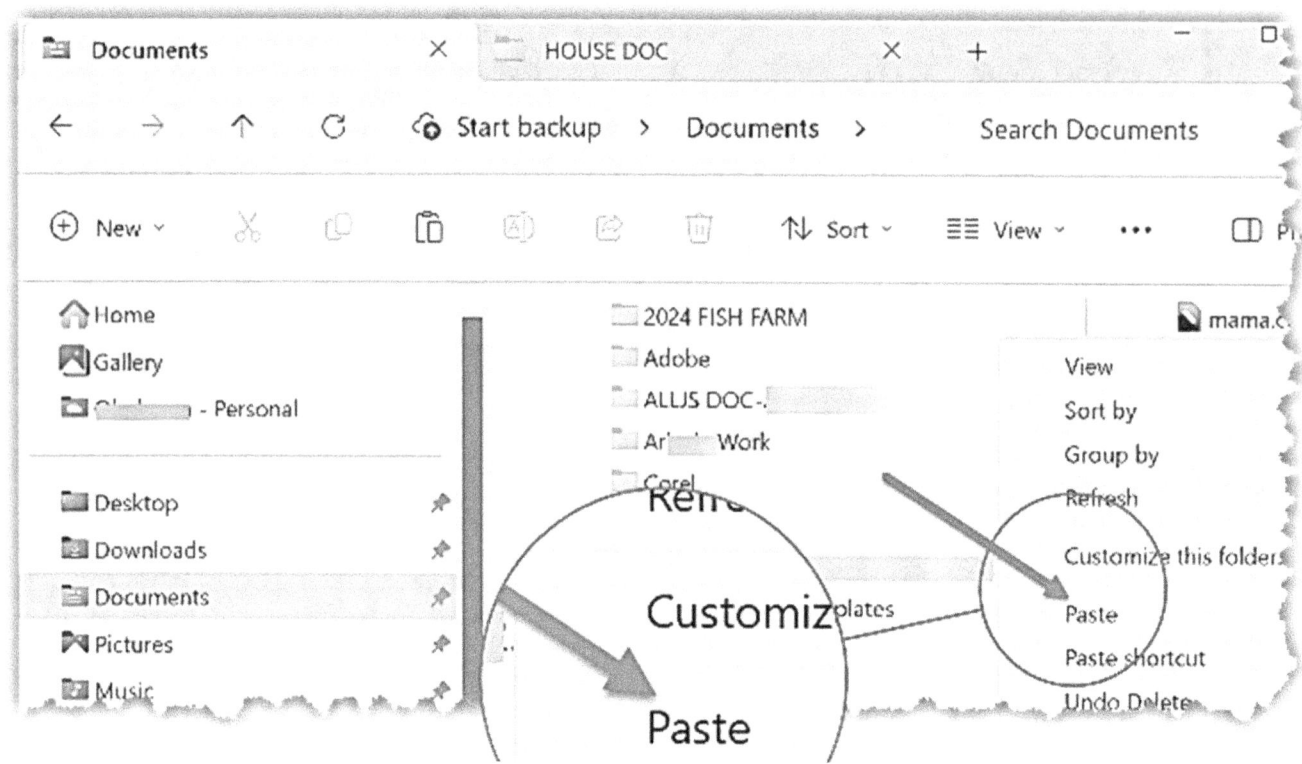

If you don't see the **Paste** option when you right-click, select **Show more options** to expand the menu.

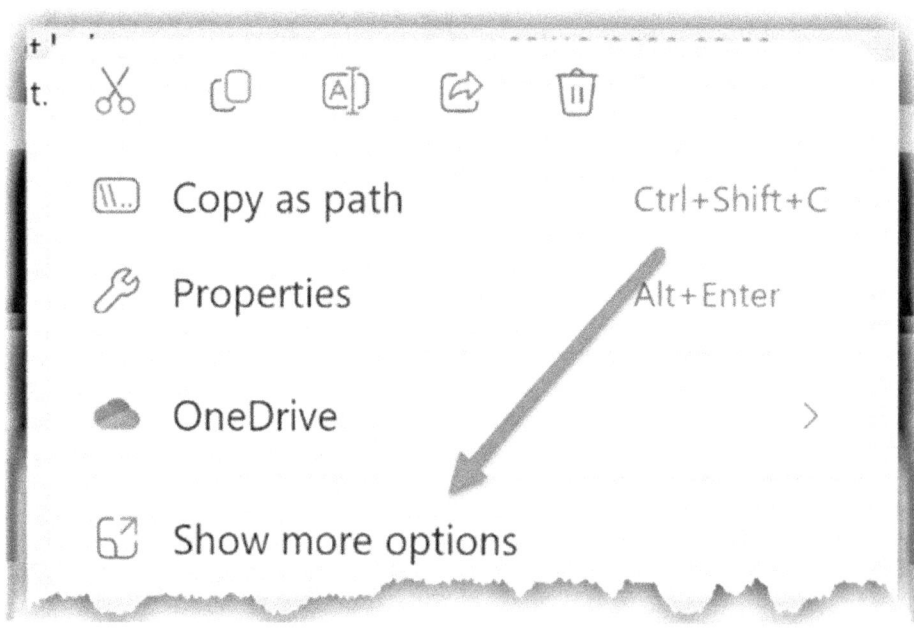

DELETING FILE(S) OR FOLDER(S)

To keep your Windows 11 workspace tidy, delete unnecessary files and folders in File Explorer. However, this has serious consequences that you should consider before doing it. Any item you delete without a backup will be lost and removed from its current location.

Clearing out unnecessary files will free up space and speed up your computer. Any deleted item will automatically be sent to the Recycle Bin by default.

How to Delete Item(s) using the Toolbar

1. Open File Explorer and locate the item(s) in the Source Folder
2. Select the Item(s) and click the **Delete** icon on the toolbar.

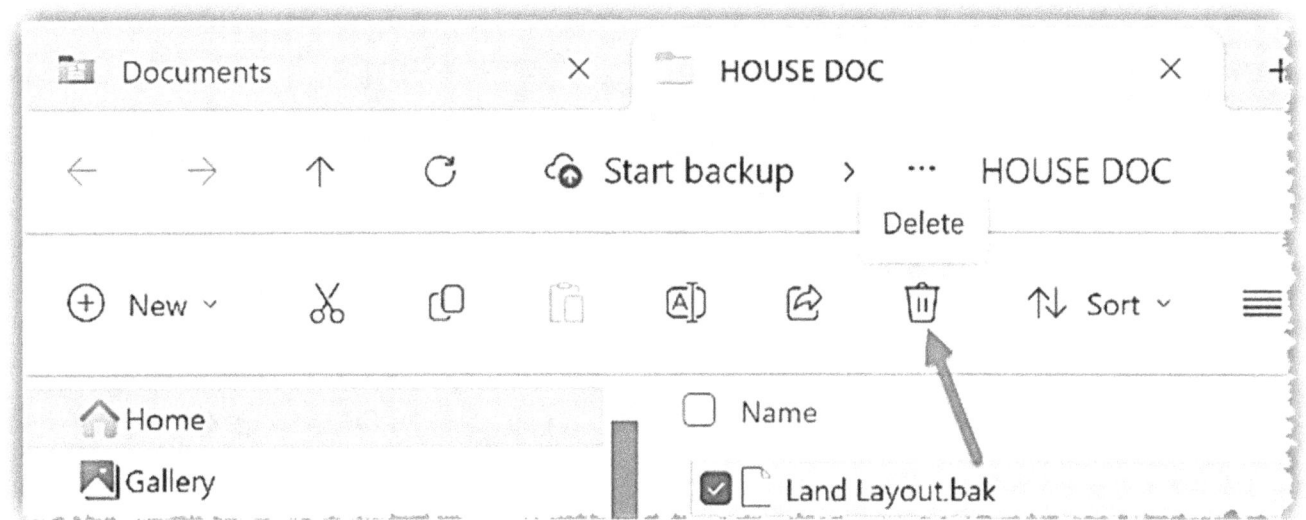

How to Delete Item(s) using the Mouse or Keyboard

Right-click on the selected item(s), and from the context menu, choose "**Delete**."

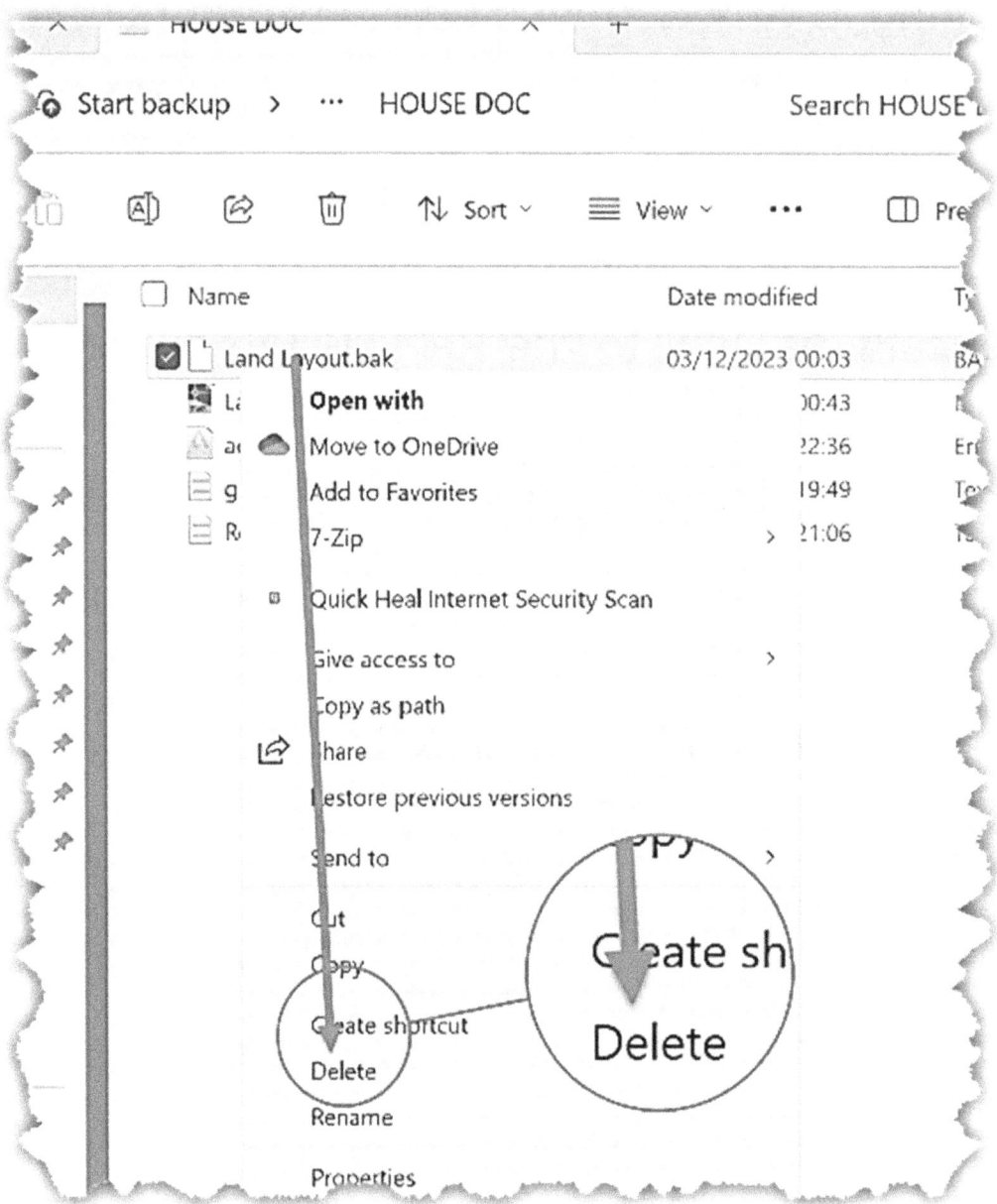

Alternatively, press the **Delete** key on your keyboard.

CREATING A FOLDER

Creating a folder in Windows File Explorer is a process that enables you to organize and manage your files effectively.

Utilizing the keyboard shortcut **Ctrl + Shift + N** is the quickest way to create a new folder in File Explorer. Once the folder is created, Windows 11 will prompt you to give the folder a name.

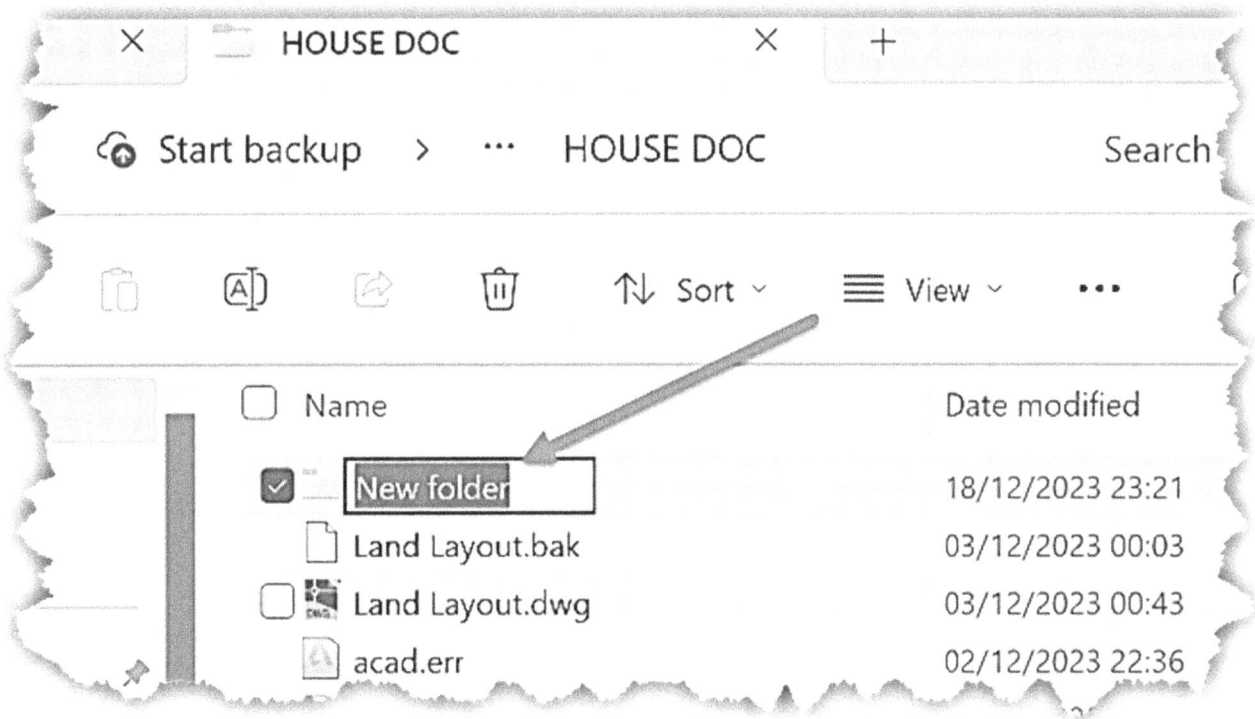

If you decide not to enter a name, the default name will be used automatically. A folder can be created inside another existing folder as much as you want to.

However, the folders you create should be named appropriately for better file organization.

Alternatively, you can use the toolbar to create a new Folder by clicking the **New** button.

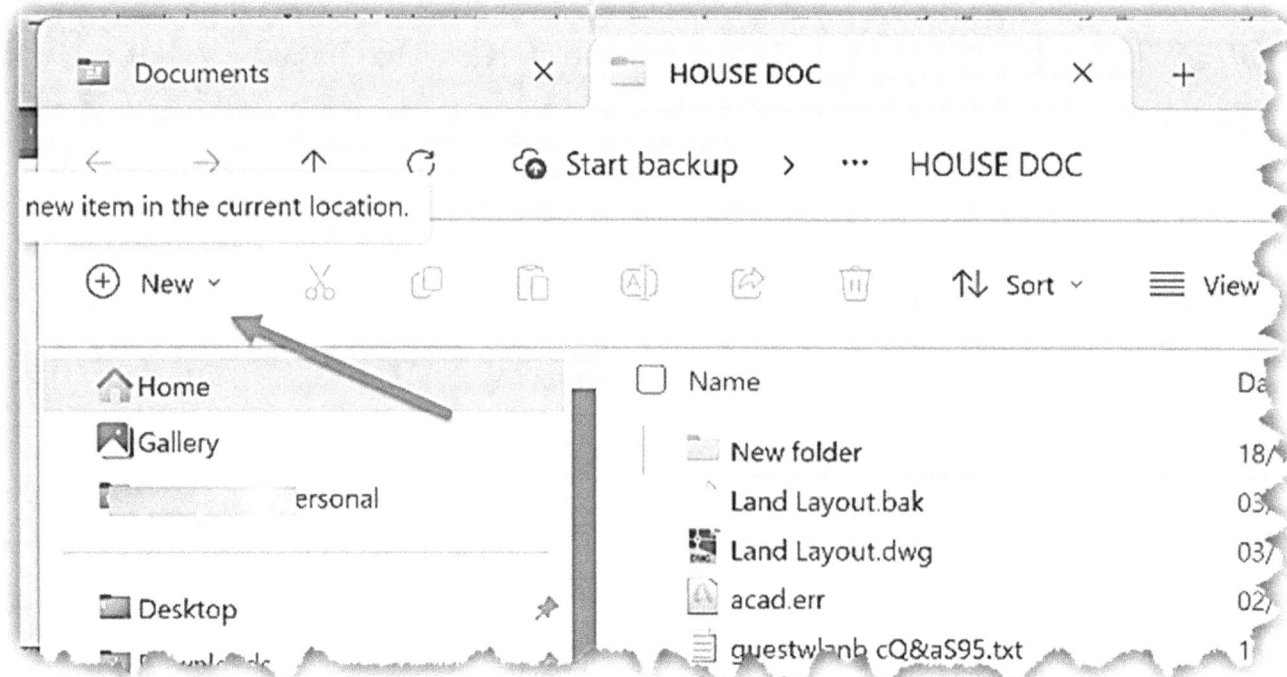

Next, you select **Folder** from the drop-down menu.

Finally, you give the new Folder a name and press the **Enter** key to complete the process.

RENAMING A FILE OR FOLDER

Renaming a folder or file in File Explorer allows you to modify the names of the folders or files to suit your requirements.

Follow these steps to rename a folder or file:

1. **Open File Explorer:** Go to the location of the folder or file you want to rename.

2. **Right-Click on the Folder:** use your mouse to Right-click on the folder or file to open the context menu.

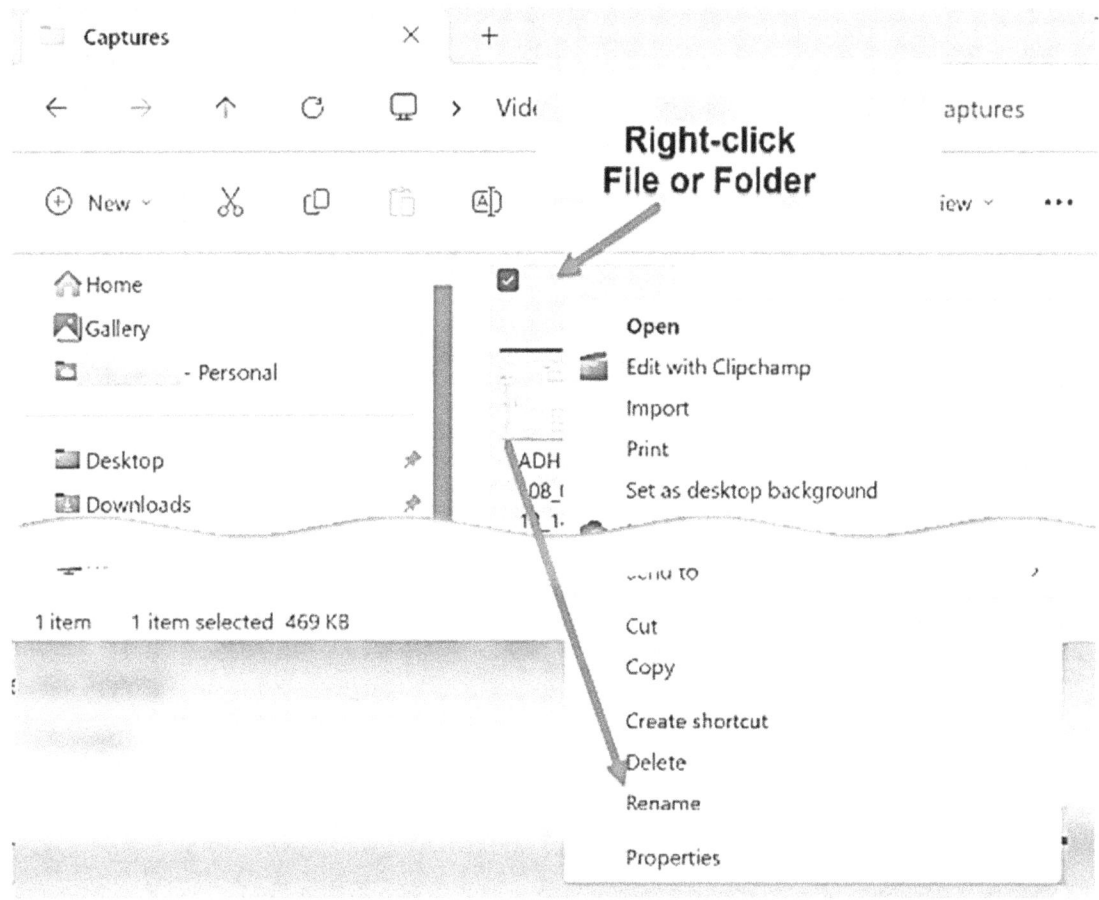

3. **Select "Rename":** In the context menu, choose the "**Rename**" option.

The current name will become editable once you select the rename option from the context menu.

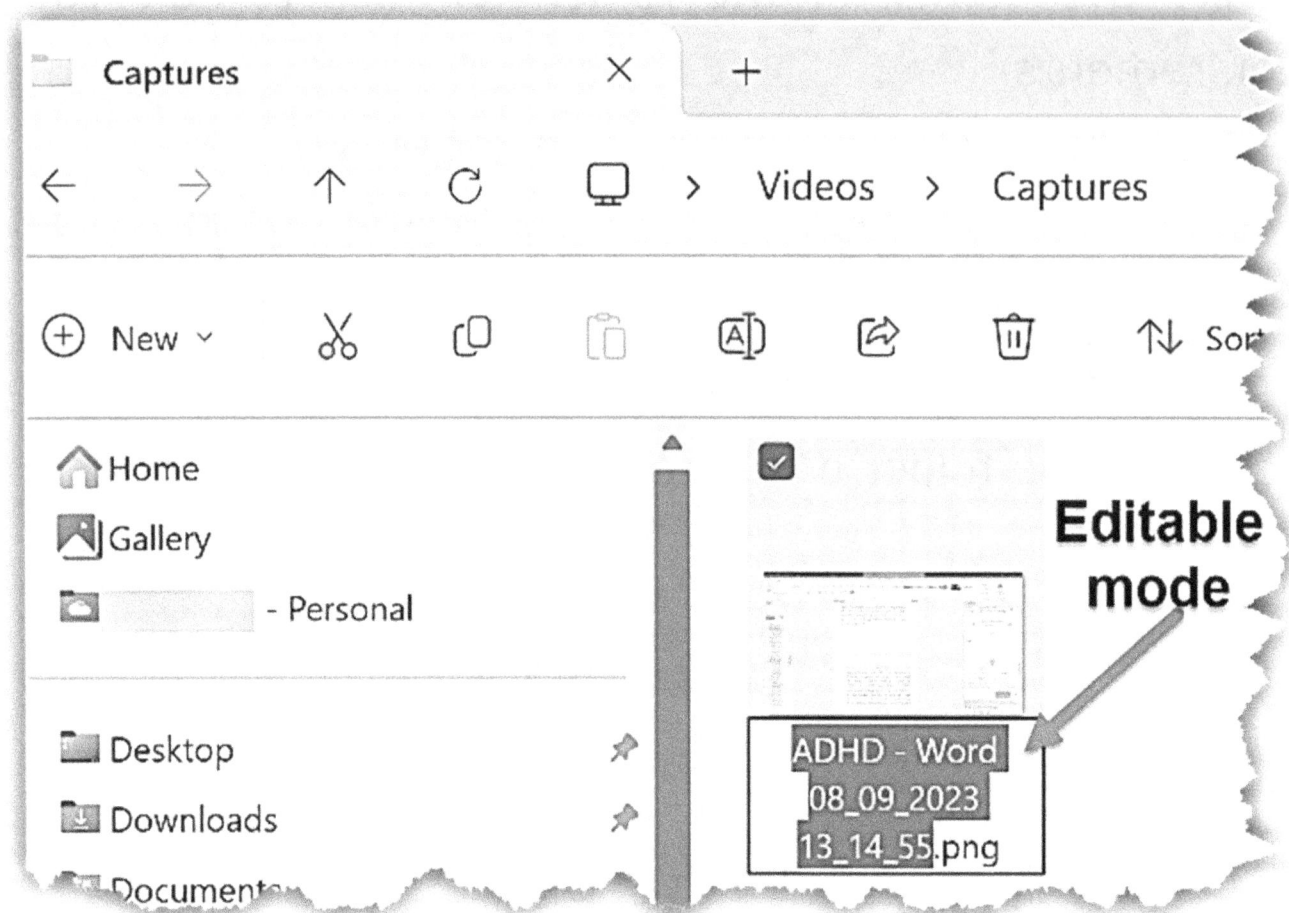

Next, enter the new name and press the **Enter** key to complete the process.

THE RECYCLING BIN

The Recycle Bin is a feature in Windows 11 that helps you better organize your computer files and folders. Several features built into the Recycle Bin allow you to restore accidentally deleted files or remove them permanently from your computer.

Instead of permanently removing items, deleted files or folders are moved to the Recycle Bin. As a result, there will be no unintentional deletions.

You can easily access the Recycle Bin from the desktop, which is symbolized by a trash can icon.

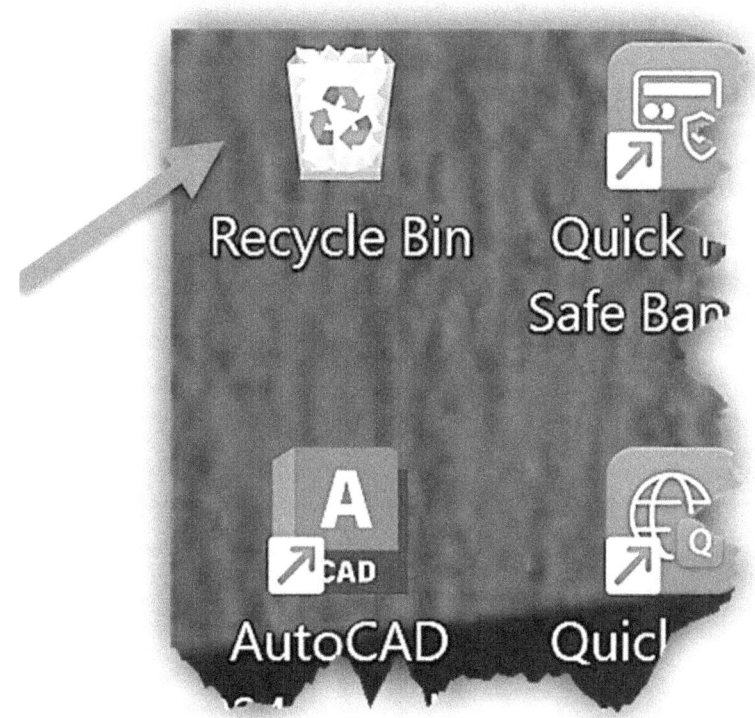

How to Open the Recycle Bin

You can open the Recycle Bin by simply double-clicking on its icon. The initial location, size, and deletion date, among other details, will be displayed in an easy-to-navigate interface.

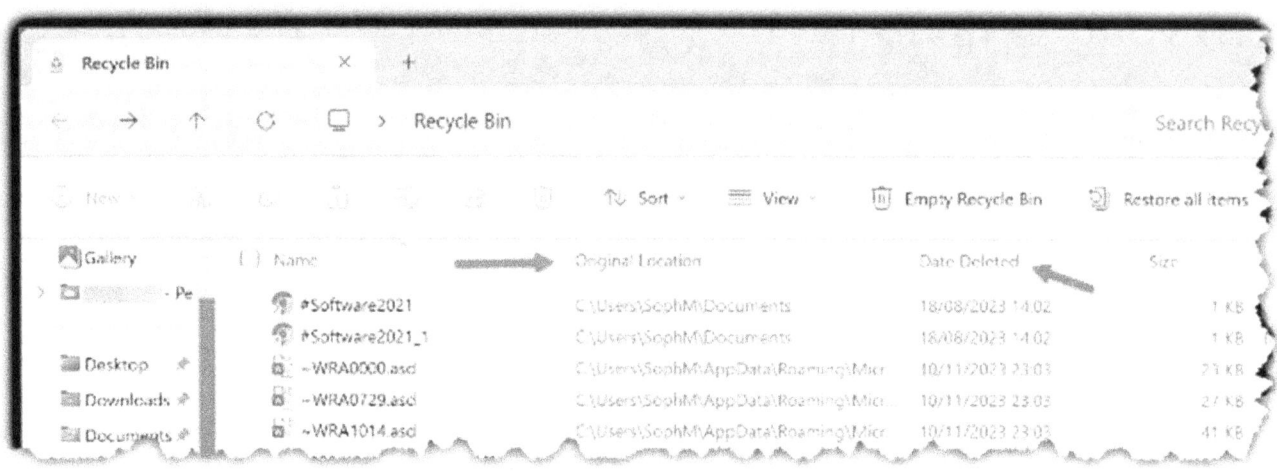

Sorting Deleted Files or Folders

You can also sort deleted items by name, type, date deleted, or original location to facilitate easy navigation and retrieval. To do this, click on the **header** for the particular criteria you want to sort.

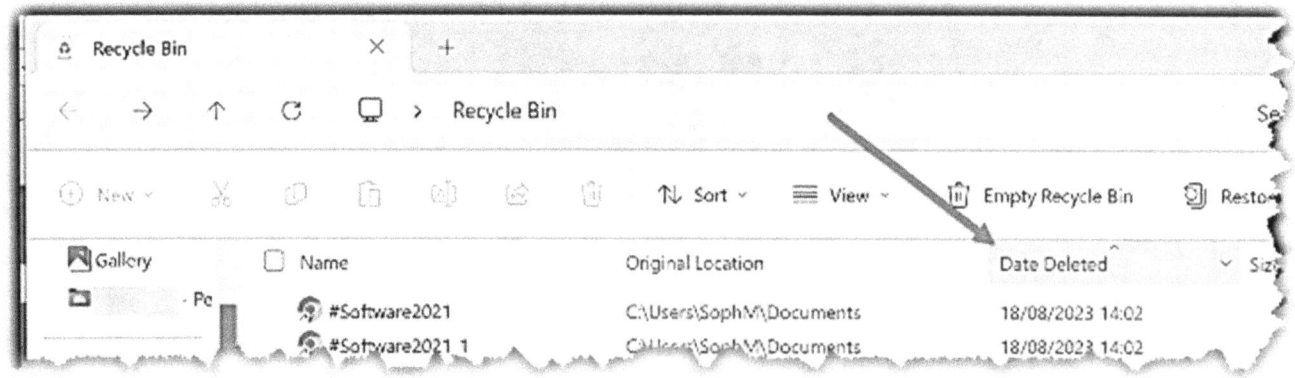

As illustrated above, the sorting is done using the **Date Deleted** criterion. This will make Windows arrange the files or folders according to their date or time of creation in ascending or descending order.

Restoring Deleted Items

Within the recycle bin window, you can retrieve any files or folders you have deleted from your computer. In order to accomplish this, you must first right-click on the item(s) in question and then select the "**Restore**".

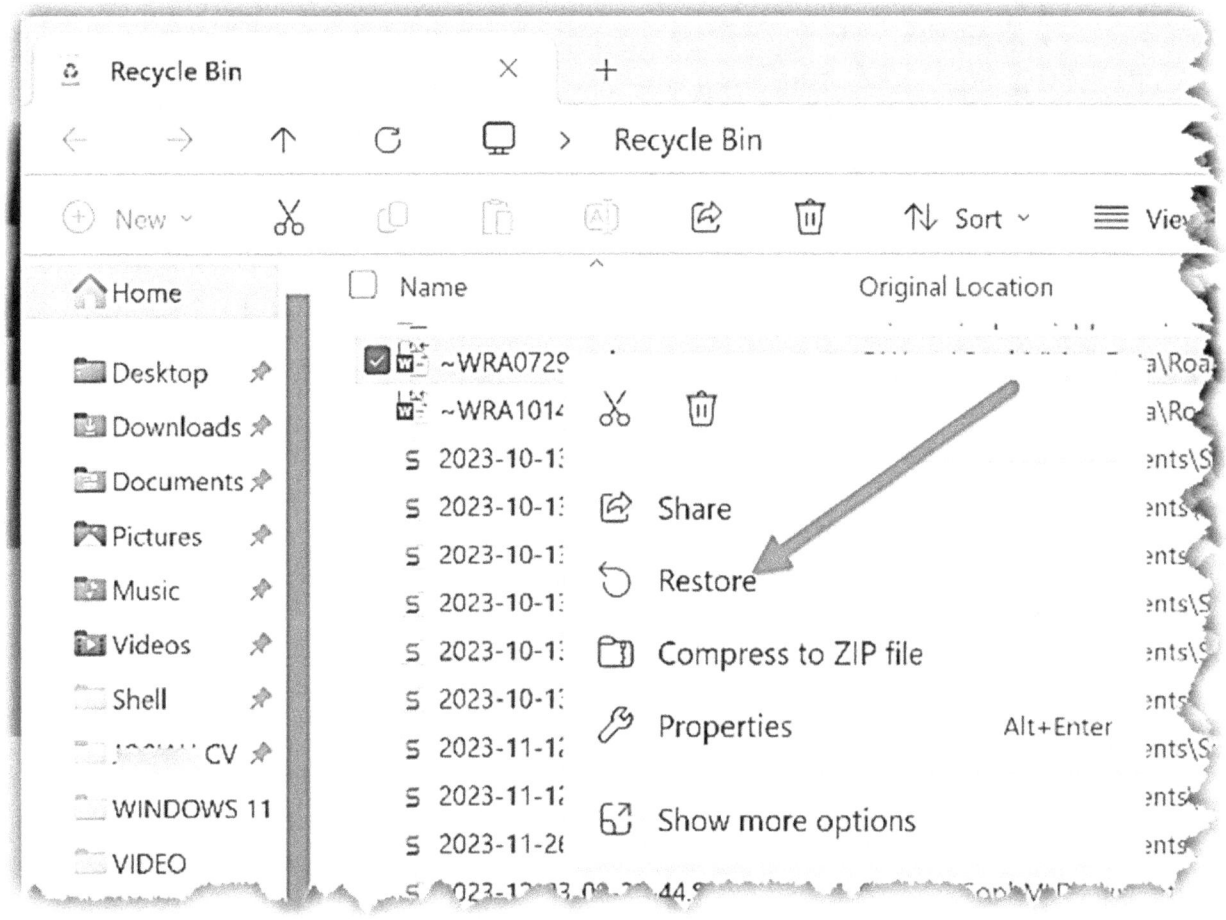

Additionally, you can restore multiple items from the recycle bin simultaneously by selecting them and then clicking the **Restore All Items** button on the toolbar.

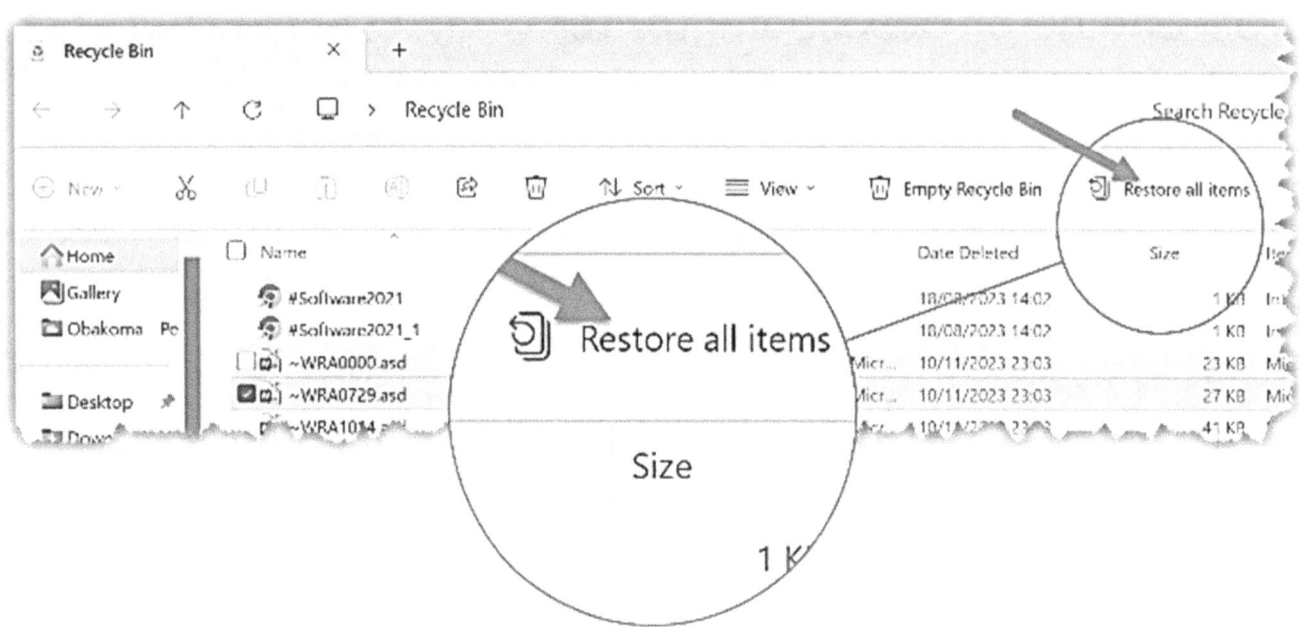

Permanently Deleting Files

Clicking "**Delete**" after right-clicking an item skips the Recycle Bin and gets rid of the file for good. Note, this action can not be undone.

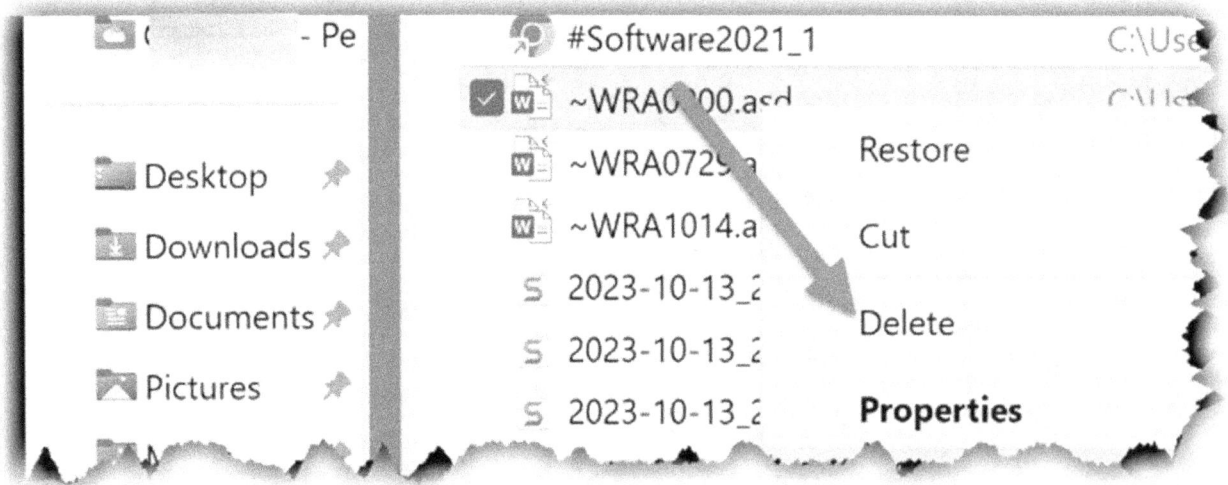

To delete multiple items, select the items and right-click to open the context menu, from which you can click the Delete option.

Emptying the Recycle Bin

Items in the recycle bin take up space on your hard drive. You can permanently delete all of these items to make room. However, you can't get these items back once they are permanently deleted in the recycle bin, so think twice before you do.

Click the Empty Recycle Bin Icon on the toolbar, and all the items will be permanently removed.

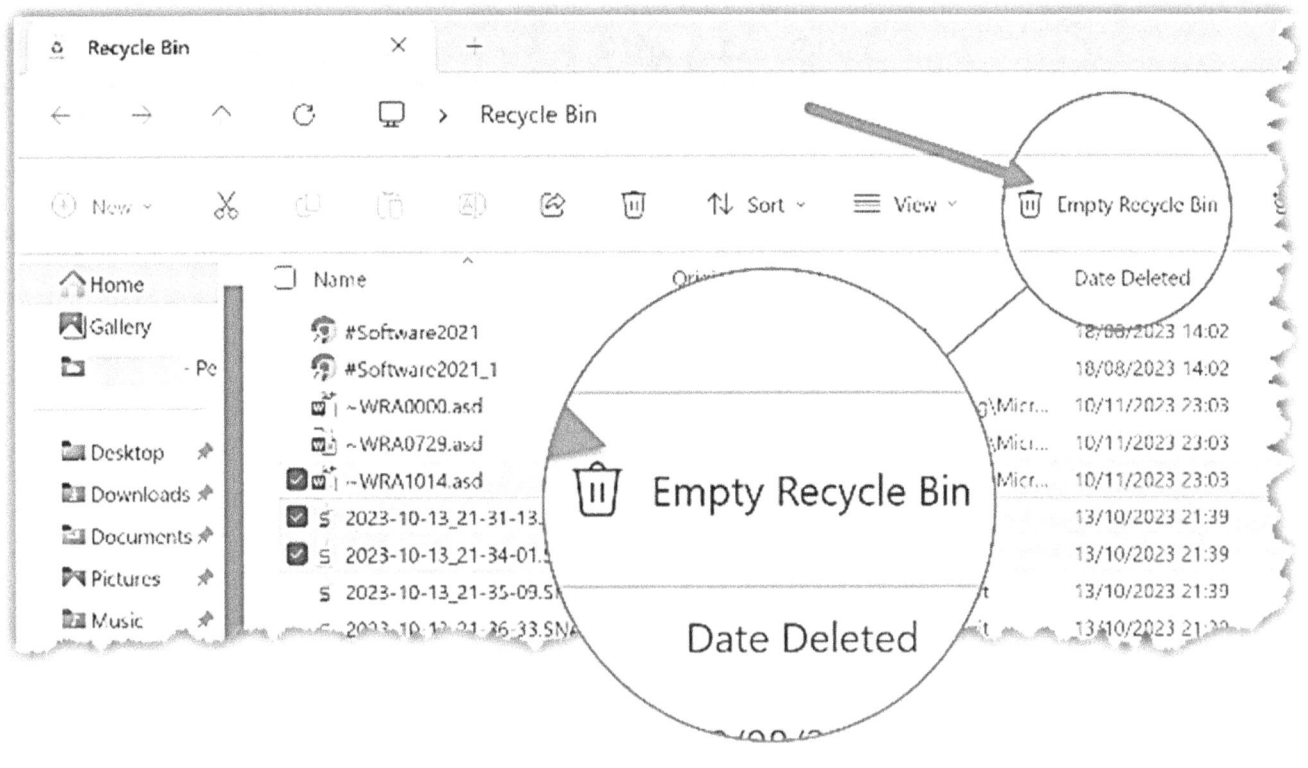

CHAPTER 8

SYSTEM NOTIFICATIONS AND QUICK SETTINGS

Notifications from your computer are essential in maintaining your connection and keeping you informed. The Windows 11 operating system has an improved notification system that lets you receive notifications and updates on your computer in real time.

To access the Windows 11 notification center, simultaneously press the **Win** and **N** keys or click the Notification icon in the taskbar's lower-right corner.

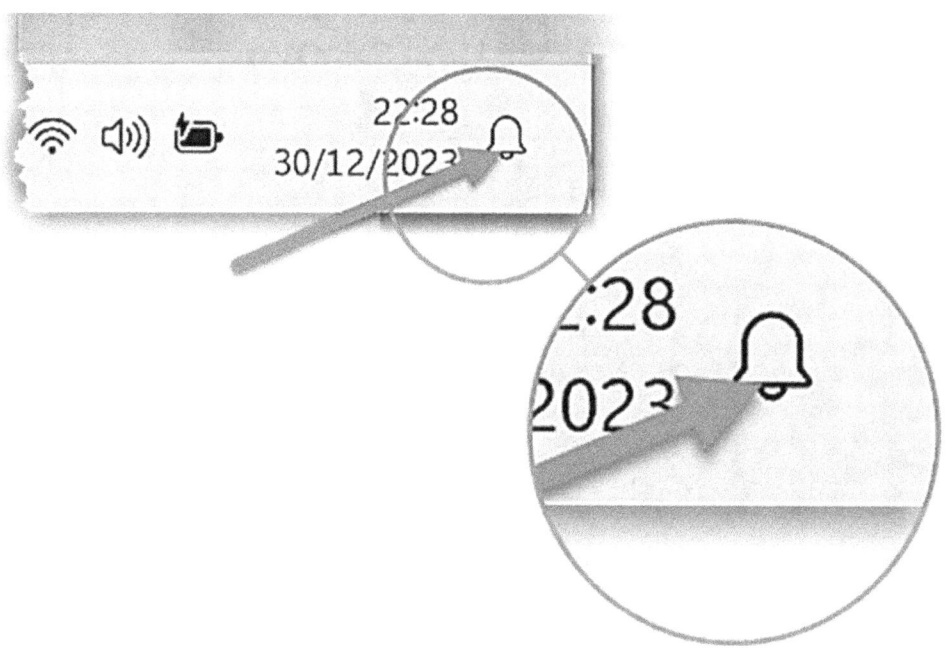

Types of Notifications in Windows 11

Even though it's important to stay updated, getting notifications all the time on your computer can be annoying. Windows 11 has a robust alert system that allows you to focus on what is important and reduce distractions.

So, let's look at the different kinds of messages and how to handle them so that you can use your computer easily and efficiently.

- **Priority Notifications**

    Prioritized notifications are the ones that are more important and require your immediate attention. Some examples of these are alarms, reminders, and messages that are considered to be urgent. They can make a sound and pop up on top of any other displayed notifications.

- **Default Notifications:**

    Default notifications are updated on a regular basis by the majority of applications, and they cover areas such as social media, email, calendar, and news information. They make a sound and appear in chronological order below priority notifications while also being displayed.

- **Silent Notifications:**

    Silent notifications refer to updates that are not essential and do not require immediate attention.

    Examples of silent notifications include suggestions, tips, and background updates. Even though they are quiet, they still appear at the bottom of the notification center.

- **Focus Assist:**

    Focus Assist is a feature that allows you to temporarily mute all notifications except those considered emergencies. It is helpful to activate this setting when you need to concentrate on a task, presentation, or game without being distracted by other things. When active, it conceals notifications that are not of high priority.

Accessing the Notification Settings

In Windows 11, you can access the settings for the system notifications through either the **Settings** app or the **Action Center**.

This is how you can accomplish it:

- **Through the Settings App:**

    1. Click on the Start button in the taskbar or press the Windows key on your keyboard.

    2. Click on the "**Settings**" icon (gear-shaped) in the Start menu.

    Alternatively, press **Win** + **I** on your keyboard to open Settings directly.

3.Select "**System**" from the left sidebar in the Settings window and click "**Notifications**".

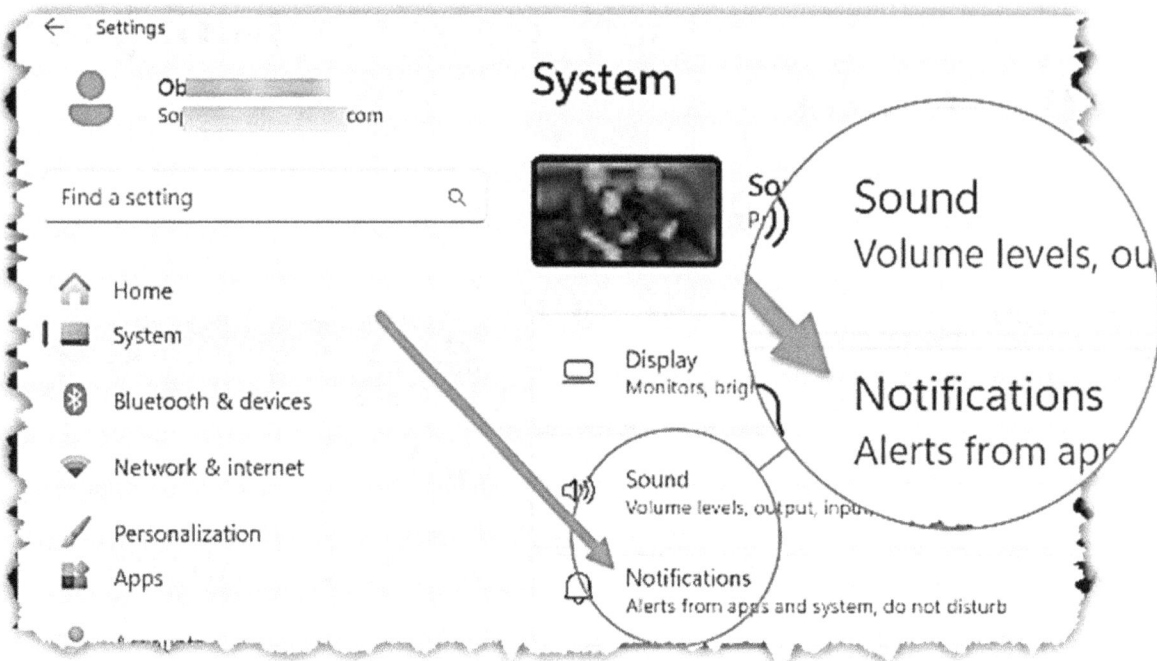

The System Notifications area customizes various notification settings, prioritizes apps, controls banners, sound settings, and manages quick actions.

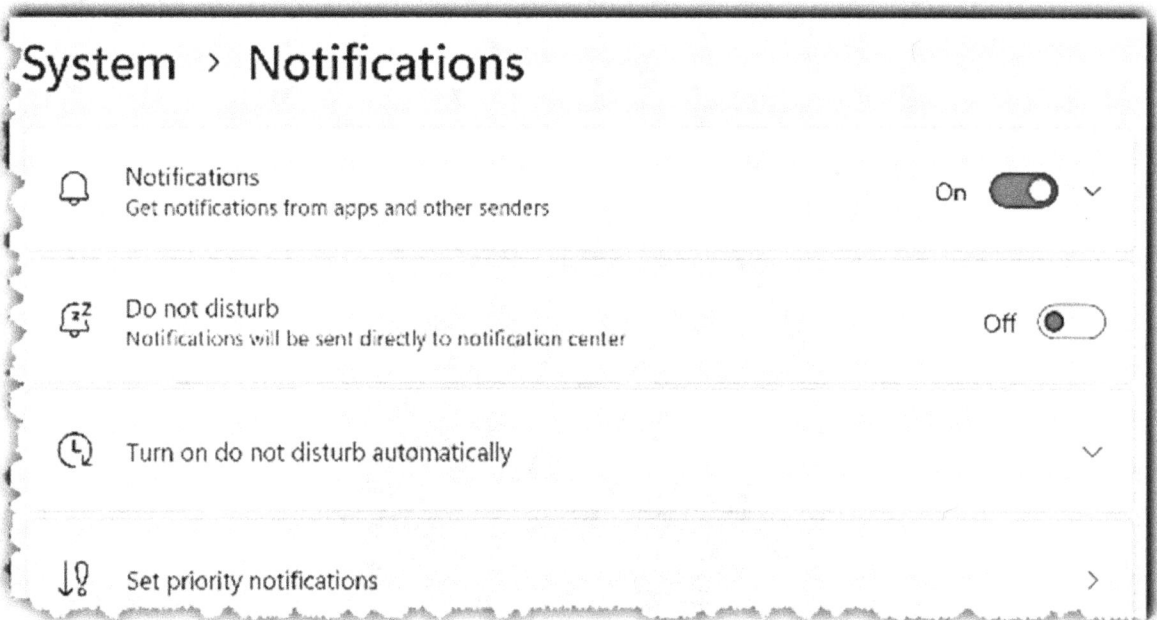

How to Turn Off/On All Your Notifications

Under the System > Notifications Settings, you can toggle **On** or **Off** the Notifications button for all Notification functionalities on your computer.

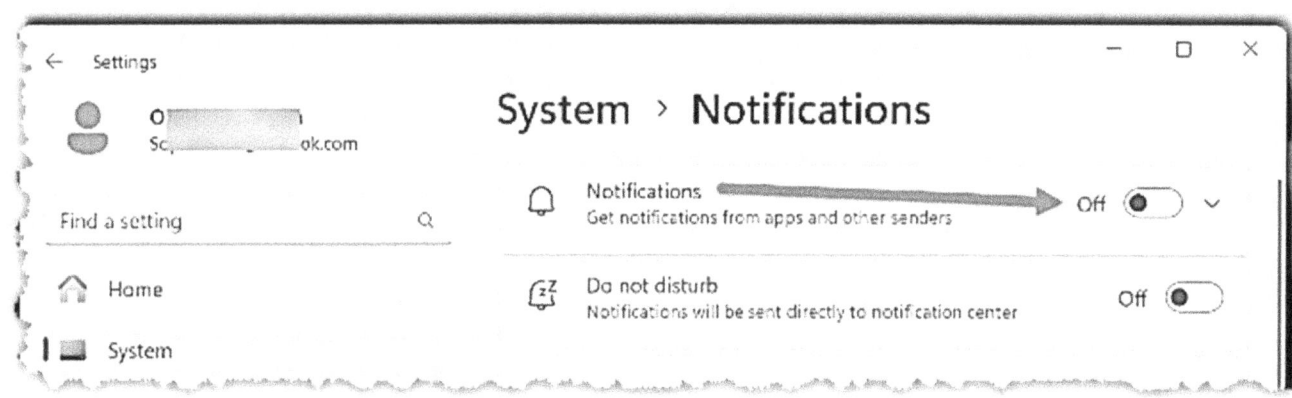

Do Not Disturb Settings

When your job requires an environment free of distractions, the **Do Not Disturb** (DND) feature will help you to mute notifications and sounds. DND gives you greater control over your digital environment, allowing you to concentrate on your work or enjoy silence and tranquility. With the Do Not Disturb setting, you can design a computing experience that is both personalized and uninterrupted.

You can access and customize the DND Settings in the System Notifications area.

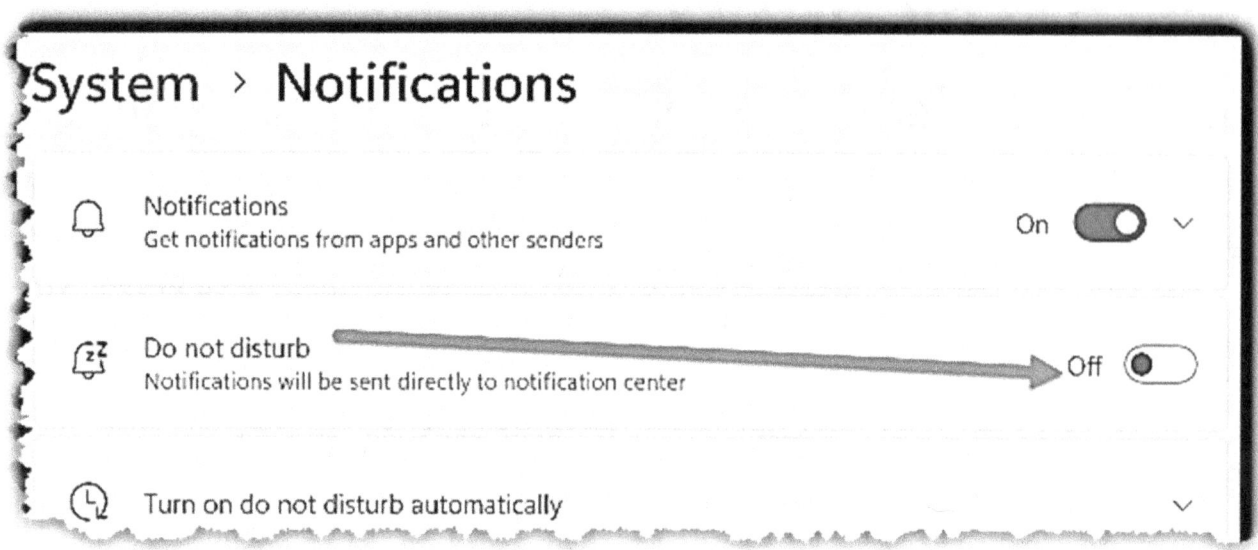

Click the Toggle button to switch the Do Not Disturb mode **On** or **Off**.

Alternatively, you can access the Do Not Disturb setting through the notification center. You will see the Do Not Disturb button on the top of the panel.

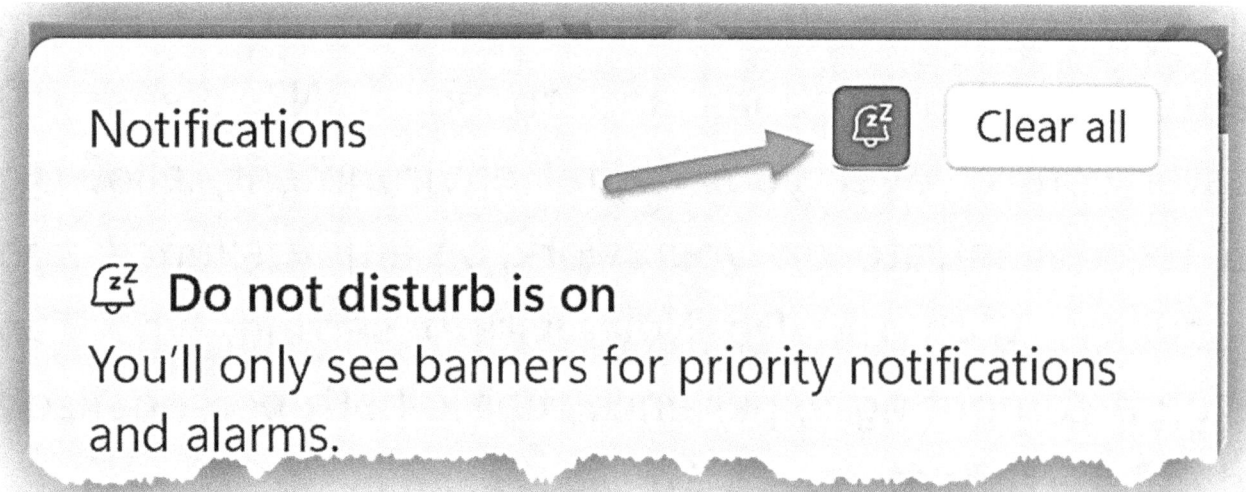

Once you click the DND button, your computer will be put in Do Not Disturb mode.

Automatic Do Not Disturb Settings

One of the features I find very useful is the "**Automatic Do Not Disturb settings**". This feature allows you to set up rules for when you want to silence notifications and focus on your work or leisure.

Note that Turning on Do Not Disturb Automatically is a standalone setting.

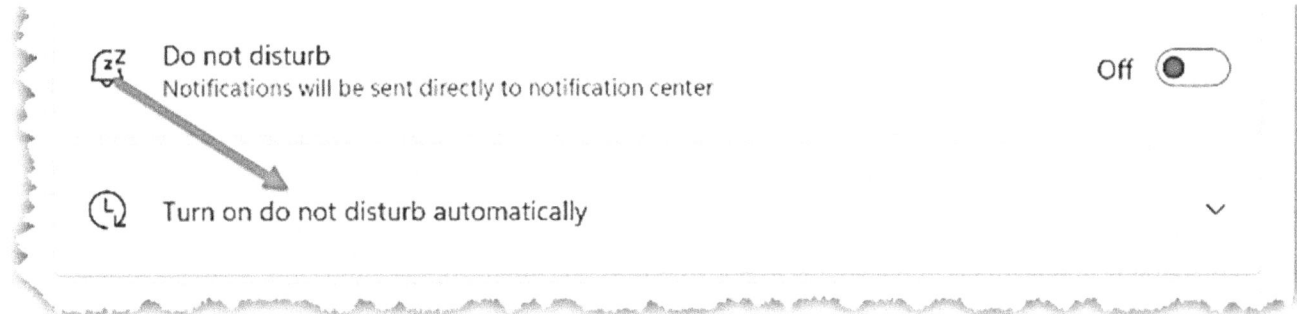

For example, when you are in a meeting, you can turn on Do Not Disturb automatically during certain hours of the day.

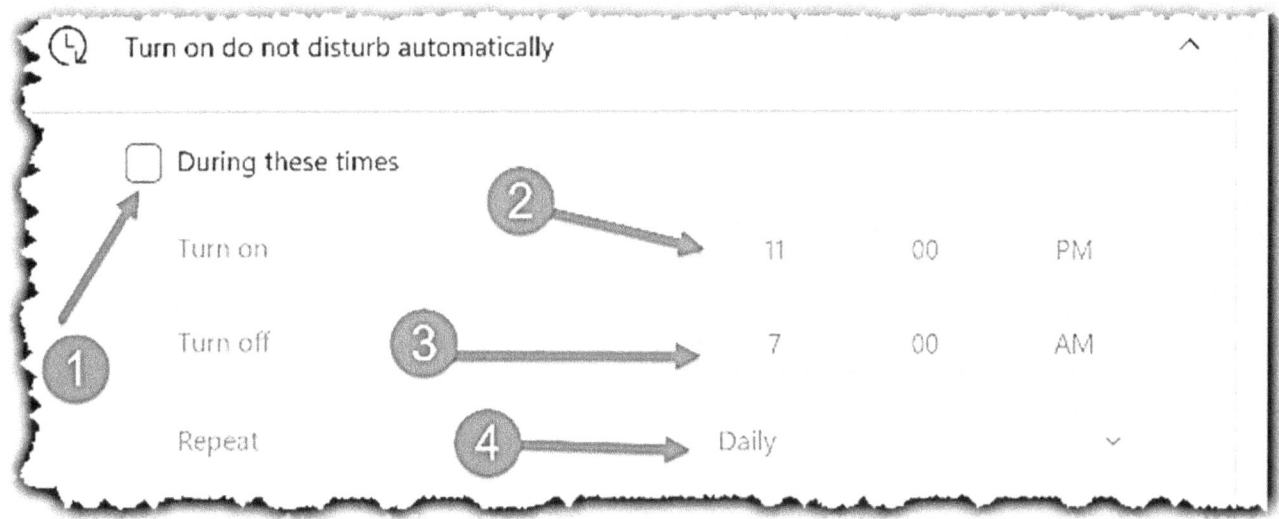

Meanwhile, you have to click the **During these times** box to use this feature.

Next, you set the time when to **Turn on** and when it should **Turn off** automatically.

If it is a process you want to repeat on its own, you can choose to repeat it: **Daily**, **Weekends,** or **Weekdays**.

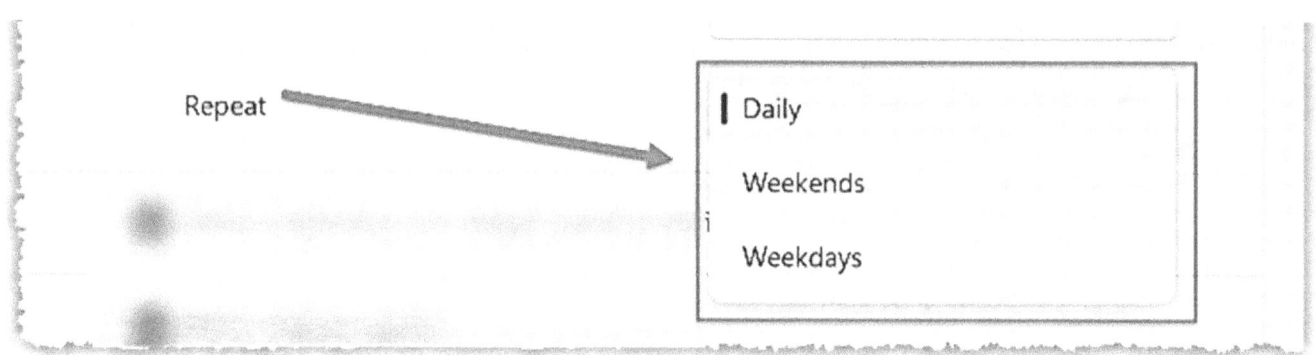

Furthermore, the Do Not Disturb settings automatically give you additional conditions to select when using your computer for a particular purpose.

- **When duplicating your display:** this setting turns on DND once you connect or share your computer screen with an external monitor (projector).

- **When playing a game:** this setting turns on DND when you are using your computer to play a game.

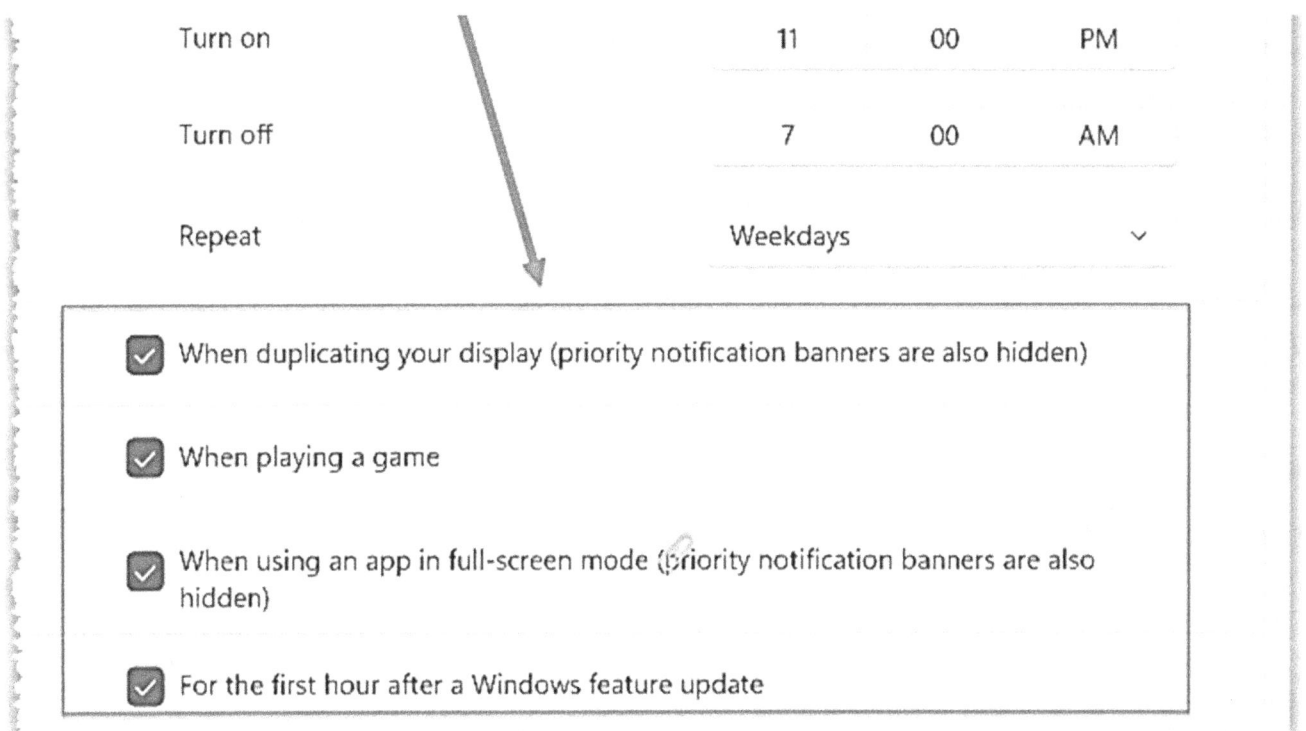

- **When using an app in full-screen mode:** this setting turns on DND when, for example, a music or video application is in full-screen mode. The idea is to continue streaming without interruption.

- **For the first hour after a Windows feature update:** this setting turns on DND after an hour when Windows 11 might have undergone a system update.

Priority Notification Settings

Setting priority to a particular program or service in Windows 11 is an excellent way to ensure you are updated with important notifications even when the Do Not Disturb mode is enabled.

Proceed to **System** > **Notifications**, then click on **Set Priority Notifications**.

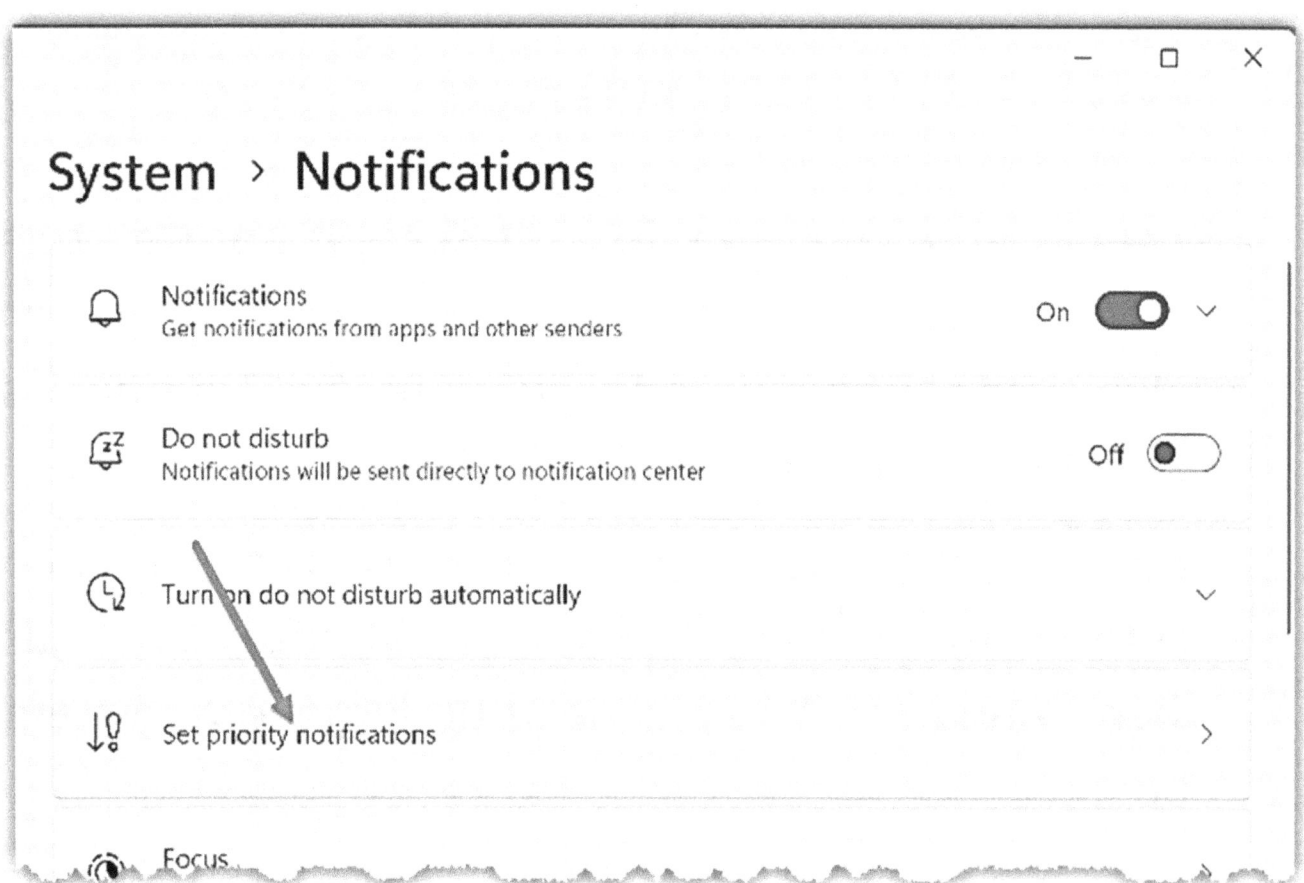

Under the **Set priority notification**, you can enable certain features and apps to be notified even in Do Not Disturb mode.

The **Calls** and **Reminders** section allows you to prioritize incoming calls and display reminders regardless of the apps used.

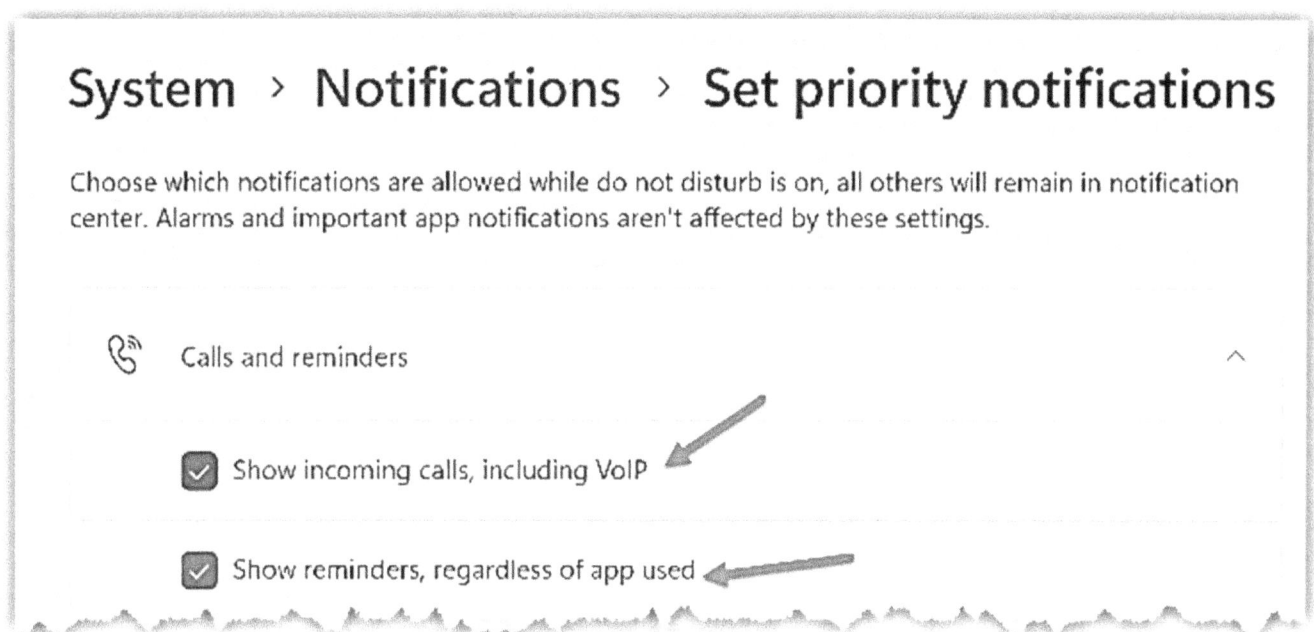

However, you can also add specific apps you like to be notified about by clicking the **Add apps** button.

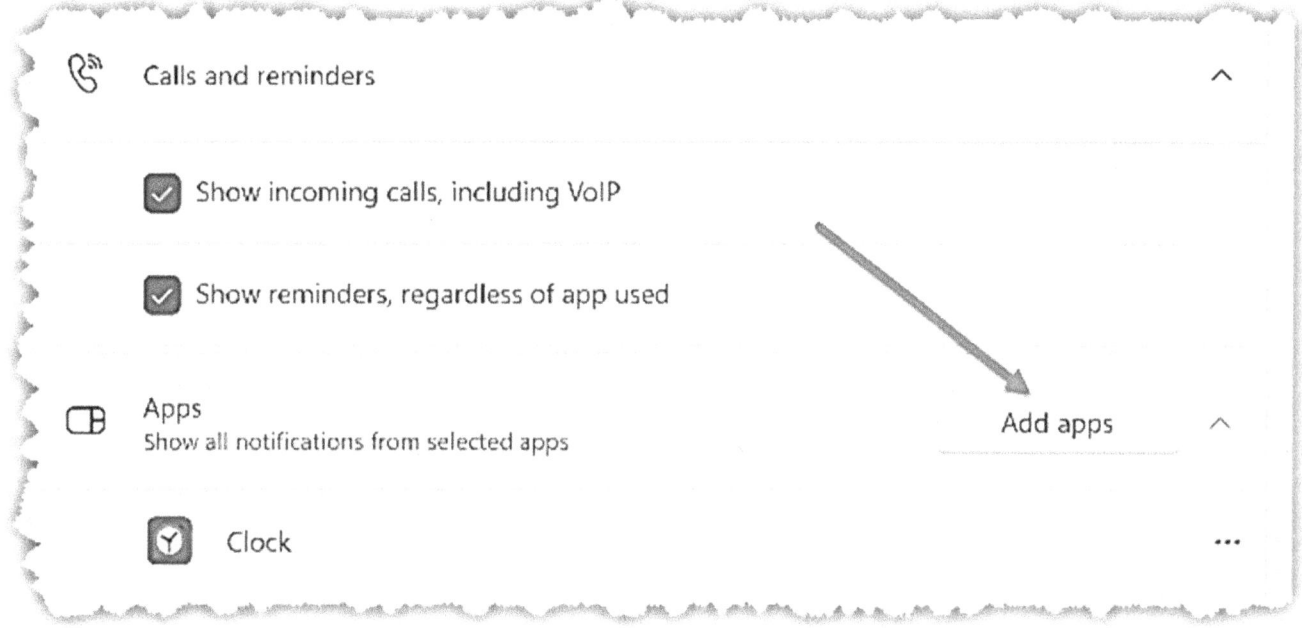

The Add apps button allows you to select applications installed on your computer that you want to get notified of even when Do Not Disturb mode is explicitly enabled.

Apps that you have prioritized will appear below the Add apps button.

To remove an app from the priority list, click the three dots on the right and select **Remove**.

Focus Mode Settings

When the need arises to focus on important tasks, such as completing homework or giving a presentation, you do not want to be distracted by notifications.

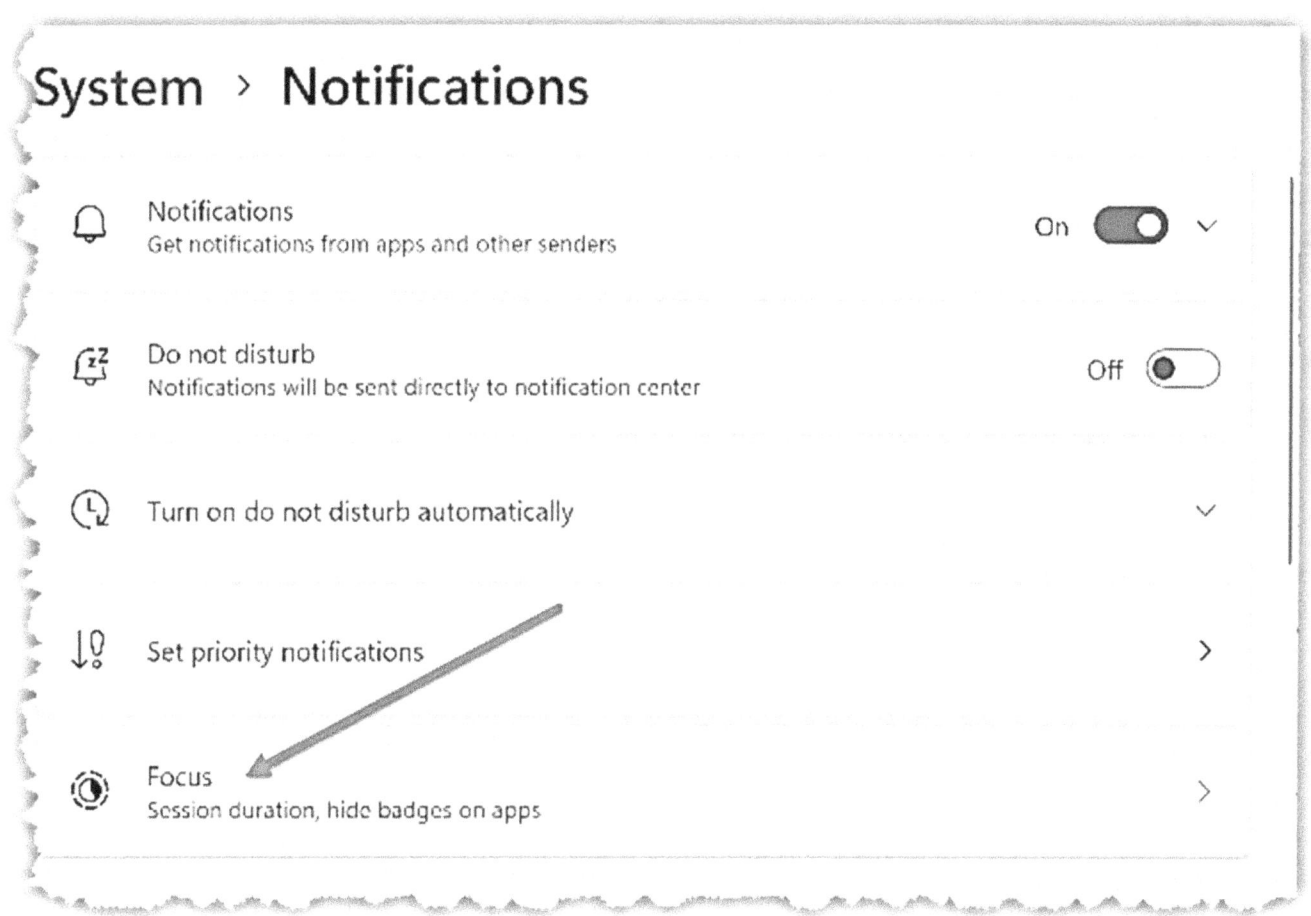

Using the **Focus** tool keeps your sounds and alerts from being activated. Think of it as a mode on your computer that says "Do Not Disturb".

When you choose the **Focus Settings** method under the System > Notifications > Focus, the following are the features you can use.

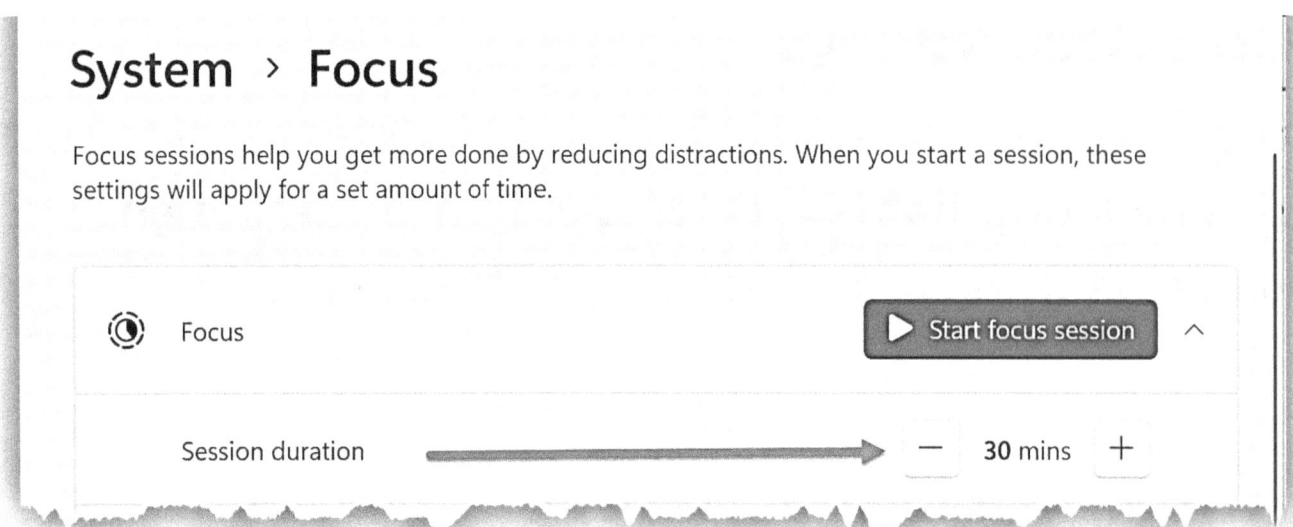

- Within the Focus setting is also the **Show the timer in the Clock app** checkbox to display a timer.

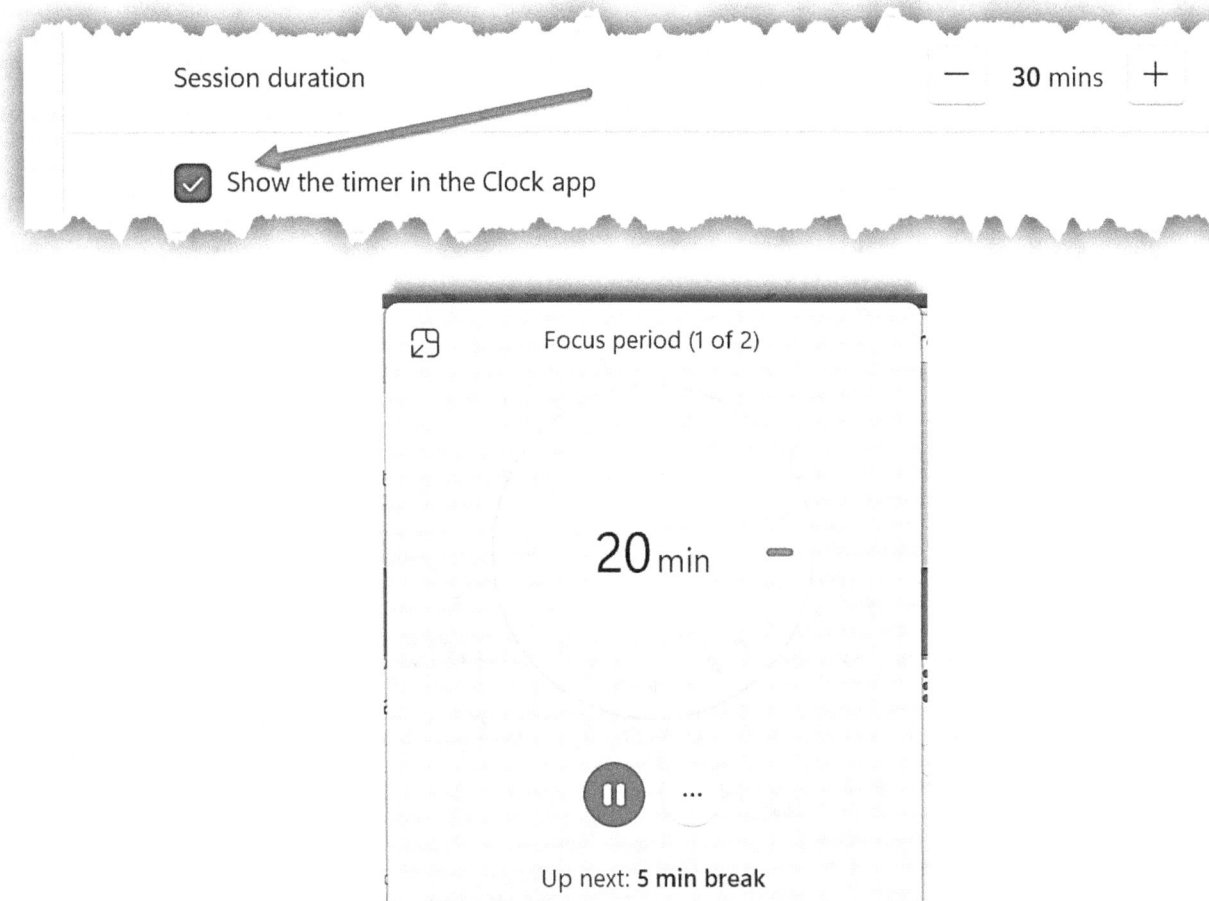

When the timer is enabled, you can set the focus period manually.

- **Badge notifications** are numerical indicators (badges) that appear on the top of an app icon. Badges show the number of unread messages, updates, or notifications within an app.

You can **hide badges** when in focus mode to allow you to concentrate on what you are doing with your computer.

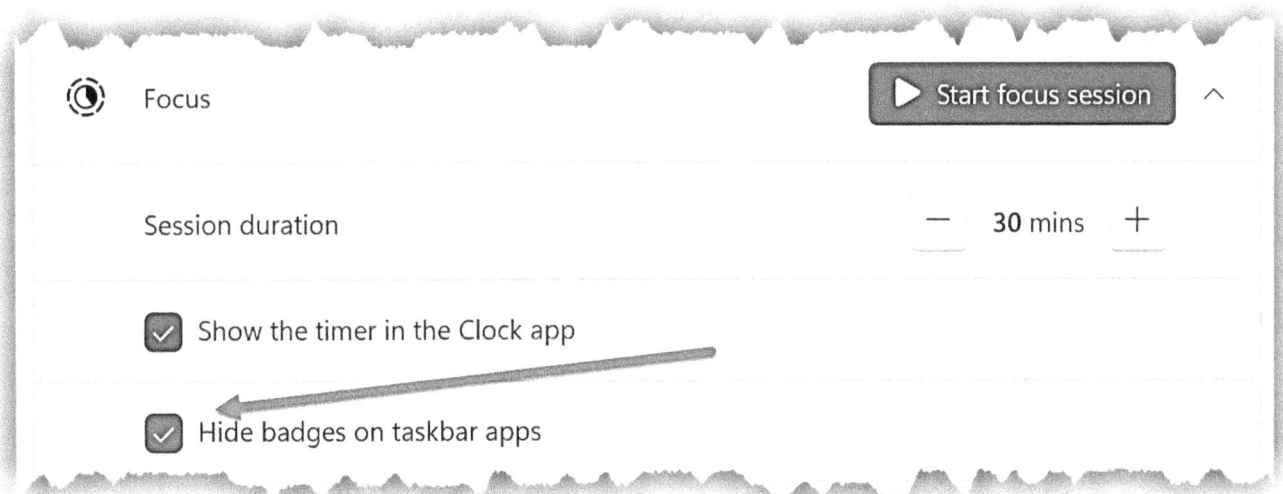

- **To Minimize Distractions,** Check the "***Show flashing on taskbar apps***" box in your notification settings to stop icons and buttons on the taskbar from flashing and taking your attention away.

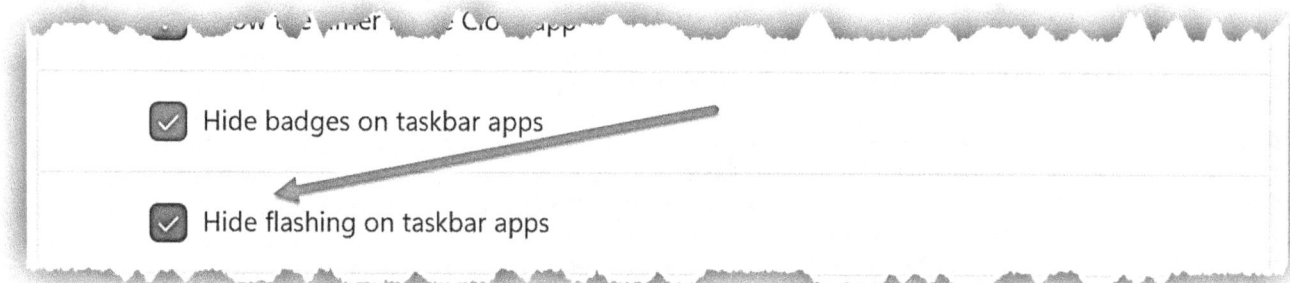

This will ensure app icons remain unnoticeable on the taskbar, even when they have updates to display.

- When the Do Not Disturb box is checked, it automatically activates the DND mode.

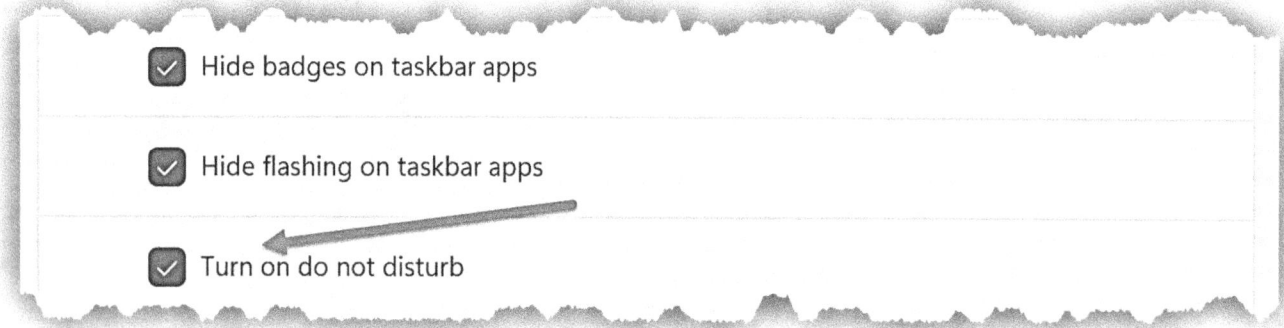

CHAPTER 9

QUICK SETTINGS PANEL

The Quick Settings panel in Windows 11 is a centralized hub that simplifies your access to critical operating system parameters.

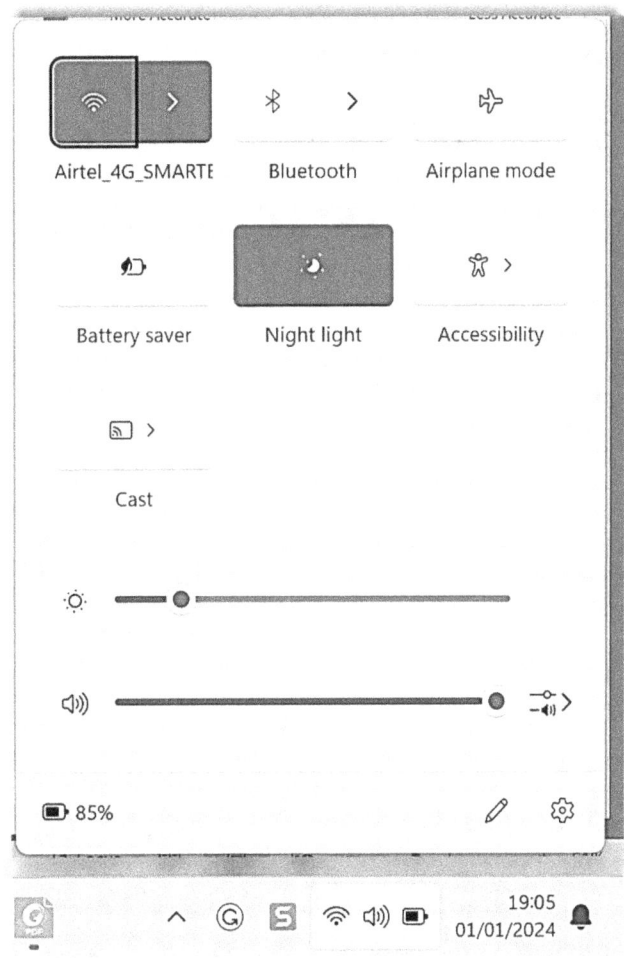

The Quick Settings panel includes buttons that, by default, allow you to activate or disable Wi-Fi, Bluetooth, and Airplane Mode quickly. You also have access to Battery Saver, Night Light, and Accessibility.

How to Access the Quick Settings Panel

1. Press **Win + A** on your keyboard to get to the Action Center. Click the sound or battery icons in the taskbar.

2. Within the Action Center, locate the Quick Settings section.

   The panel shows settings you use often, like Wi-Fi, Bluetooth, Focus Assist, etc.

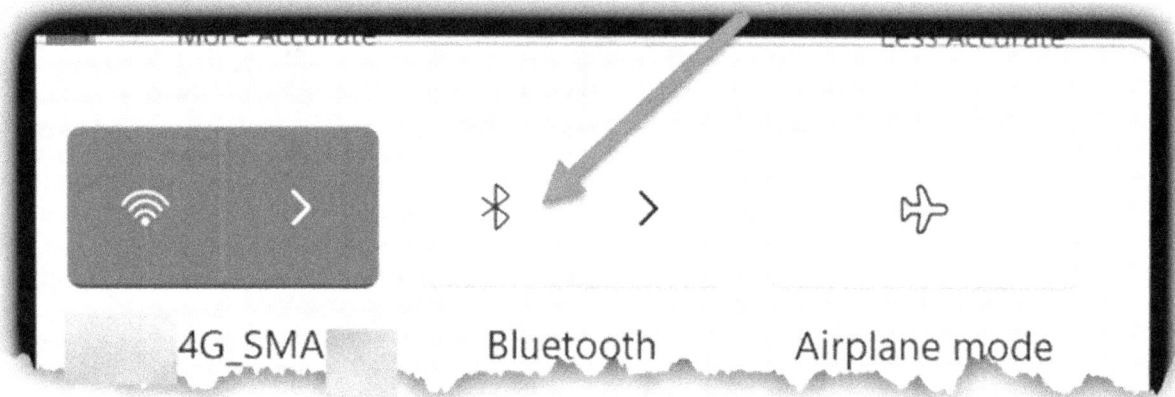

If you click on any of the icons in the Quick Settings section, you can change the settings linked to them. This makes it easy to handle important tasks without going through complicated menus.

Wi-Fi and Bluetooth Device Setting

Network settings you can carry out include Wi-Fi, Bluetooth, and Airplane mode. You can only use the Wi-Fi and Bluetooth settings if your computer hardware is active and the software installed.

The Wi-Fi network button is on the top left corner of the quick settings panel.

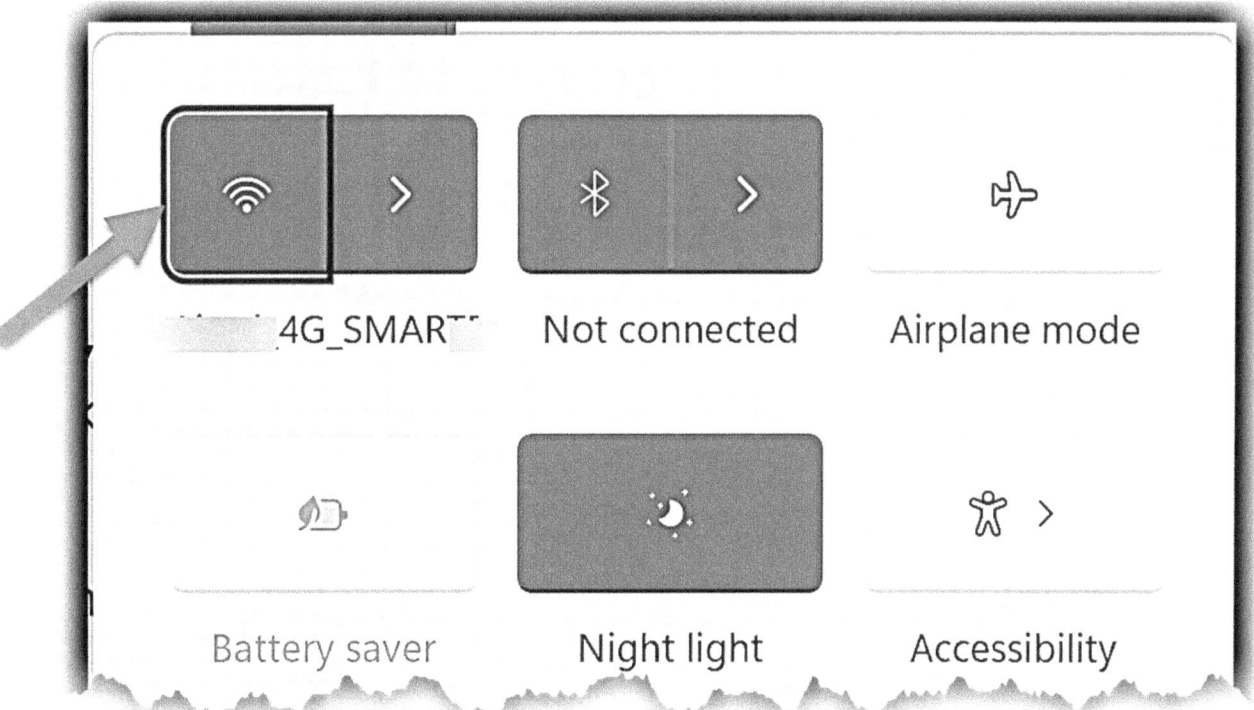

The identity of the Wi-Fi network that your computer is connected to appears below the Wi-Fi button.

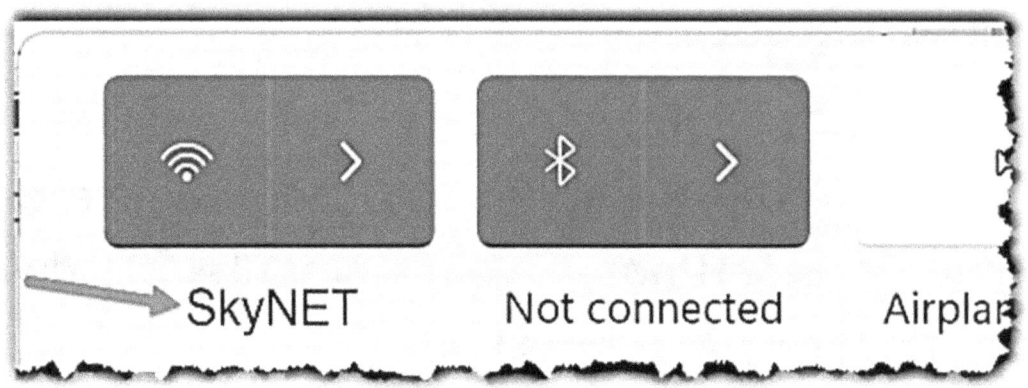

Similarly, you can use the Bluetooth button to select the Bluetooth device you want to connect to your computer.

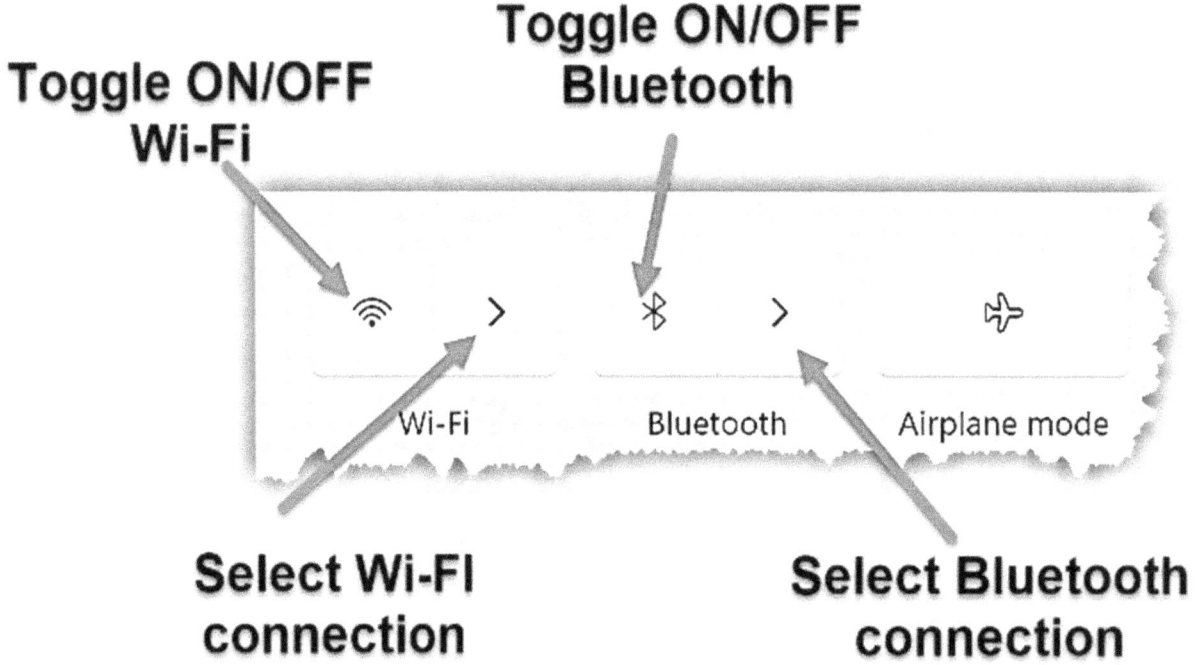

The Wi-Fi and Bluetooth icons allow you to turn these features off or on. When you click the arrow button beside the Wi-Fi or Bluetooth icon, you gain access to the available Wi-Fi network and Bluetooth devices, respectively.

Airplane Mode Setting

Airplane mode is a setting that allows you to turn off all forms of wireless communication, including Wi-Fi, Bluetooth, cellular data, and GPS. Airplane mode can help you save the battery's life and prevent interference with equipment on an aircraft.

The Quick Settings panel is the easiest way to access and toggle airplane mode on Windows 11

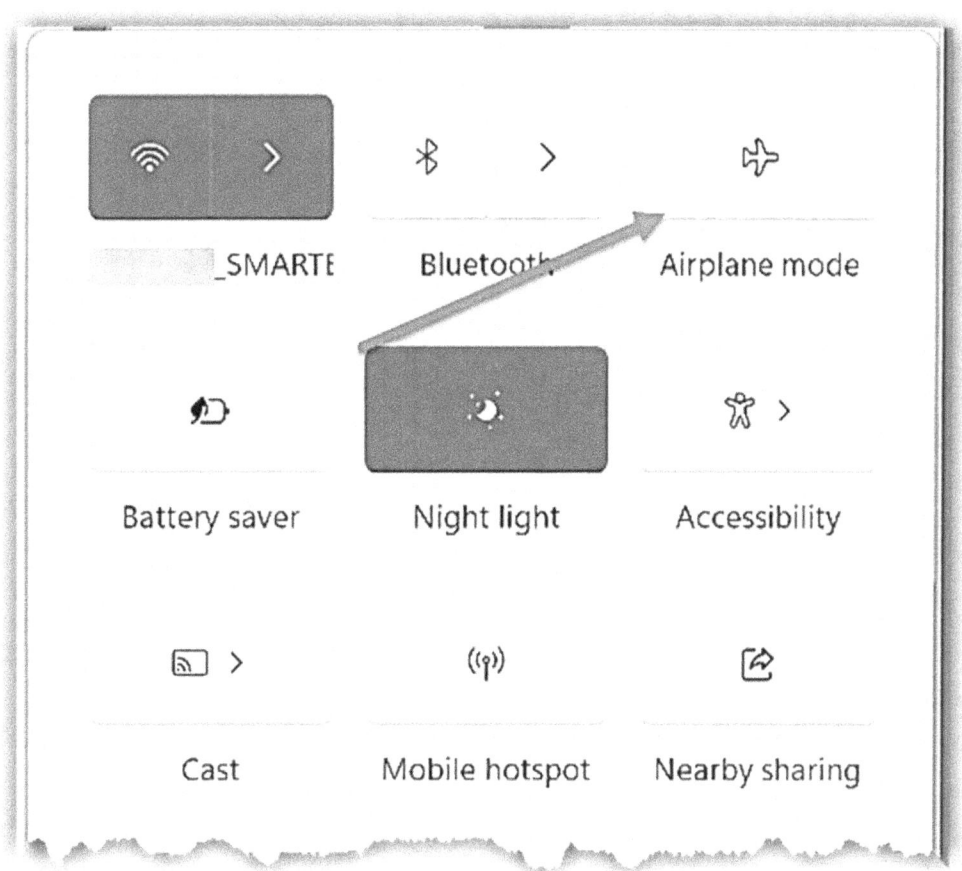

Click the airplane button to turn on airplane mode using the quick settings panel. To turn it off, click on the button again.

Battery Saver Setting

Battery Saver is a feature that you can use to reduce the power your computer consumes. This option extends the life of your battery by reducing your computer's background activity and raising the screen brightness.

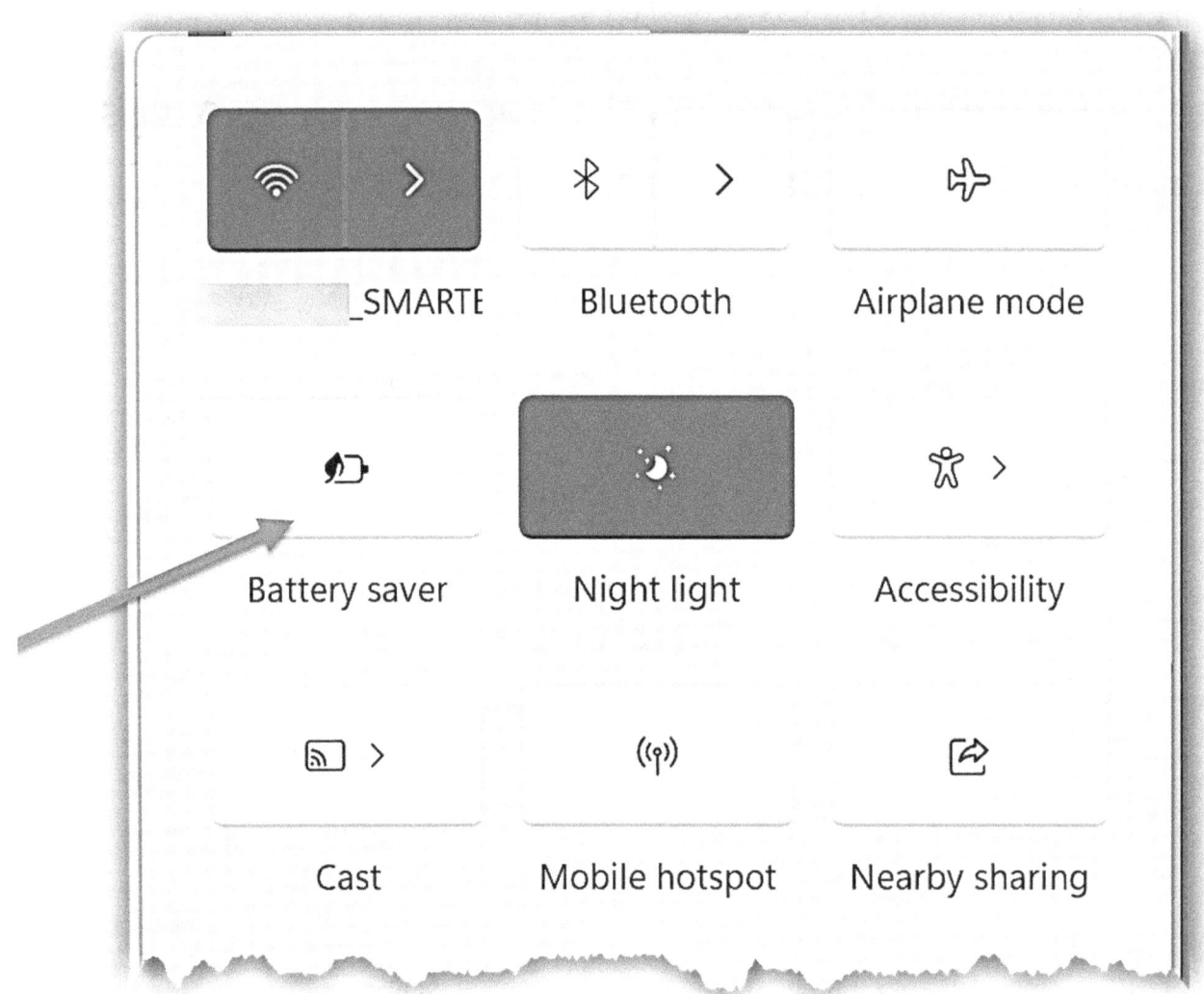

As illustrated above, you can manually turn the battery saver on or off through the quick settings panel by clicking the battery saver button.

When the battery saver mode is activated, a leaf icon appears at the edge of the battery icon, as shown below.

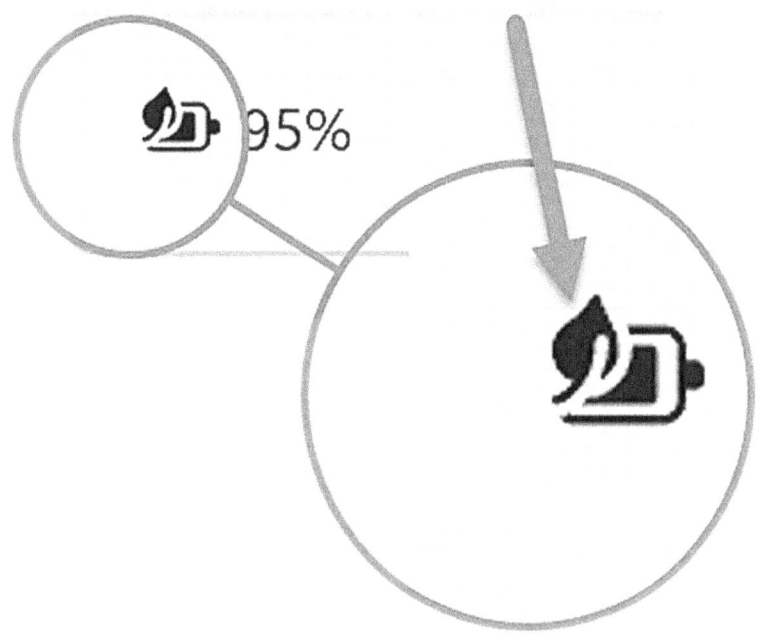

Night light Setting

The Night Light setting allows you to change the color temperature of your screen to a warmer hue. With this setting enabled while using your computer, you can relax and have no difficulty falling asleep when necessary.

Click the Night light button to turn the setting on or off.

When the Night light setting is off, your screen appears much brighter but warmer when enabled.

However, you can also use the slider with a sun icon to change your screen temperature.

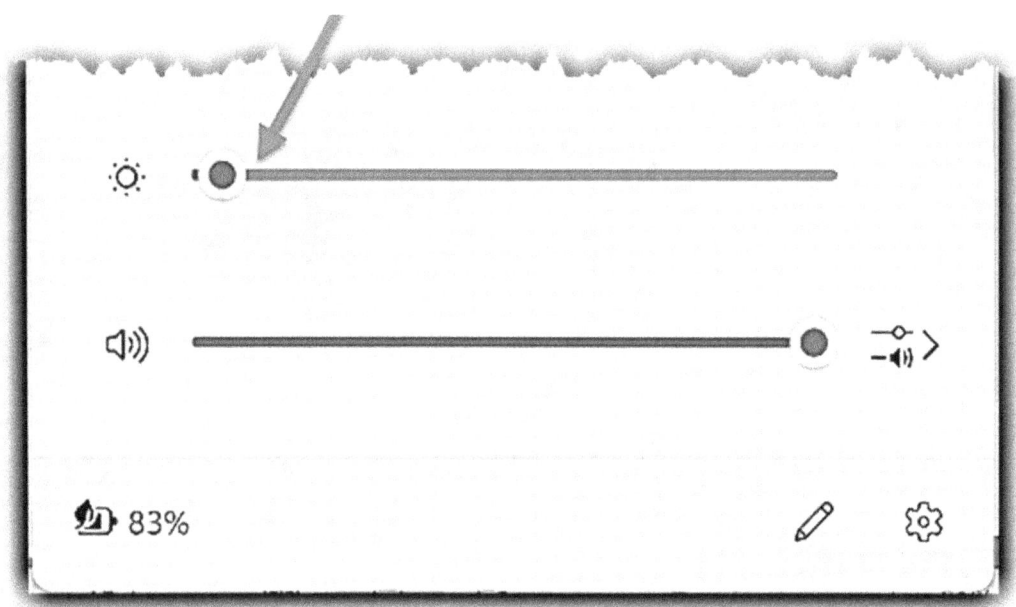

When you click and drag the slider, you will notice that the brightness of your screen increases as you slide toward the right but increases as you slide toward the left.

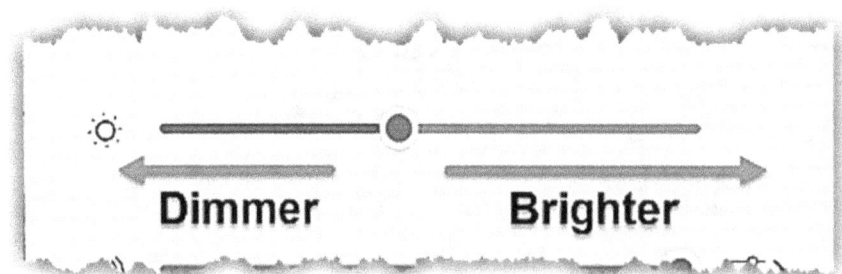

Accessibility Setting

The Accessibility setting allows you to access many other options on the quick settings panel. To access the accessibility features, click the button to open a menu with various options.

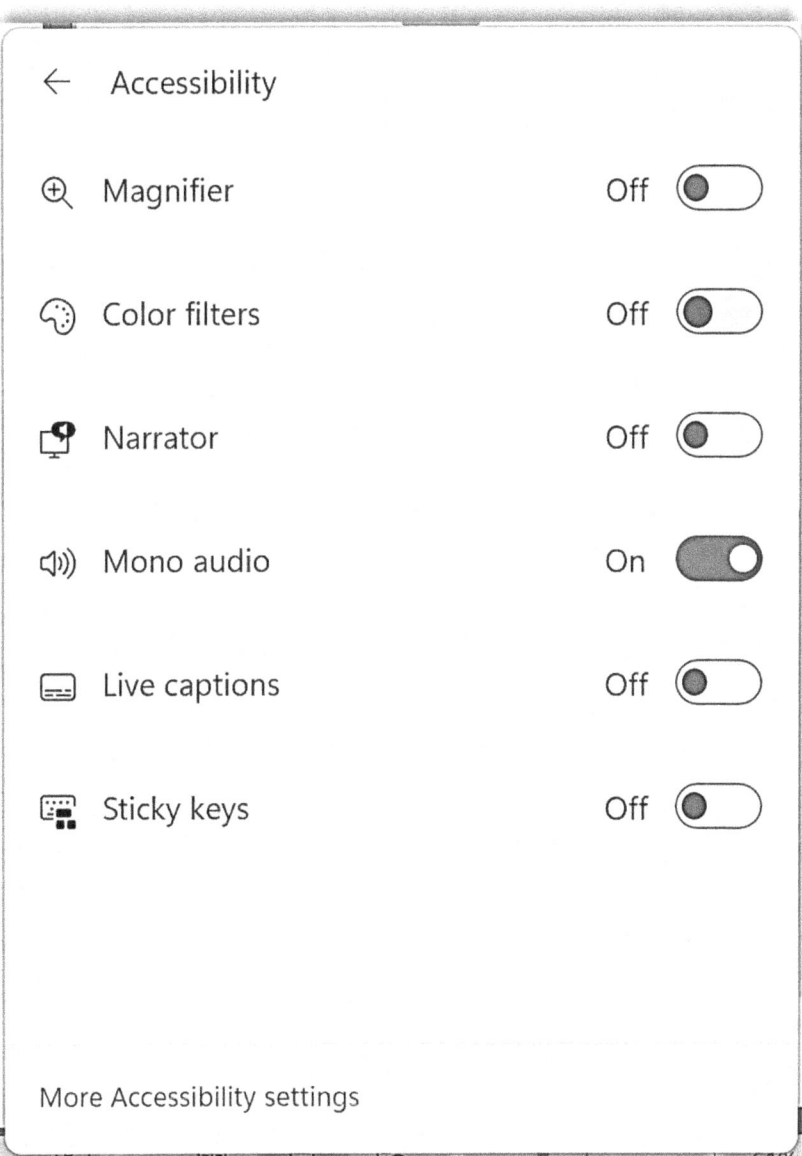

You toggle on or off any of these options using your mouse to click on them.

- **Magnifier**

  This feature enlarges the content on your screen, making it easier to view and read.

  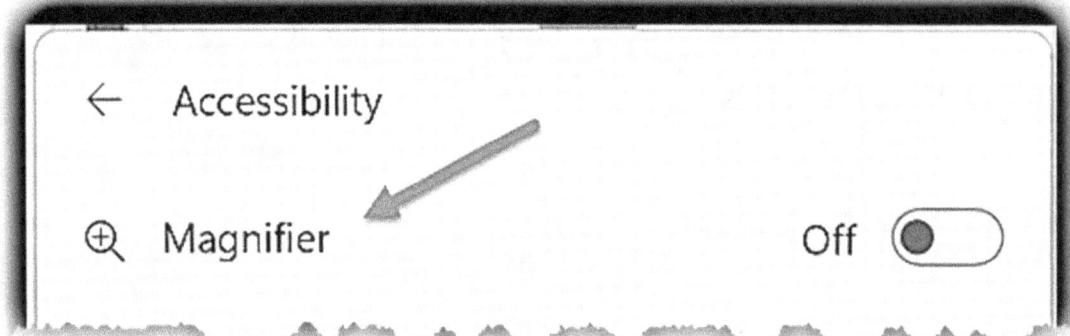

  You can adjust the magnification level and the zoom mode by using the Magnifier app on your screen when the magnifier setting is enabled.

  The minus or the plus icon zooms in or zooms out the contents on your screen for a preferred view.

- **Color Filters**

  This feature allows you to apply various color schemes to your screen, including grayscale, inverted, and colorblind-friendly color schemes.

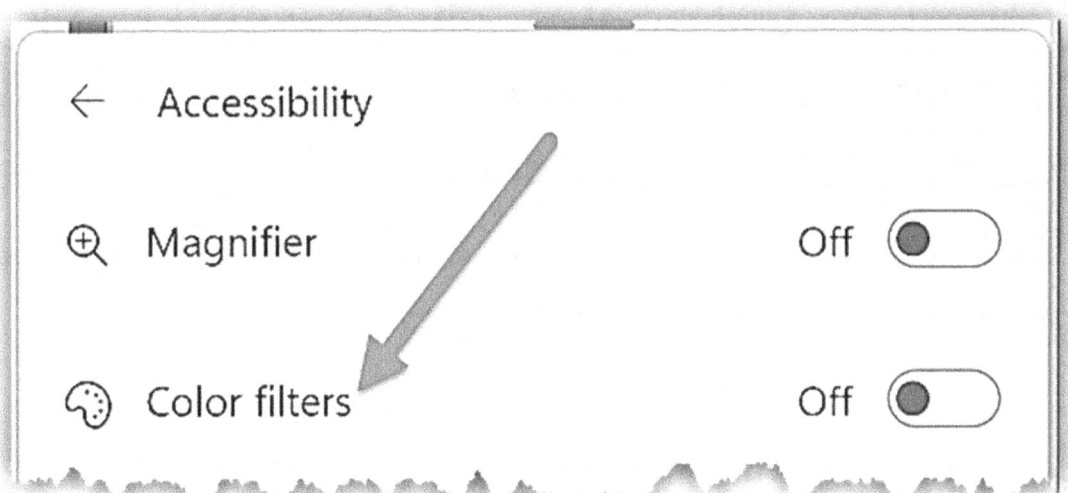

Using color filters can help reduce the strain on your eyes, especially when looking at the screen for a long time. It enhances the screen contrast and makes reading letters and words simpler.

- **Narrator**

When you enable the narrator feature, your computer will verbally communicate on-screen text and elements to you.

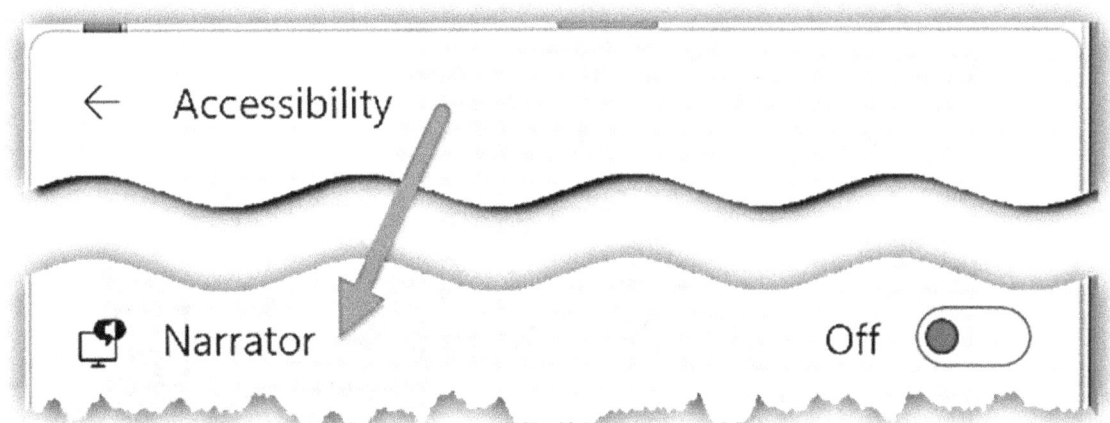

With the help of Narrator, people with low vision or trouble learning can easily access the Windows 11 interface. This feature also allows you to navigate your device, browse the web, and access applications without looking at your screen.

Screen Casting (Wireless Display) Setting

Screen casting is one of the features on the quick settings panel that allows you to mirror your computer display or screen onto another device like TVs, monitors, or projectors without a cable connection.

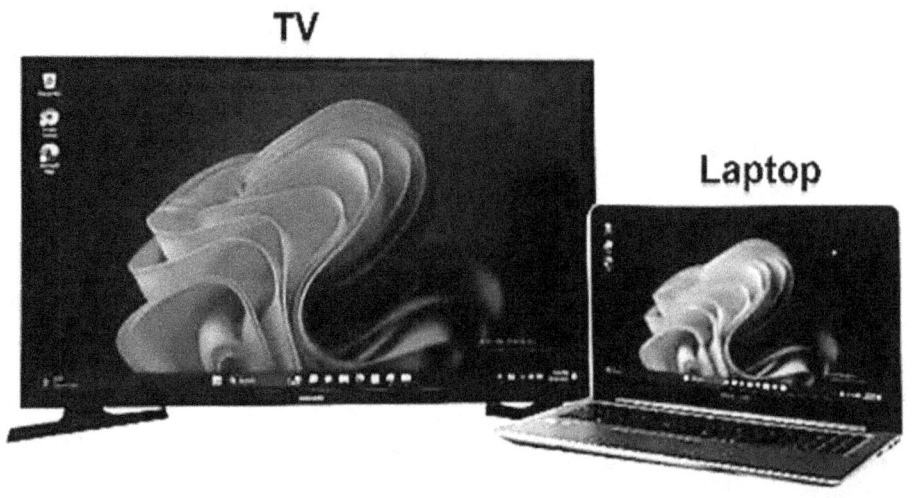

This can be helpful for various purposes, including presentations and entertainment.

To cast your computer screen, click the "**Cast**" option in the quick settings panel. Immediately, the quick settings panel will scan for any available devices within its range.

You will be presented with a list of available devices supporting casting, from which you can choose the one you wish to connect.

To terminate the casting process, click the "Cast" option again, select "Disconnect," or use the keyboard shortcut ⊞ + K

Mobile Hotspot Setting

The Mobile Hotspot button on the quick settings panel lets you easily share your internet connection with other devices via Bluetooth or Wi-Fi.

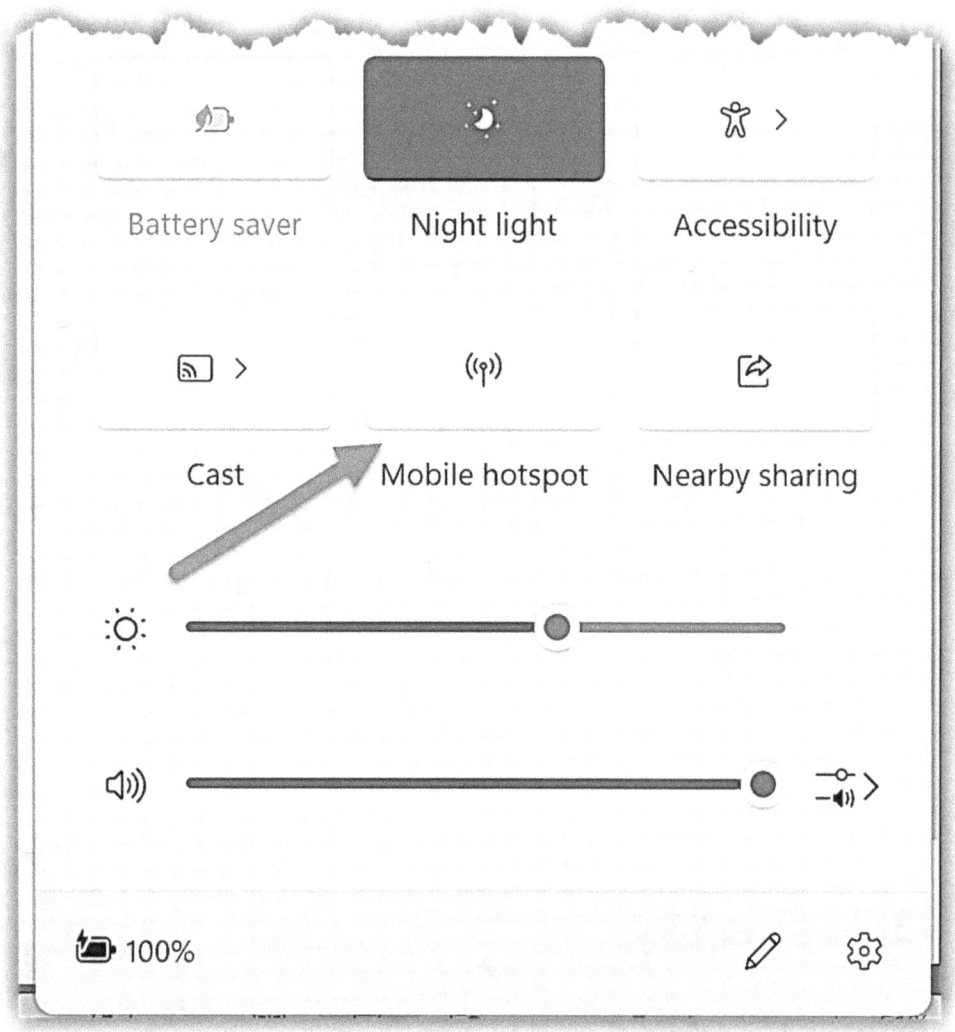

It is useful when you find yourself in circumstances where a wireless network is unavailable or attempting to reduce the amount of data consumed by your mobile plan.

To begin, click the "Mobile Hotspot" button in the quick settings panel. This will successfully activate the mobile hotspot.

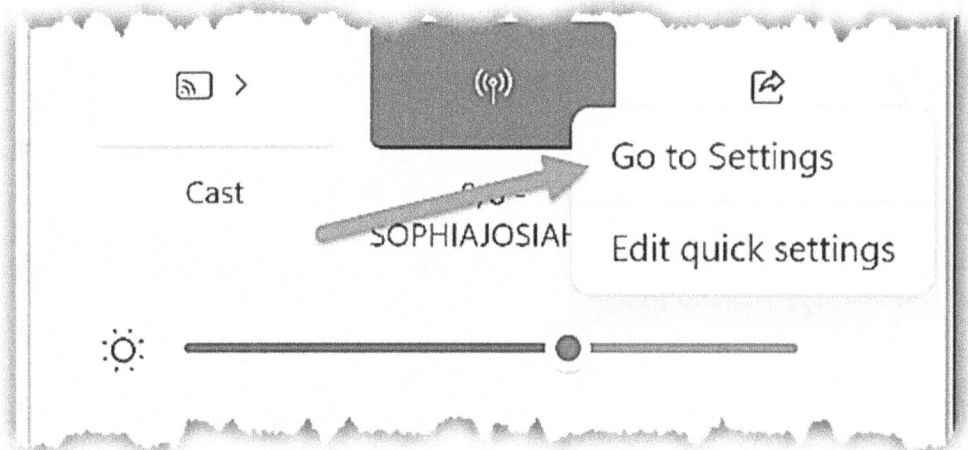

However, you may need to set some parameters to enable other devices to connect with your computer. Right-click and select the **Go to Settings** option to allow you to change the hotspot settings.

In the Settings app, changes you can carry out include changing the hotspot name or password after clicking on the Edit button.

Moreover, you need to keep track of the devices connected to your internet connection by selecting the devices you wish to share your internet with. This is especially important when you are dealing with several different options.

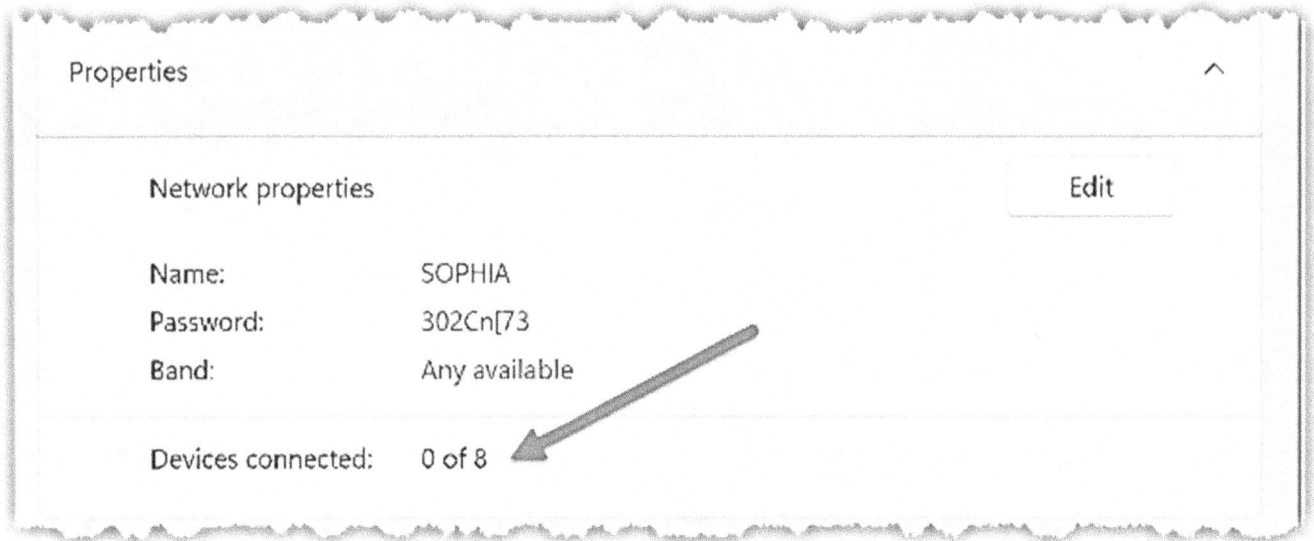

To deactivate the mobile hotspot, go back to the quick settings panel and click the mobile hotspot button again.

Limitation and Risk of Mobile Hotspot

However, some limitations and risks are associated with turning on your mobile hotspot when using a laptop, even though it has some benefits.

- The rate at which your battery will drop will be higher and may require the computer to be plugged into a power source.

- When activating the hotspot, the next thing you should do is ensure you know your mobile data usage and limits.
- How well and fast your internet connection works may depend on the number of devices connected and what those devices do.
- Exercise care when dealing with security; a strong password is necessary. You can lower your risk of getting malware or being hacked by using antivirus software and only letting devices and people you trust connect to publicly accessible Wi-Fi.

Nearby Sharing

The Nearby Sharing option in the quick settings panel allows you to send files, photos, links, and more to nearby devices with Bluetooth and Nearby Sharing enabled.

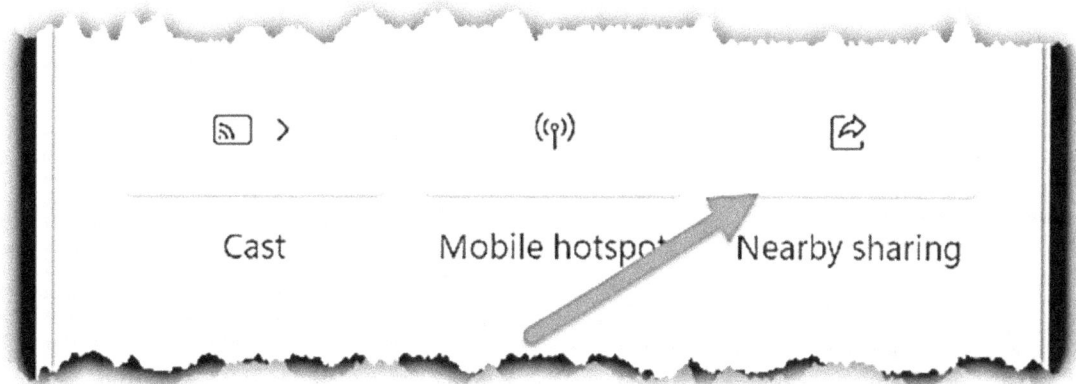

When enabled, you can change who can see you and what you want by right-clicking the **Nearby Sharing** button.

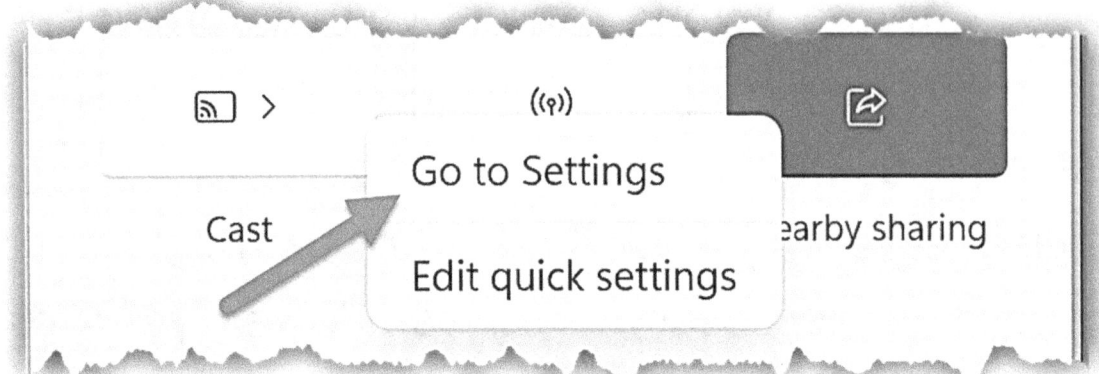

From the options, click on **Go To Settings** to access and manage the Nearby Sharing setting.

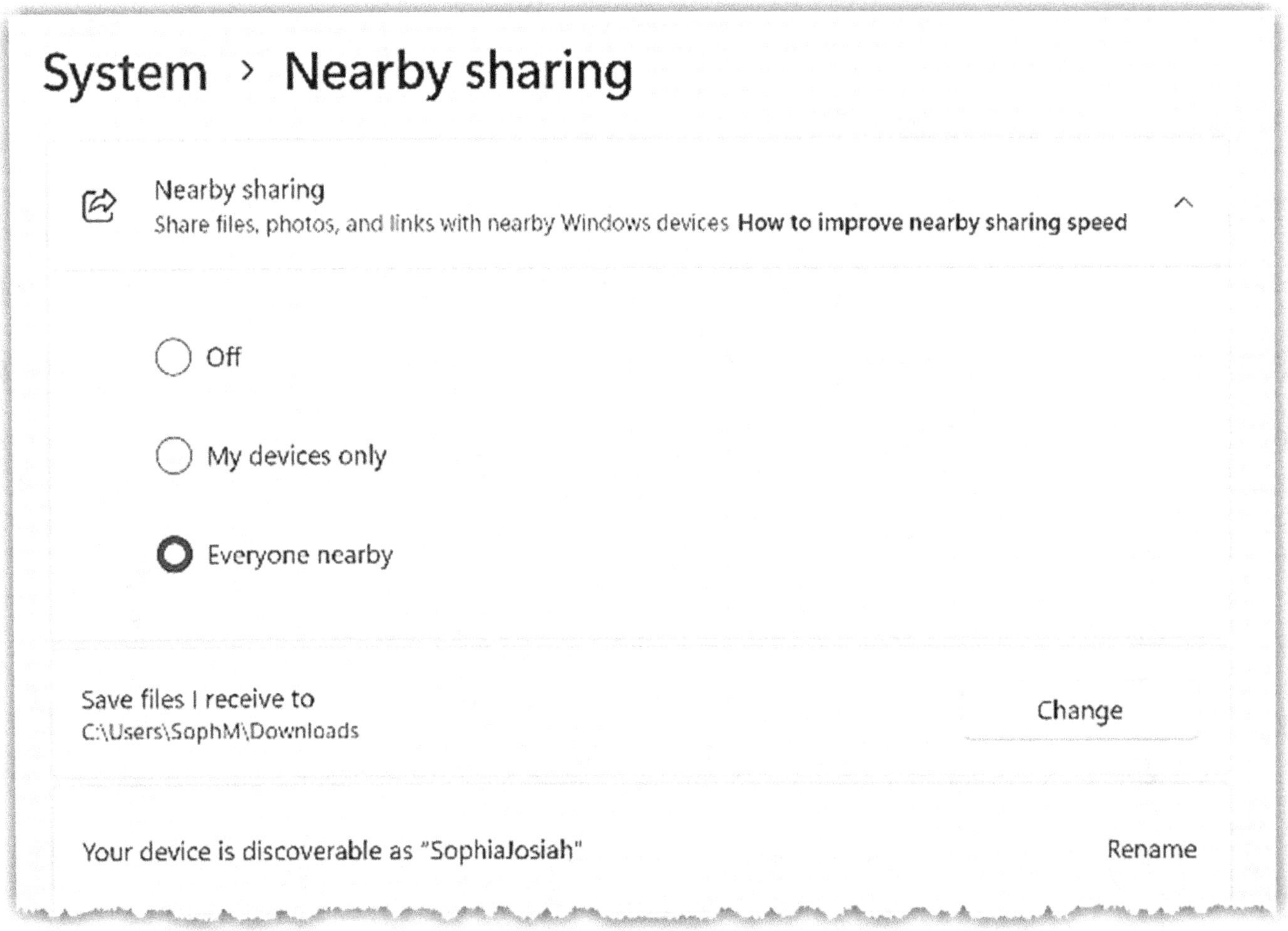

You can use the settings windows to decide on devices that can see your device and its identity.

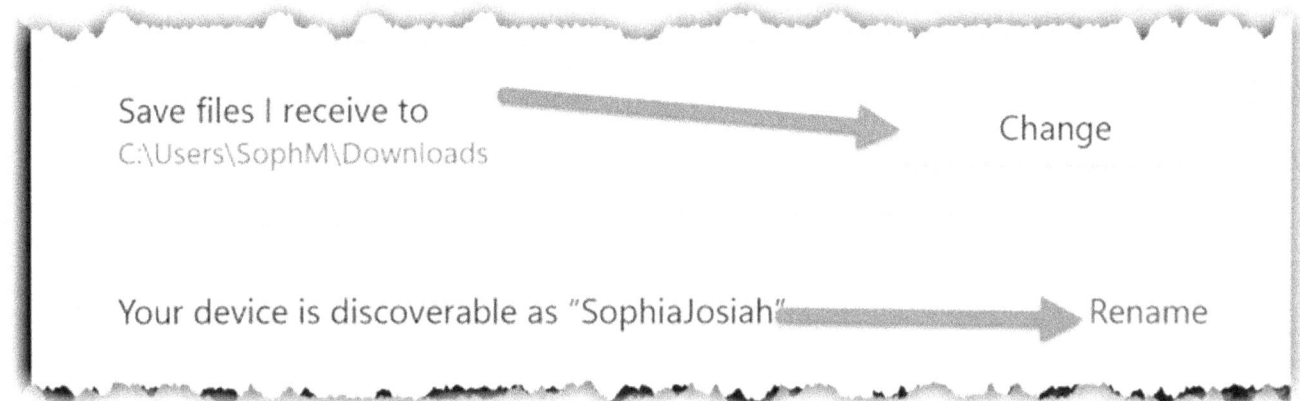

You can also set the folder or location on your computer where the files you want to receive will be stored using the change button.

Audio Volume Control

The volume control is a slider located at the bottom of the quick settings panel.

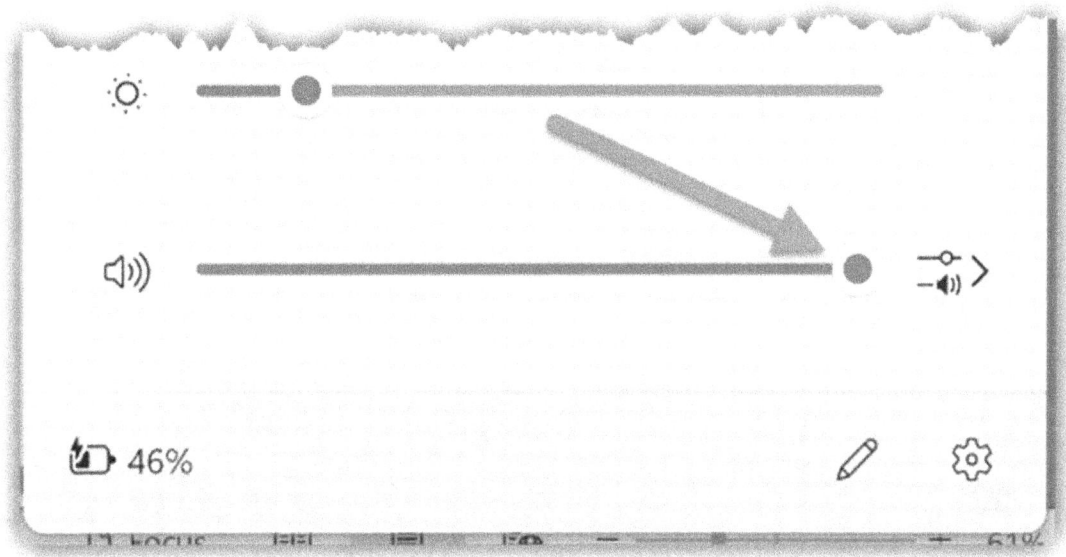

With the volume control slider, you can adjust the sound level of your speakers or headphones.

However, clicking the speaker icon will mute or unmute your computer speakers or headphones connected to your computer.

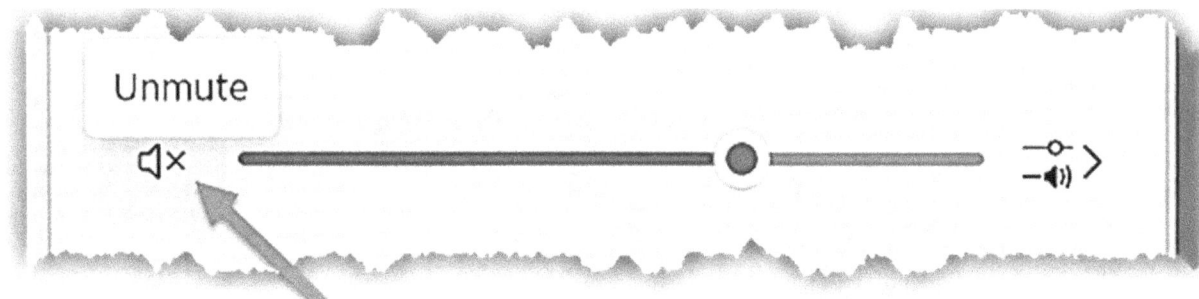

The Volume Mixer

The volume mixer allows you to adjust the sound levels of applications and devices connected to your computer. You can access the volume mixer through the quick settings panel when you click the **Select a sound output** icon.

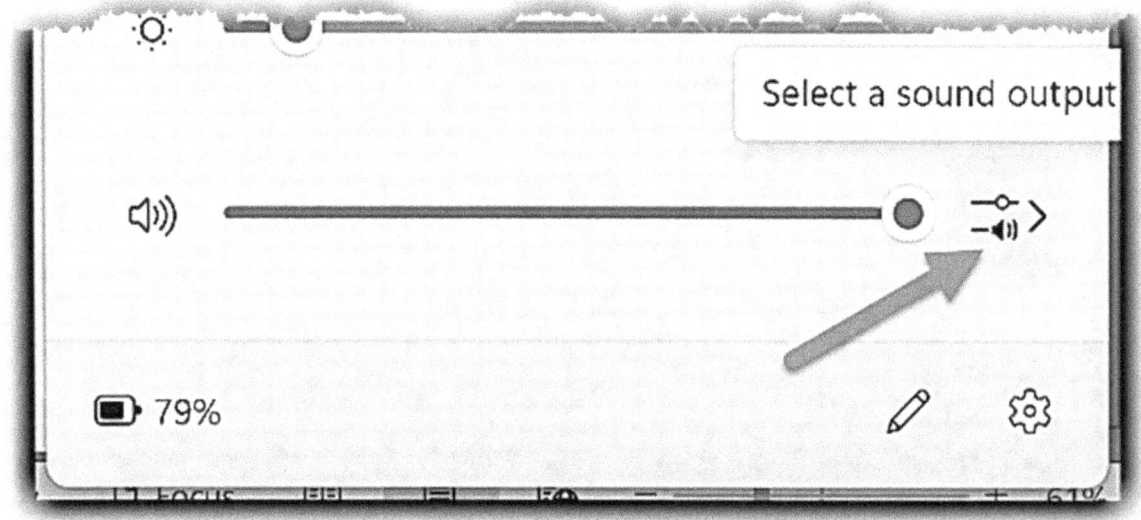

Alternatively, you can right-click the speaker icon in the taskbar and select **Open volume mixer**.

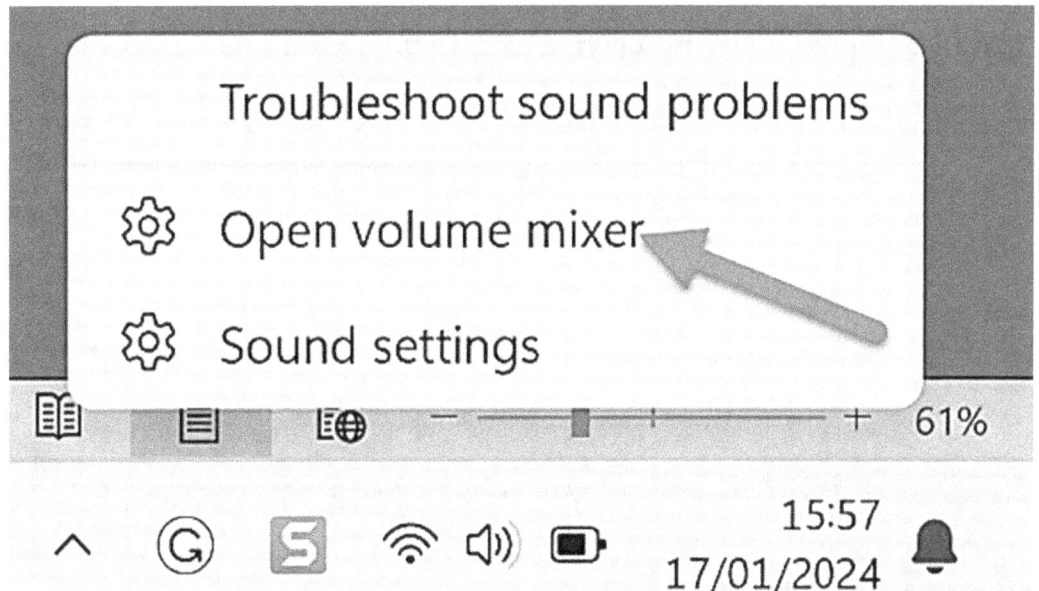

The number of sliders that appear corresponds to the different sound sources on your computer, such as your speakers, microphone, music player, browser, etc.

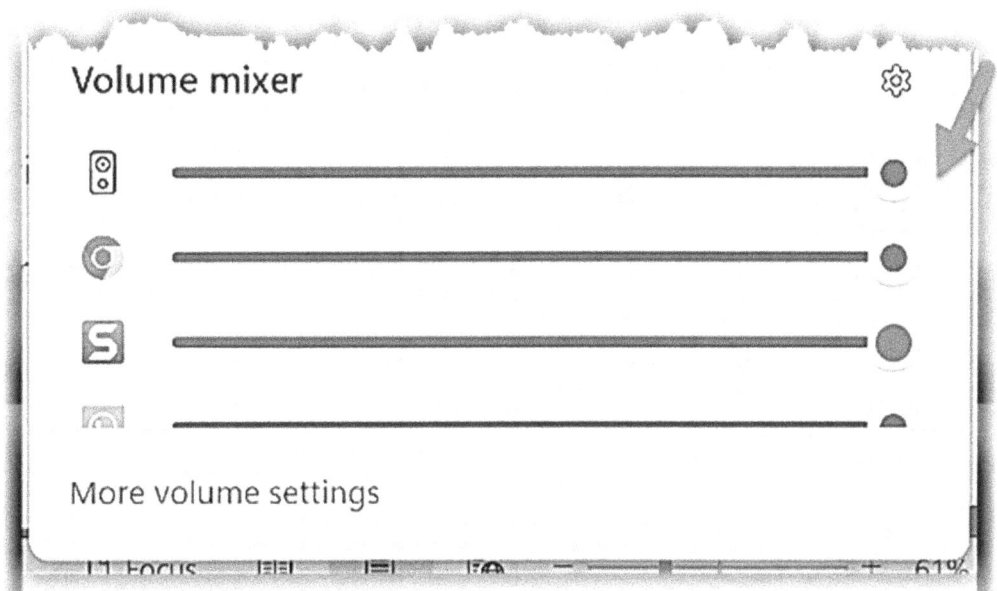

You can drag the sliders toward your left or right to adjust the volume of each source.

To mute the sound from any application, simply click on its icon in the Quick Settings panel. When you want to unmute the app, click the speaker icon directly beneath the application's icon, as shown in the illustration below.

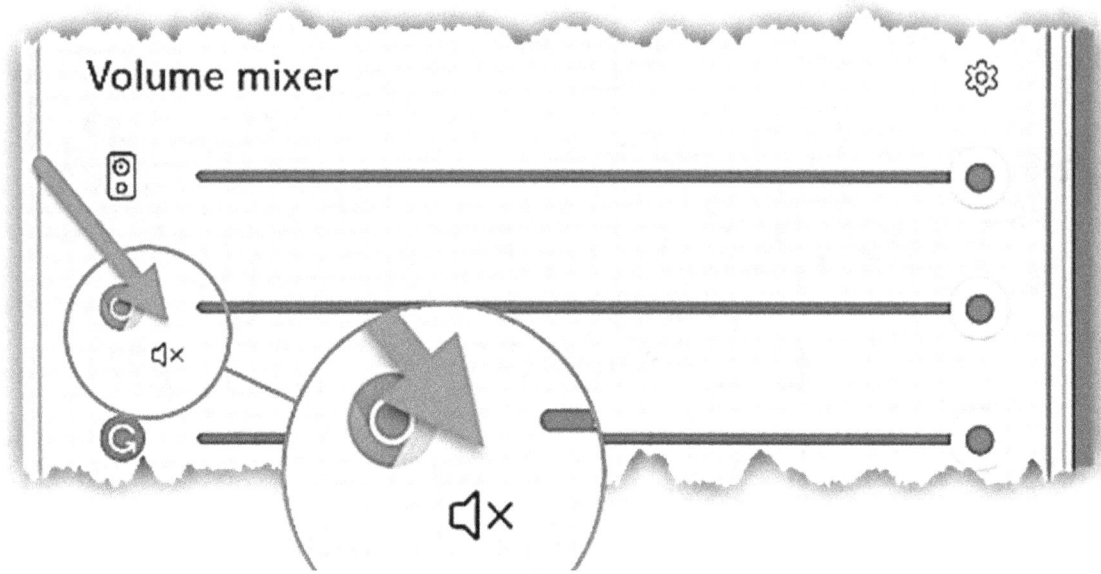

When working with multiple audio applications or devices, the volume mixer will help you balance the sound levels of the different devices.

For example, you can lower the volume of your browser while watching a video and raise the volume of your music player while listening to music.

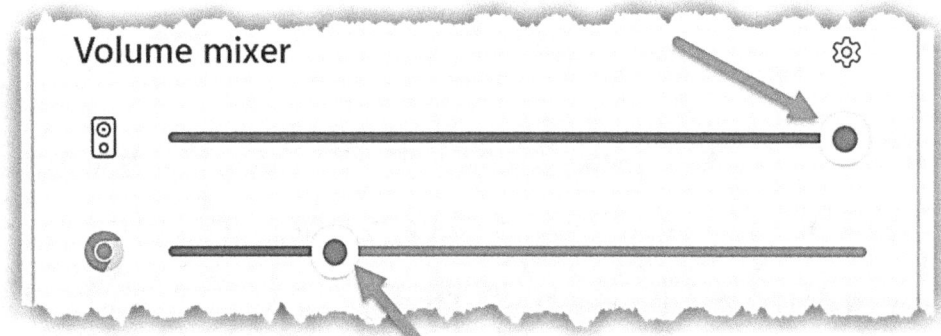

EDITING THE QUICK SETTINGS PANEL

The Quick Settings panel in Windows 11 offers a level of customization. If you want to prioritize your frequently used settings or hide those you rarely touch? Simply click the pencil icon located at the bottom of the panel.

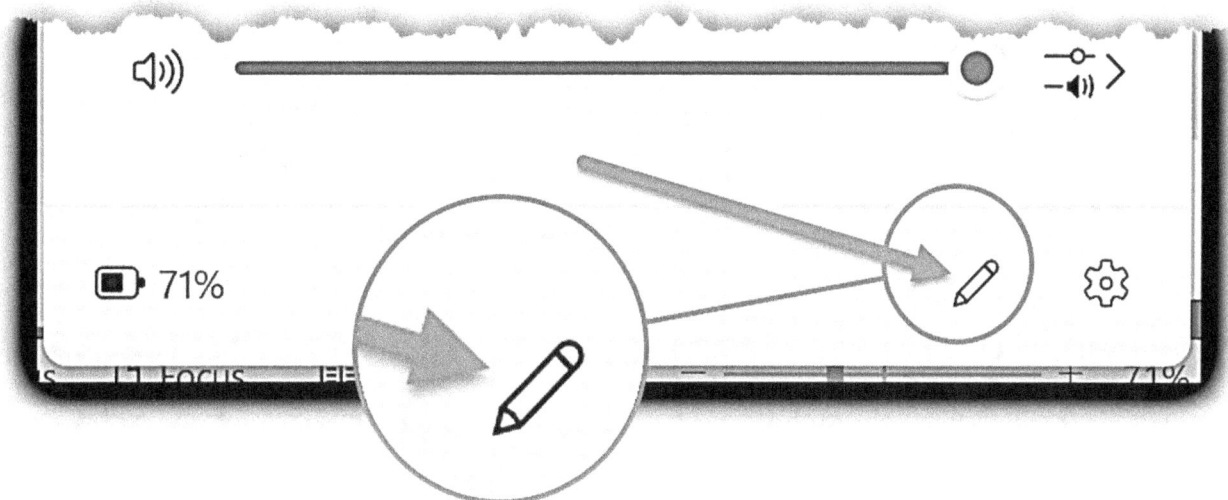

This will make the quick settings panel editable, allowing you to pin or unpin your items.

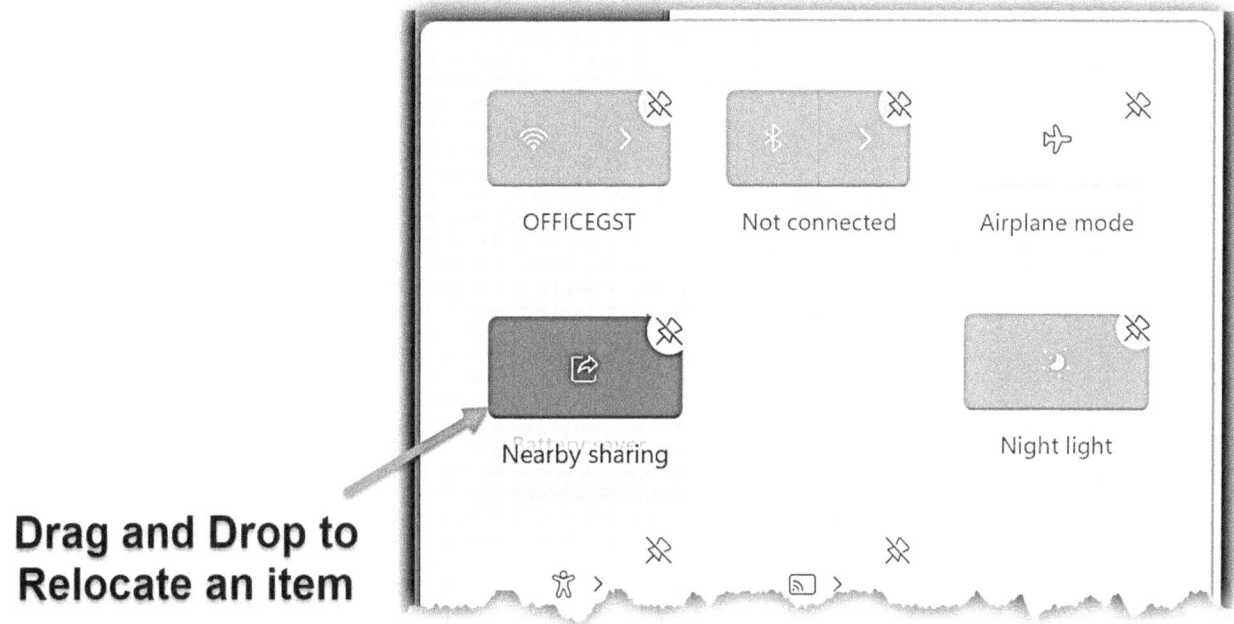

Drag and Drop to Relocate an item

To delete an item from the quick setting panel while in editable mode, click the pin icon for that particular item, as shown in the illustration.

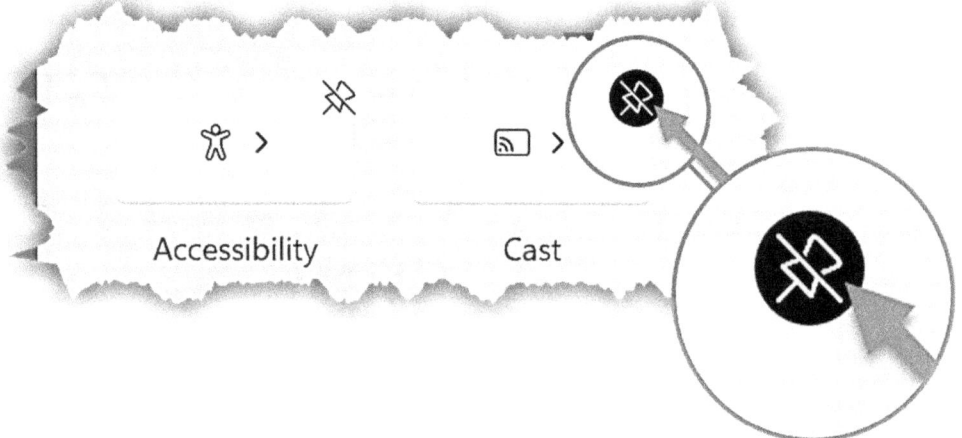

However, to pin an item on the quick settings panel, ensure you are in editable mode, then click the add icon at the bottom of the panel.

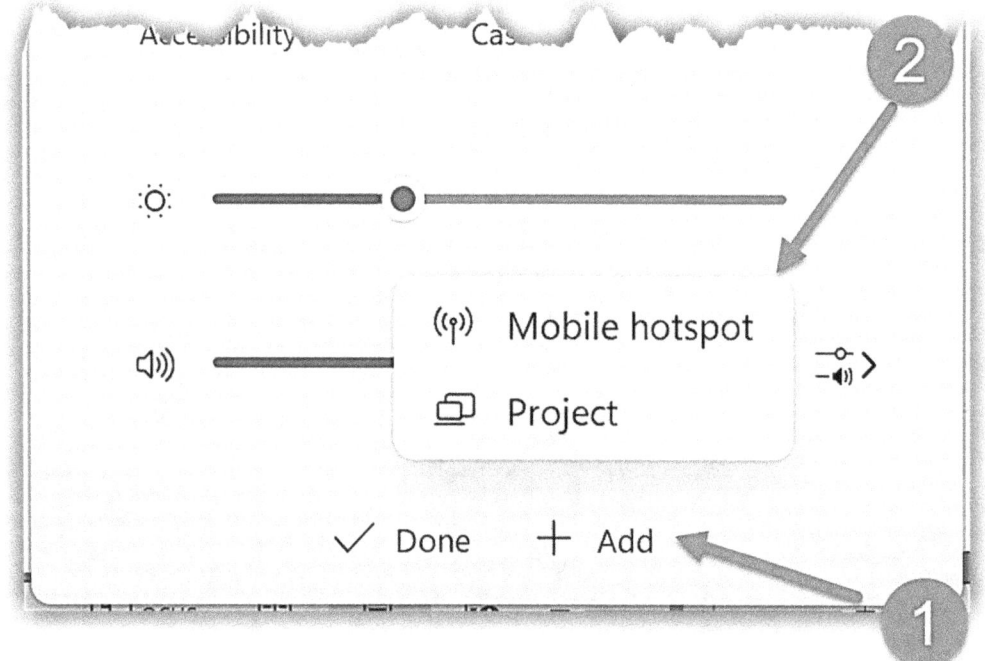

Once you click the add icon, select any item from the menu to make it appear on the panel.

CHAPTER 10

FILE SHARING IN WINDOWS 11

Sharing digital files, like documents, photos, videos, or software, with others or devices over a network is called file sharing.

Windows 11's file-sharing features make sharing your folders and files with other devices connected to the same network easy. This allows you to work on projects with coworkers, send files to loved ones, or access data from any device.

Benefits of File Sharing:

- **Collaboration**: You and others can collaborate on real-time projects regardless of location.

- **Accessibility**: You can access your files from any device to which you can access the internet.

- **Storage Efficiency**: When using multiple devices, duplicate files are avoided.

- **Resource Sharing**: You can also share additional devices linked to your network, such as printers and scanners.

Choosing the Right Sharing Method

Windows 11 provides several options for the sharing of files, each of which has its own set of benefits and drawbacks:

- **Local Network Sharing:** Ideally suited for sharing inside a network at home or in the workplace. Although it is simple to set up, you must link all the devices to the same network.

- **Cloud Storage:** You can share files with other users using online services such as OneDrive or Google Drive. Not only is it accessible from any device, but it may also require internet connectivity, and storage constraints exist.

- **Remote Desktop Connection:** This allows you to access your entire computer remotely, including your files. Even if it is secured, additional settings and technical knowledge are nonetheless required.

- **FTP Server:** This is a specialized software that creates internet-accessible to public servers. Users with usernames and passwords can download server files. This method is handy for sending huge files that are difficult to email or store.

Security Considerations for File Sharing

File sharing can expose your computer or files to potential security issues. Before you share, consider the following:

- **Who do you want to share with**?: You should only share with people or groups that you can trust.

- **What are you going to share?:** If it is not absolutely required, do not disclose any sensitive information.

- **Which access level are you granting to the user**?: To meet your needs, select between read-only or read-and-write rights.

- **Password protection:** You can add an extra layer of safety by enabling password protection.

- **Antivirus and Firewall:** Protecting your system against malicious software and unauthorized access should be your priority.

FILE AND PRINTER SHARING

In Windows 11, you must first activate the "Network Discovery and File Sharing" option to share files and folders on a personal computer with other computers or devices connected to the same network.

Your computer can see other computers and devices on the same network if the "Network Discovery" setting is activated. Other computers on the same network can also see your computer if they are in the same workgroup.

What is a Workgroup

A "workgroup" is a collection of computers connected to the same network. Computers in the same workgroup can easily communicate with each other.

Sharing resources like folders or printers is more manageable when communicating with other computers without restrictions. You will fully understand these basic ideas as we go through the details of Windows 11 networking in this chapter.

How to Check Your Computer Workgroup

By default, your computer is in a workgroup labeled "WORKGROUP," making it easier to set up a network because you don't have to do any complicated configurations.

So, we will be looking at some of the steps you can take to check your device workgroup details:

Follow these steps to examine your device workgroup profile:

1. Click the Start menu on the taskbar.

2. Type "**Settings**" into the search bar.

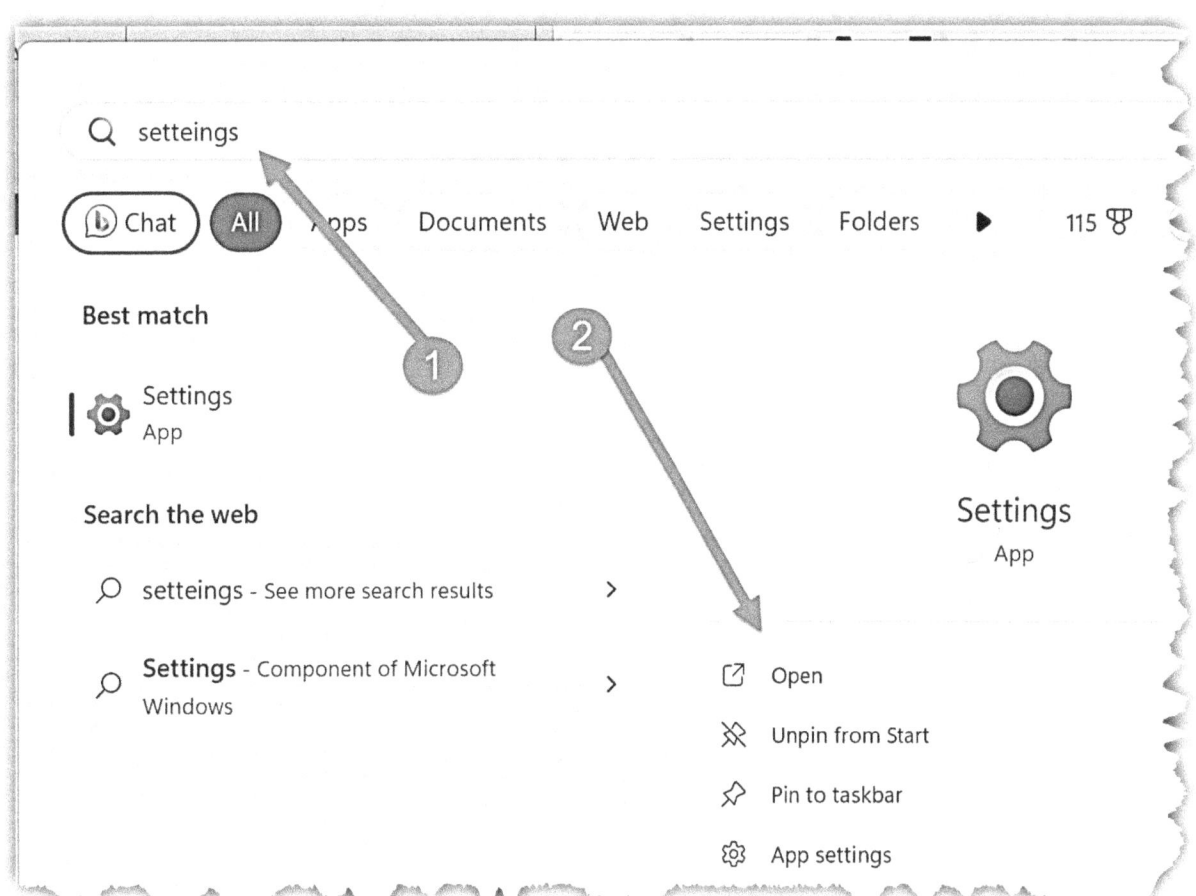

3. Click on Open to continue.

4. In the Systems window, click the search bar and enter "**ABOUT**." When done, click the enter button on your keyboard.

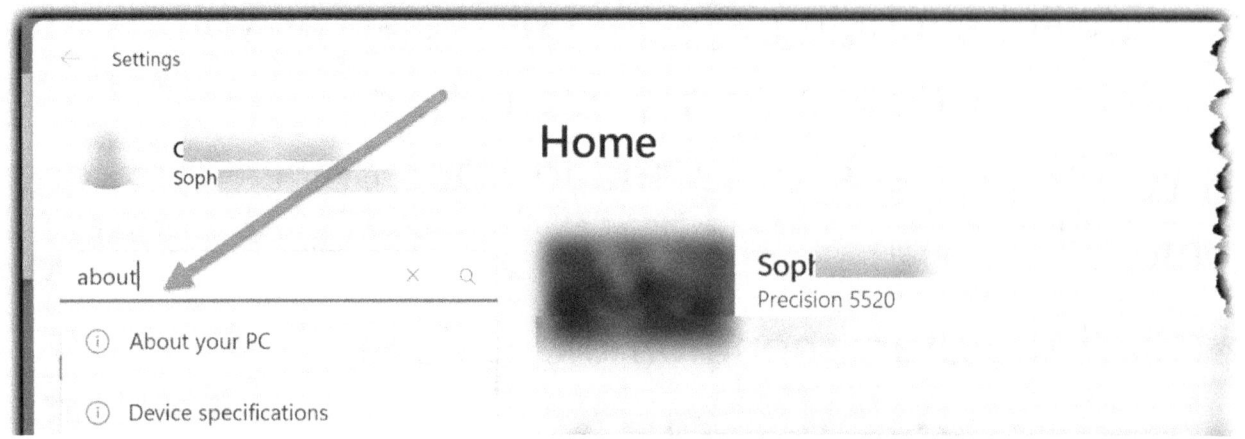

5. Click on **Doman or Workgroup,** as illustrated below.

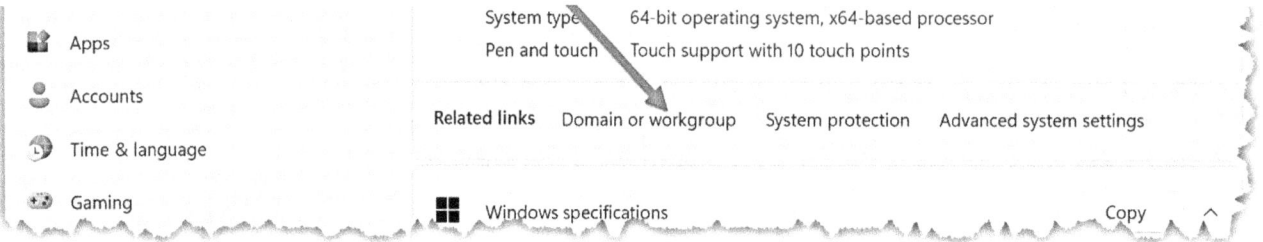

Immediately, your system properties window will pop up.

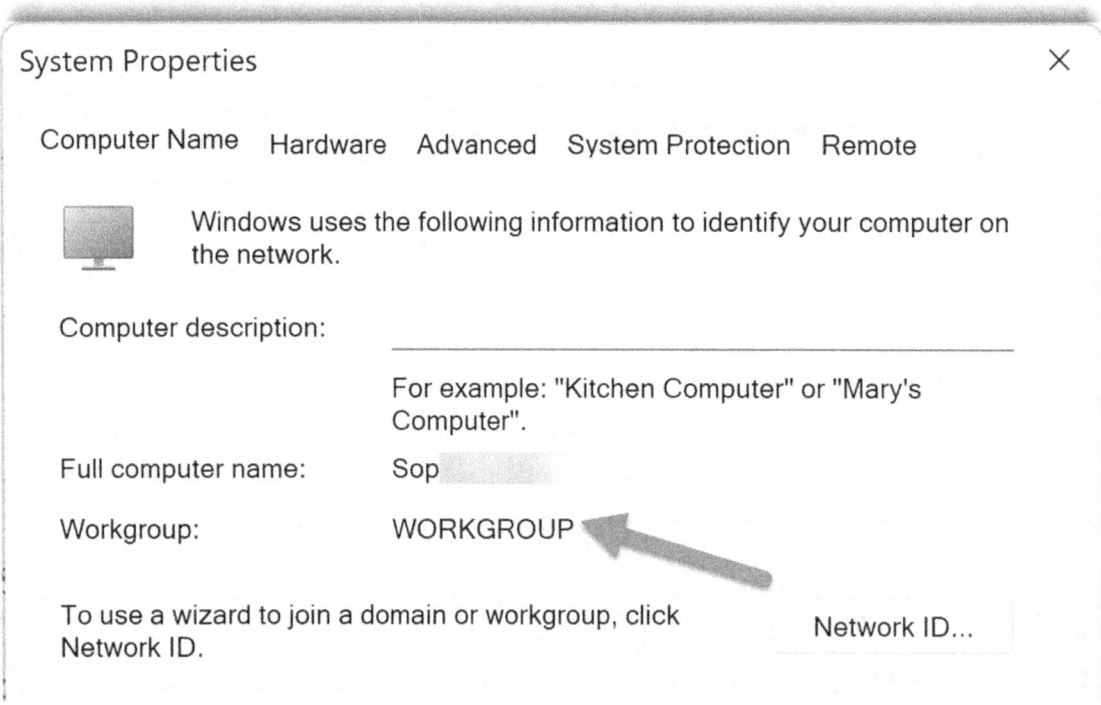

How to Check Your Computer Name

The name of your computer helps other system users identify you on a network, which allows sharing files and printing. Here are three easy ways to do it:

1. Using the Settings app:

Proceed to the Settings menu by clicking the Start button (the Windows logo) and then the gear icon.

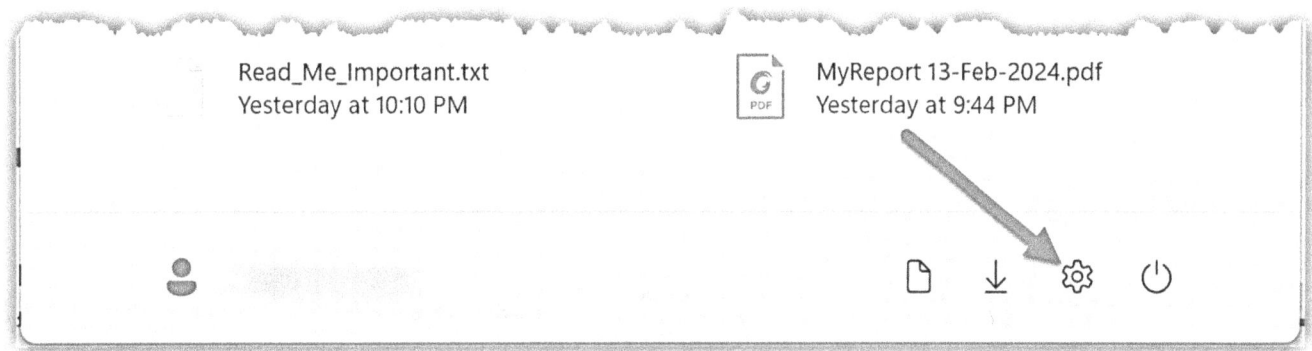

On the windows that appear, choose **System**, then scroll down and click **About**.

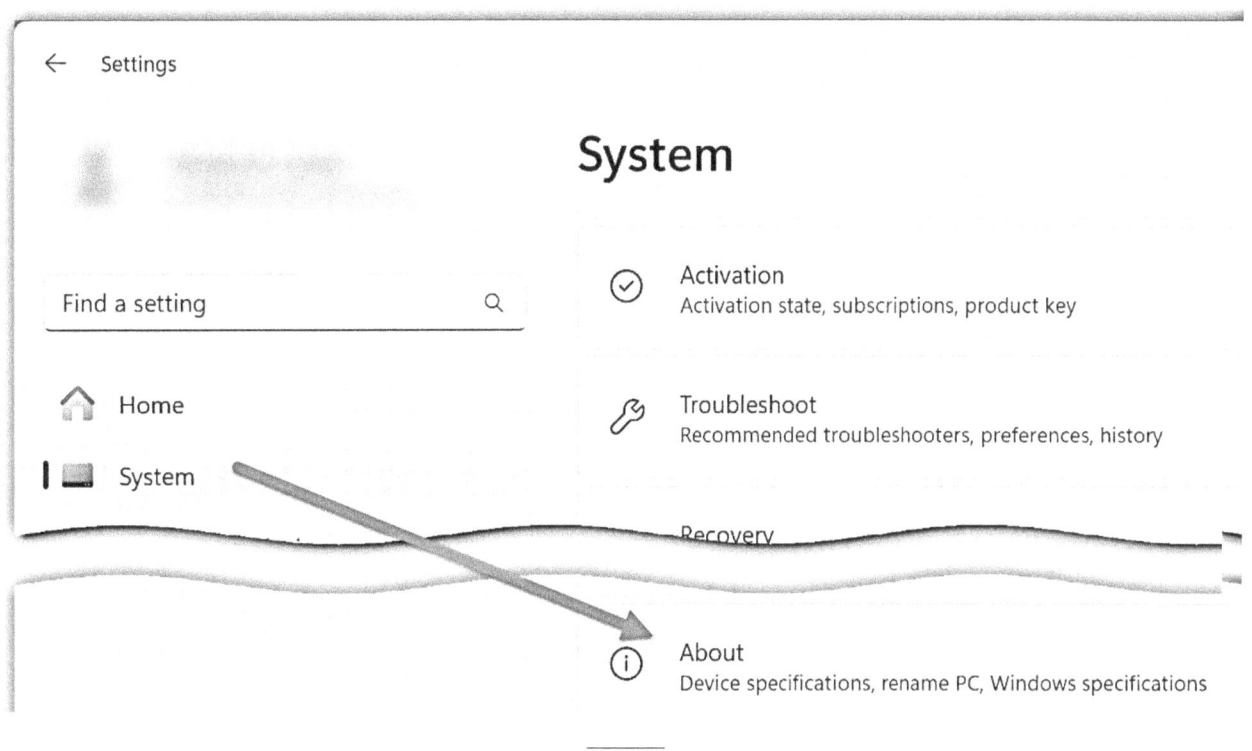

You will see your computer name next to the **Device name**.

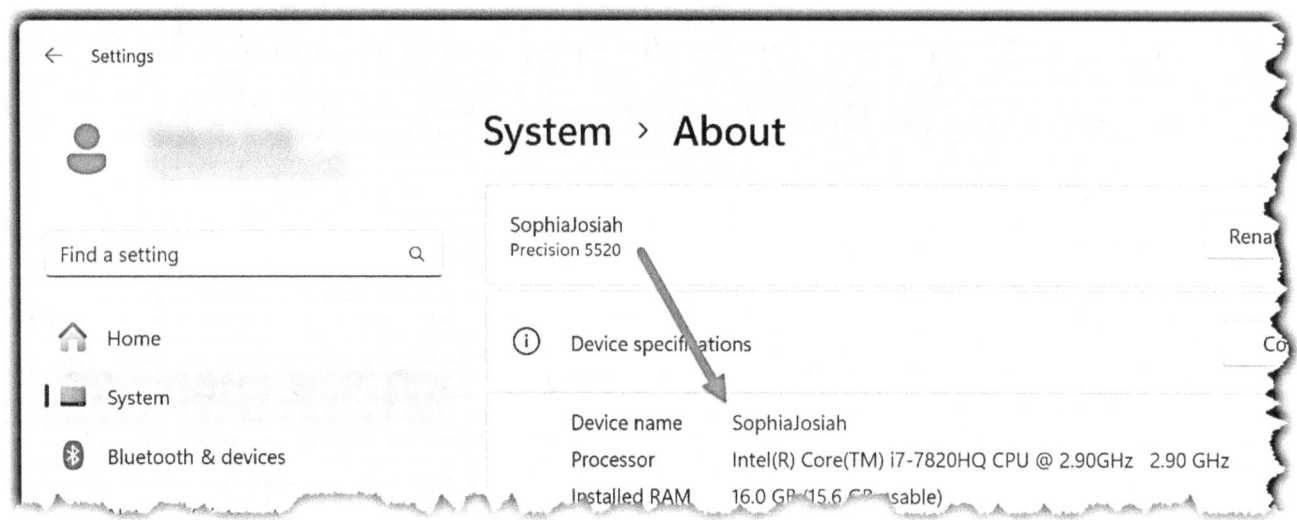

2. Using the Search bar:

Click the start menu, type "**About your PC**" in the search bar, and press Enter.

When you click on the option that comes up, the name of your computer will show up next to the device's name.

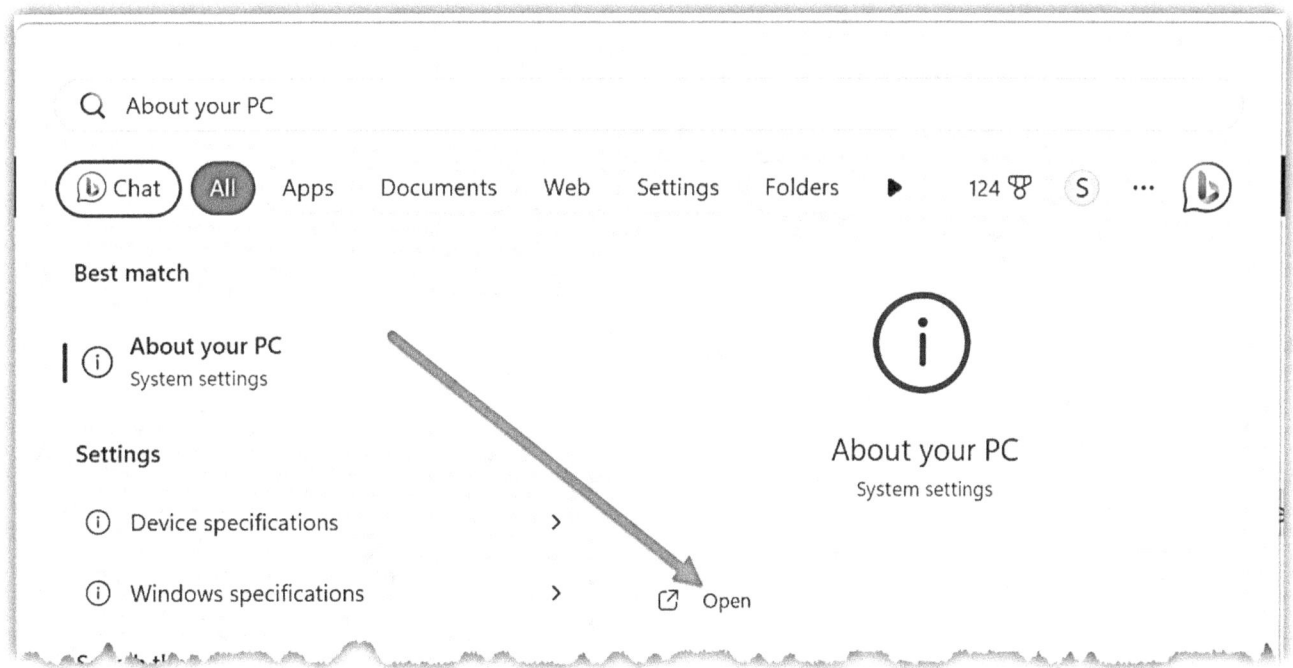

3. Using the Run command:

Press the **Windows key** and **R** simultaneously to open the Run dialog.

Type "**cmd**" and press Enter.

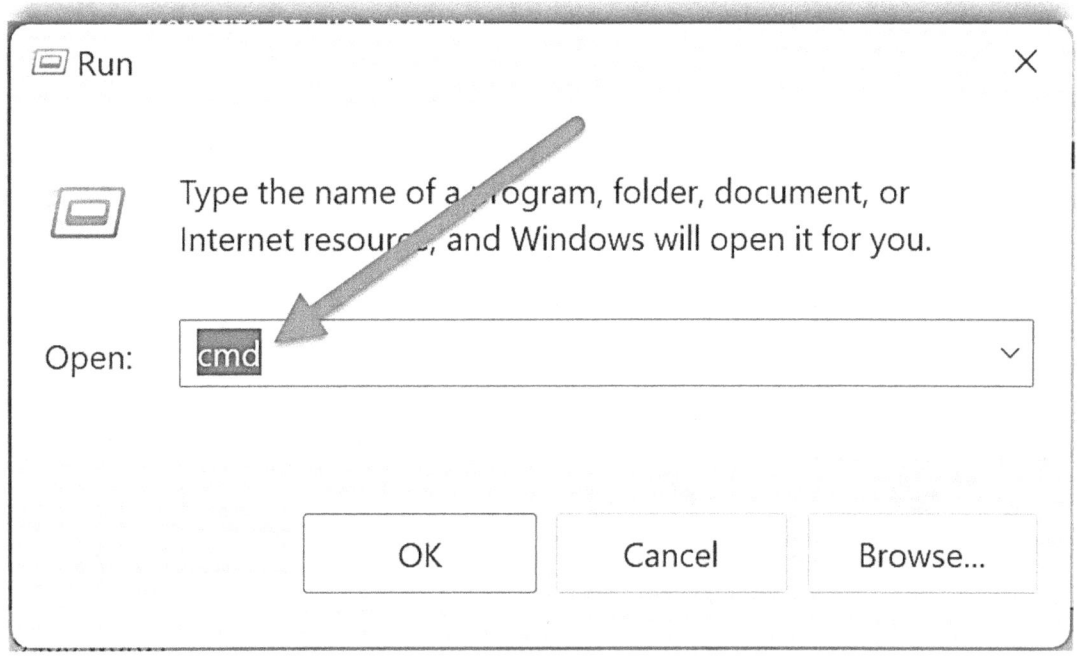

Next, type "**hostname**" in the command window and press Enter.

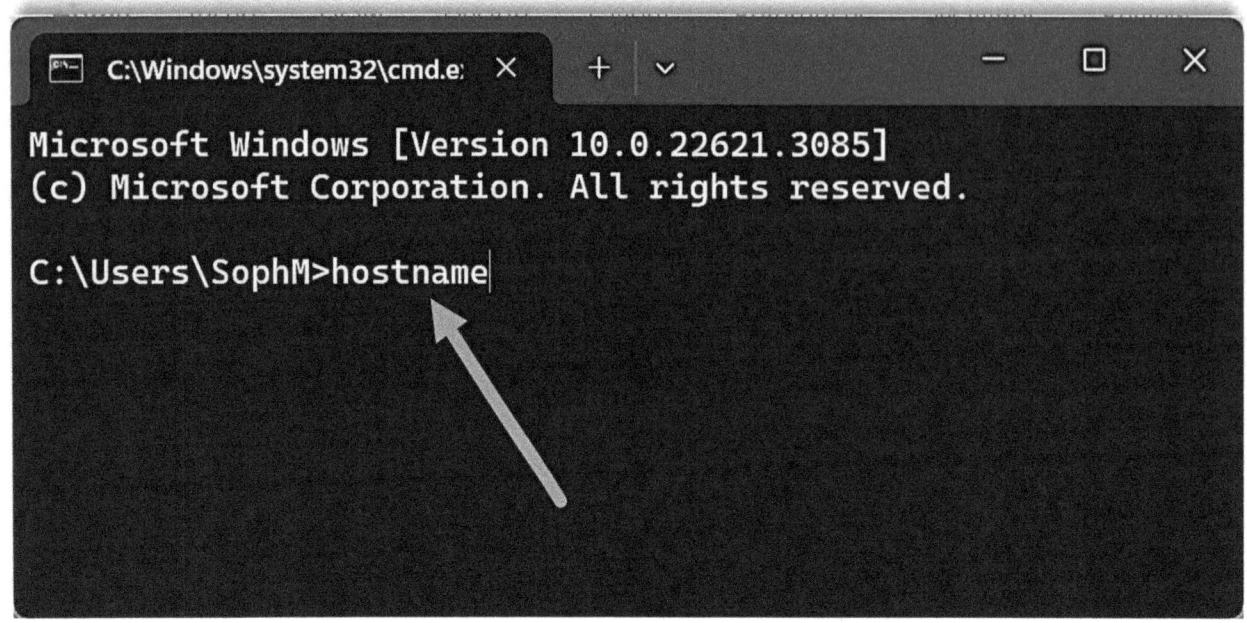

Your **computer name** will appear instantly.

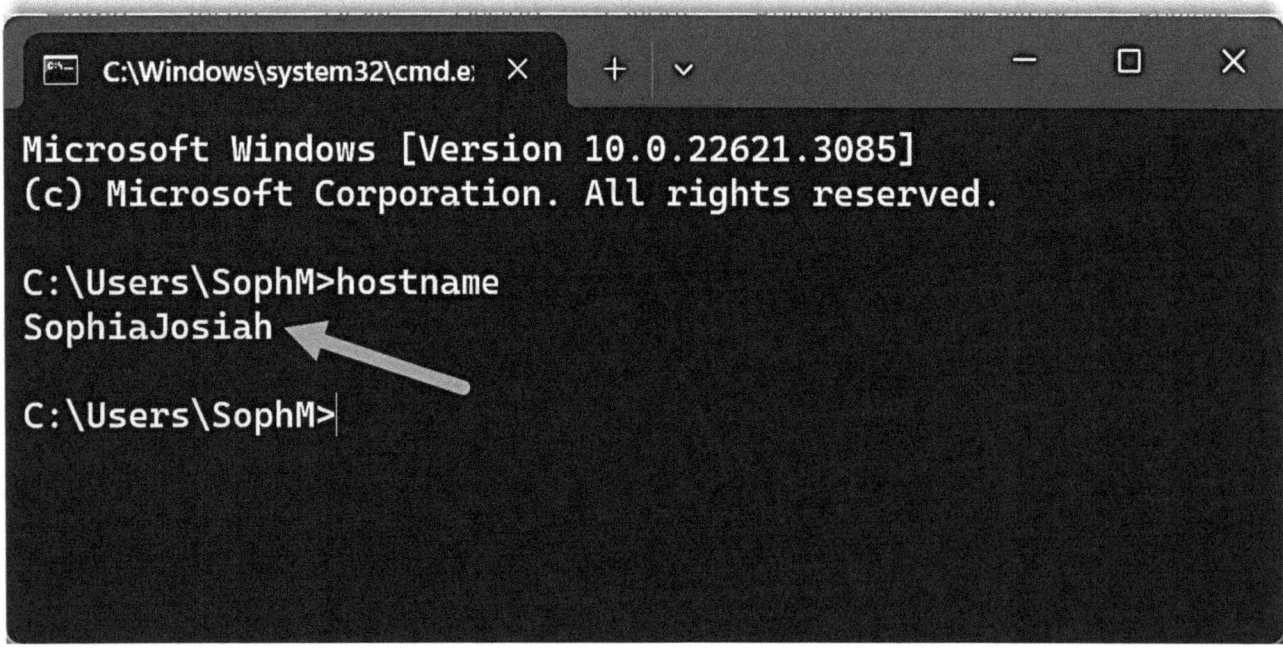

How to Change the Name of Your Computer

Altering the name of your computer is another option if you do not like the one set by default.

Repeat the procedures in the Settings app, and then select "**Rename this PC**" from the menu that appears.

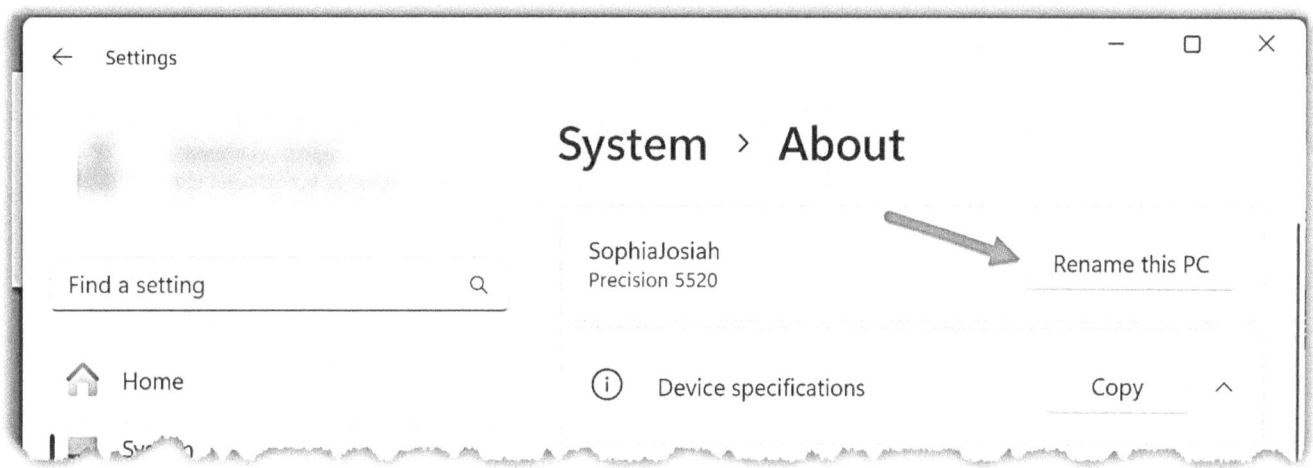

Enter the new name and then click the **Next** button.

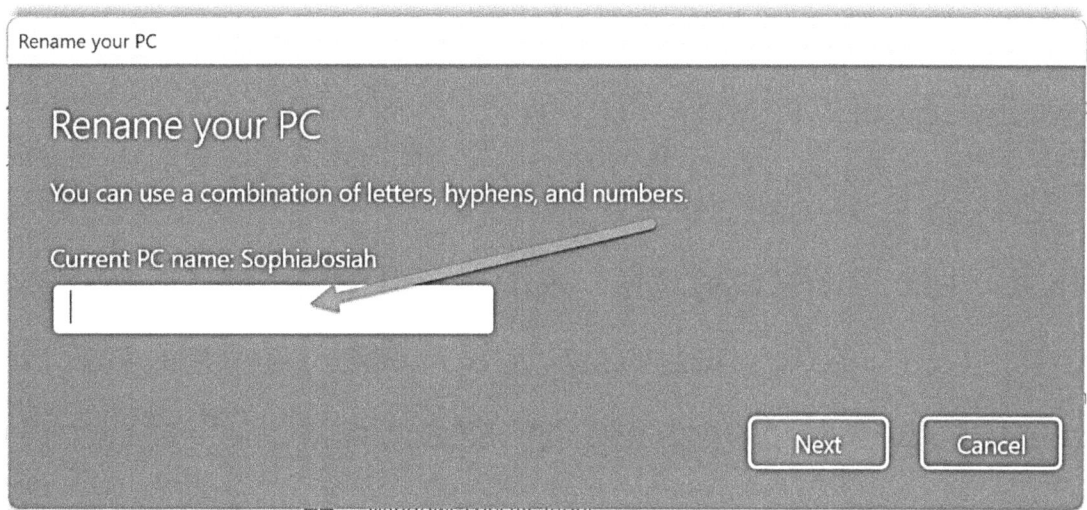

Follow the window instructions to complete the process.

How to Activate Files and Printers Sharing

Sharing files and printers is also like teaching your computer how to get along with other people. By turning this option on, your computer can be seen by other devices on your network. This lets you share files and printers.

How to activate it:

1. Go to the Start menu and look for "**Control Panel**." Alternatively, use the search bar to look for it.

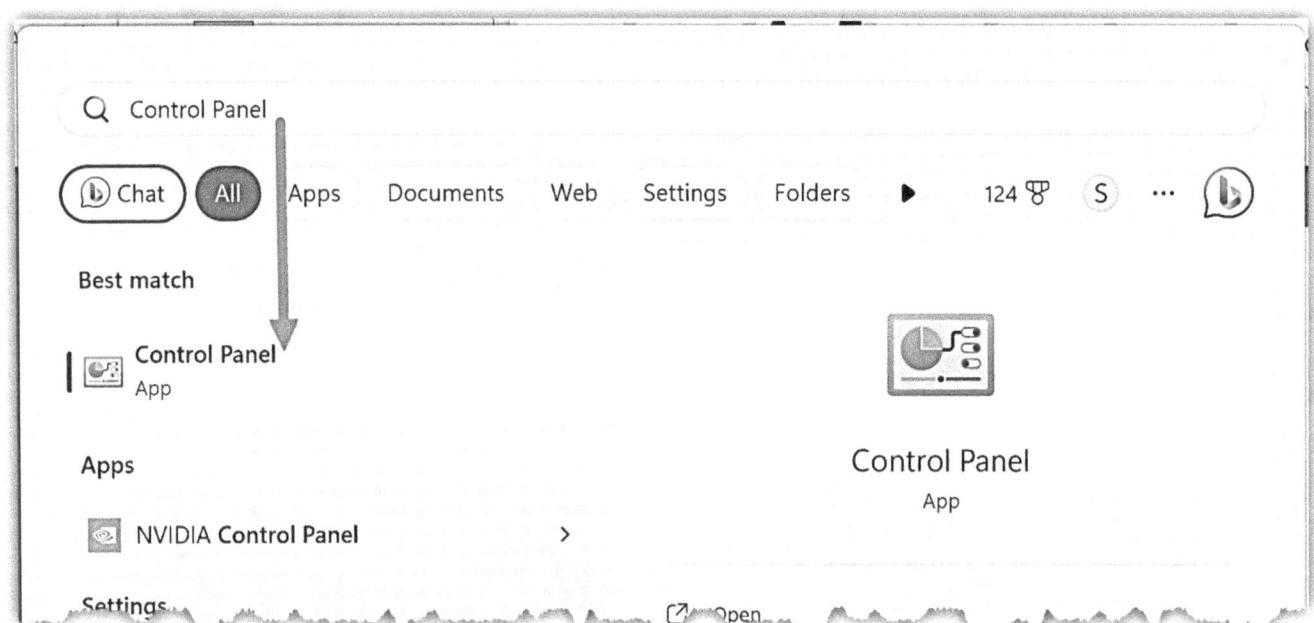

2. Click on "**Network and Sharing Center**" to continue. Alternatively, use the search bar in the control panel window to search for "Network and Sharing Center".

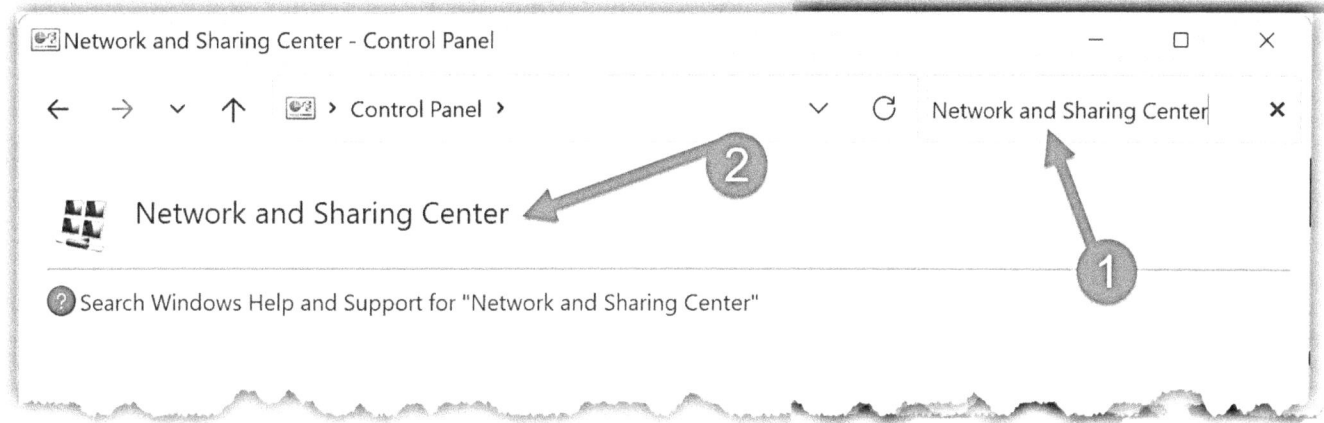

3. Select "**Change advanced sharing settings**" from the list on the left.

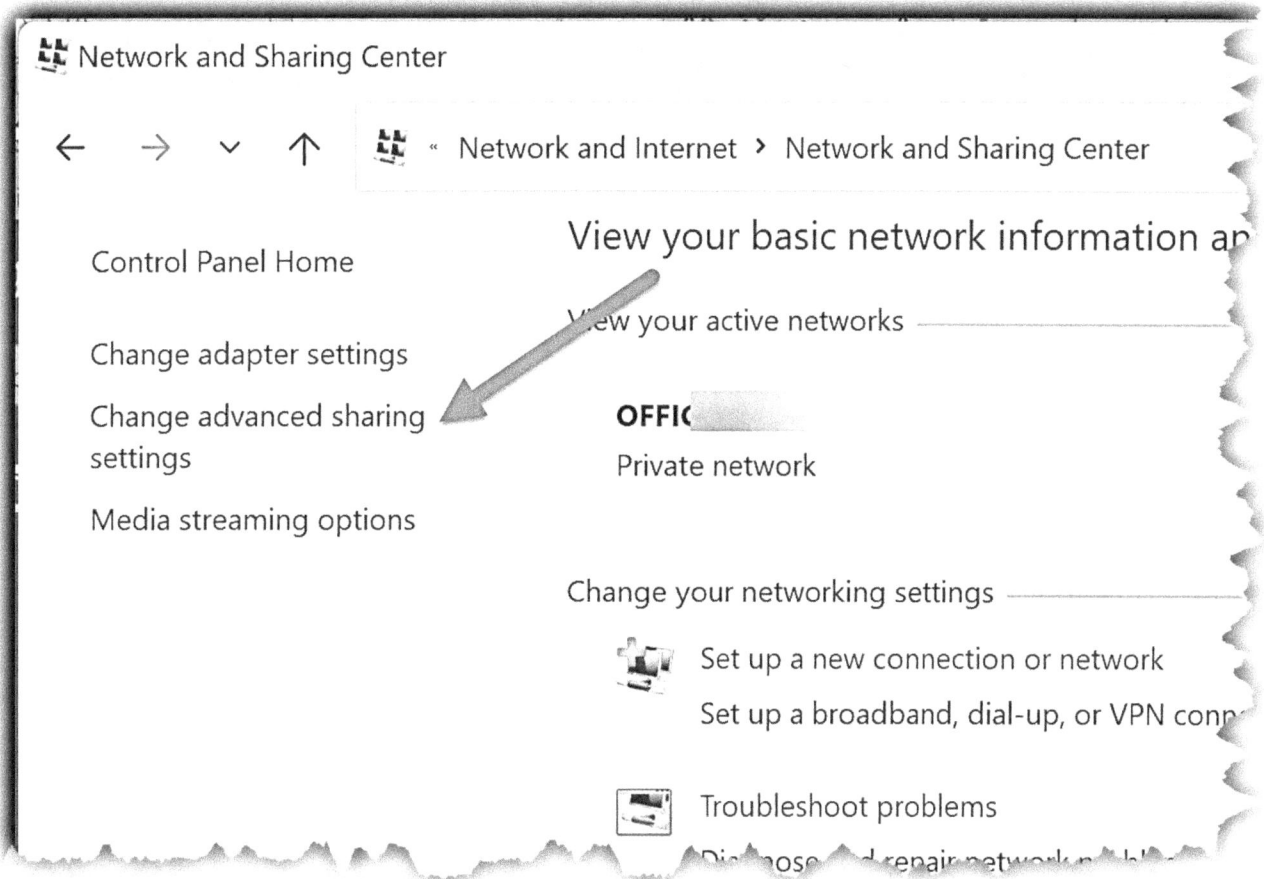

4. Make sure "**Network discovery**" and "**File and Printer sharing**" are enabled under the "**Private network**," tab, which is best for home networks.

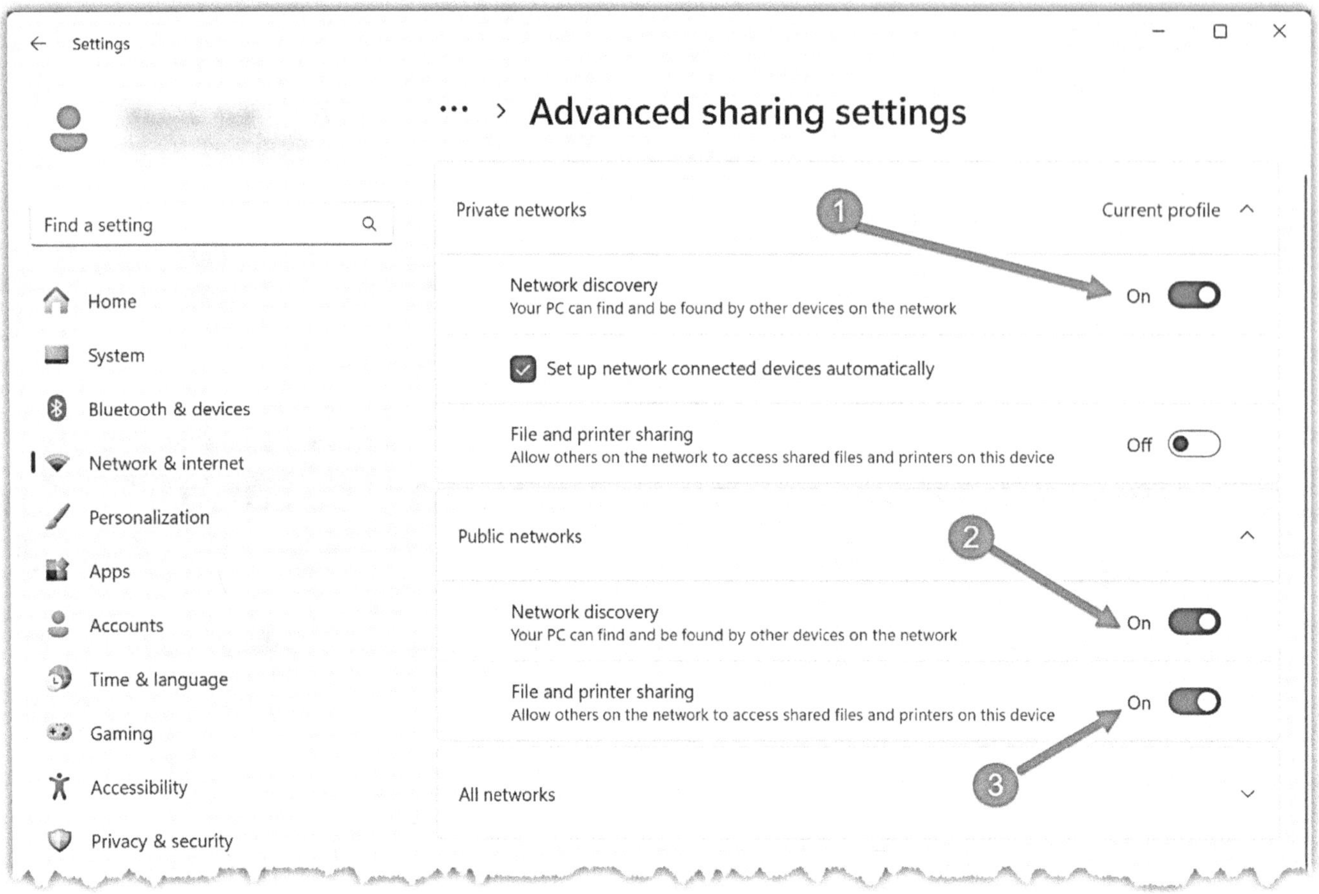

[Screenshot of Windows Settings showing Advanced sharing settings with Private networks (1), Public networks (2), and File and printer sharing toggle (3).]

HOW TO SHARE YOUR FILES

You can search for the file using the search box in the Start menu or go to the file explorer to locate the file you want to share. Click the file to highlight it.

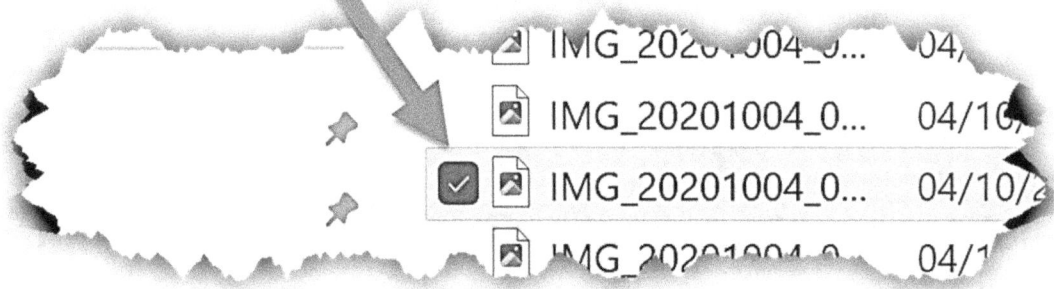

To share more than one file, click on each one separately while holding down the "Ctrl" key.

214

To choose everything in between, you can also click the first file, hold down "**Shift**," and then click the last file in the group.

Next, you right-click and select **Share** from the menu.

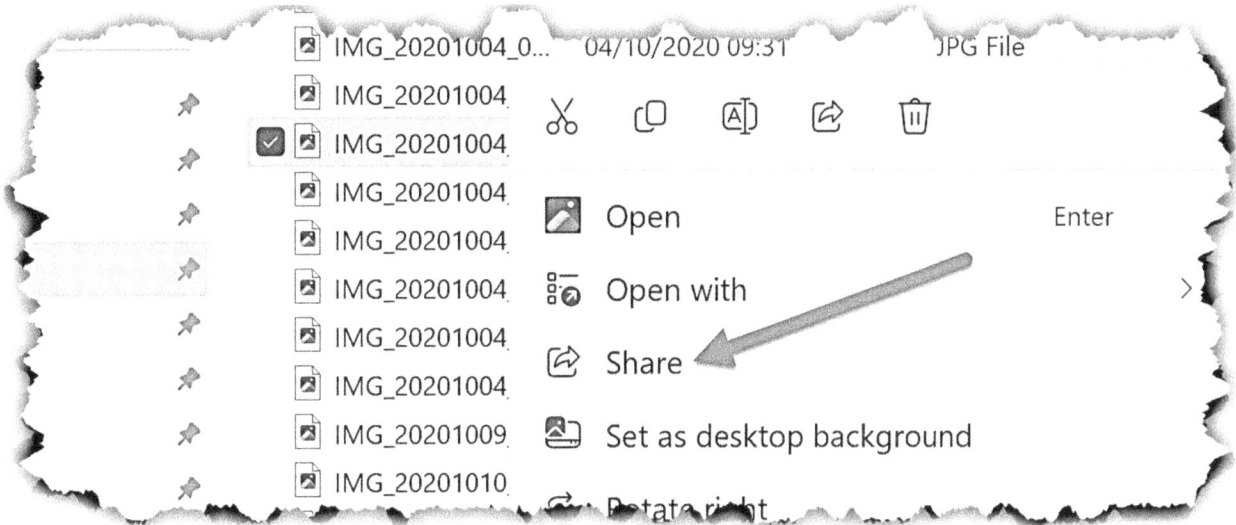

Alternatively, click the **share** button on the toolbar once the file(s) is selected, as illustrated below.

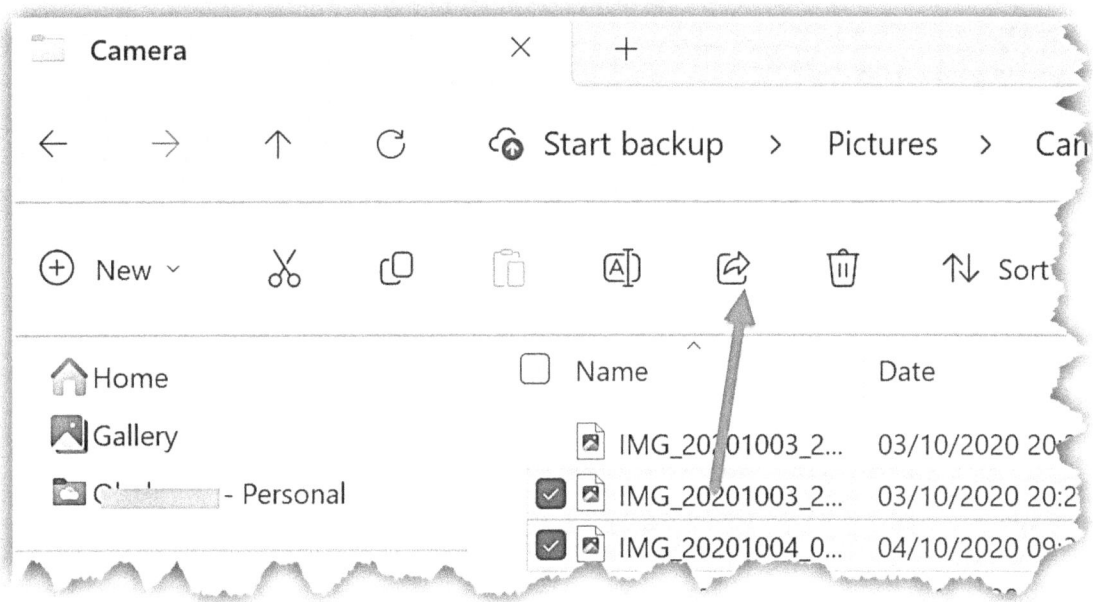

Determining the Destination of the Files

Once you click the share button, Windows 11 will present you with a list of alternatives. The email option allows you to attach your files to an email for quick delivery.

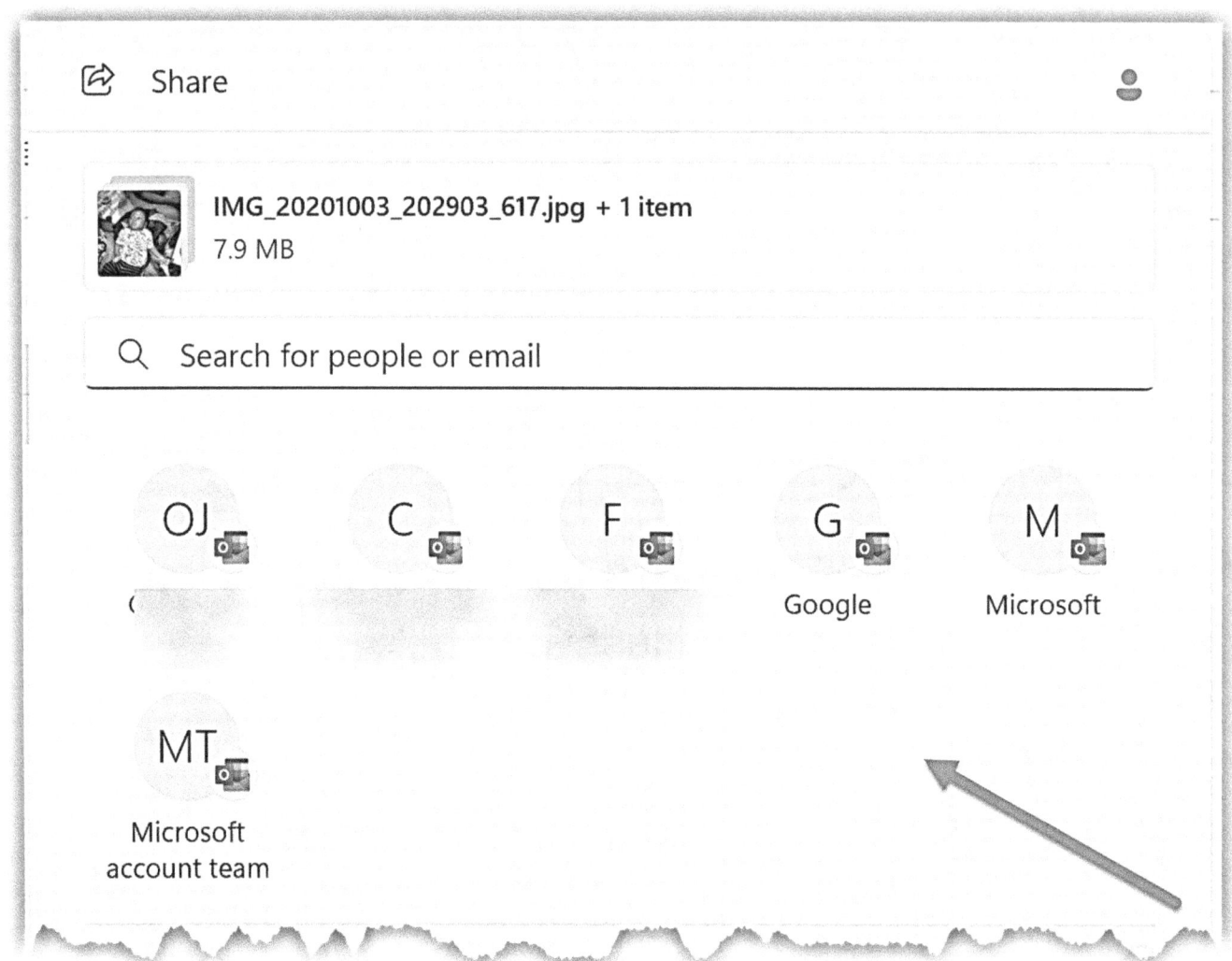

- **Social Media**: This option allows you to share your creations instantly on platforms like Facebook or Twitter.

- **Nearby Share:** You can share your files with a nearby device using a wireless connection.

NEARBY FILE SHARING

The Nearby Share feature in Windows 11 allows you to quickly share your files and folders to nearby devices using Bluetooth or Wi-Fi without requiring an internet connection or additional storage devices.

Nevertheless, you must activate the Nearby Share feature on your computer and that of the device receiving the data, which is within proximity (around 10 meters).

You can activate it by going to **Settings** > clicking on **System** > then scrolling down and selecting **Nearby Sharing**.

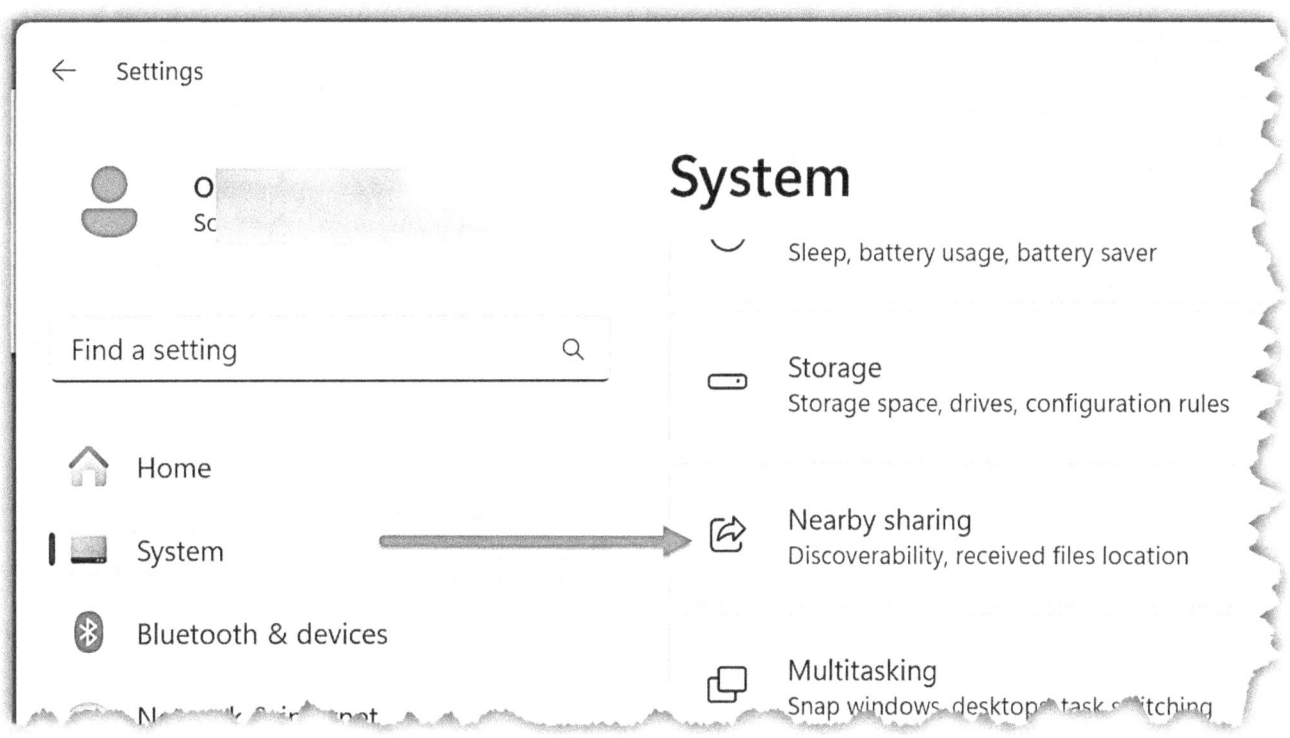

Next, you select the options available that suit your needs.

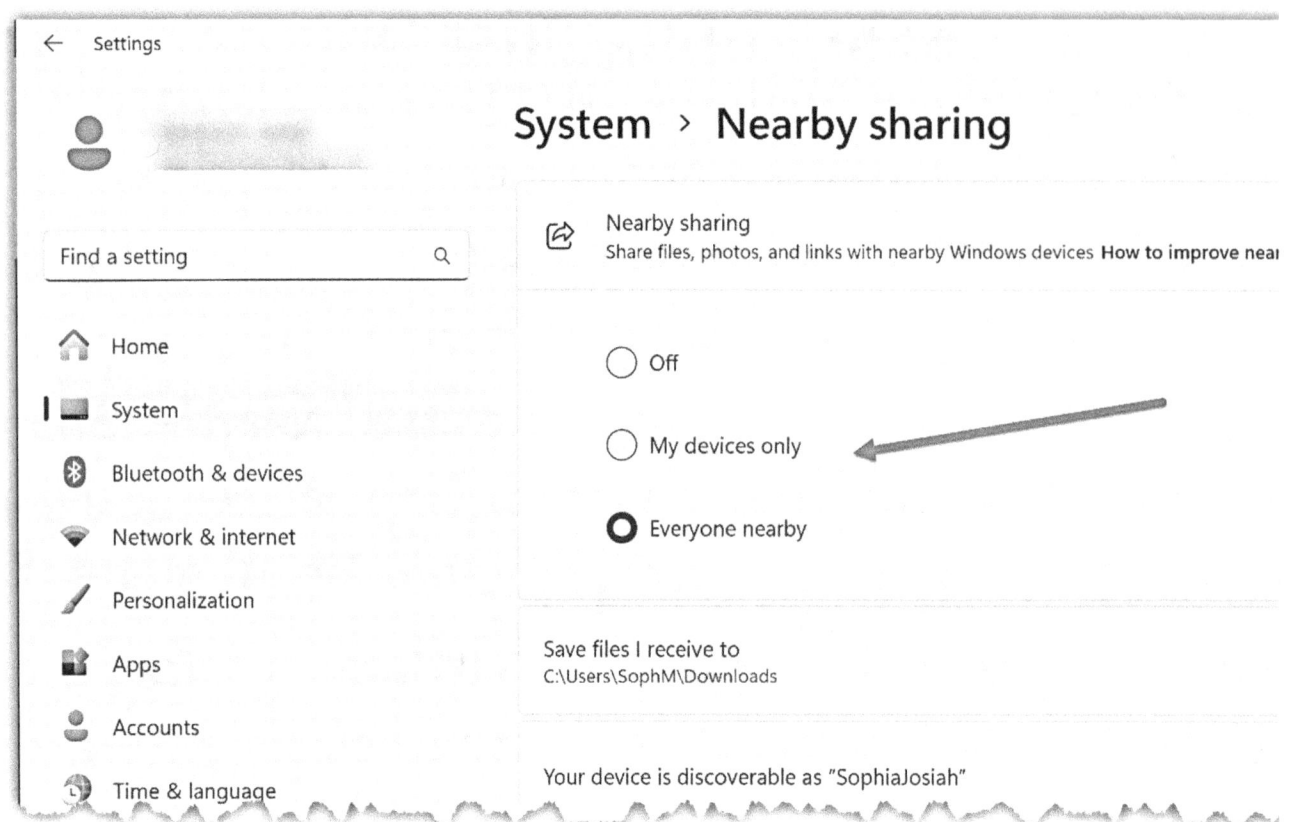

My devices only — This option limits your computer to sending and receiving data with other Microsoft-linked devices.

Everyone nearby — This feature enables you to send and receive files from any device close to you.

All your transfers are saved In your "Downloads " folder by default.

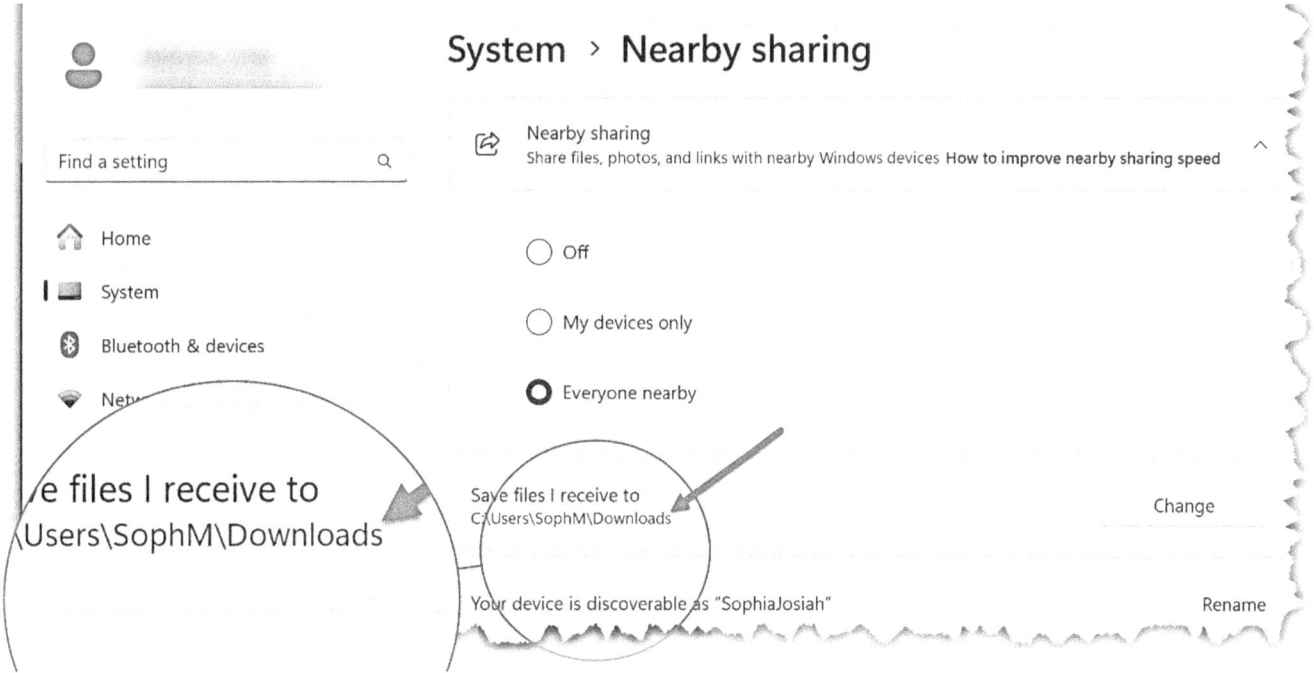

Click the **Change** button to use a different folder on your computer to save the files you receive.

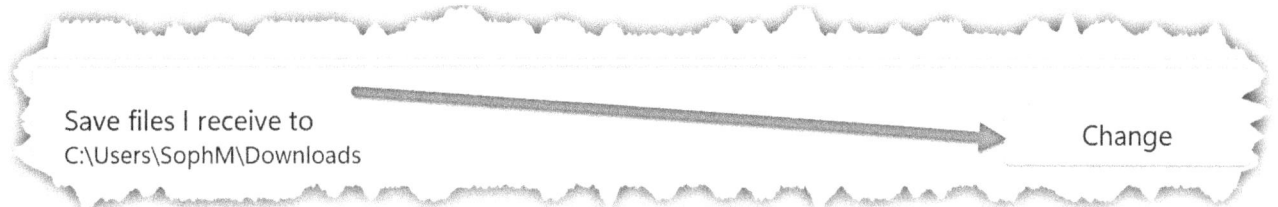

When the nearby sharing feature is activated, its button on the quick action panel will be highlighted.

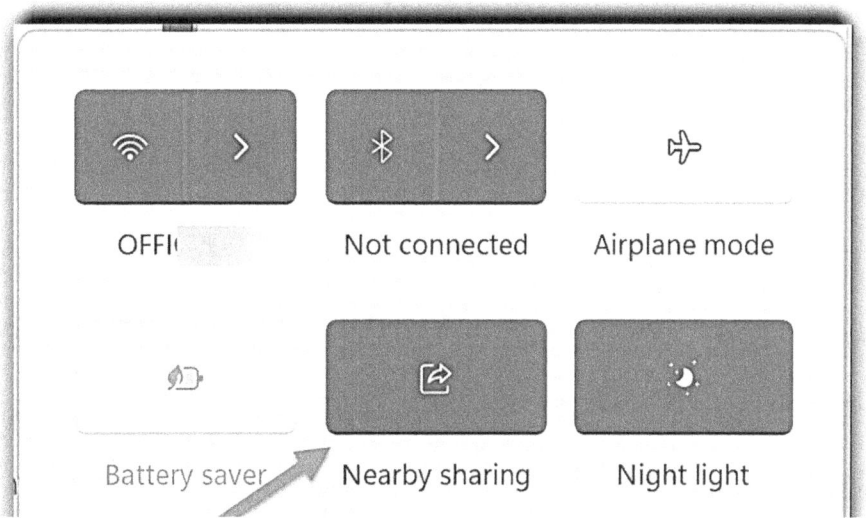

How to Use Nareby Share

- Ensure both your device and the device that is receiving the data have the Nearby Share feature activated.

- Navigate through your files and select the one that you wish to share.

- You can either use the "**Share**" button in File Explorer or right-click the file and select "**Share**."

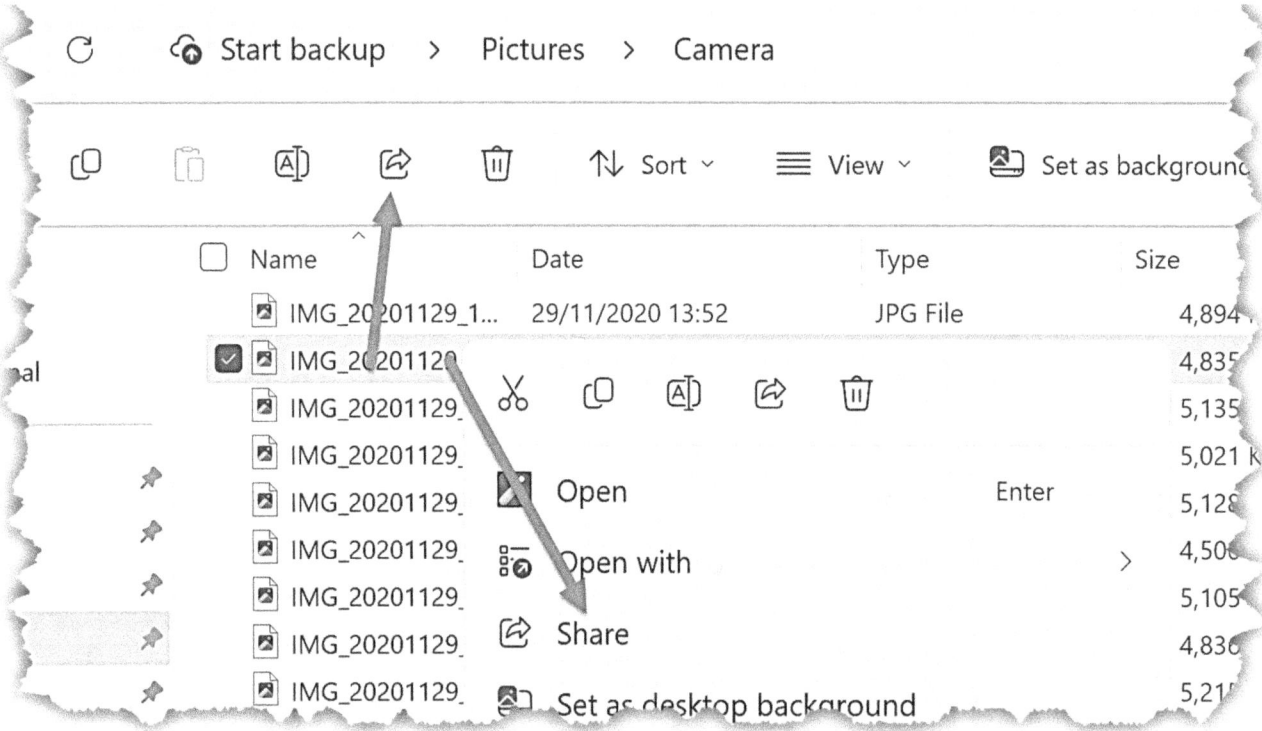

Your computer will automatically detect any nearby devices with the feature enabled. Choose the recipient you want to share from the window that pops out. The file will be transferred through Bluetooth or Wi-Fi, depending on the best available connection.

The receiving device will get a notification about the incoming file. So, the user on the other end will have to accept the transfer, and the file will be saved in the Downloads folder by default.

ONEDRIVE FILE SHARING

With information and files snowballing, it can be challenging to keep track of everything. While things like hard drives and USB sticks have been helpful, they have their downsides. They can get lost or damaged easily, and it's not always easy to access them when you need to.

Imagine having a secure vault that you can reach from anywhere in the world using any device you have. That's pretty much what cloud storage offers. Your data is stored on servers far away and can be accessed as long as your computer is connected to the internet.

Here are some of the benefits:

- **Accessibility**: Any internet device, laptop, phone, or tablet can access your data. This eliminates the risk of file loss and large hard drives.

- **Collaboration:** You can share files and folders with your coworkers, friends, or family members so that everyone can work on them together simultaneously. This means you can edit and collaborate on documents in real time, making teamwork more accessible.

- **Backup and Recovery:** When you use cloud storage, your data is automatically copied and saved in a secure place online. This means that even if someone hacks into your computer or device, your important files are still safe and accessible.

- **Scalability:** You can quickly get more storage space with just a few clicks by upgrading your plan. This means you don't have to worry about managing many different drives or running out of storage space on your devices.

- **Security:** Microsoft's cloud service keeps your data safe and is often even stronger than the ones you might have on your own devices. So you can trust that your data is well protected.

Advantages of Using OneDrive

If you have Windows 11 on your computer, you already have OneDrive installed and ready to use. You don't need to do anything extra. While many options exist for storing your files in the cloud, OneDrive stands out because it works seamlessly with Windows 11. This means it fits right into your Windows 11 experience without any issues. Plus, it offers some unique benefits that make it a great choice for keeping your files safe and accessible.

- **Automatic File Syncing:** With OneDrive, if you make changes to a file on one device, those changes will also appear on all your other devices. This means you will always have the most up-to-date version of your files, whether you are using your computer, phone, or any other device.

- **Integration with Windows Features:** You can save your documents straight to OneDrive from Microsoft Office apps like Word or Excel. This makes it simple to find and open your files using File Explorer, just like you would with any other file on your computer.

- **Offline Access:** You can still work on your files even if you don't have internet. This means you can access and edit these files, online or offline, whenever needed.

- **Personal Vault:** You can add an extra layer of protection to your important files by using two-factor authentication. This means you will need to provide two different forms of verification to access your files, making them more secure from unauthorized access.

- **Microsoft 365 Integration:** With a Microsoft 365 subscription, you can use extra features to make your files even safer. These include advanced security measures, tools to detect ransomware, and keeping a history of file changes over time. So, if anything goes wrong, you can always return to an earlier version.

Comparing OneDrive to the Competition

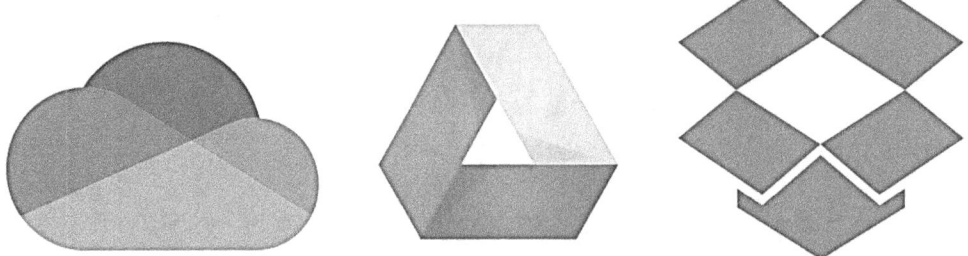

- **Storage**: OneDrive gives you 5GB of free storage, and if you need more, you can choose from paid plans that go up to 6 TB.

Google Drive starts with 15GB for free, and Dropbox begins with 2GB.

- **Pricing**: OneDrive plans are often cheaper than those of its competitors, especially if you want Microsoft 365.

- **Integration**: OneDrive works well with Windows 11 and other Microsoft apps. However, Google Drive might be better if you are more into Android. And Dropbox is great if you use different devices and platforms.

- **Security**: All the extensive cloud services take security seriously, but OneDrive gets an extra boost from Microsoft's expertise in this area.

OneDrive Files and Folders

You will spot the OneDrive icon on the right side of your taskbar. It looks like a cloud, so it's pretty easy to recognize.

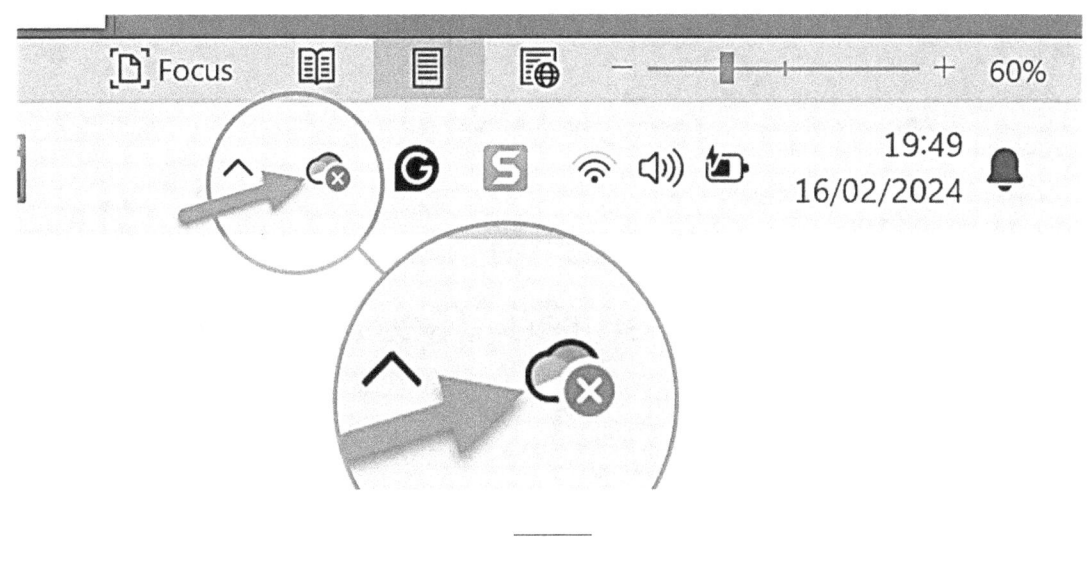

OneDrive has a simple, easy-to-understand layout that helps you quickly find your files and folders.

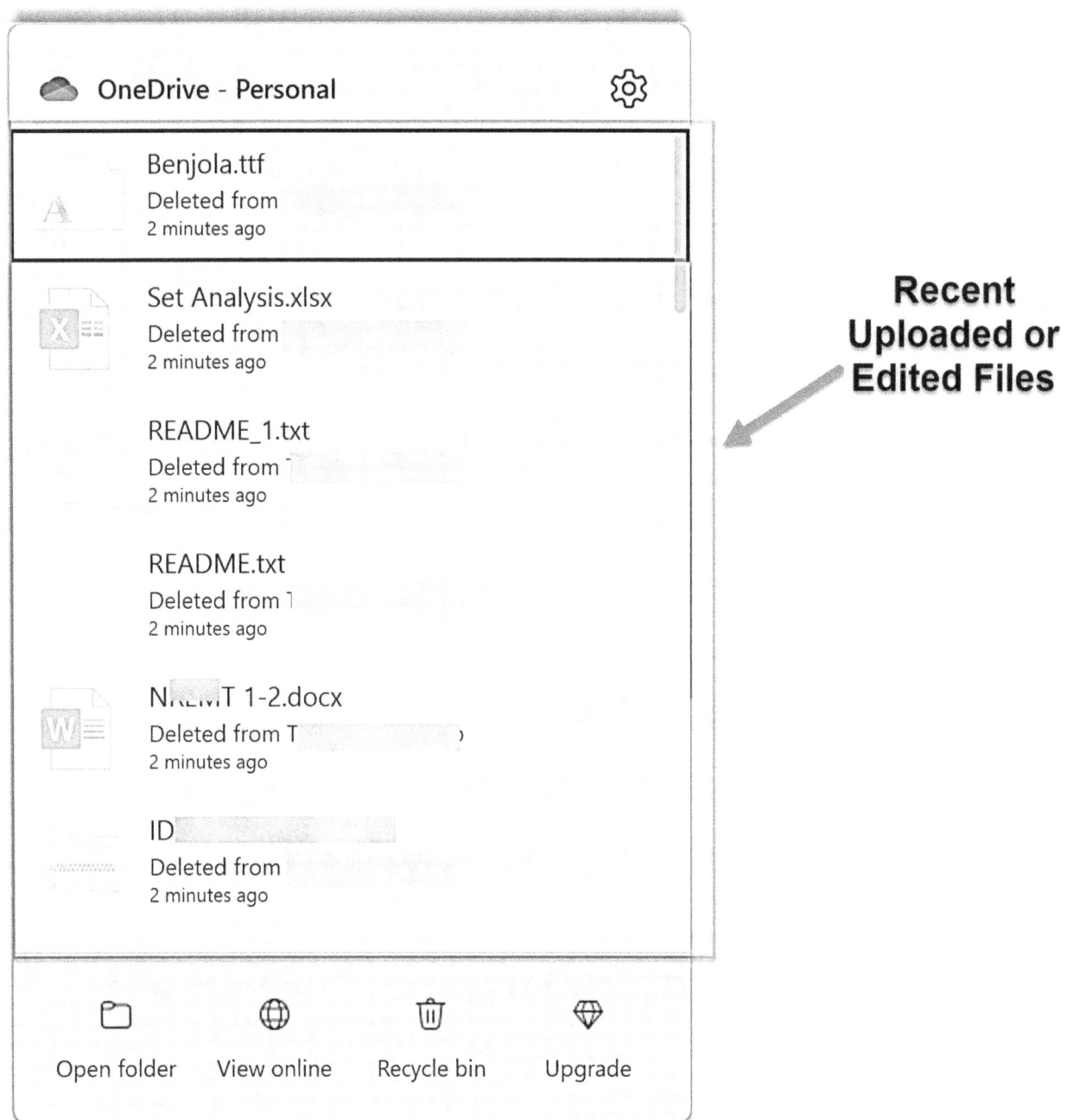

Once you click the OneDrive icon, you can see the recently uploaded or edited files on the panel, as illustrated above.

At the bottom of the OneDrive panel, there are some helpful links you can use:

- **Open folder**: This lets you quickly open the OneDrive folder on your computer.

- **View online**: Click here to see your OneDrive dashboard on the internet.

- **Recycle bin**: This link takes you to your OneDrive Recycle bin online, where you can find deleted files.

- **Upgrade**: If you need more space or features, use this link to upgrade your OneDrive subscription.

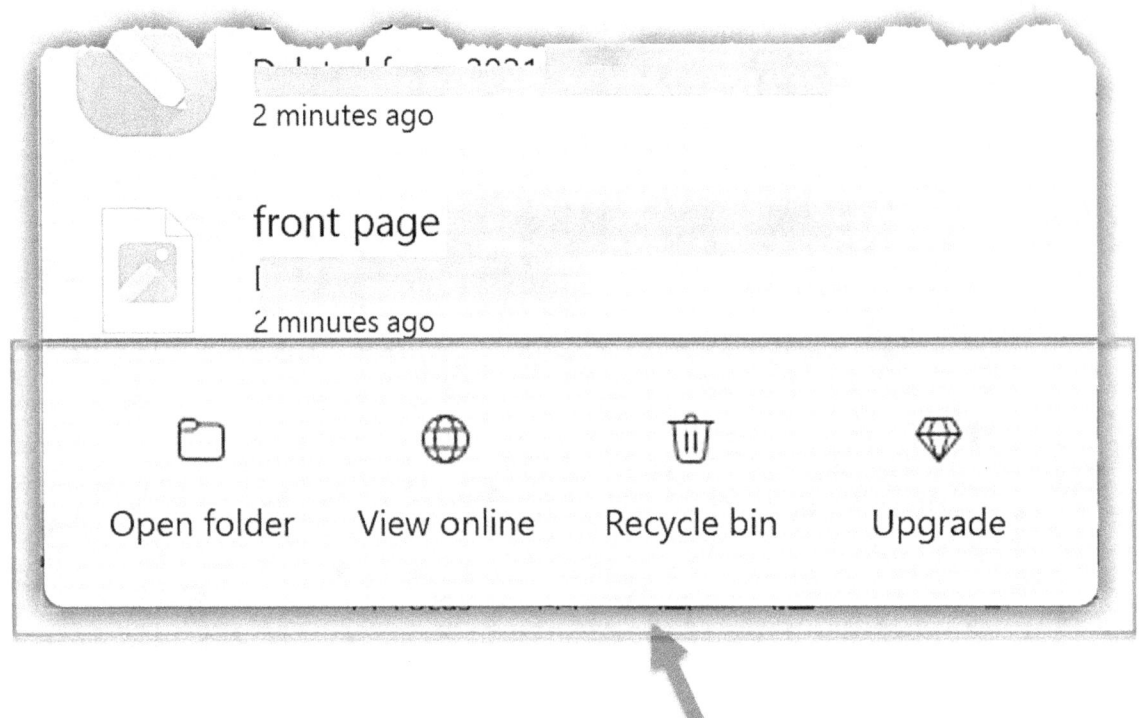

When you click on the Open folder, it gives you access to OneDrive folder on your computer.

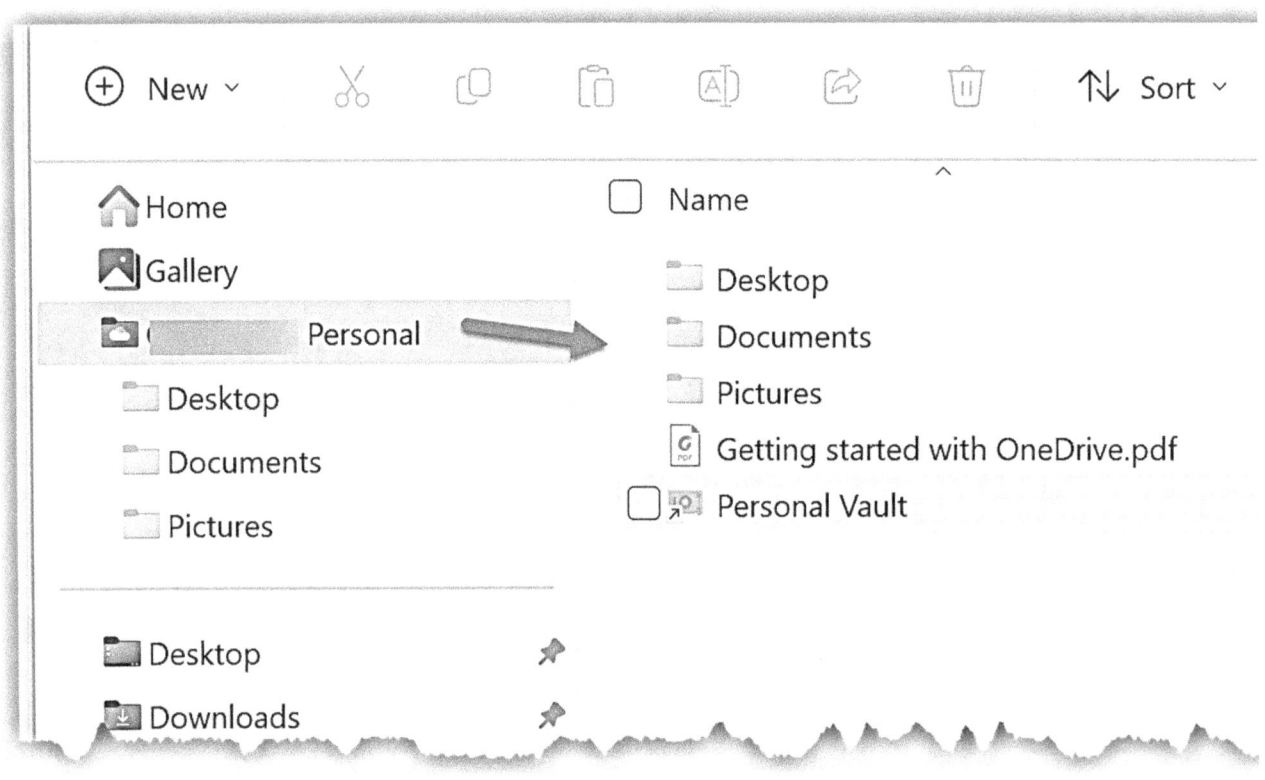

You can quickly move your files or folders to and from the OneDrive folder by copying and pasting them.

When you are connected to the internet, the files in your regular file explorer automatically sync with your OneDrive cloud, so you always have the latest versions.

If you want to delete files from your OneDrive folder, you can do it just like you would with any other files in your regular file explorer.

OneDrive Personal Vault

Think of Personal Vault as a secret and super secure section inside your OneDrive. Getting into it is like going through a security check. It uses two-factor authentication, meaning you need your password and a unique code sent to your phone or email to get in. This extra step makes it much harder for anyone who shouldn't be there to get access, even if they somehow know your password.

File Explorer allows you to access and manage the contents of Personal Vault, even though it has its own very secure internal storage space.

Here's how you can access your Personal Vault through File Explorer:

- **Open File Explorer:** Click on the File Explorer icon on your taskbar.

- **Navigate to your OneDrive:** Look for your OneDrive folder in the list on the left side of the window.

- Find the "Personal Vault" folder: You'll see a folder called "**Personal Vault**" with a lock icon next to it. This means it's extra secure.

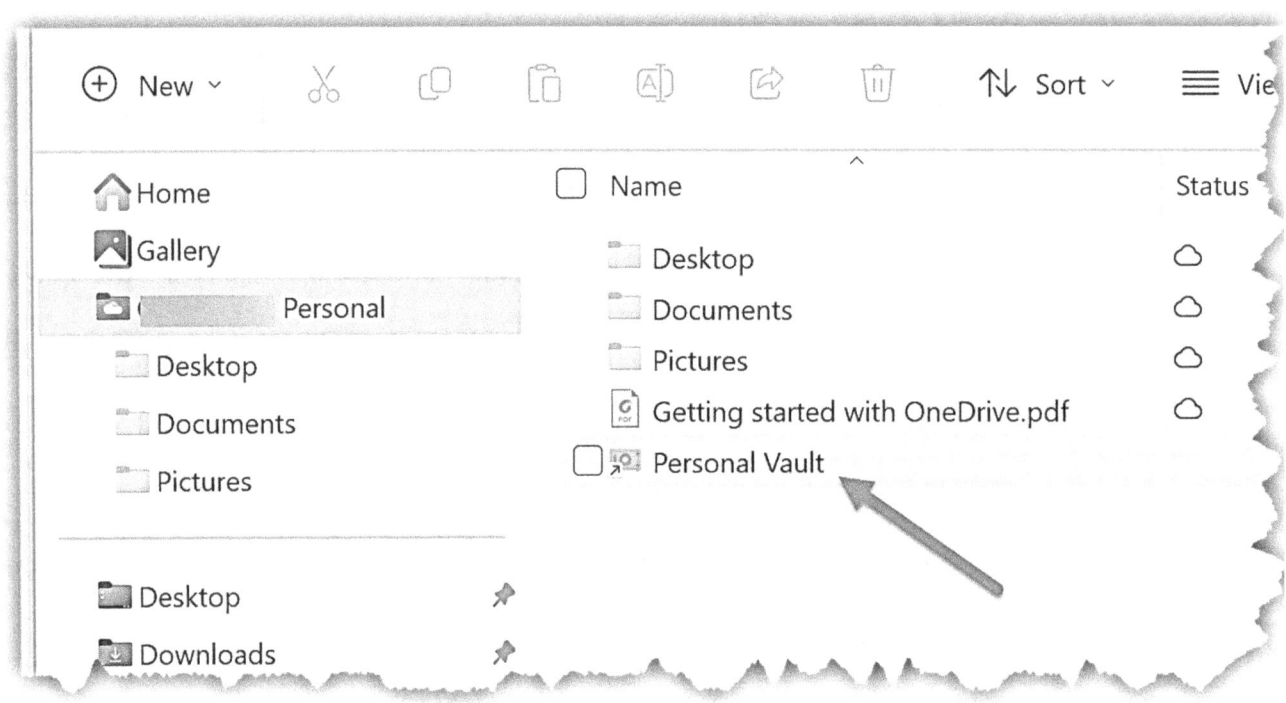

- You can't open the files in this folder directly from File Explorer. If you click on it, you'll be taken to the OneDrive app and asked for two-factor authentication before you can see what's inside.

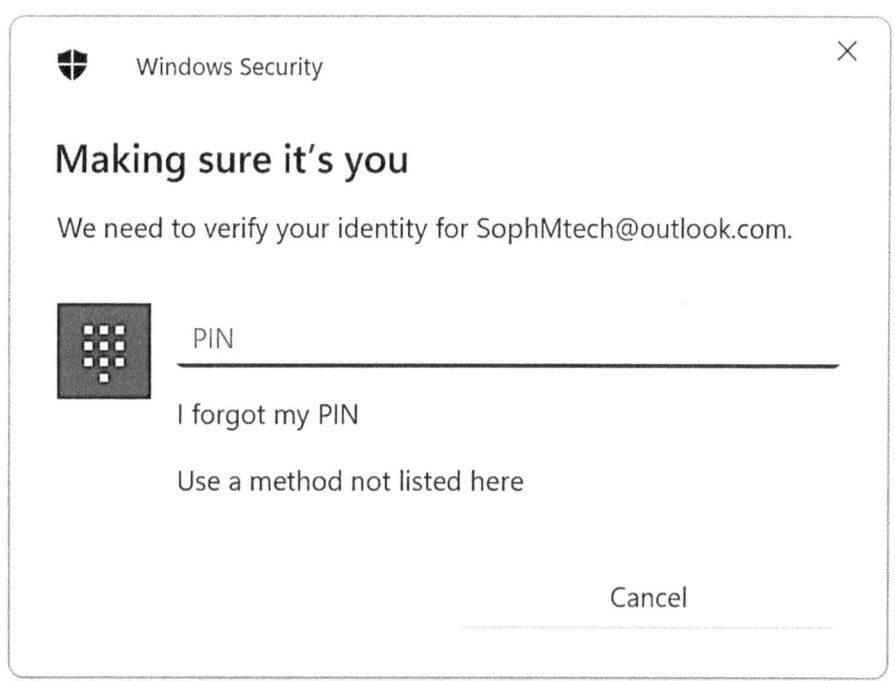

Meanwhile, note that you cannot open files from your Personal Vault when you are not connected to the internet.

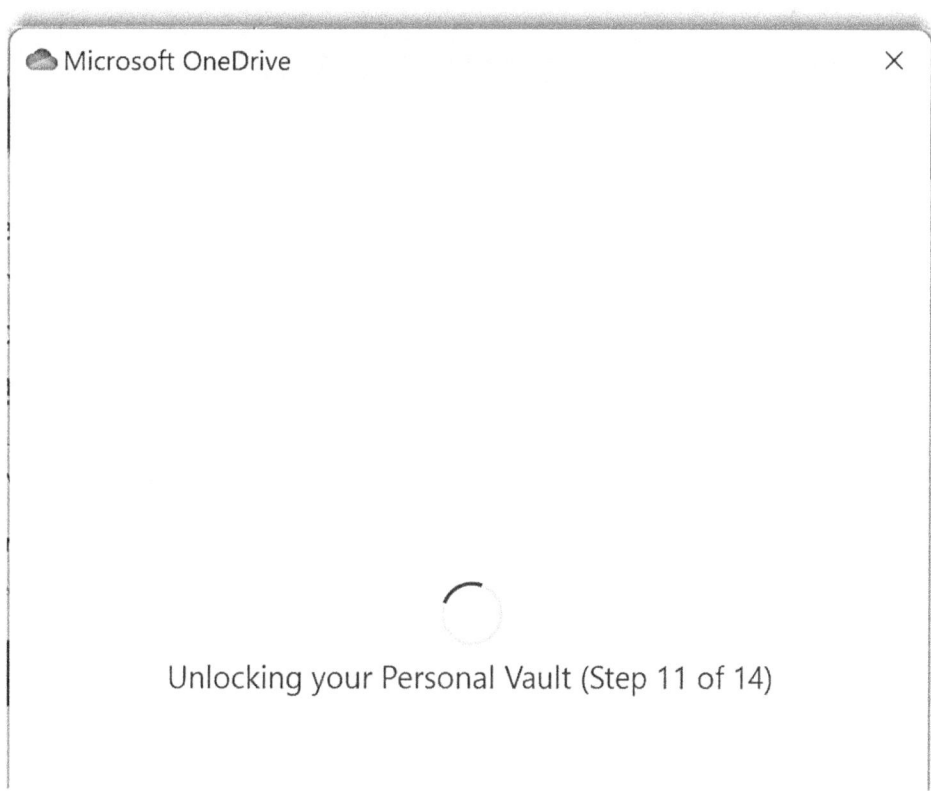

CHAPTER 11

BASIC INTERNET CONNECTION

The internet is a gigantic digital library with knowledge on practically any subject. You are open to a universe of information at your disposal with just a few clicks, thanks to the tools that Windows 11 provides, which enable you to connect to this network easily.

Types of Internet Connections

- **Wired connection:** In this type of connection, you connect your computer to your modem or router using an ethernet (wired) connection, which is the traditional method.

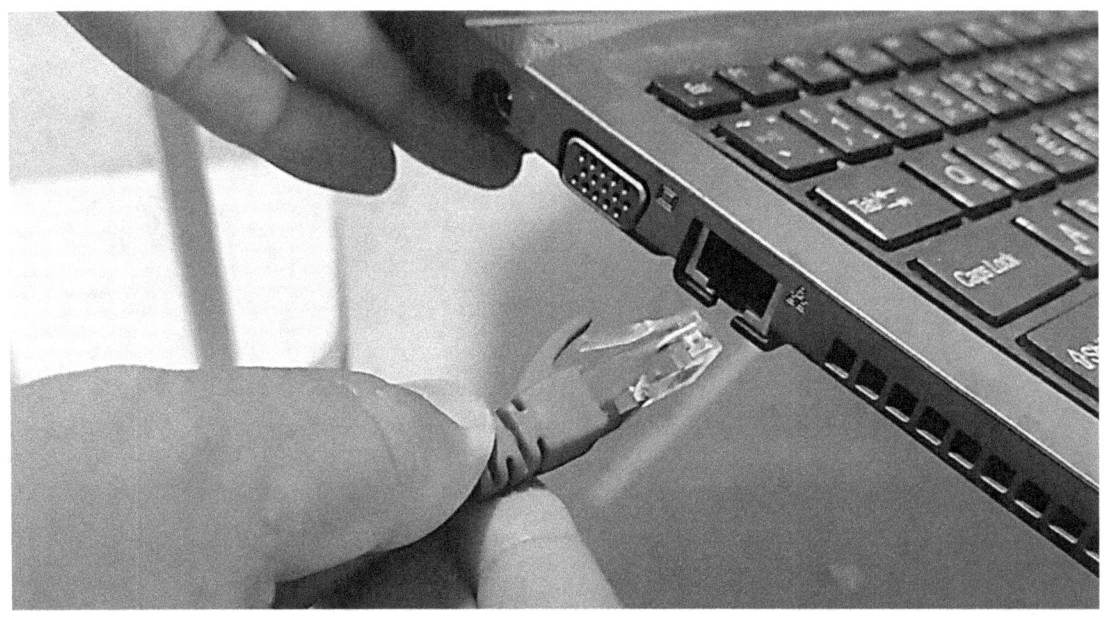

Wired connections are known to be very dependable and provide the highest possible speeds.

- **Wireless connection:** Wi-Fi allows you to move about freely while maintaining your internet connection. You are required to establish a connection between your computer and a wireless router, which is a device that transmits signals for your device to pick up. The speed of Wi-Fi might vary depending on how far away you are from the router. Still, it is helpful for activities such as accessing social media, sending emails, and surfing the internet.
- **Mobile hotspot:** Your smartphone data can be used to connect your computer to the internet through a wireless network. Your mobile device will function as a gateway to the internet. It is useful when you are out and need to connect to the internet using your laptop or other devices.

When determining whether or not to connect to the internet, it is essential to consider that the connection speed, dependability, and security are all key factors.

How to Add a Hidden or Private Wi-Fi Network Manually

Wi-Fi networks can be configured to be hidden or restricted. This might be due to concerns over network security, or it could simply be the preference of the network owner. You must enter specific parameters, such as a username and password, to connect to these restricted networks. These networks are also known as "private networks."

Here is how to manually add a Wi-Fi network on your Windows 11 PC or laptop:

Method 1: Using Settings

1. Open the Start menu and click on "**Settings**."
2. Click on "**Network & internet**" located in the left sidebar. Ensure the Wireless button is enabled
3. Under "**Network settings**," click on "Manage known networks."

4. Click on "**Manage known networks**".

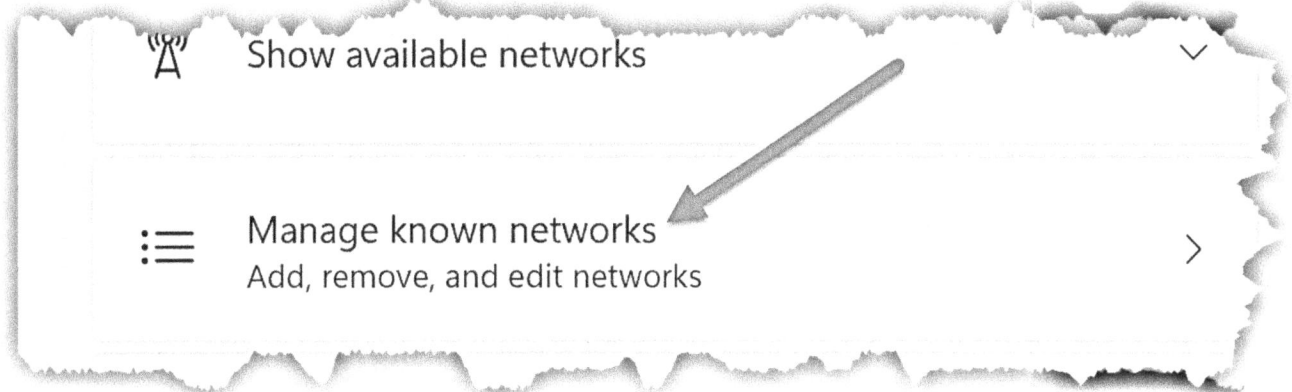

5. Click on the "**Add network**" button.

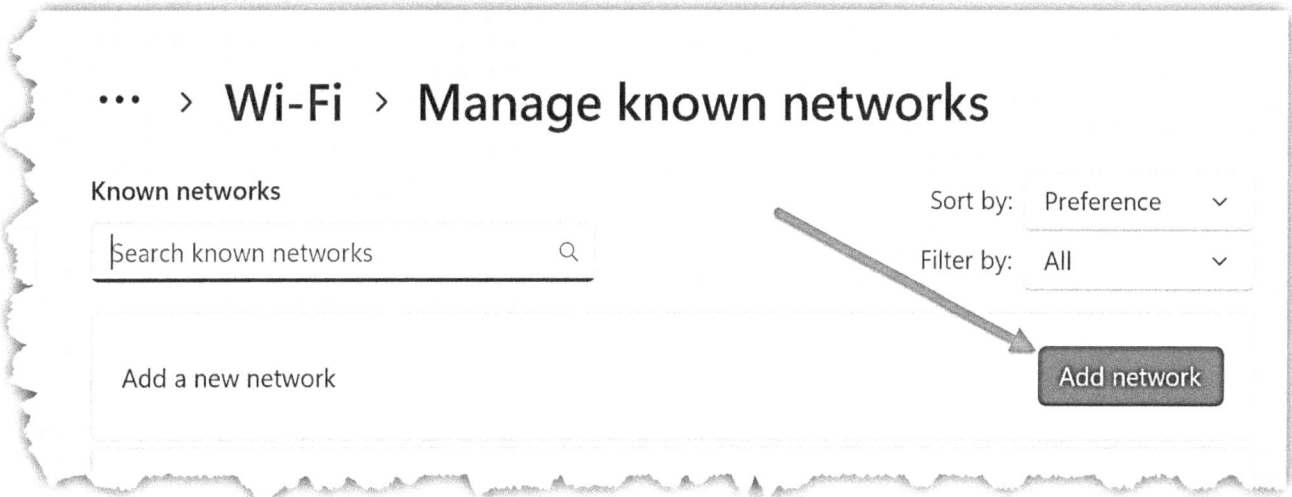

6. Enter the network name.
7. Choose the appropriate security type from the dropdown menu (WPA2-Personal, WPA3-Personal, etc.).
8. Enter the network password in the "Security key" field.
9. **Connect automatically**: Check this box if you want to connect to this network automatically whenever it's in range.

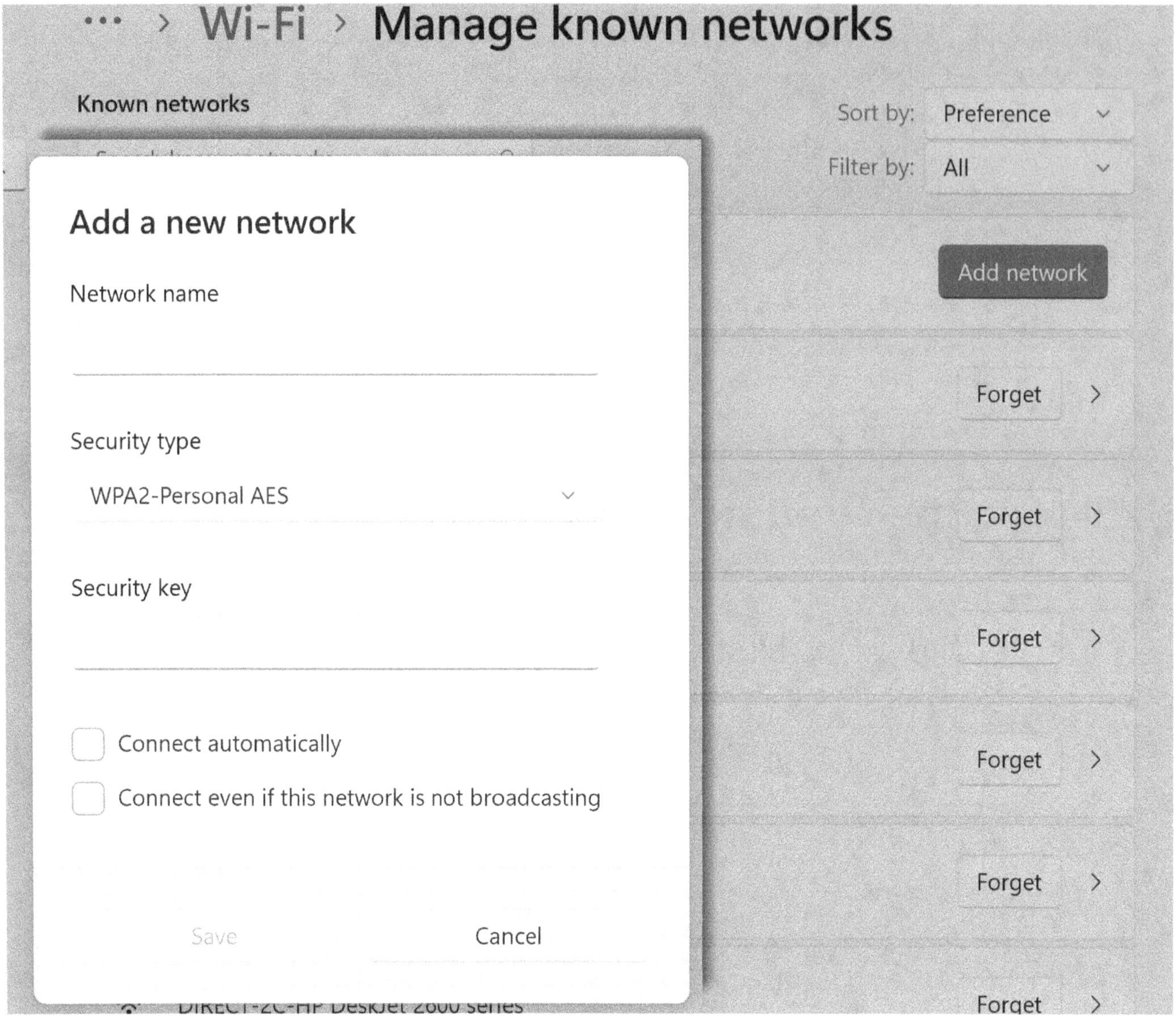

10. Click "**Save**" to store your changes.

Method 2: Using Control Panel (Optional)

1. Open the Start menu and search for "**Control Panel**."

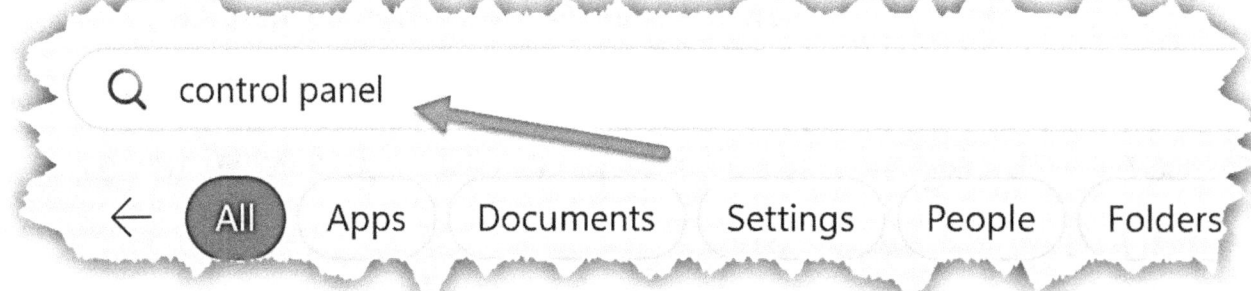

2. Click on "**Network and Internet**" and then "**Network and Sharing Center**."

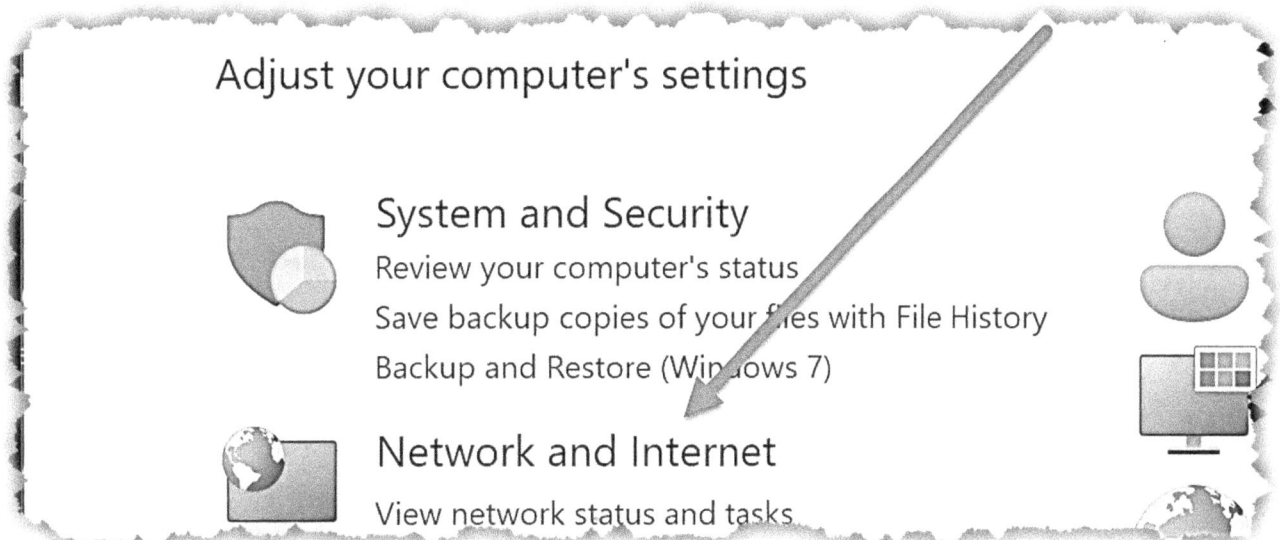

3. Click on "**Set up a new connection or network**."

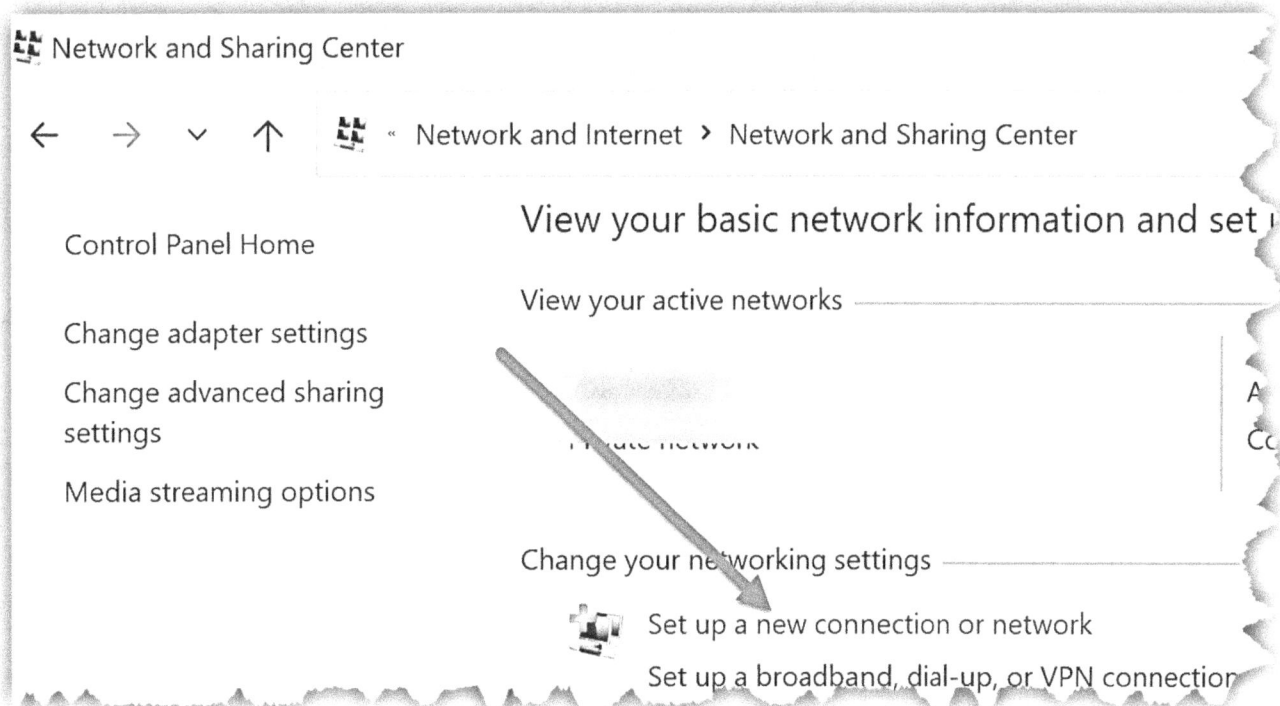

4. Choose "**Manually connect to a wireless network**" and click "**Next**."

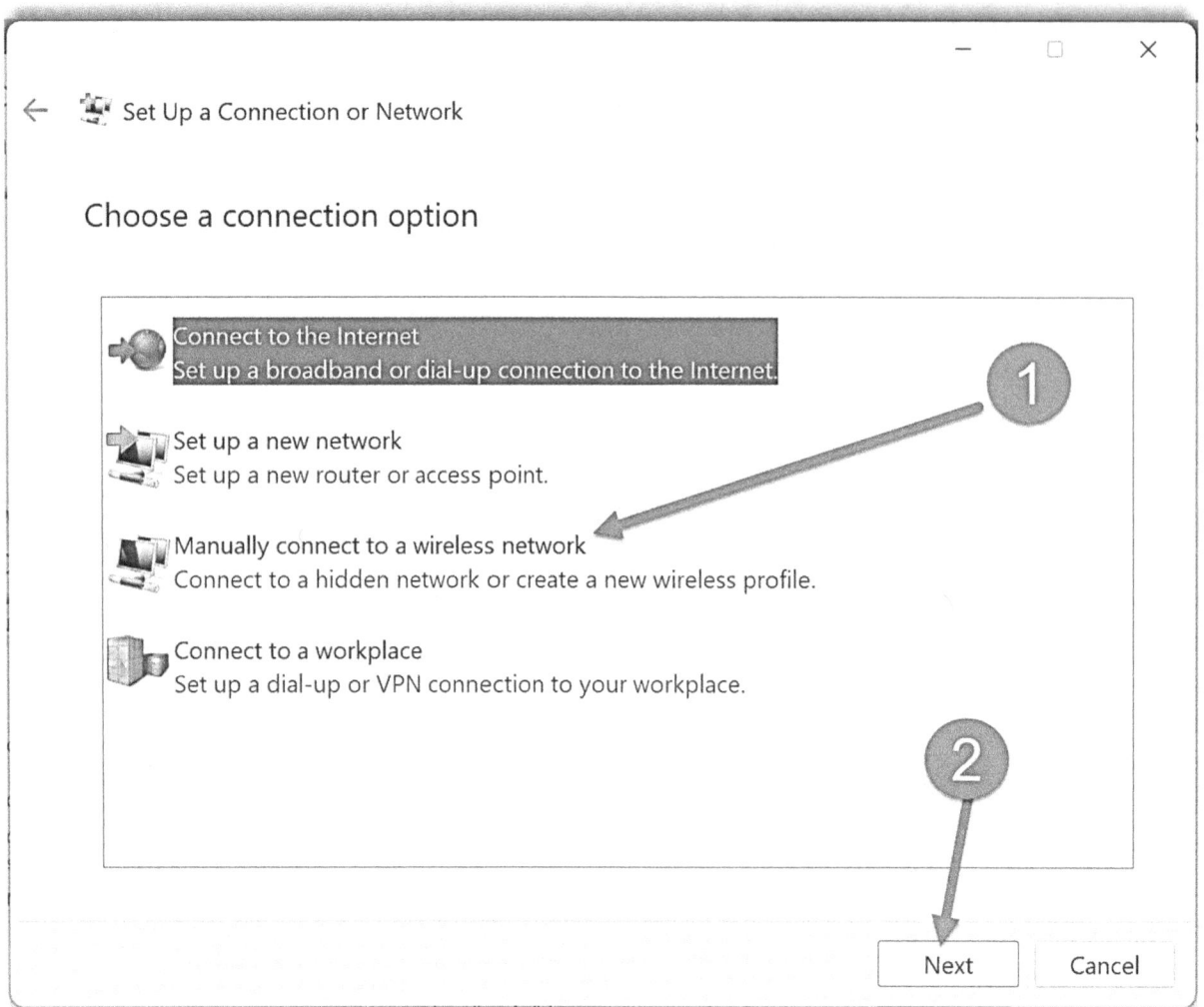

5. Enter the **network name** (SSID) and security type, similar to Method 1. If the network is hidden, ensure the "network name (SSID)" is entered.
6. Follow steps 7-9 from Method 1 to configure additional settings and save your network profile.

SECURING YOUR CONNECTION

Exploring the digital world is similar to walking into uncharted territory. Whether you are using the internet to communicate with others, download applications, or browse the web, it is important to be aware of the possible dangers that may be there. You can defend yourself against potential threats hiding in the shadows if you know these hazards and have the appropriate resources.

The internet can be a safe refuge of knowledge and opportunities, but it also contains potential dangers such as:

- **Malware**: Programs with malicious intent can damage computers, steal data, or impede operations. This category includes malware such as viruses, spyware, and ransomware.
- **Phishing**: Cybercriminals send emails or set up websites that seem official in order to deceive you into giving them personal information or visiting dangerous links.
- **Cyberattacks** refer to attempts to obtain unauthorized access to your computer or network, which often result in data breaches or disruptions.

- **Identity theft**: This is an act of stealing your personal information for the goal of doing fraudulent acts, such as accessing accounts or conducting financial transactions.

Nevertheless, you have some different lines of defense available to you, such as:

- **Strong Passwords:** A strong and secure password is your first line of protection against hackers. Instead of using a simple password, such as birthdays or names of loved ones, you should use more complicated combinations of letters, numbers, and symbols with your password.

   You can use a password manager to store and create one-of-a-kind passwords for each account safely.

- **Firewalls**: These are system software that filters incoming and outgoing traffic, which also prohibit questionable activities. They perform the function of digital gatekeepers.

- **Antivirus and Anti-malware Software:** You should invest in reliable security software to search your system for any dangers and eliminate them. Always keep it up to date for the best possible protection.

- **Suspicious Links and Attachments:** Never open an attachment or click on a link in an email from someone you do not know, no matter how official it seems. Before clicking on a link, hover over it to see where it leads.

- **Software Updates:** Hackers may take advantage of security holes in outdated software. Update your Windows 11 operating system and apps as soon as they become available.

CHAPTER 12

EXPLORING MICROSOFT EDGE IN WINDOWS 11

By default, Microsoft Edge is installed on your computer when you install Windows 11, giving you access to the vast expanse of the internet.

To open Microsoft Edge, you go to the start menu and search for the application.

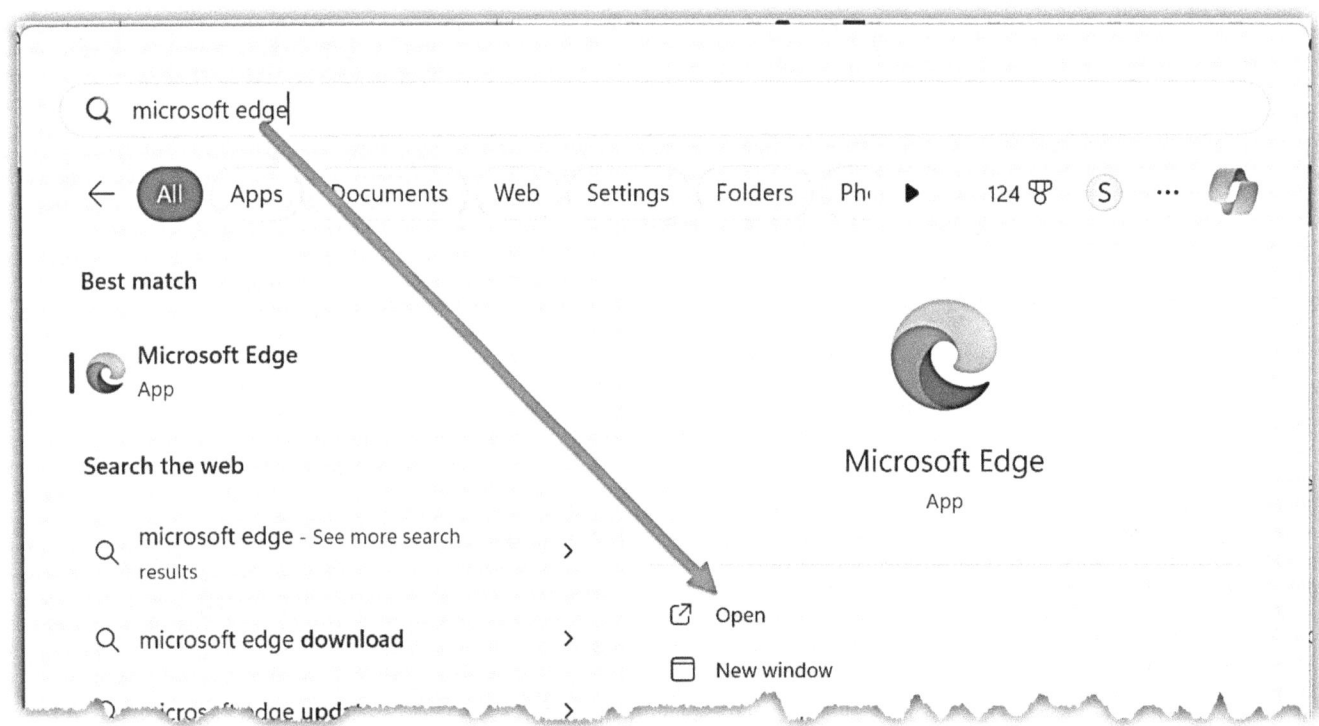

Another method is to click the icon on the taskbar.

Below is what the Microsoft Edge interface looks like

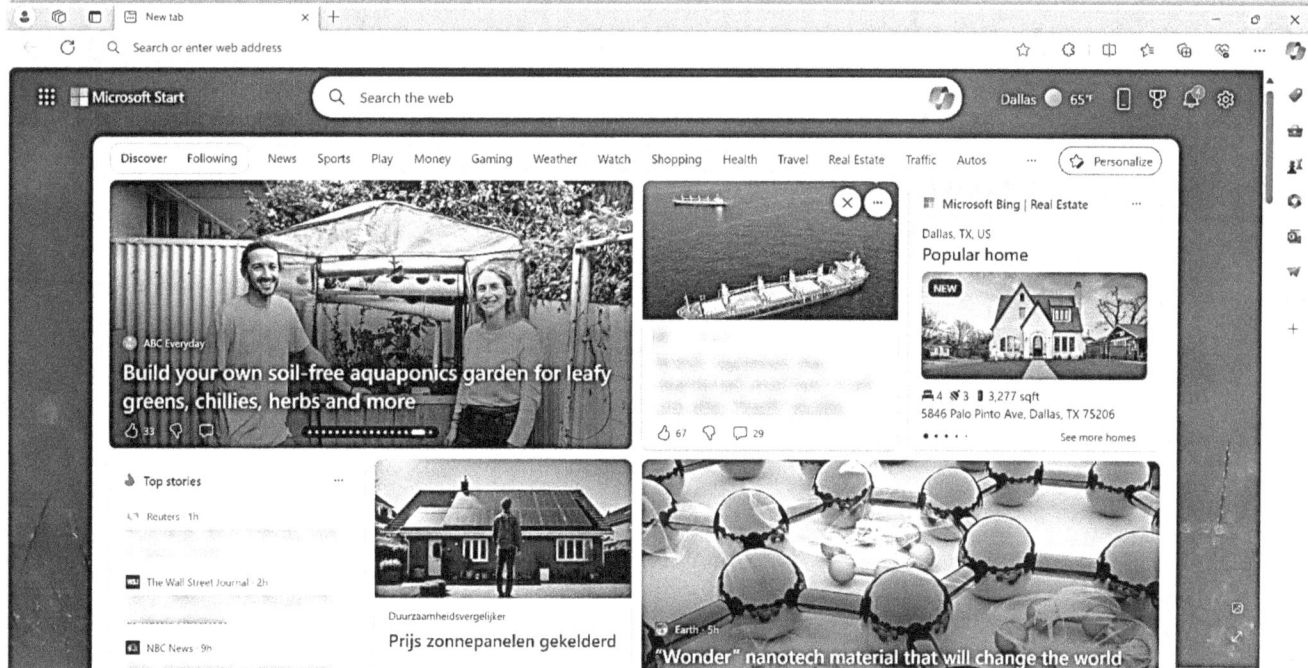

What you see when you open Microsoft Edge is not a typical webpage. Instead, it is something completely different. It's a homepage that's tailored just to your preferences.

This page contains several unique sections, each providing you with the most recent news, the current weather conditions in your region, and the most recent updates from the world of sports. You can find all of these sections on this page.

The Microsoft Edge Browser & Tab Controls

The browser controls are in the top left corner, which includes the Page refresh button and the Page Forward/Page Back buttons.

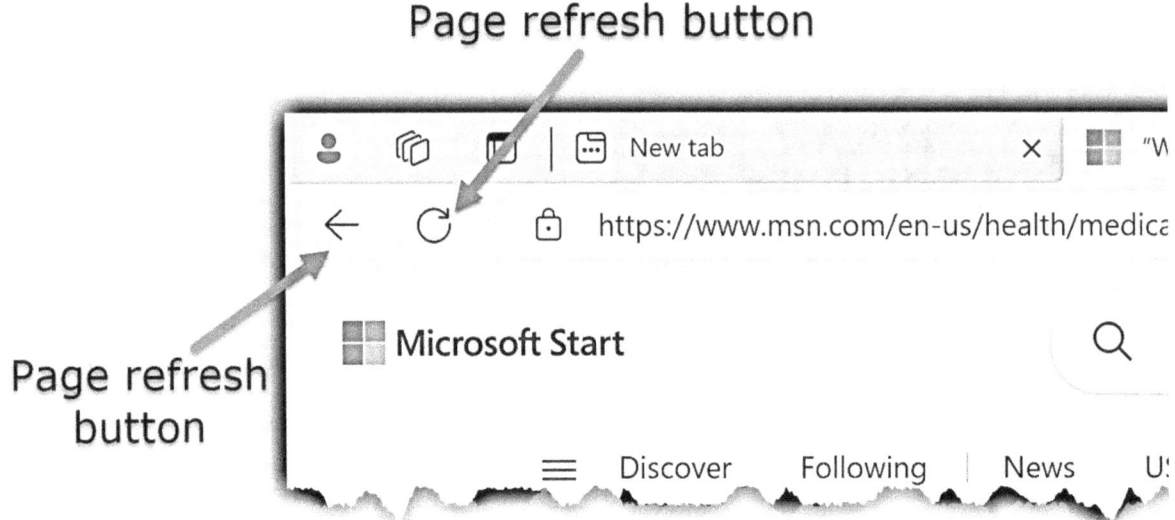

The Search Field and Address Bar

The majority of online browsers, including Microsoft Edge, provide a streamlined experience for browsing the entire internet compared to other browsers.

The address bar is the most important part of your browsing experience because it serves as your one-stop shop for navigating the internet.

In the address bar, you type the **web address** of the information you want online.

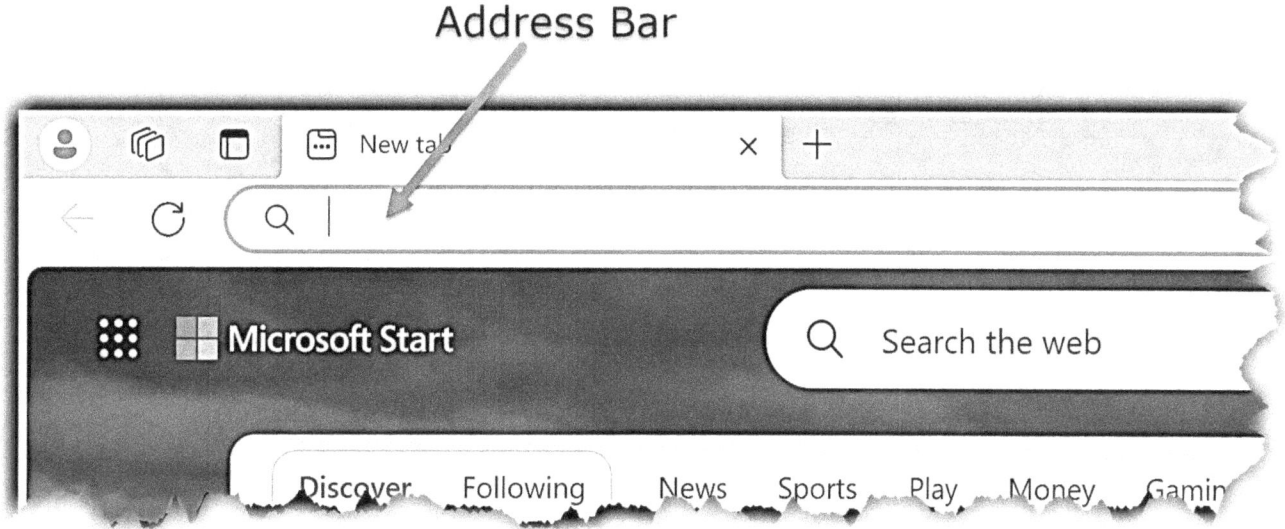

If you are unsure of the website but have a clear idea of what you are looking for, type your search query directly into the address bar.

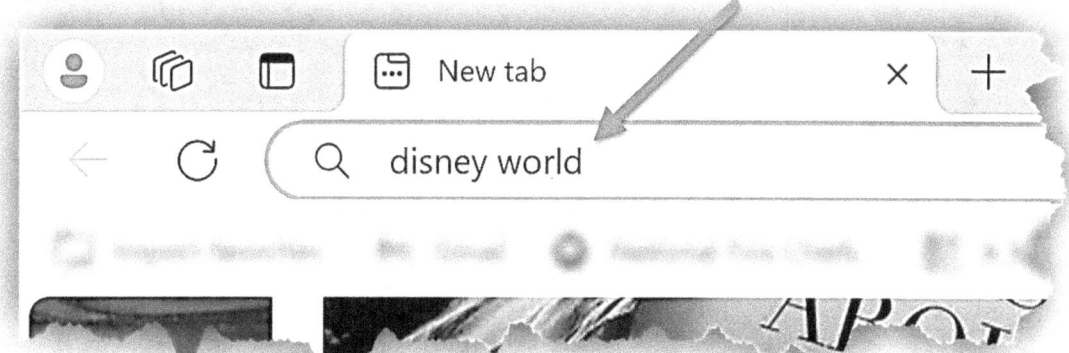

Edge will suggest relevant websites or execute a web search using your default search engine.

Accessing the Microsoft Edge Menu

The menu bar has undergone some modification in Microsoft Edge, which is a departure from previous versions and favors a more minimalist approach.

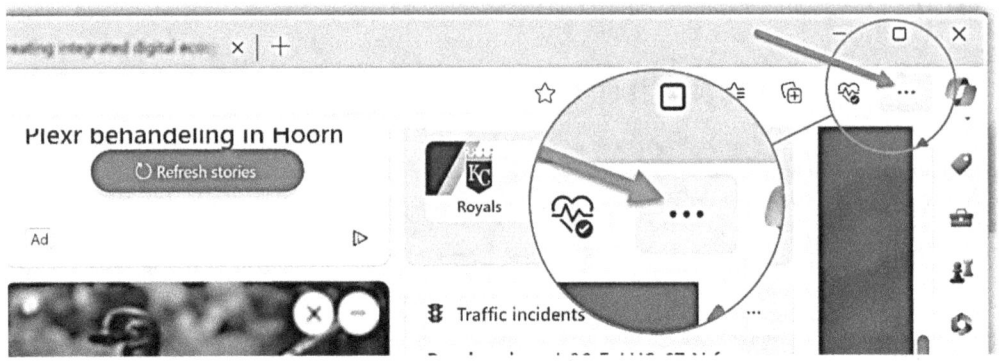

When you click on these **three dots**, a dropdown list or menu will appear, giving you quick access to various options, including settings, extensions, history, downloads, and more.

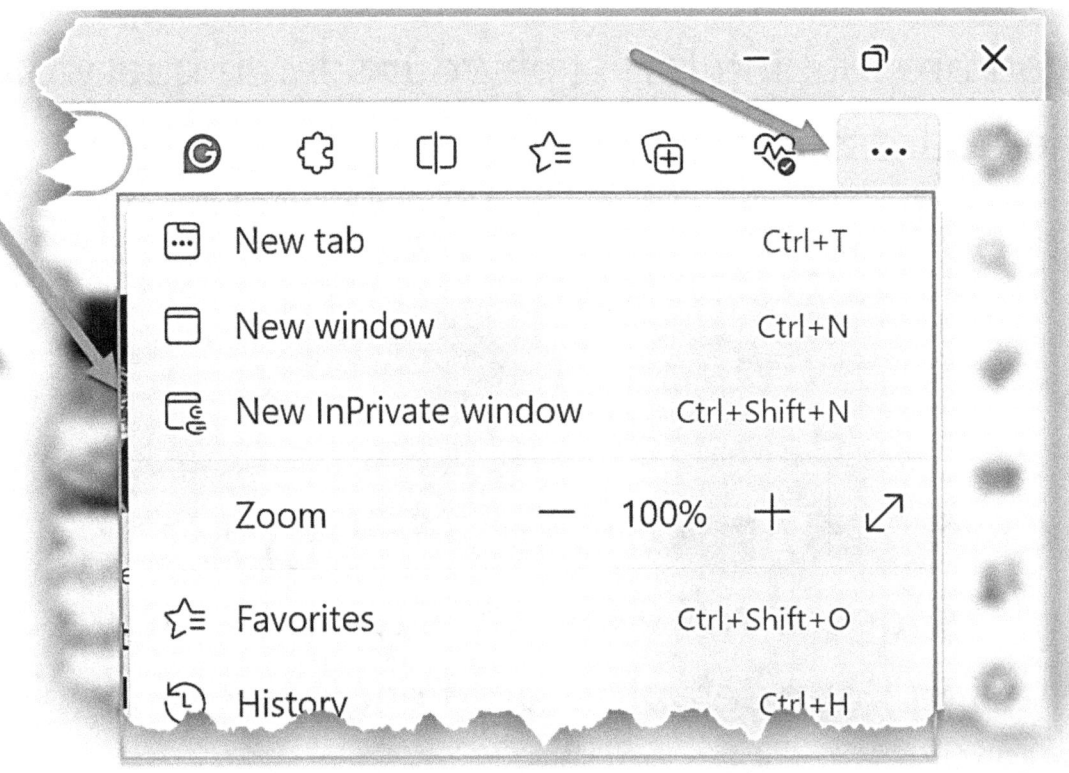

Microsoft Edge Browser Tabs

Tabs are a concept that Microsoft Edge uses to support multitasking. Each of these tabs is like a separate folder inside the main folder. They represent a different page you can open separately to view multiple websites simultaneously in the same browser window.

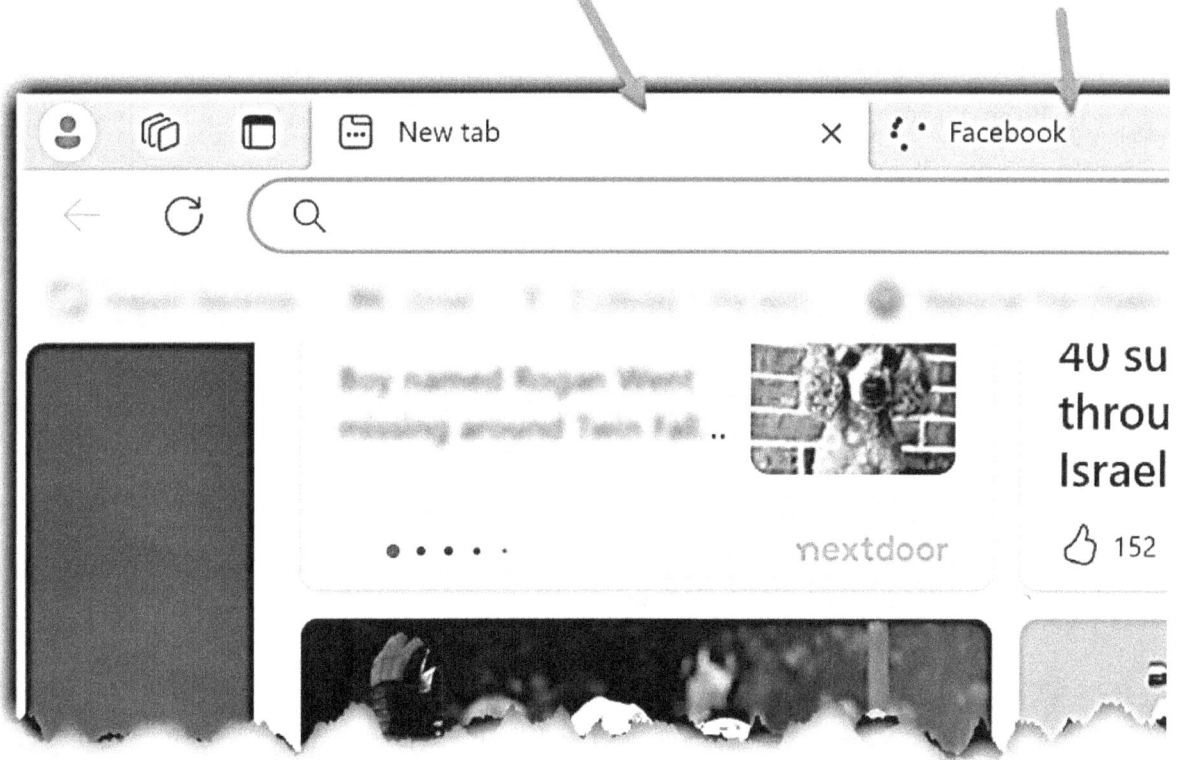

This keeps you from having to open and close new browser windows all the time, which speeds up your browsing experience. You can easily switch between tabs by clicking on them. This keeps all of your online activities in order and easy to find.

Microsoft Edge Favourites Tabs

The Favorites bar is your unique way to get to the websites you visit most often. This eliminates the need to enter long URLs over and over. To make it easy to get to your favorite websites, add them to the Favorites bar by clicking on the Favorite (star) icon, as illustrated below.

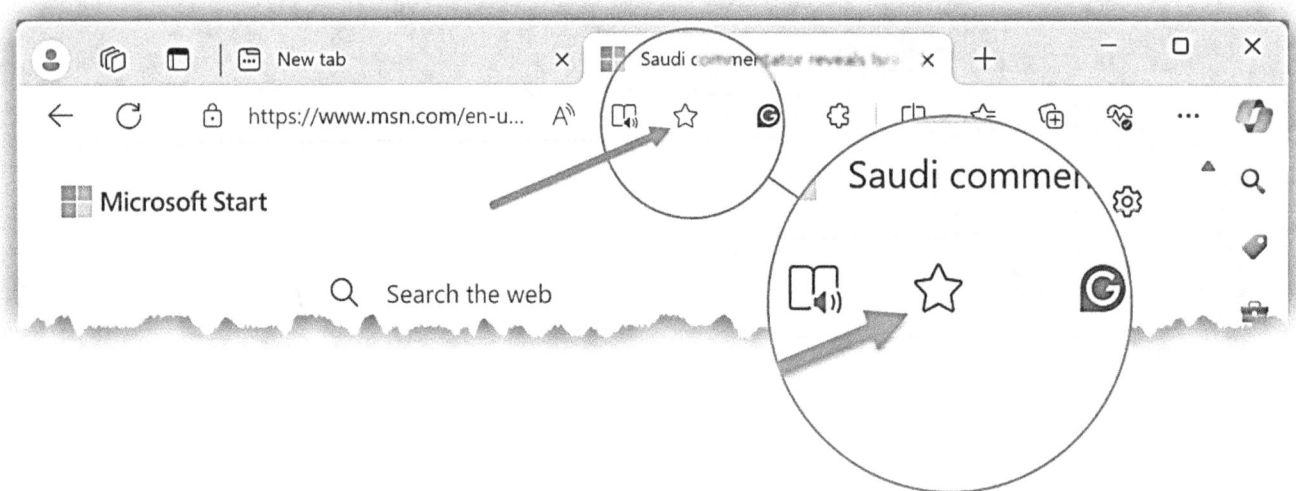

The favorite bar is similar to having a customized toolbar at the top of your browser window, populated with shortcuts to the websites you visit the most frequently.

A list of these websites is displayed when you start Microsoft Edge.

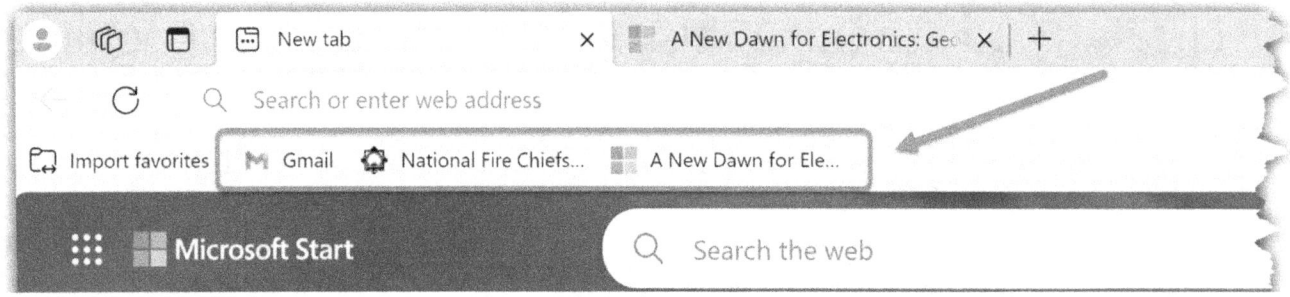

Each tab represents a separate web page, enabling you to open and explore multiple websites concurrently. This eliminates the need to constantly open and close browser windows, minimizing clutter and maximizing efficiency.

How to Display the Favorites Bar

1. Locate and click the three-dotted menu icon representing the Settings in the Edge window's upper-right corner.

2. From the dropdown menu, navigate to the "**Settings**" option.

3. Select the "Appearance" category on the right panel within the Settings panel.

4. Scroll down to **Show Favorite Bar** under the "Customize toolbar" section, and in the dropdown menu, select **Always,** as illustrated below.

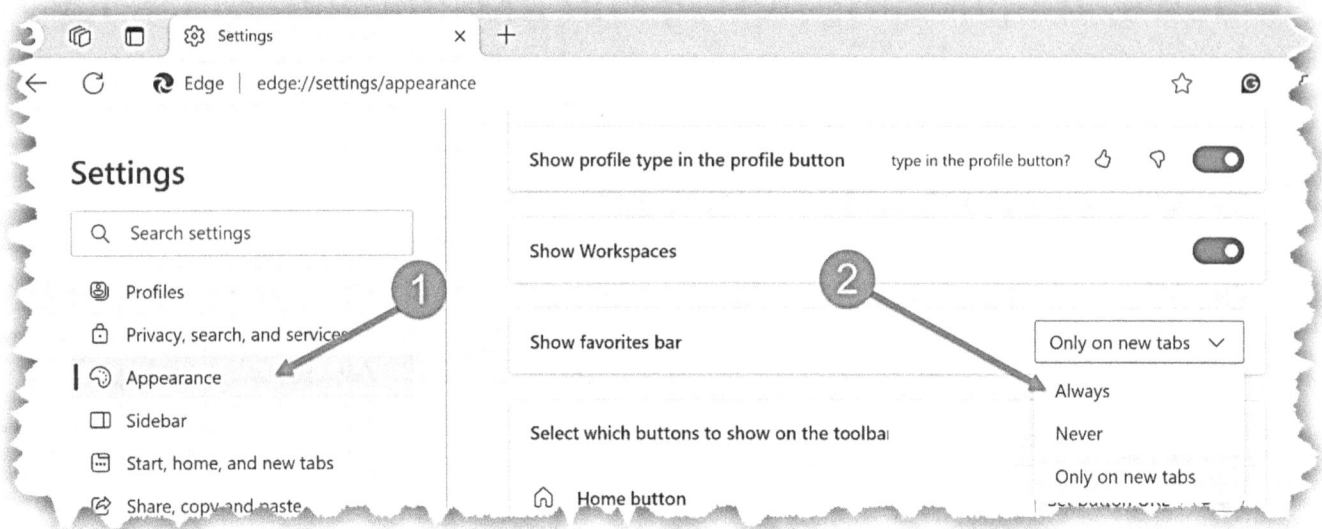

- **Always**: If you choose this option, the Favorites bar will always be visible, giving you easy access to the websites you have bookmarked.

- **Only on new tabs:** If you choose this option, the Favorites bar will only show up on newly opened tabs. This makes it easy to get to your favorites when you start a new viewing session.

- **Never**: If you choose this option, the Favorites bar will be completely hidden.

MICROSOFT EDGE EXTENSION BAR

The Extension bar in Microsoft Edge functions similarly to a toolbox, which allows you to add and use specialized tools to enhance your browsing experience.

Although it is optional, you can decide whether or not to make use of it. You can add new features and capabilities to Edge by adding browser extensions.

Some examples of these extensions are ad blockers and translation tools. This is an excellent method for personalizing your web browser to meet your requirements and ensuring that it functions as you need.

How to Enable the Extension Icon

Activating the extension icon on the Microsoft Edge browser allows you to toggle installed extensions on or off. To do this, you follow the steps below;

1. Open Microsoft Edge.
2. Click on the three-dot menu in the top-right corner.

3. Select Settings.

4. Scroll down and click on Appearance.

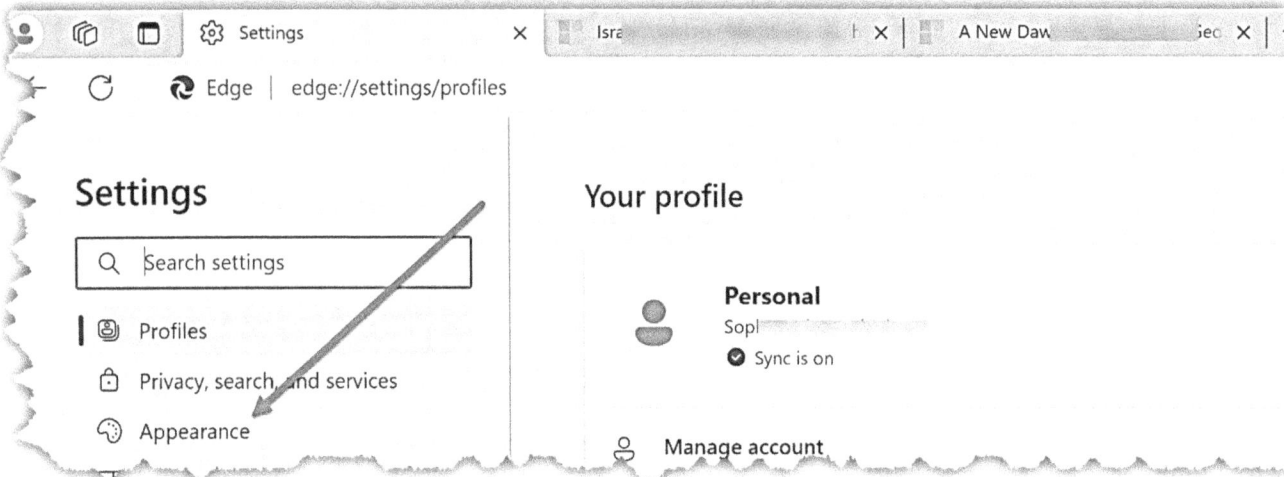

5. Scroll down to the Extension button and click on the drop-down menu to select your options.

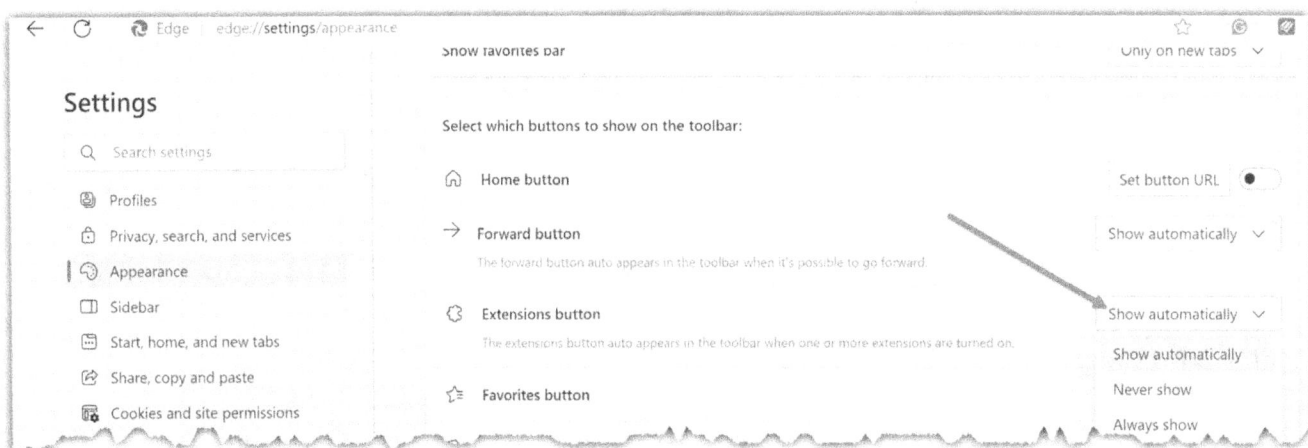

In this case, you can select **Show automatically** or **Always show**.

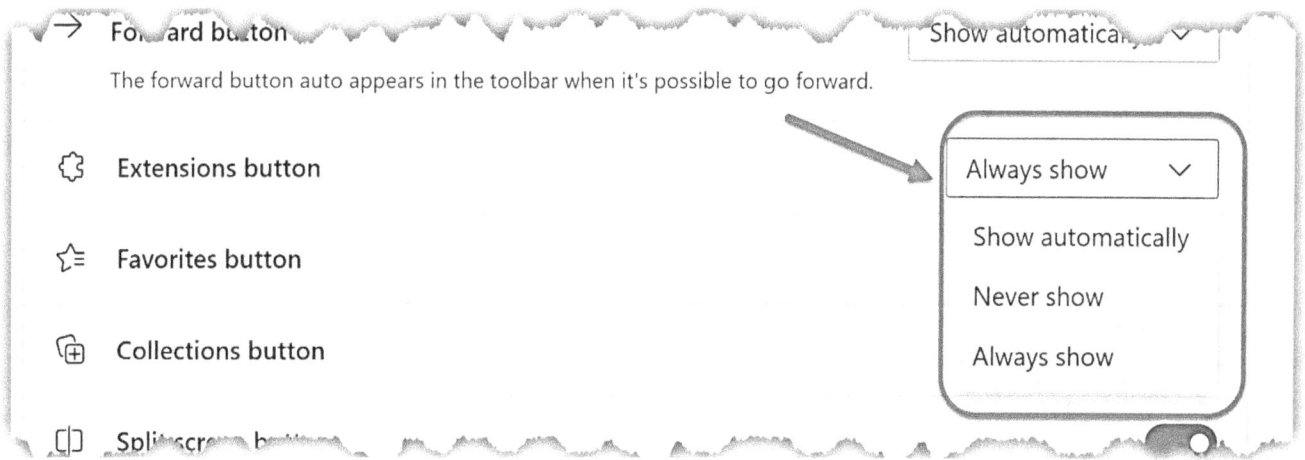

The extension bar only appears if an extension or the extension icon is enabled.

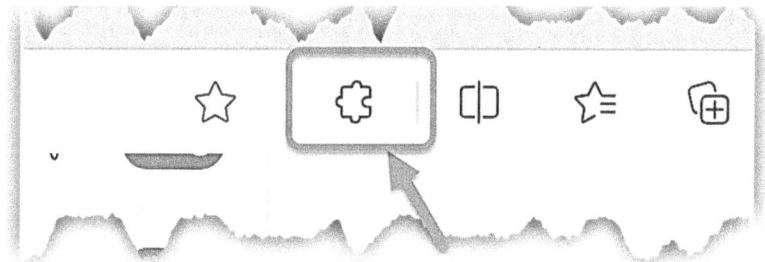

Frequently Installed Extensions

Having prepared the extension bar, let us look at some of the most common extensions you can add to the Microsoft Edge browser to boost productivity.

- **Grammarly**

With the Grammarly Extensions, you can fix spelling and grammar mistakes as you write. It is as if you have a helpful editor there while you write, checking for clarity, correctness, and the absence of errors.

- **AdBlock Plus**

AdBlock Plus is an extension that can prevent intrusive adverts and improve your web browsing experience. It's almost like having your assistant that blocks irrelevant adverts so you can get down to business when you're surfing the web.

- **Evernote Web Clipper**

Evernote Web Clipper Extensions make it simple to save webpages and articles for subsequent use as a reference. Like a digital scrapbook, it allows you to gather and arrange content from the internet with only a few clicks.

- **LastPass**

LastPass Extensions manages your passwords securely and simply across all of your devices. It is similar to having a safe place where you can keep all of your passwords, making it simple to access your accounts without having to remember various passwords.

Installing and Removing Extensions

Adding extensions is possible through the Microsoft Store as well as through other reliable sources.

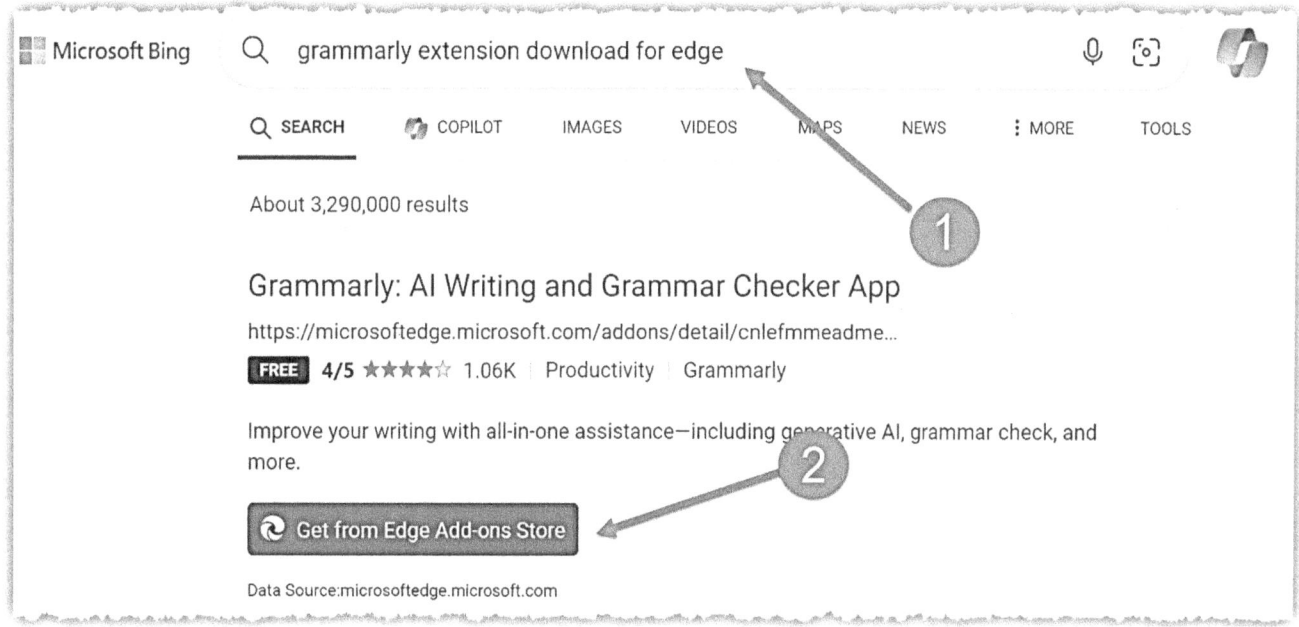

It is important to carefully review the permissions that the extension requires before installing it.

Start by searching for the extension using the search field, then click the **Get from Add-ons Store button**.

Follow the on-screen instructions and have the extension installed on your browser.

You can uninstall an extension from your browser by going to the Extensions settings page. This is the case if you no longer require the extension or if it could potentially compromise your security.

Extensions Settings Page

The extension settings page allows you to personalize your browser with extensions.

There are two main ways to get to the Extensions settings page in Microsoft Edge. You either go through the **Extension icon** or use the **Address Bar**.

For the Extension icon method, you right-click the Extension icon and click on **Manage extensions**.

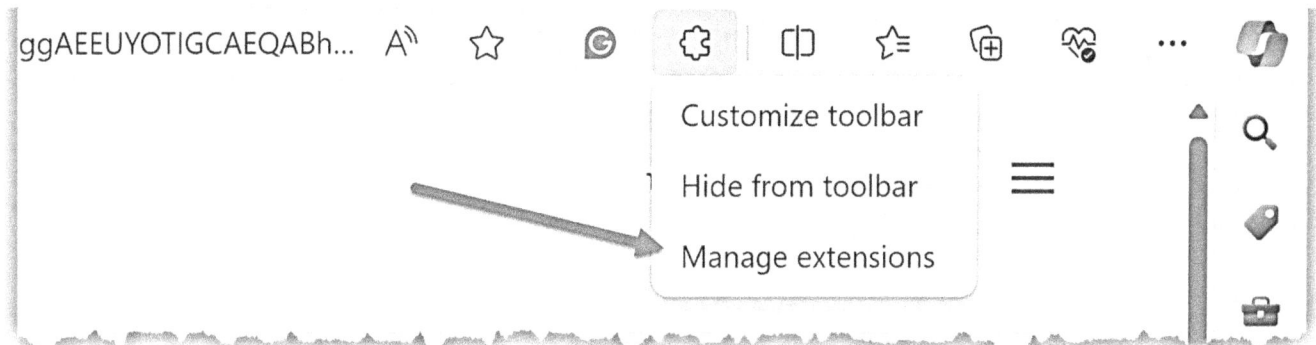

The address bar method requires you to type **edge://extensions** and press Enter.

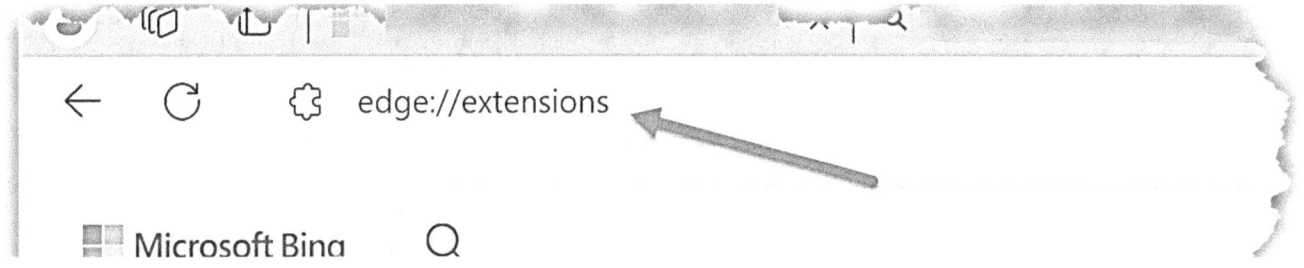

This will take you directly to the Extensions settings page.

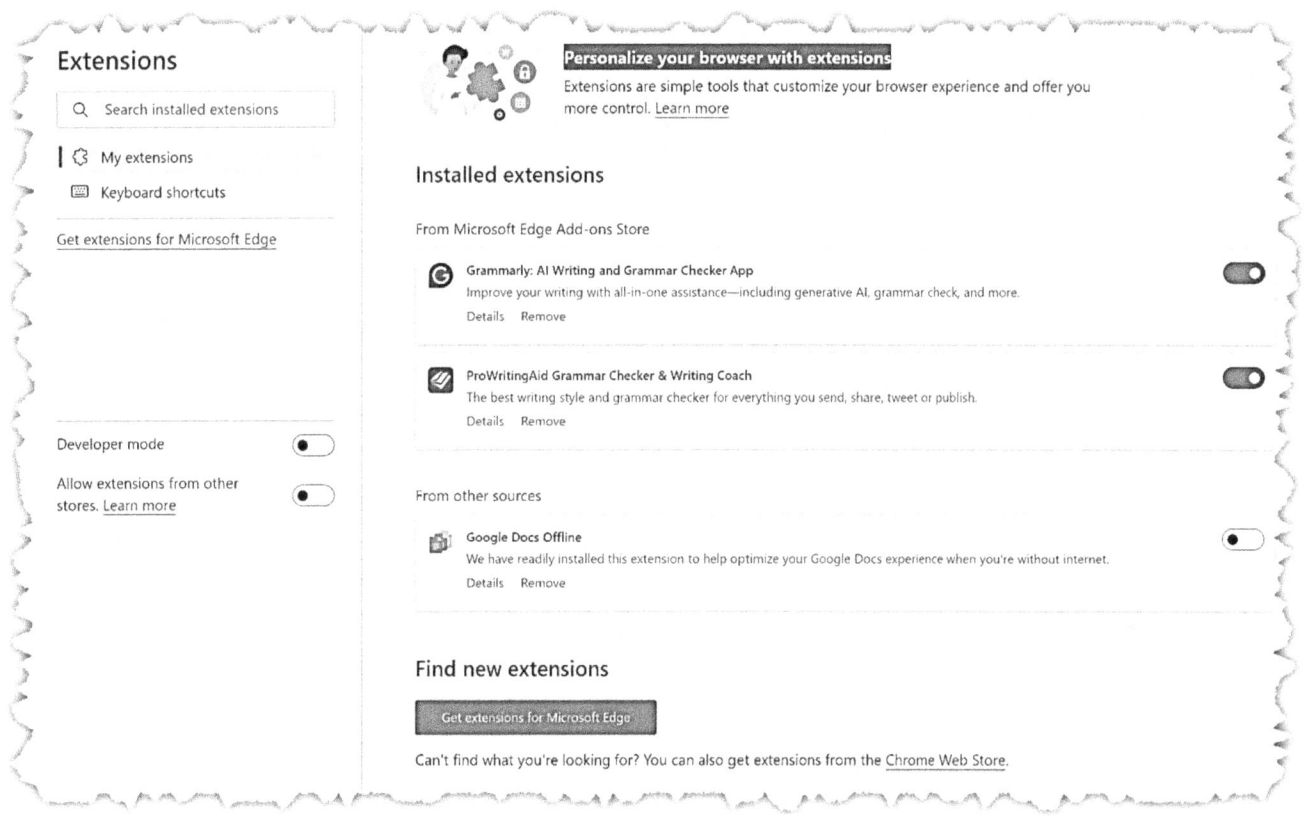

On the extension page, you can decide to turn on or off an extension you have installed.

The toggle button is use to toggle your extensions on or off.

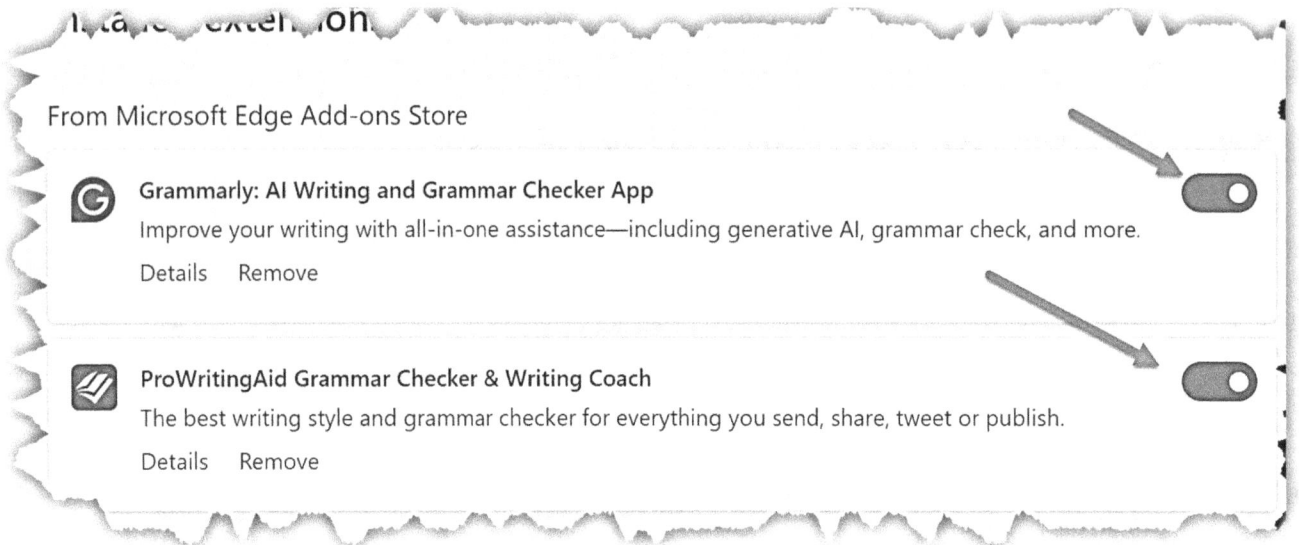

CHAPTER 13

SECURING YOUR WINDOWS 11

Many knowledge and opportunities are available in the vast digital realm; nevertheless, possible dangers remain hidden. This chapter will look into the most efficient strategies for strengthening your digital defenses, ensuring that your computer experience is safe and secure.

IMPORTANCE OF WINDOWS UPDATES

Keeping your Windows 11 computer updated is like giving it a shield of protection. Just like wearing armor to stay safe from enemies, your computer needs updates to defend against bad guys like hackers who try to break in.

These Windows Updates work like patches for your armor, fixing any weak spots and making it stronger.

Setting up your computer to update automatically is the simplest way to guarantee it will remain secure. This ensures that your computer will always receive the most recent patches without requiring any action.

Here are the steps you should follow:

1. Open the **Settings app** through the Start menu.

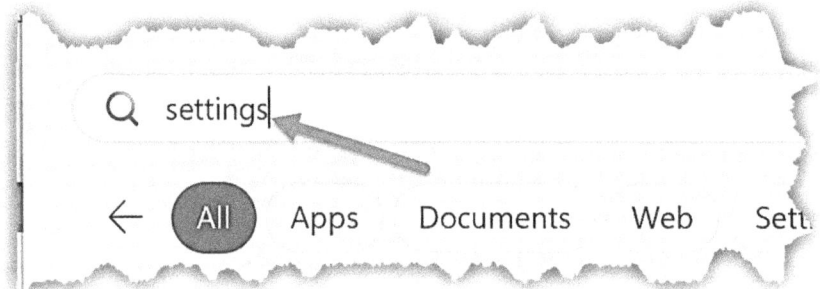

2. Click on "Windows Update".

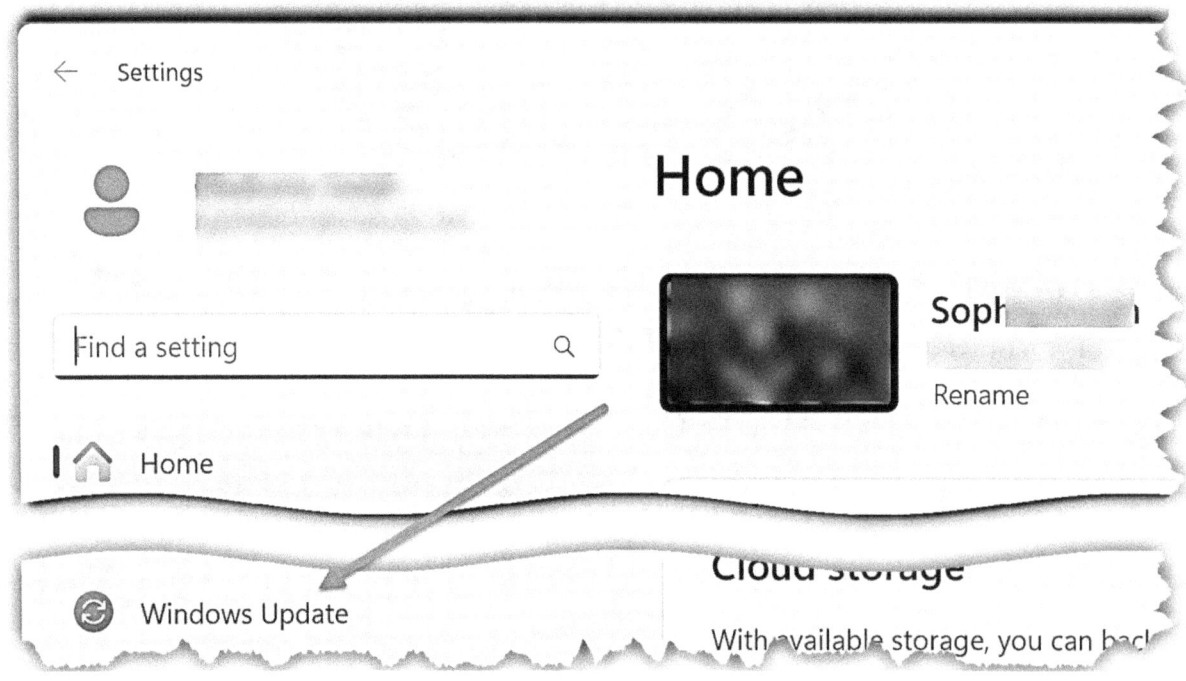

3. Click on "**Advanced**" options.

4. Toggle on the **Get Lastest Update** button.

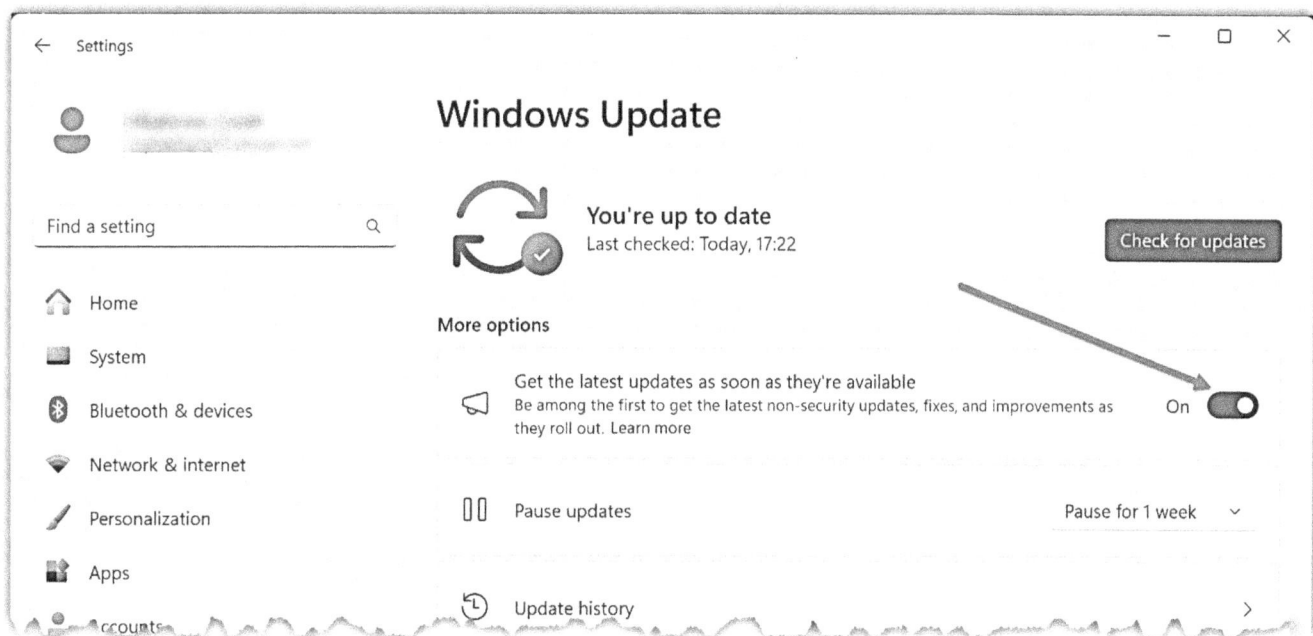

Under **Windows Updates** > **Advanced Options**, you have more update settings that give you better control of your computer.

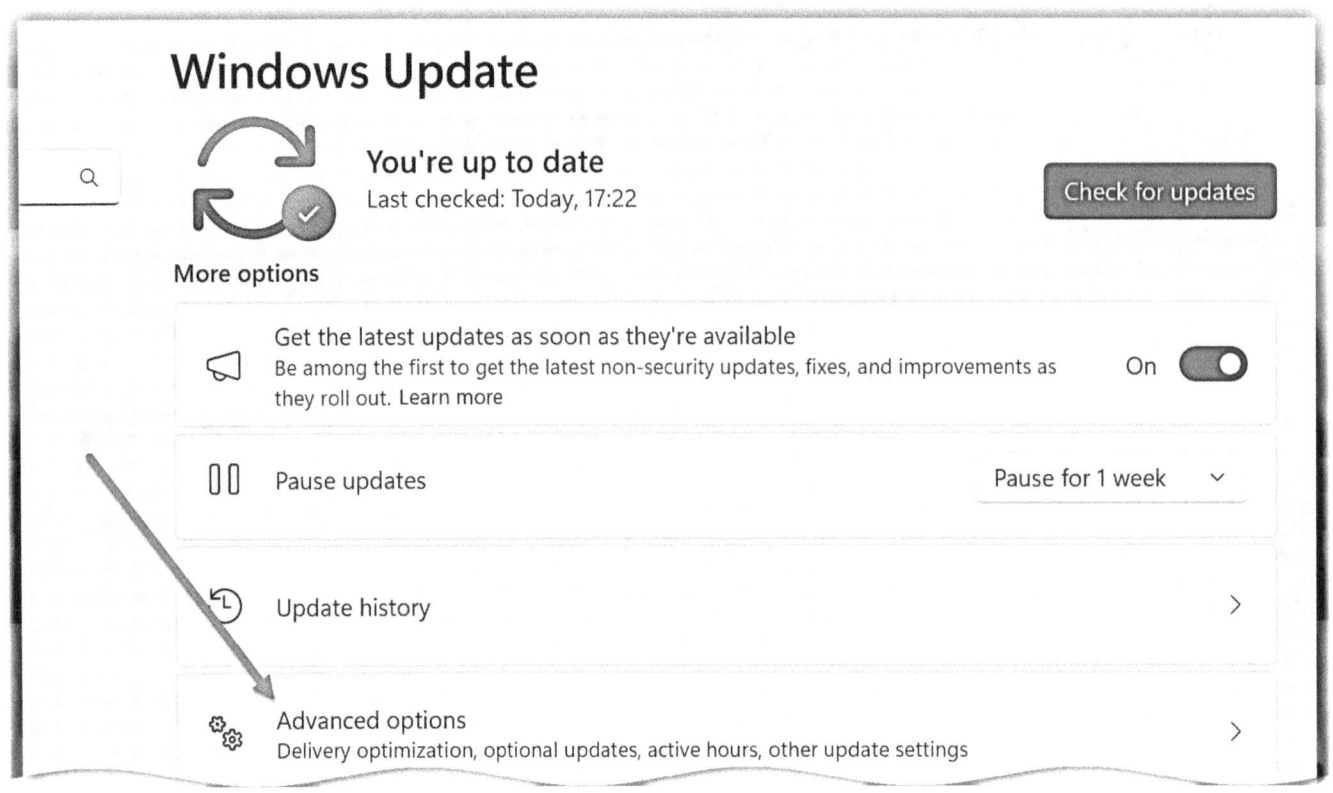

1. The option "**Receive updates for other Microsoft products**" allows the Windows Update process to download and install updates for Windows and other Microsoft programs installed on your device.

2. The "**Get me up to Date**" enables the Windows Update process to determine when and how to obtain the most recent updates for your Windows device.

When you enable this feature, Windows will restart your device and complete any updates that are still outstanding, even when your computer is actively engaged. Meanwhile, you will be alerted fifteen minutes before your computer gets forced to restart.

For example, if you use a laptop with a low battery, the restart information may ask you to put it in the charger before the installation begins.

However, don't enable this setting if you will be working on a task that may be affected when your computer is forced to restart.

3. The **"Download updates over metered connections"** setting lets you control how Windows Update operates when your computer is connected to a network with metered data.

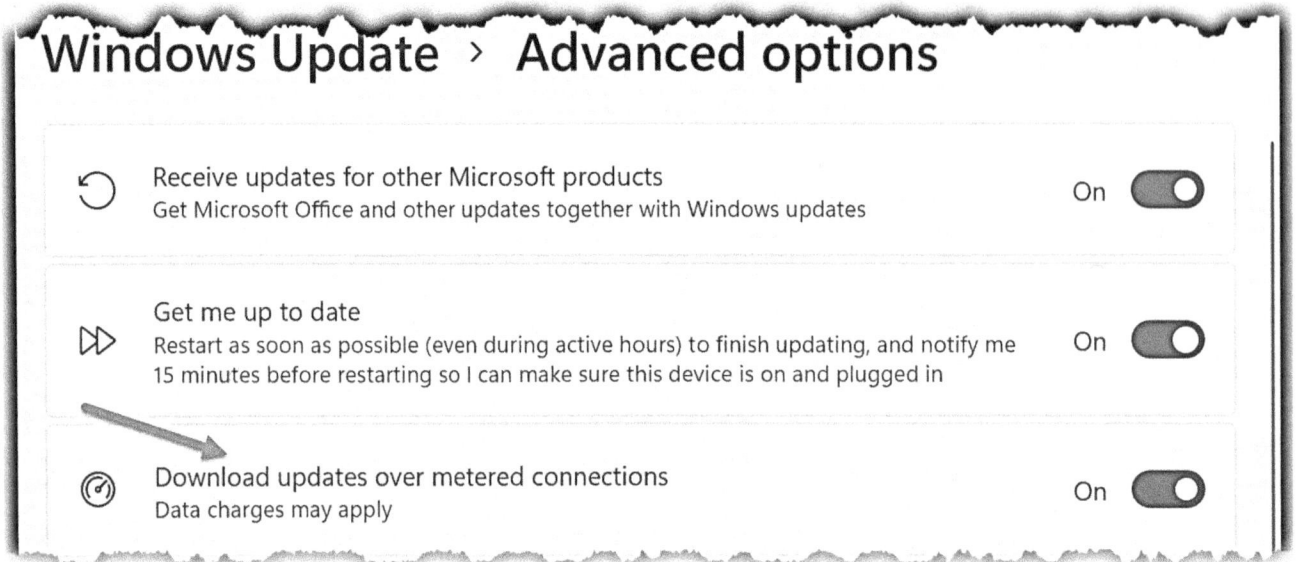

In most cases, a metered connection is chosen to conserve data and avoid exceeding your internet limit, especially when utilizing a mobile hotspot or a capped connection.

Windows 11 and the Microsoft Store will cease downloading updates for the operating system and applications over metered connections when this setting is enabled.

THIRD-PARTY ANTIVIRUS PROGRAM

Having an antivirus tool installed on your computer serves as a diligent watchdog, always searching for potential dangers and eliminating them before they can cause any damage.

The antivirus software that comes with Windows 11 by default is Microsoft Defender. It can protect your computer from viruses, malware, and other online threats, but knowing what it can not do is important.

Even if Microsoft Defender provides some level of security, it may not be sufficient to deal with the ever-evolving arsenal of cyber dangers now available. These are some of its limitations:

- **Limited detection capabilities:** Some sophisticated forms of malware and phishing efforts might be able to get through Microsoft Defender.

- **Limited real-time protection:** There is a possibility that certain functionalities, such as parental controls and advanced firewalls, are missing.

- **Potential performance impact:** Depending on the resources available to your system, Microsoft Defender may cause your computer to run more slowly.

The easiest way to add additional layers of protection to your computer is to think about using third-party antivirus software.

Some scenarios in which a third-party antivirus program might prove to be beneficial include:

- If you use the internet frequently, you will likely be exposed to potential dangers from data downloading, viewing websites, and participating in other activities that take place online.

- If you place high importance on advanced features such as parental controls, protection against identity theft, and robust firewalls, offer additional layers of security than traditional security measures.

- If performance is a priority for you, some third-party apps are designed to have minimal impact on your system, ensuring smooth operation.

Popular Third-Party Antivirus Options

You need to consider an alternative to Microsoft Defender, which is included in the pre-installed software on Windows 11. Next, we will examine some of the most well-known antivirus programs offered by third-party technology businesses. This list, however, does not contain everything.

Bitdefender Antivirus Plus

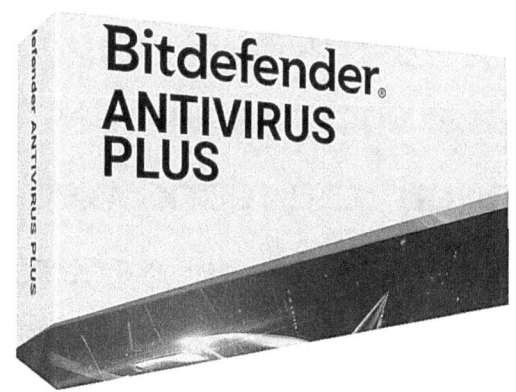

- **Features**: Provides protection in real-time, identifies malicious software, prevents ransomware from running, incorporates parental controls, and analyses vulnerabilities.

- **Pricing**: A free trial is available, while paid options begin at $39.99 annually for the most basic level.

- **Pros**: These features include a user-friendly interface, excellent protection against various threats, and assistance in optimizing speed.

- **Cons**: The free version has limited features and some advanced features cost extra.

Norton 360 Deluxe

- **Features**: This software is capable of identifying malicious software such as viruses and ransomware, keeping an eye on the dark web, incorporating a password manager and a secure virtual private network (VPN), and offering parental controls. Real-time protection is another feature it provides.

- **Pricing**: Offers a free trial, with premium options beginning at $69.99 for a year.

- **Pros**: In addition to offering a comprehensive security package that incorporates other features, it also provides exceptional customer service.

- **Cons**: Can consume a significant amount of system resources, and some functions might not be required for individuals with very minimal needs.

Kaspersky Anti-Virus

- **Features**: Provides security in real-time, identifies and eliminates harmful malware and ransomware, integrates secure tools for managing money, does vulnerability checks, and offers parental controls.

- **Pricing**: A trial version is free, while paid alternatives start at $29.99 yearly for the most basic level.

- **Pros**: The device contains powerful detecting capabilities, is suitable for individuals with advanced skills, and is affordable.

- **Cons**: Compared to some of the other competitors, the user interface might be less user-friendly for those who are just starting out, and there might be fewer additional capabilities.

ESET NOD32 Antivirus

- **Features**: The software delivers lightweight performance, detects malware and ransomware, provides real-time security, and includes protection against phishing.

- **Pricing**: A free trial is available, while paid options begin at $39.99 annually for the most basic level.

- **Pros**: The detection rate is excellent, the impact on system performance is negligible, and the value for the money is satisfactory.

- **Cons**: The basic interface does not have many modification possibilities, and there are limited additional features.

Avast Free Antivirus

- **Features**: The software provides protection in real-time, identifies malicious software and phishing attacks, incorporates browser extensions, and offers a fundamental firewall.

- **Pricing**: A free version is available, and paid plans with more features begin at $49.99 annually for the upgraded version.

- **Pros**: It offers a free version, provides enough protection at the primary level, and has an intuitive user interface.

- **Cons**: The free edition has fewer features, and advertisements may pop up, while the paid version may be more expensive.

BEST PRACTICES FOR ONLINE SAFETY

Although a powerful antivirus tool is necessary, it is equally important to supplement it with your alertness to achieve the highest possible level of online security. A few essential procedures are as follows:

- **Be cautious with websites:** It is best to avoid unknown or questionable websites, particularly those that promise free downloads or deals that appear too good to be true.

- **Embrace strong passwords:** Make sure each of your online accounts has a unique and strong password, and think about using a password manager to store your passwords securely.

- **Beware of email attachments:** When you receive attachments from unknown sources or ones that include dubious file formats, you should not open them (e.g., .exe, .zip).

- **Be mindful of social media:** Exercise caution with the information you disclose to the public and refrain from clicking unknown links or downloading files from sources you do not trust.

- **Stay informed:** Follow reputable security resources by updating yourself on emerging online threats and scams.

USER ACCOUNTS

Creating distinct user accounts lets you keep your work-related data and apps separate from personal ones in a shared computer environment, such as in an office or home.

A User Account is a significant feature that grants access to anyone using your computer while keeping your privacy and security. This is made possible by creating additional user accounts.

Creating a user account for someone you want to use on your computer requires you to establish their login credentials, such as usernames, passwords, or personal identification numbers (PINs).

Users can set their own desktop background, themes, and program preferences, making it easier for them to work. Personal files and documents are also stored in separate areas of each user's account.

How to Create a User Account

1. Open "**Settings**" from the Start Menu.

2. Navigate to "**Accounts**" and select "**Other users**."

3. Click "**Add account**" to create a new user.

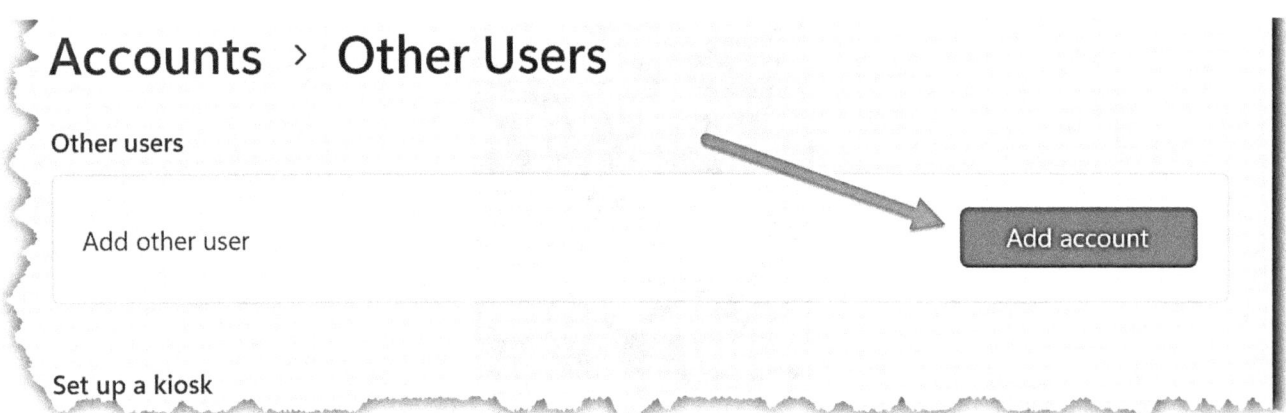

4. Follow the on-screen instructions to set up the new account.

PARENTAL CONTROLS

Having separate user accounts within a computer is necessary for families to set up effective parental restrictions. Creating separate user accounts is crucial for implementing adequate parental controls for families. As a parent, you can monitor your children's activities, restricting access to certain apps or websites based on age appropriateness.

How to Create a Family Account

1. Open the Settings app and click on **Accounts**.

2. Scroll down and click on **Family** in the left pane.

3. Click on **Add someone** in the right pane.

1. Enter the email address of the child for whom you want to create a user account.

If you don't have a Microsoft account for the user, click on the **Create one for a child** link.

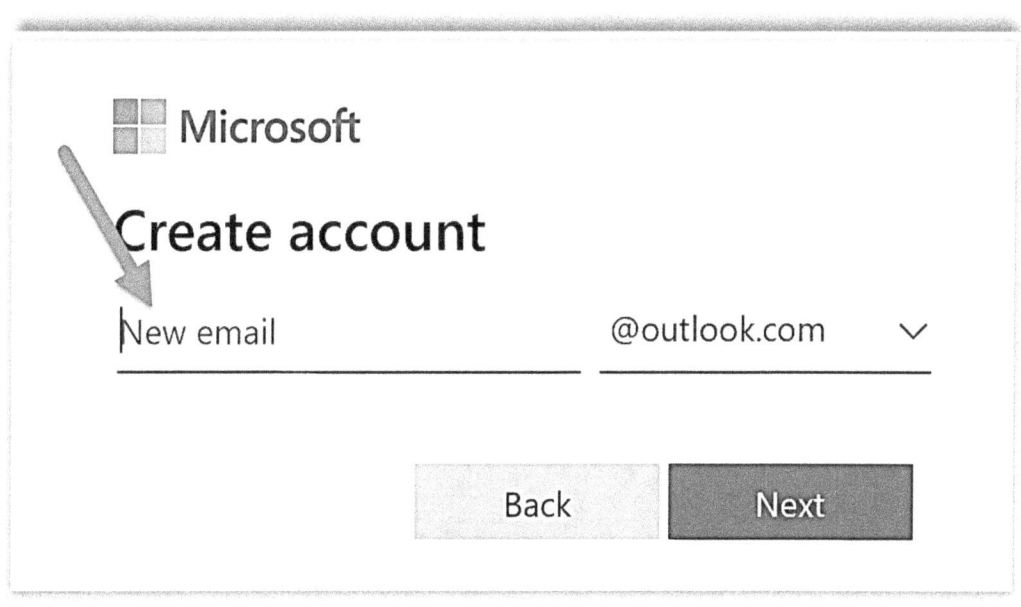

2. Choose whether to add a child or an adult to your family account.

3. Enter the email address or phone number of the person you want to add and click Next.

4. If the person already has a Microsoft account, they will receive an email or a text message with a link to join your family. If they don't have a Microsoft account, they will be prompted to create one.

5. Once they accept your invitation, they will be added to your family account. You can view and manage their online activity, screen time, content restrictions, and more from the Settings or Microsoft Family Safety apps.

www.ingramcontent.com/pod-product-compliance
Lightning Source LLC
Chambersburg PA
CBHW062100220526
45471CB00010B/3549